高等院校英语专业英美文学系列丛书

英美文学选读

主　编　冯正斌　师新民

西北工业大学出版社

【内容简介】《英美文学选读》为英语专业三、四年级及英美文学专业研究生研读及课程教材,共分英国文学、美国文学两个部分。英国部分19个章节、美国部分21个章节,主要内容有作者简介、作品导读、作品选读、难点注释、术语解释等。全书章节安排合理,共选择30位著名作家的作品,每单元评注一位作家的作品,注解内容充实,可帮助读者加深对作品的理解。

图书在版编目(CIP)数据

英美文学选读/冯正斌,师新民主编. —西安:西北工业大学出版社,2016.3
ISBN 978-7-5612-4702-0

Ⅰ.①英… Ⅱ.①冯… ②师… Ⅲ.①英语—阅读教学—研究生—教材②英国文学—文学欣赏③文学欣赏—美国 Ⅳ.①H319.4:I

中国版本图书馆CIP数据核字(2016)第062611号

出版发行:西北工业大学出版社
通信地址:西安市友谊西路127号　邮编:710072
电　　话:(029)88493844　88491757
网　　址:www.nwpup.com
印　刷　者:陕西宝石兰印务有限责任公司
开　　本:787 mm×1 092 mm　1/16
印　　张:23.25
字　　数:571千字
版　　次:2016年4月第1版　2016年4月第1次印刷
定　　价:59.00元

前　言

随着全球化进程的日益加剧,掌握一门外语成为了21世纪人们必不可少的技能之一。作为世界最通用的语言之一的英语更是成为了人们学习外语的重要选择。然而语言的学习是一个复杂的过程,尤其对于专业学习者来说,恰当的学习材料是成功的关键。文学作为语言世界最经典、最浓缩的文化形式自然是学习者最值得信赖、依托的素材,它是整个语言使用民族的历史、文化、哲学、风俗等最完美的见证,尤其是代表作家、优秀作者的作品。

市场上现有的英美文学选读教材都各具特色,各有优点,但是大多数作品的选择还停留在两战之间这个时间段,对于近代的作家涉猎较少。另外,有的选读面向的读者群不是十分明确,有的缺少适当的注解和术语解释。本《英美文学选读》的编写明确了读者群,以英语专业三、四年级学生及文学专业的研究生为主要读者群,对于理解难点进行了适当的注解,并且对每一位作家有作者简介,对每部作品也进行了导读。在编写过程中力求做到以下几个方面:

1. 内容选择新颖,在多年授课的基础上,选择英语文学界享有盛誉的代表篇目。

2. 章节安排合理,共选择30位著名作家的作品,每单元评注一位作家的作品。

3. 注解内容充实,帮助读者加深对作品的理解。

4. 导读内容详实,对每位作家加以简单明了的介绍,并在作品前加以导读,辅助读者更好地把握作品的内涵。

5. 整体构思新颖,本书不同于同类作品的两个方面:在选择作品时尽量把握难度,使本书既有相应的学术含量,又最大可能地扩大读者群;在注解方面,尽量兼备创新评论和准确性,避免人云亦云。

本书由西安科技大学人文与外国语学院冯正斌副教授、师新民教授主编,冯正斌负责英国部分1~15章及美国部分1~16章的编写;师新民负责英国部分16~19章及美国部分17~21章的编写。

在本书编写过程中,教育界的同仁及出版社的编辑老师对本书提出了宝贵的意见和建议,在此特表示诚挚的谢意!由于本书的编写量大、涉及面广,书中难免有不妥甚至谬误之处,诚请广大同仁、读者指正。

编　者

2016年1月

TABLE OF CONTENTS

THE BRITISH PART

Chapter 1 William Shakespeare 3
Chapter 2 John Milton 12
Chapter 3 Daniel Defoe 19
Chapter 4 Jonathan Swift 29
Chapter 5 William Wordsworth 38
Chapter 6 Samuel Taylor Coleridge 44
Chapter 7 Jane Austen 50
Chapter 8 Charles Dickens 58
Chapter 9 Alfred Tennyson 72
Chapter 10 Thomas Hardy 77
Chapter 11 George Bernard Shaw 87
Chapter 12 Joseph Conrad 97
Chapter 13 E. M. Forster 110
Chapter 14 Thomas Stearns Eliot 118
Chapter 15 James Joyce 126
Chapter 16 D. H. Lawrence 133
Chapter 17 William Golding 150
Chapter 18 Doris Lessing 167
Chapter 19 Vidiadhar Surajprasad Naipaul ... 177

THE AMERICAN PART

Chapter 1	Nathaniel Hawthorne	189
Chapter 2	Walt Whitman	199
Chapter 3	Emily Elizabeth Dickinson	204
Chapter 4	Mark Twain	207
Chapter 5	Henry James	213
Chapter 6	Sherwood Anderson	228
Chapter 7	F. Scott Fitzgerald	239
Chapter 8	William Faulkner	254
Chapter 9	Ernest Miller Hemingway	266
Chapter 10	Ezra Pound	272
Chapter 11	Wallace Stevens	277
Chapter 12	Robert Frost	282
Chapter 13	William Carlos Williams	287
Chapter 14	Eugene Gladstone O'Neill	292
Chapter 15	Tennessee Williams	300
Chapter 16	John Lawrence Ashbery	309
Chapter 17	Arthur Miller	316
Chapter 18	Joseph Heller	329
Chapter 19	Toni Morrison	341
Chapter 20	Maxine Hong Kingston	350
Chapter 21	Amy Tan	362
Bibliography		366

THE BRITISH PART

Chapter 1 William Shakespeare

作者简介

William Shakespeare(26 April, 1564 (baptised) - 23 April, 1616) was an English poet and playwright, widely regarded as the greatest writer in the English language and the world's pre-eminent dramatist. He is often called England's national poet and the "Bard of Avon."

Shakespeare was born and brought up in Stratford-upon-Avon. At the age of 18, he married Anne Hathaway, with whom he had three children: Susanna, and twins Hamnet and Judith. Between 1585 and 1592, he began a successful career in London as an actor, writer, and part-owner of a playing company called the Lord Chamberlain's Men, later known as the King's Men. He appears to have retired to Stratford around 1613 at age 49, where he died three years later. Shakespeare was buried in the chancel of the Holy Trinity Church two days after his death.

Shakespeare produced most of his known works between 1589 and 1613. His early plays were mainly comedies and histories, genres he raised to the peak of sophistication and artistry by the end of the 16th century. He then wrote mainly tragedies until about 1608. In his last phase, he wrote tragicomedies, also known as romances, and collaborated with his extant works, including some collaborations, consist of about 38 (or 39) plays, 154 sonnets, two long narrative poems, *Venus* and *Adonis* and *The Rape of Lucrece*. *The Merchant of Venice*, *A Midsummer Night's Dream*, *Twelfth Night* and *As You Like It* are considered as his four great comedies. *Hamlet*, *King Lear*, *Othello*, and *Macbeth* are considered as four great tragedies. *King John*, *Richard* II, *Henry* IV and *Henry* V are his histories. His plays have been translated into every major living language and are performed more often than those of any other playwright.

Shakespeare's work has made a lasting impression on later theatre and literature. In particular, he expanded the dramatic potential of characterisation, plot, language, and genre. Shakespeare influenced novelists such as Thomas Hardy, William Faulkner, and Charles Dickens. Shakespeare has also inspired many painters, including the Romantics and the Pre-Raphaelites. The psychoanalyst Sigmund Freud drew on Shakespearean psychology, in particular that of Hamlet, for his theories of human nature. In Shakespeare's day, English grammar, spelling and pronunciation were less standardized than they are now, and his use of language helped shape modern English. Therefore, it was prefaced with a poem by Ben Jonson, in which Shakespeare is hailed, presciently, as "not of an age, but for all time."

威廉·莎士比亚(1564年4月26日(受洗)—1616年4月23日)是一位英国诗人和剧作家,被公认为是最伟大的英语作家和世界杰出的剧作家。他通常被称为英国的民族诗人和"艾冯诗人"。

莎士比亚出生和成长在艾冯河畔斯特拉特福德。18岁时,他与安妮·海瑟薇结婚并和她有了三个孩子:苏珊娜、双胞胎哈姆内特和朱迪思。从1585年到1592年,莎士比亚前往伦敦开始他的演员和作家生涯,且小有成就,他还与人合开了一家名为宫内大臣的剧团,后又更名为国王剧团。据传在约1613年,约49岁的莎士比亚退休回到斯特拉特福德。3年后,他便在那儿去世了。莎士比亚死后两天,被葬在圣三一教堂的圣坛。

莎士比亚的创作主要集中在1589年到1613年间。他的早期剧本主要是喜剧和历史剧,在16世纪末到达了复杂性和艺术性的顶峰。然后,直到大约1608年,他主要创作悲剧。在他人生最后阶段,他写了悲喜剧,也被称为爱情剧,他的现存作品,包括一些合作,作品共有约38或39部戏剧,154首十四行诗,两个长叙事诗歌,《维纳斯和阿多尼斯》和《鲁克丽思受辱记》。《威尼斯商人》、《仲夏夜之梦》、《第十二夜》和《皆大欢喜》被称为他的四大喜剧。《哈姆雷特》、《李尔王》、《奥赛罗》和《麦克白》被称为他的四大悲剧。《约翰王》、《理查德二世》、《亨利四世》以及《亨利五世》是他的历史剧。他的剧本被译成多种语言,并比其他任何戏剧都要更频繁地被搬上舞台。

莎士比亚的作品对以后的戏剧和文学有着深远的影响。值得一提的是,他扩大了人物塑造、情节、语言和流派的戏剧潜力。莎士比亚也影响了包括托马斯·哈代、威廉·福克纳和查尔斯·狄更斯在内的小说家。他还激励了许多画家,包括浪漫派和前拉斐尔派画家。精神分析学家弗洛伊德运用了莎士比亚的心理学,特别是《哈姆雷特》中的人性理论。在莎士比亚的时代,英语语法、拼写和发音与现在相比还不太标准,所以,他对语言的应用促进了现代英语的塑造。因此,在本·琼森的一首诗的开头,他预见性地称赞莎士比亚为"不是一个时代,而是永恒。"

作品及导读

作品 1

Hamlet

导 读

Hamlet is a tragedy written by William Shakespeare between 1599 and 1602. Set in the Kingdom of Denmark, the play dramatizes the revenge Prince Hamlet exacts on his uncle Claudius for murdering King Hamlet, Claudius's brother and Prince Hamlet's father, and then succeeding to the throne and taking as his wife Gertrude, the old king's widow and Prince Hamlet's mother. The play vividly portrays both true and feigned madness — from overwhelming grief to seething rage — and explores themes of treachery, revenge, incest, and moral corruption.

At the beginning of Act 3, Claudius is questioning Rosencrantz and Guildenstern as to whether they have discovered the cause of Hamlet's "turbulence and dangerous lunacy." They respond that Hamlet professes himself to be "distracted". Yet, a serious question arises as to whether Prince Hamlet may in fact be manipulating everyone else into believing him insane. Guildenstern echoes Polonius's previous observation that there is a method to this madness, implying once again that Hamlet may very well be in full control of his emotions. In the mean time, Polonius suggests, and Claudius agrees, that the two should hide and observe Hamlet and Ophelia, to determine whether it be "the affliction of love or no." When Hamlet enters, delivering his most poignant soliloquy, he reveals an inner torment and struggle with his inability to avenge his father's murder. At the end of this soliloquy as he meets with Ophelia, Hamlet's anger against women resurfaces. He states that although he did love her once because of her beauty. He now believes that the same beauty to be another aspect of dissembling womanhood and wants to banish her from his thoughts. King Claudius enters, with Polonius, stating that Hamlet's condition is not that of love, and demanding that he be sent speedily to England to avoid his danger to the state.

《哈姆雷特》是莎士比亚在 1599 到 1602 之间的写的悲剧。背景设在丹麦王国,该剧戏剧化地呈现了复仇王子哈姆雷特向他的叔叔克劳迪斯复仇的故事,因为他谋杀哈姆雷特的父亲然后继承了王位,并娶了老国王的遗孀,也就是哈姆雷特的母亲格特鲁德为妻。该剧生动地刻画了真实和假装的疯狂——铺天盖地而来的悲痛到沸腾的愤怒——探讨了背叛、报复、乱伦道德腐败等主题。

第三幕的一开始,克劳迪斯质问罗森格兰兹和吉尔登斯登他们是否已经发现了哈姆雷特

"狂暴的和危险的精神失常"的原因。他们回应,哈姆雷特声称自己是"心烦意乱"。然而,一个严重的问题出现了,那就是哈姆雷特王子是否实际上是在操纵其他人去相信他疯了。吉尔登斯登根据波洛尼厄斯先前的观察,他们认为哈姆雷特很可能完全控制他的情绪。同时,波洛尼厄斯建议,克劳迪斯同意他们两个应该隐秘观察哈姆雷特和欧菲莉亚,确定他的疯癫是否出于"爱的悲痛"。当哈姆雷特出场,他做了最深刻的独白,他显示出报复杀父仇人的内心的痛苦与挣扎。在独白的最后,随着他与欧菲莉亚的会面,哈姆雷特对女人的愤怒再次浮现。他指出,虽然他曾因为她的美貌爱她,他现在认为,同样的美丽掩饰女人的另一个方面并想把她从他的大脑中驱逐掉。克劳迪斯王在普罗尼尔斯陪同下出场了,认为哈姆雷特的状况不是出于爱,并要求急需将他派送到英国,以避免他对国家造成危险。

选 文

(*Act 3, Scene 1, lines 55 - 86, Hamlet*)

HAMLET
To be, or not to be? that is the question —
Whether 'tis nobler in the mind to suffer
The slings and arrows of outrageous fortune,
Or to take arms against a sea of troubles,
And by opposing end them? To die, to sleep —
No more — and by a sleep to say we end
The heartache and the thousand natural shocks
That flesh is heir to, 'tis a consummation
Devoutly to be wish'd! To die, to sleep.
To sleep, perchance to dream ay, there's the rub,
For in that sleep of death what dreams may come
When we have shuffled off this mortal coil,
Must give us pause. There's the respect
That makes calamity of so long life.
For who would bear the whips and scorns of time,
Th' oppressor's wrong, the proud man's contumely,
The pangs of despis'd love, the law's delay,
The insolence of office, and the spurns
That patient merit of th' unworthy takes,
When he himself might his quietus make
With a bare bodkin? Who would fardels bear,
To grunt and sweat under a weary life,
But that the dread of something after death,
The undiscover'd country from whose bourn
No traveller returns, puzzles the will

And makes us rather bear those ills we have
Than fly to others that we know not of?
Thus conscience does make cowards of us all,
And thus the native hue of resolution
Is sicklied o'er with the pale cast of thought,
And enterprises of great pith and moment
With this regard their currents turn awry,
And lose the name of action. — Soft you now!

作品 2

Romeo and Juliet

导读

  This is the famous "balcony scene". Romeo and Juliet confess their love. Having left the feast, Romeo decides to find Julie. He leaps down into the Capulet orchard. In the orchard, Juliet appears at a window. Romeo compares her to the morning sun. Juliet, musing to herself and unaware that Romeo is in her garden, asks why Romeo must be Romeo — a Montague, and therefore an enemy to her family. She says that if he would refuse his Montague name, she would give herself to him; or if he would simply swear that he loved her, she would refuse her Capulet name. Romeo responds to her plea, surprising Juliet. She wonders how he found her and he tells her that love led him to her. Juliet worries that Romeo will be murdered if he is found, but Romeo refuses to budge, claiming that Juliet's love would make him immune to his enemies. Juliet admits she feels as strongly about Romeo as he professes he loves her, but she worries that perhaps Romeo will prove inconstant or false, or will think Juliet too easily won. Romeo begins to swear to her, but she stops him, concerned that everything is happening too quickly. He reassures her, and the two confess their love again. She tells Romeo that she will send someone to him the next day to see if his love is honorable and if he intends to wed her. She appears at the window once more to set a time when her emissary should meet him: they settle on nine in the morning. They exult in their love for another moment before saying good night.

  这是著名的"阳台诉情"。罗密欧与茱丽叶互诉爱意。离开宴席后,罗密欧决定找到茱丽叶。他跳进凯普莱特定族的庭院。在庭院里,茱丽叶出现在窗边。罗密欧把她比作早晨的太阳。茱丽叶在与自我进行对话,并没有意识到罗密欧在她的花园里,她问罗密欧为什么一定要是罗密欧——蒙特奇家族,也是她家族的宿敌。她说,如果罗密欧舍弃蒙特奇家族,那她就会与他在一起;或者如果罗密欧发誓爱她,那她便可放弃凯普莱特的名字。罗密欧回应了她的诉求,这使茱丽叶收到了惊吓。她想知道他怎样找到她,而罗密欧告诉茱丽叶,爱引领着方向。

茱丽叶担心罗密欧被发现了就会大难临头,但罗密欧不愿离开,他坚信茱丽叶的爱能让他无坚不摧。茱丽叶也承认对罗密欧也有同样的爱意,但她担心罗密欧心思多变,或移情于人,又担心自己是否很容易赢得芳心。罗密欧向她发誓,但茱丽叶制止了,她担心一切都发生都太快。罗密欧又向茱丽叶做了保证,两人又互诉爱意。茱丽叶跟罗密欧说她第二天会派人确认罗密欧是否矢志不渝,是否有意娶她。她再次出现在窗前,约定她的密使与罗密欧会面的时间。时间定在早上九点。在道晚安前,两人再次因爱意而欣喜若狂。

选 文

(Act 2, Scene 2, lines 1-78, Romeo and Juliet)

(SCENE 2)

[Enter ROMEO]

ROMEO

He jests at scars that never felt a wound.

[JULIET appears above at a window]

But, soft! What light through yonder window breaks?

It is the east, and Juliet is the sun.

Arise, fair sun, and kill the envious moon,

Who is already sick and pale with grief,

That thou her maid art far more fair than she:

Be not her maid, since she is envious;

Her vestal livery is but sick and green

And none but fools do wear it; cast it off.

It is my lady, O, it is my love!

O, that she knew she were!

She speaks yet she says nothing: what of that?

Her eye discourses; I will answer it.

I am too bold, 'tis not to me she speaks:

Two of the fairest stars in all the heaven,

Having some business, do entreat her eyes

To twinkle in their spheres till they return.

What if her eyes were there, they in her head?

The brightness of her cheek would shame those stars,

As daylight doth a lamp; her eyes in heaven

Would through the airy region stream so bright

That birds would sing and think it were not night.

See, how she leans her cheek upon her hand!

O, that I were a glove upon that hand,

That I might touch that cheek!

◁ ◁ ◁ ◁ **THE BRITISH PART**

JULIET

Ay me!

ROMEO

She speaks:

O, speak again, bright angel! for thou art

As glorious to this night, being o'er my head

As is a winged messenger of heaven

Unto the white-upturned wondering eyes

Of mortals that fall back to gaze on him

When he bestrides the lazy-pacing clouds

And sails upon the bosom of the air.

JULIET

O Romeo, Romeo! Wherefore art thou Romeo?

Deny thy father and refuse thy name;

Or, if thou wilt not, be but sworn my love,

And I'll no longer be a Capulet.

ROMEO

[Aside] Shall I hear more, or shall I speak at this?

JULIET

'Tis but thy name that is my enemy;

Thou art thyself, though not a Montague.

What's Montague? it is nor hand, nor foot,

Nor arm, nor face, nor any other part

Belonging to a man. O, be some other name!

What's in a name? that which we call a rose

By any other name would smell as sweet;

So Romeo would, were he not Romeo call'd,

Retain that dear perfection which he owes

Without that title. Romeo, doff thy name,

And for that name which is no part of thee

Take all myself.

ROMEO

I take thee at thy word:

Call me but love, and I'll be new baptized;

Henceforth I never will be Romeo.

JULIET

What man art thou that thus bescreen'd in night
So stumblest on my counsel?

ROMEO

By a name
I know not how to tell thee who I am:
My name, dear saint, is hateful to myself,
Because it is an enemy to thee;
Had I it written, I would tear the word.

JULIET

My ears have not yet drunk a hundred words
Of that tongue's utterance, yet I know the sound:
Art thou not Romeo and a Montague?

ROMEO

Neither, fair saint, if either thee dislike.

JULIET

How camest thou hither, tell me, and wherefore?
The orchard walls are high and hard to climb,
And the place death, considering who thou art,
If any of my kinsmen find thee here.

ROMEO

With love's light wings did I o'er-perch these walls;
For stony limits cannot hold love out,
And what love can do that dares love attempt;
Therefore thy kinsmen are no let to me.

JULIET

If they do see thee, they will murder thee.

ROMEO

Alack, there lies more peril in thine eye
Than twenty of their swords: look thou but sweet,
And I am proof against their enmity.

JULIET

I would not for the world they saw thee here.

ROMEO

I have night's cloak to hide me from their sight;
And but thou love me, let them find me here:
My life were better ended by their hate,
Than death prorogued, wanting of thy love.

相关链接

1. **Iambic pentameter**: A poetic line consisting of five verse feet, with each foot an iamb — that is, an unstressed syllable followed by a stressed one. Iambic pentameter is the most common verse line in English poetry.

2. Sonnet, A fourteen-line poem, usually composed in iambic pentameter, employing one of several rhyme schemes. There are two major types of sonnets, upon which all other variations of the form are based: the "Petrarchan" or "Italian" sonnet and the "Shakespearean" or "English" sonnet. An Italian sonnet consists of an octave rhymed "abbaabba" and a "sestet" rhymed either "cdecde", "cdccdc", or "cdedce". The octave poses a question or problem, relates a narrative, or puts forth a proposition; the sestet presents a solution to the problem, comments upon the narrative, or applies the proposition put forth in the octave. The Shakespearean sonnet is divided into three quatrains and a couplet rhymed "abab" "cdcd" "efefgg". The couplet provides an epigrammatic comment on the narrative or problem put forth in the quatrains.

十四行诗：一首诗有14行，通常以五步抑扬格写成，采用其中一种韵律格式。十四行诗有两种主要形式，在此基础上创作出其他形式：意大利十四行诗和莎士比亚十四行诗，意大利十四行诗由一个韵律为"abbaabba"的8行诗和一个韵律为"cdecde"、"cdccdc"或"cdedce"的6行诗组成。8行诗中提出一个问题与叙述一个故事或提出一个建议，而6行诗则提出问题的解决办法，对叙述做出评论或者运用所提出的建议。莎士比亚的十四行诗分成3个4行诗和一个对句，其韵律为"abab cdcd efef gg"。对句是对前面12行诗中、4行诗中的叙述或者提出的问题进行警醒评论。

Chapter 2 John Milton

作者简介

John Milton (1608 – 1674) was an English poet, political commentator and thinker. As the representative of the puritan literature, during his writing career, he created dozens of famous works which included *Lycidas* (1637), *Areopagitica* (1644), *Paradise Lost* (1667), *Paradise Regained* (1671), and *Samson Agonistes* (1671). Among these works, *Paradise Lost* was the most famous one, because it was called one of "the greatest three epics" in the west, with the other two being *La Oivina Commedies* and the *Homer*.

Milton was born in a wealthy puritan family in London, which enabled him to get a good education in early years. First, he was taught by tutor at home. After that, he was sent to the St. Paul's School in London, where he began the study of Latin and Greek, and the classical languages left an imprint on his poetry in English. In 1625, Milton attended Cambridge and graduated with a Master of Arts degree in 1632. During Cambridge time, Milton was on good terms with Edward King, for whom he later wrote *Lycidas*.

Then, Milton went home for years of self-directed private study. He read both ancient and modern works of theology, philosophy, history, politics, literature and science and had command of Latin, Greek, Hebrew, French and Italian, which made him become the most learned poet among all of the English poets. After years of private study, he traveled to Europe, which supplemented his study with new and direct experience of artistic and religious traditions, especially Roman Catholicism. In 1639, he came back to England because the Civil War almost broke out, and he created many works like the *Areopagitica* to support the resolution. Upon the Restoration in May 1660, he was arrested and put into the prison but later he was released. From then on, he began his creation of the third period. During this period, although he gradually became blind, he created the most famous work *Paradise Lost*, which was one of the greatest three epics. Later, he also created *Paradise Regained* and *Samson Agonistes*. On the day before his 66th birthday, November 8, 1674, Milton died of gout-fever.

约翰·弥尔顿(John Milton, 1608—1674)英国诗人、政论家和思想家。作为清教徒文学的代表,在他的写作生涯中,他创作了大量的著作,其中包括《利西达斯》(1637)、《论出版自由》(1644)、《失乐园》(1667)、《复乐园》(1671)和《力士参孙》(1671)。其中,《失乐园》最为著名,它与《神曲》和《荷马史诗》并称为西方的"三大史诗"。

弥尔顿出生于伦敦一个富裕的清教徒家庭,这使得他早年可以接受很好的教育。首先,他由家庭教师在家授课。之后,他被送进伦敦的圣保罗学校,在那里,他开始了拉丁文和希腊语的学习,古典语言在他的英语诗歌中留下了印记。1625年,弥尔顿进入剑桥大学,并于1632年取得文学学士学位后毕业。在剑桥岁月里,他与爱德华国王关系要好,后来还为他写了《利西达斯》一诗。

之后,弥尔顿回家进行了多年的自主学习。他博览古今群书,其中包括神学、哲学、历史、政治、文学和科学方面的书籍,还掌握了拉丁语、希腊语、希伯来语、法语和意大利语,这使他成为英国诗人中最博学的诗人。在这之后,他去欧洲游历,这为他的学习增添了许多关于艺术和宗教传统的新的和直接的经验,尤其是罗马天主教义。1639年,由于英国革命即将爆发,他回到英国并创作许多作品来支持革命,例如:《论出版自由》。1660年5月王政复辟,他被捕入狱,但很快就被释放。自此之后,他开始了第三个时期的创作。在这个时期,他逐渐失明,但是他创作了三大史诗之一的最著名的作品《失乐园》。之后,他还创作了《复乐园》和《力士参孙》。1674年11月8日,他66岁生日的前一天,他由于痛风病逝。

作品及导读

作品 1

Paradise Lost

导 读

In the first part of this poem, the poet John Milton points out the theme of the work in general. The theme is that people lose the paradise they have once owned because they violate the order of gods. Then, the poet explains the reason why people lose their footings — they are attacked by the snake that is adjoined by Satan. Satan have once summoned a lot of angels and controlled them to rebel gods. At last, they are expelled to the mundane by gods, being thrown into the endless abyss. After describing this event briefly, the poet tells us the central part of the event — the detailed description of the experience after Satan and his angels being thrown into the hell. And the hell mentioned here is not the "center" of the earth, but the most deserted area which is also called "chaos". Being struck by thunder and lightning, Satan and his angels finally fall into the Lake of Fire. After a while, Satan wakes up and awakens the angel who is rank only second to him, and then they discuss and analyze the crushing defeat jointly. Satan awakes all the angels that are trapped in dizziness, does the nose counts, clears up the battle array, and declares the name of the generals. Satan comforts them by giving a speech and inspires them that it is possible to reenergize the heaven. Eventually, he tells them that, according to an old prediction or hearsay from the heaven, a new world and a new life will be created. According to the old god-father's opinion, the angels exist before the world is created. As a result, they decide to call a plenary meeting to discuss the prediction and find out the solution. All his angels itch to try it, build up a tall and rugged palace in the hell, and sit there to hold a meeting.

在《失乐园》的第一卷,诗人约翰·弥尔顿先扼要点明本书的主题:人失去曾经拥有的乐园,是由于违背了天神命令。然后叙述他失足的主要原因在于撒旦所变化的蛇。撒旦曾经召集了许多天使军在他手下反叛天神,结果全被天神下令逐出天界,落入无垠的深渊。本诗简略地交代这事之后,便直叙事件的中心,描述撒旦和他所率领的天使进入地狱之中。这儿所描写的地狱不在地的"中心",而在天外的冥荒,最恰当的莫过于称它为"混沌"。撒旦和他的天军在这儿被雷电轰击而惊倒在炎炎的火湖里,过了一段时间之后,他从眩晕中清醒过来,并叫起倒在他身边的一个地位仅次于他的天使,共同商量这次惨败的事。撒旦唤醒了一个个处于同样的眩晕中的天军,于是他们起身,清点人数,整理阵容,宣布将领名单。撒旦以演说安慰他们,鼓舞他们,他说天界有望光复;最后告诉他们,根据一个古老的预言或天上的传闻,有一个新的世界和一种新的生物将被创造出来;根据古代教父们的看法,天使军在这个世界创造出来之前就存在了。于是他们决定召开全体会议,探讨这个预言并商量对策。因此他的党徒们都跃跃欲试,顷刻之间,就在地狱中筑起巍峨的撒旦的万魔殿,他们就坐在那里召开会议。

选 文

(Excerpt)

Nine times the space that measures day and night
To mortal men, he with his horrid crew
Lay vanquished, rolling in the fiery gulf
Confounded though immortal: But his doom
Reserved him to more wrath; for now the thought
Both of lost happiness and lasting pain
Torments him; round he throws his baleful eyes
That witnessed huge affliction and dismay
Mixed with obdurate pride and steadfast hate:

At once as far as Angels ken, he views
The dismal situation waste and wild.
A dungeon horrible, on all sides round
As one great furnace flamed, yet from those flames
No light, but rather darkness visible
Served only to discover sights of woe,
Regions of sorrow, doleful shades, where peace
And rest can never dwell, hope never comes
That comes to all; but torture without end
Still urges, and a fiery deluge, fed
With ever-burning sulphur unconsumed:
Such place Eternal Justice has prepared
For those rebellious, here their prison ordained
In utter darkness, and their portion set
As far removed from God and light of Heaven
As from the center thrice to th' utmost pole.
Oh how unlike the place from whence they fell!
There the companions of his fall, o'erwhelmed
With floods and whirlwinds of tempestuous fire,
He soon discerns; and, weltering by his side
One next himself in power, and next in crime,
Long after known in Palestine, and named
Beelzebub. To whom th' Arch-Enemy,
And thence in Heaven called Satan, with bold words
Breaking the horrid silence thus began.

"If thou beëst he — but O how fallen! how changed
From him, who in the happy realms of light
Clothed with transcendent brightness, didst outshine
Myriads, though bright! if he whom mutual league,
United thoughts and counsels, equal hope,
And hazard in the glorious enterprise,
Joined with me once, now misery hath joined
In equal ruin: into what pit thou seest
From what height fallen, so much the stronger proved
He with his thunder, and till then who knew
The force of those dire arms? Yet not for those
Nor what the potent Victor in his rage
Can else inflict do I repent or change,

Though changed in outward luster; that fixed mind
And high disdain, from sense of injured merit,
That with the mightiest raised me to contend,
And to the fierce contentions brought along
Innumerable force of spirits armed
That durst dislike his reign, and me preferring,
His utmost power with adverse power opposed
In dubious battle on the plains of Heaven,
And shook his throne. What though the field be lost?
All is not lost; the unconquerable will,
And study of revenge, immortal hate,
And courage never to submit or yield:
And what is else not to be overcome?
That glory never shall his wrath or might
Extort from me. To bow and sue for grace
With suppliant knee, and deify his power
Who, from the terror of this arm so late
Doubted his empire — that were low indeed;
That were an ignominy and shame beneath
This downfall; since by fate the strength of gods
And this empyreal substance, cannot fail,
Since, through experience of this great event
In arms not worse, in foresight much advanced,
We may with more successful hope resolve
To wage by force or guile eternal war
Irreconcilable, to our grand Foe,
Who now triumphs, and in th' excess of joy
Sole reigning holds the tyranny of Heaven."
So spake th' apostate Angel, though in pain,
Vaunting aloud, but racked with deep despair:
And him thus answered soon his bold compeer.
"O Prince, O Chief of many throned powers,
That led th' embattled seraphim to war
Under thy conduct, and in dreadful deeds
Fearless, endangered Heavens perpetual King;
And put to proof his high supremacy,
Whether upheld by strength, or chance, or fate,
Too well I see and rue the dire event,
That with sad overthrow and foul defeat

◂ ◂ ◂ ◂ **THE BRITISH PART**

Hath lost us Heaven, and all this mighty Host
In horrible destruction laid thus low,
As far as Gods and heavenly essences
Can perish: for the mind and spirit remains
Invincible, and vigor soon returns,
Though all our glory extinct, and happy state
Here swallowed up in endless misery.
But what if he our Conqueror, (whom I now
Of force believe almighty, since no less
Than such could have o'rerpowered such force as ours)
Have left us this our spirit and strength entire,
Strongly to suffer and support our pains,
That we may so suffice his vengeful ire,
Or do him mightier service as his thralls
By right of war, whate'er his business be
Here in the heart of Hell to work in fire,
Or do his errands in the gloomy Deep;
What can it the avail though yet we feel
Strength undiminished, or eternal being
To undergo eternal punishment?"
Whereto with speedy words th' Arch-Fiend replied:
"Fall'n Cherub, to be weak is miserable,
Doing or suffering: but of this be sure,
To do aught good never will be our task,
But ever to do ill our sole delight,
As being the contrary to his high will
Whom we resist. If then his providence
Out of our evil seek to bring forth good,
Our labor must be to pervert that end,
And out of good still to find means of evil;
Which ofttimes may succeed so as perhaps
Shall grieve him, if I fail not, and disturb
His inmost counsels from their destined aim.
But see! the angry Victor hath recalled
His ministers of vengeance and pursuit
Back to the gates of Heaven: the sulphureous hail
Shot after us in storm, o'erblown hath laid
The fiery surge that from the precipice
Of Heaven received us falling; and the thunder,

Winged with red lightning and impetuous rage,
Perhaps hath spent his shafts, and ceases now
To bellow through the vast and boundless deep.
Let us not slip th' occasion, whether scorn,
Or satiate fury yield it from our Foe.
Seest thou yon dreary plain, forlorn and wild,
The seat of desolation, void of light,
Save what the glimmering of these livid flames
Casts pale and dreadful? Thither let us tend
From off the tossing of these fiery waves,
There rest, if any rest can harbour there,
And, re-assembling our afflicted powers,
Consult how we may henceforth most offend
Our enemy, our own loss how repair,
How overcome this dire calamity,
What reinforcement we may gain from hope,
If not, what resolution from despair."

Chapter 3 Daniel Defoe

作者简介

Daniel Defoe (1660 – 1731), the son of James Foe, was born in London and educated at the Stoke Newington Academy. He traveled widely in France, Spain, Italy and Germany, and then established himself as a hosiery merchant. Then he tried his hands in politics and became one of the best-informed political and economic pamphleteers of his time.

His first important work was *An Essay upon Projects*(1697), followed by *The True-Born Englishman*(1701), an immensely popular satirical poem attacking the prejudice against a king of foreign birth and his Dutch friends. His political work and writing finally brought upon him official wrath and caused him to be fined, imprisoned and pilloried, and became bankrupt. He was soon secured to release, and was employed as a secret agent by Robert Harley, the Troy politician and Speaker of the House of Common. Defoe traveled around the country gathering information and wrote many pamphlets. Later, he issued a triweekly news journal entitled *The Review*. The journal is historically important as it established the form of the periodical essay. He has been regarded as the pioneer of modern journalist, for he not only ran *The Review* by himself, but also wrote articles on various subjects of politics, crime, religion, marriage, psychology and the supernatural. His pamphlets led to his persecution by the Whigs and to a brief imprisonment. He then started a new trade journal, *Mercator*. In his late fifties, Defoe began to produce fiction at incredible speed. First came *The Life and Strange Surprising Adventures of Robinson Crusoe* (1719), then *Captain Singleton* (1720); in 1722 appeared *Moll Flanders*, and then *Roxana* (1724) and *A New Voyage round the World* (1725). He died in his lodgings, probably whilst in hiding from his creditors. He was buried in Bun hill Fields, London.

Defoe's influence on the English novel and prose writing is enormous. He is a master of plain prose and powerful narrative, with a journalist's curiosity and love of realistic details; his peculiar gifts make him one of the greatest reporters of his time, as well as a great imaginative writer.

丹尼尔·笛福(1660—1731),出生于伦敦一小工商业家庭,詹姆斯·福之子。他就读于一所宗教学校,并改其姓"福"为"笛福"。他曾广泛游历于法国、西班牙、意大利及德国,此后成为一名羊毛织品商。接着,他尝试涉足政治领域,并成为当时最具盛名的政治和经济学小册子作家之一。

他的首部重磅作品《论开发》出版于1697年,紧接着于1701年出版了《真正的英国人》——一首流传极广的讽刺诗,旨在为外籍的信奉新教的威廉三世及其荷兰朋友辩护。他的政治性作品最终引起官方愤怒,也导致他被罚款、监禁、落为笑柄谈资,然后破产。不久之后他被释放,被特洛伊政治家及下议院发言人罗伯特·哈利雇佣为秘密情报员。笛福游走于各国搜集舆论并且杜撰了多部小册子。随后,他创办了名为《评论》的新闻杂志,该杂志因作为英国第一份定期出版的刊物而具有历史性的重要意义。他不但独自经营《评论》杂志,而且撰写涵盖政治、犯罪、宗教、婚姻、心理学和超自然等多种话题的文章,所以被称为"现代新闻报道之父"。他的小册子著作导致他受到辉格党的迫害及短期监禁。随后他开始经营一份新的贸易杂志——《经商全书》。笛福在其50岁后期,开始以让人难以置信的速度创作小说。首先出版的是《鲁滨逊漂流记》(1719),随后陆续出版了《辛格顿船长》(1720)、《摩尔弗兰德斯》(1722)、《罗克萨那》(1724)、《新环球游记》(1725)。他死于其寓所内,也许当时是在躲避他的债权人。随后葬于伦敦的邦西田园。

笛福对于英国小说及散文写作的影响巨大。他在平缓的散文及有力的叙述上造诣深厚,并富有新闻者的好奇心、热衷于真实细节。他独特的天赋使得他成为当时最伟大的记者之一,同时也是一位极其伟大、富有想象力的作家。

作品及导读

作 品 1

The Life and Strange Surprising Adventures of Robinson Crusoe
(*Chapter 4. First Weeks on the Island*)

导 读

Robinson Crusoe, a young Englishman, goes against his parents' wishes and runs off to sea to seek his fortune. After some times, he became the owner of a sugar plantation, and aligned himself with other planters to undertake a trip to Africa in order to bring back a shipload of slaves. After surviving a storm, he was thrown upon shore only to find he was the only survivor of the wreck. Overcoming his despair, he fetches arms, tools, and other supplies from the ship before it breaks apart and sinks. He proceeds to build a fenced-in habitation near a cave which he excavates himself. He keeps a calendar by making marks in a wooden cross which he has built. He hunts, grows corn and rice, dries grapes to make raisins for the winter months, learns to make pottery and raises goats, all using tools created from stone and wood which he harvests on the island. He also adopts a small parrot. He reads the Bible and becomes religious, thanking God for his fate in which nothing is missing but human society. Later he acquires a companion, whom he rescues from cannibals and names "Friday". After encountering with pirates and mutineers, Crusoe and Friday manage to escape from the island. Finally Crusoe returns to England safely and finds that in his absence he has become a wealthy man. Years later he revisits his island, now populated by marooned sailors, to establish a regular colony there.

This chapter (First Weeks on the Island) will mainly introduce the practical problems in his life on the island, such as how he considers the security, the sunshine, the health and the view to the sea when he chooses the location of tents, and how he makes the medicine for himself as well as how to remember time accurately. The author tries to give a vivid description of the details and also uses the very simple languages to record the life of Robinson on the island objectively. The character of Robinson Crusoe is representative of the rising English bourgeoisie. He is very optimistic, full of fighting spirit and shows a strong will of his self struggle.

鲁滨逊,一个年轻的英国小伙,违背父母的劝告,逃到海外寻找财富。后来,他变成了种植园主,并且与其他种植者结盟,到非洲购买奴隶。途中遇上风暴,漂流到南美附近的无人荒岛。他很快战胜了忧郁失望的心情,从沉船上搬来枪械和工具,修建住所、记录时间、制造工具、种植谷类、驯养山羊、饲养鹦鹉、阅读《圣经》,这使得他变得有宗教信仰,感谢上帝,即使他失去了一切。之后,他有一个同伴——星期五,是他从食人族那里救回的。遇见一些海盗和暴徒后,他们设法逃离荒岛。最后,他乘船返回英国,并且成为巨富。多年后,他重返已被孤立水手居住的岛上,旨在建立一个有秩序的殖民地。

本章(荒岛第一周)主要针对他在荒岛上生存的实际问题,比如选址搭建帐篷时考虑到的安全、卫生、阳光等,非常贴近生活。再如他如何制药为自己做万全准备,以及记时间如何精确。作者的描写不厌其烦,语言朴实无华。客观的记载了发生在荒岛上的事情。鲁滨逊的形象是资产阶级上升时期的典型代表。他十分乐观,充满了斗志,体现了自我奋斗的精神。

选 文

My thoughts were now wholly employed about securing my self against either savages, if any should appear, or wild beasts, if any were in the island; and I had many thoughts of the method how to do this, and what kind of dwelling to make, whether I should make me a cave in the earth, or a tent upon the earth. And, in short, I resolved upon both, the manner and description of which, it may not be improper to give an account of.

I soon found the place I was in was not for my settlement, particularly because it was upon a low moorish ground near the sea, and I believed would not be wholesome, and more particularly because there was no fresh water near it, so I resolved to find a more healthy and more convenient spot of ground.

I consulted several things in my situation which I found would be proper for me: 1st, health, and fresh water I just now mentioned; 2dly, shelter from the heat of the sun; 3dly, security from ravenous creatures, whether men or beasts; 4thly, a view to the sea, that if God sent any ship in sight, I might not lose any advantage for my deliverance, of which I was not willing to banish all my expectation yet.

In search of a place proper for this, I found a little plain on the side of a rising hill, whose front towards this little plain was steep as a house-side, so that nothing could come down upon me from the top. On the side of this rock there was a hollow place worn a little way in like the entrance or door of a cave, but there was not really any cave or way into the rock at all.

On the flat of the green, just before this hollow place, I resolved to pitch my tent. This plain was not above an hundred yards broad, and about twice as long, and lay like a green before my door, and at the end of it descended irregularly every way down into the low-grounds by the sea-side. It was on the N. N. W. side of the hill, so that I was sheltered from the heat every day, till it came to a W. and by S. sun, or thereabouts, which in those countries is near the setting.

Before I set up my tent, I drew a half circle before the hollow place, which took in about ten yards in its semi-diameter from the rock, and twenty yards in its diameter, from its beginning and ending.

In this half circle I pitched two rows of strong stakes, driving them into the ground till they stood very firm like piles, the biggest end being out of the ground about five foot and a half, and sharpened on the top. The two rows did not stand above six inches from one another.

Then I took the pieces of cable which I had cut in the ship, and I laid them in rows one upon another, within the circle, between these two rows of stakes, up to the top, placing other stakes in the inside, leaning against them, about two foot and a half high, like a spur to a post, and this fence was so strong, that neither man or beast could get into it or over it. This cost me a great deal of time and labor, especially to cut the piles in the woods, bring them to the place, and drive them into the earth.

The entrance into this place I made to be not by a door, but by a short ladder to go over the top, which ladder, when I was in, I lifted over after me, and so I was completely fenced in, and fortified, as I thought, from all the world, and consequently slept secure in the night, which otherwise I could not have done, though, as it appeared afterward, there was no need of all this caution from the enemies that I apprehended danger from.

Into this fence or fortress, with infinite labor, I carried all my riches, all my provisions, ammunition and stores, of which you have the account above, and I made me a large tent, which, to preserve me from the rains that in one part of the year are very violent there, I made double, viz. one smaller tent within, and one larger tent above it, and covered the uppermost with a large tarpaulin which I had saved among the sails.

And now I lay no more for a while in the bed which I had brought on shore, but in a hammock, which was indeed a very good one, and belonged to the mate of the ship.

Into this tent I brought all my provisions, and every thing that would spoil by the wet, and having thus enclosed all my goods, I made up the entrance, which till now I had left open, and so passed and re-passed, as I said, by a short ladder.

When I had done this, I began to work my way into the rock, and bringing all the earth and stones that I dug down out through my tent, I laid them up within my fence in the nature of a terra, that so it raised the ground within about a foot and a half, and thus I made me a cave just behind my tent, which served me like a cellar to my house.

It cost me much labor, and many days, before all these things were brought to perfection, and therefore I must go back to some other things which took up some of my thoughts. At the same time it happened after I had laid my scheme for the setting up my tent and making the cave, that a storm of rain falling from a thick dark cloud, a sudden flash of lightning happened, and after that a great clap of thunder, as is naturally the effect of it. I was not so much surprised with the lightning as I was with a thought which darted into my mind as swift as the lightning itself — oh my powder! My very heart sunk within me, when I thought, that at one blast all my powder might be destroyed, on which, not my defence only, but the providing me food, as I thought, entirely depended; I was nothing near so anxious about my own danger, though, had the powder took fire, I had never known who had hurt me.

Such impression did this make upon me, that after the storm was over, I laid aside all my works, my Building, and fortifying, and applied my self to make bags and boxes to separate the powder, and keep it a little and a little in a parcel, in hope, that whatever might come, it might not all take fire at once, and to keep it so apart that it should not be possible to make one part fire another. I finished this work in about a fortnight, and I think my powder, which in all was about 240 pounds weight, was divided in not less than a hundred parcels; as to the barrel that had been wet, I did not apprehend any danger from that, so I placed it in my new cave, which in my fancy I called my kitchen, and the rest I hid up and down in holes among the rocks, so that no wet might come to it, marking very carefully where I laid it.

In the interval of time while this was doing I went out once at least every day with my gun, as well to divert my self, as to see if I could kill any thing fit for food, and as near as I could to acquaint my self with what the island produced. The first time I went out I presently discovered that there were goats in the island, which was a great satisfaction to me; but then it was attended with this misfortune to me, viz. that they were so shy, so subtle, and so swift of foot, that it was the most difficult thing in the world to come at them. But I was not discouraged at this, not doubting but I might now and then shoot one, as it soon happened, for after I had found their haunts a little, I laid wait in this manner for them: I observed if they saw me in the valleys, though they were upon the rocks, they would run away as in a terrible fright; but if they were feeding in the valleys, and I was upon the rocks, they took no notice of me, from whence I concluded, that by the position of their optics, their sight was so directed downward, that they did not readily see objects that were above them; so afterward I took this method, I always climbed the rocks first to get above them, and then had frequently a fair mark.

The first shot I made among these creatures, I killed a she-goat which had a little kid by her which she gave suck to, which grieved me heartily; but when the old one fell, the kid stood stock still by her till I came and took her up, and not only so, but when I carried the old one with me upon my shoulders, the kid followed me quite to my enclosure, upon which I laid down the dam, and took the kid in my arms, and carried it over my pale, in hopes to have bred it up tame, but it would not eat, so I was forced to kill it and eat it my self; these two supplied me with flesh a great while, for I eat sparingly; and saved my provisions (my bread especially) as much as possibly I could.

Having now fixed my habitation, I found it absolutely necessary to provide a place to make a fire in, and fuel to burn; and what I did for that, as also how I enlarged my cave, and what conveniences I made, I shall give a full account of in its pace; but I must first give some little account of myself, and of my thoughts about living, which it may well be supposed were not a few.

I had a dismal prospect of my condition, for as I was not cast away upon that island without being driven, as is said, by a violent storm quite out of the course of our intended voyage, and a great way, viz. some hundreds of leagues out of the ordinary course of the trade of mankind, I had great reason to consider it as a determination of heaven, that in this desolate place, and in this desolate manner I should end my life; the tears would run plentifully down my face when I made these reflections, and sometimes I would expostulate with myself, why providence should thus completely ruin its creatures, and render them so absolutely miserable, so without help abandoned, so entirely depressed, that it could hardly be rational to be thankful for such a life.

But something always returned swift upon me to check these thoughts, and to reprove me; and particularly one day walking with my gun in my hand by the sea-side, I was very pensive upon the subject of my present condition, then reason as It were expostulated with me the other way, thus, well, you are in a desolate condition it is true, but pray remember, where are the rest of you? Did not you come eleven of you into the boat, where are the ten? Why were not they saved and you lost? Why were you singled out? Is it better to be here or there? And then I pointed to the sea. All evils are to be considered with the good that is in them, and with what worse attends them.

Then it occurred to me again, how well I was furnished for my subsistence, and what would have been my case if it had not happened, which was an hundred thousand to one, that the ship floated from the place where she first struck and was driven so near to the shore that I had time to get all these things out of her. What would have been my case, if I had been to have lived in the condition in which I at first came on shore, without necessaries of life, or necessaries to supply and procure them? Particularly said I aloud, (though to myself) what should I have done without a gun, without ammunition, without any tools to make any thing, or to work with, without clothes, bedding, a tent, or any manner of covering, and that now I had all these to a sufficient quantity, and was in a fair way to provide my self in such a manner, as to live without my gun when my ammunition was spent, so that I had a tolerable view of subsisting without any want as long as I lived; for I considered from the beginning how I would provide for the accidents that might happen, and for the time that was to come, even not only after my ammunition should be spent, but even after my health or strength should decay.

I confess I had not entertained any notion of my ammunition being destroyed at one blast, I mean my powder being blown up by lightning, and this made the thoughts of it so surprising to me when it lightened and thundered, as I observed just now.

And now, being about to enter into a melancholy relation of a scene of silent life, such perhaps as was never heard of in the world before, I shall take it from its beginning, and continue it in its order. It was, by my account, the 30th of Sept. when, in the manner as above said, I first set foot upon this horrid island, when the sun being, to us, in its autumnal equinox, was almost just over my head, for I reckoned my self, by observation, to be in the latitude of 9 degrees 22 minutes north of the line.

After I had been there about ten or twelve days, it came into my thoughts, that I should lose my reckoning of time for want of books and pen and ink, and should even forget the Sabbath days from the working days. But to prevent this I cut it with my knife upon a large post, in capital letters, and making it into a great cross I set it up on the shore where I first landed, viz. I came on shore here on the 30th of Sept. 1659. Upon the sides of this square post I cut every day a notch with my knife, and every seventh notch was as long again as the rest, and every first day of the month as long again as that long one, and thus I kept my calendar, or weekly, monthly, and yearly reckoning of time.

In the next place we are to observe, that among the many things which I brought out of the ship in the several voyages, which, as above mentioned, I made to it, I got several things of less value, but not all less useful to me, which I omitted setting down before; as in particular, pens, ink, and paper, several parcels in the captain's, mate's, gunner's, and carpenter's keeping, three or four compasses, some mathematical instruments, dials, perspectives, charts, and books of navigation, all which I huddled together, whether I might want them or no, also I found three very good Bibles which came to me in my cargo from England, and which I had packed up among my thing, some Portuguese books also, and among them two or three popish prayer-books, and several other books, all which I carefully secured. And I must not forget, that we had in the ship a dog and two cats, of whose eminent history I may have occasion to say something in its place, for I carried both the cats with me, and as for the dog, he jumped out of the ship of himself and swam on shore to me the day after I went on shore with my first cargo, and was a trusty servant to me many years; I wanted nothing that he could fetch me, nor any company that he could make up to me, I only wanted to have him talk to me, but that would not do. As I observed before, I found pen, ink and paper, and I husbanded them to the utmost, and I shall chew, that while my ink lasted, I kept things very exact, but after that was gone I could not, for I could not make any ink by any means that I could devise.

And this put me in mind that I wanted many things, notwithstanding all that I had amassed together, and of these, this of ink was one, as also spade, pickaxe, and shovel to dig or remove the earth, needles, pins, and thread; as for linen, I soon learned to want that without much difficulty. This want of tools made every work I did go on heavily, and it was near a whole year before I had entirely finished my little pale or surrounded habitation: The piles or stakes, which were as heavy as I could well lift, were a long time in cutting and preparing in the woods, and more by far in bringing home, so that I spent some times two days in cutting and bringing home one of those posts, and a third day in driving it into the ground; for which purpose I got a heavy piece of wood at first, but at last bethought my self of one of the iron crows, which however though I found it, yet it made driving those posts or piles very laborious and tedious work. But what need I have been concerned at the tediousness of any thing I had to do, seeing I had time enough to do it in, nor had I any other employment if that had been over, at least, that I could foresee, except the ranging the Island to seek for food, which I did more or less every day.

I now began to consider seriously my condition, and the circumstance I was reduced to, and I drew up the state of my affairs in writing, not so much to leave them to any that were to come after me, for I was like to have but few heirs, as to deliver my thoughts from daily poring upon them, and afflicting my mind; and as my reason began now to master my despondency, I began to comfort my self as well as I could, and to set the good against the evil, that I might have something to distinguish my case from worse, and I stated it very impartially, like debtor and creditor, the comforts I enjoyed, against the miseries I suffered, thus: —

Evil:

I am cast upon a horrible desolate Island, void of all hope of recovery.

I am singled out and separated, as it were, from all the world to be miserable.

I am divided from mankind, a solitaire, one banished from humane society.

I have not clothes to cover me.

I am without any defence or means to resist any violence of man or beast.

I have no soul to speak to, or relieve me.

Good:

But I am alive, and not drowned as all my ship's company was.

But I am singled out too from all the ship's crew to be spared from death; and he that miraculously saved me from death, can deliver me from this condition.

But I am in a hot climate, where if I had clothes I could hardly wear them.

But I am cast on an Island, where I see no wild beasts to hurt me, as I saw on the coast of Africa. And what if I had been shipwrecked there?

But God wonderfully sent the ship in near enough to the shore, that I have gotten out so many necessary things as will either supply my wants, or enable me to supply my self even as long as I live.

Upon the whole, here was an undoubted testimony, that there was scarce any condition in the world so miserable, but there was something negative or something positive to be thankful for in it; and let this stand as a direction from the experience of the most miserable of all conditions in this world, that we may always find in it something to comfort our selves from, and to set in the description of good and evil, on the credit side of the accompt.

Having now brought my mind a little to relish my condition, and given over looking out to sea to see if I could spy a ship, I say, giving over these things, I began to apply my self to accommodate my way of living, and to make things as easy to me as I could.

I have already described my habitation, which was a tent under the side of a rock, surrounded with a strong pale of posts and cables, but I might now rather call it a wall, for I raised a kind of wall up against it of turfs, about two foot thick on the out-side, and after some time, I think it was a year and half, I raised rafters from it leaning to the rock, and thatched or covered it with bows of trees, and such things as I could get to keep out the rain, which I found at some times of the year very violent.

I have already observed how I brought all my goods into this pale, and into the cave which I had made behind me. But I must observe too, that at first this was a confused heap of goods, which as they lay in no order, so they took up all my place, I had no room to turn my self; so I set my self to enlarge my cave and works farther into the earth, for it was a loose sandy rock, which yielded easily to the labor I bestowed on it; and so when I found I was pretty safe as to beasts of prey, I worked side-ways to the right hand into the rock, and then turning to the right again, worked quite out and made me a door to come out, on the out-side of my ale or fortification. This gave me not only egress and regress, as it were a back way to my tent and to my storehouse, but gave me room to stow my goods.

And now I began to apply my self to make such necessary things as I found I most wanted, as particularly a chair and a table, for without these I was not able to enjoy the few comforts I had in the world, I could not write, or eat, or do several things with so much pleasure without a table. So I went to work; and here I must needs observe, that as reason is the substance and original of the mathematics, so by stating and squaring every thing by reason, and by making the most rational judgment of things, every man may be in time master of every mechanic art. I had never handled a tool in my life, and yet in time by labor, application, and contrivance, I found at last that I wanted nothing but I could have made it, especially if I had had tools; however I made abundance of things, even without tools, and some with no more tools than an adze and a hatchet, which perhaps were never made that way before, and that with infinite labor: For example, if I wanted a board, I had no other way but to cut down a tree, set it on an edge before me, and hew it flat on either side with my axes, till I had brought it to be thin as a plank, and then dub it smooth with my adze. It is true, by this method I could make but one board out of a whole tree, but this I had no remedy for but patience, any more than I had for the prodigious deal of time and labor which it took me up to make a plank or board. But my time or labor was little worth, and so it was as well employed one way as another.

However, I made me a table and a chair, as I observed above, in the first place, and this I did out of the short pieces of boards that I brought on my raft from the ship: But when I had wrought out some boards, as above, I made large shelves of the breadth of a foot and half one over another, all along one side of my cave, to lay all my tools, nails, and ironwork, and in a word, to separate every thing at large in their places, that I might come easily at them; I knocked pieces into the wall of the rock to hang my guns and all things that would hang up. So that had my cave been to be seen, it looked like a general magazine of all necessary things, and I had every thing so ready at my hand, that it was a great pleasure to me to see all my goods in such order, and especially to find my stock of all necessaries so great.

And now it was that I began to keep a journal of every day's employment, for indeed at first I was in too much hurry, and not only hurry as to labor, but in too much discomposure of mind, and my journal would have been full of many dull things: For example, I must have said thus. Sept. the 30th. After I got to shore and had escaped drowning, instead of being thankful to God for my deliverance, having first vomited with the great quantity of salt water which was gotten into my stomach, and recovering my self a little, I ran about the shore, wringing my hands and beating my head and face, exclaiming at my misery, and crying out, I was undone, undone, till tried and faint I was forced to lye down on the ground to repose, but durst not sleep for fear of being devoured.

Some days after this, and after I had been on board the ship, and got all that I could out of her, yet I could not forbear getting up to the top of a little mountain and looking out to sea in hopes of seeing a ship, then fancy at a vast distance I spied a sail, please my self with the hopes of it, and then after looking steadily till I was almost blind, lose it quite, and sit down and weep like a child, and thus encrease my misery by my folly.

But having gotten over these things in some measure, and having settled my household stuff and habitation, made me a table and a chair, and all as handsome about me as I could, I began to keep my journal, of which I shall here give you the copy (though in it will be told all these particulars over again) as long as it lasted, for having no more ink I was forced to leave it off.

4 Jonathan Swift

作者简介

Jonathan Swift, Irish author and journalist, dean of St. Patrick's Cathedral (Dublin) from 1713, the foremost prose satirist in English language. He was born in Dublin. His father, Jonathan Swift St., a lawyer and an English civil servant, died seven months before his son was born. His mother returned to England, leaving him to her wealthy brother-in-law, Uncle Godwin. Between the year of 1674 and 1682, Swift studied at Kilkenny Grammar School and in 1682 – 1689, he studied at Trinity College in Dublin. In 1689, he was employed by Sir William Temple, a powerful English statesman, as secretary and personal assistant. He met Esther Johnson when she was 8 years old and acted as her tutor and mentor, giving her the nickname "Stella". In 1690, Swift left Temple for Ireland because of his health, but returned to Moor Park the following year. In 1692, Swift received his M. A. from Hertford College, Oxford.

In 1702, he received his Doctor of Divinity degree from Trinity College, Dublin and traveled to England accompanied by Esther Johnson who was twenty years old. And in 1704, he began to write satire, his work *A Tale of the Tub* is a satire on corruptions in religion and learning, and *Battle of the Books* is a mock-epic on the debate between Ancients and Moderns. He became the editor of the *Examiner* when Tory came to power in 1710 and published the political pamphlet *The Conduct of the Allies*, in 1711. In 1714, with the dismal of Tory, Swift's best move was to leave England and he returned to Ireland in disappointment, a virtual exile, to live "like a rat in a hole". During the year of 1726 to 1745, he began writing his masterpiece such as *Gulliver's Travels*, *The Death of Mrs. Johnson*, *A Modest Proposal*. In 1745, Swift died and was buried in his own cathedral by Esther Johnson's side, the bulk of his fortune (twelve thousand pounds) was left to found St. Patrick's Hospital for Imbeciles.

乔纳森·斯威夫特，爱尔兰作家和记者，从1713年开始担任圣帕特里克大教堂(都柏林)的院长，是英语语言界最著名的讽刺散文作家。乔纳森·斯威夫特生于爱尔兰都柏林的一个贫苦家庭。他父亲是定居爱尔兰的英格兰人,早在他出生前七个月就已去世。斯威夫特由叔父抚养长大,就读于著名的都柏林三一学院(以天主教的"三位一体"命名)。十五岁时获得三一学院的学士学位。1674年至1682年,斯威夫特曾在基尔肯尼预科学校学习,1689年,斯威夫特前往英国,做了穆尔庄园主人威廉·邓波尔爵士的私人秘书,直到1699年邓波尔去世。1692年,他荣获文学士。

1702年,他在都柏林三一学院接受了他的神学博士学位,并同20岁的埃丝特·约翰逊前往英国。随后在1704年,他开始写讽刺小说,他的《一只桶的故事》讲述了宗教和学习的腐败,《书籍之战》讲述了古人和现代人之间的辩论。1714年托利党失势,他回到爱尔兰,任都柏林圣帕特里克教堂主持牧师,同时着手研究爱尔兰现状,积极支持并投入争取爱尔兰独立自由的斗争,但一个个美好的梦想最后都破灭了。晚年的斯威夫特内心十分孤独,只和屈指可数的几个朋友交往。他将自己积蓄的三分之一用于各种慈善事业,用三分之一的收入为弱智者盖了一所圣帕特里克医院。他的亲人去世,头昏耳聋,然而,斯威夫特本人也被疾病折磨得不成样子,但是,仍然一直坚持写作(直到逝世),许多人甚至认为他已完全疯了。在1726年到1745年之间是斯威夫特文学创作的主要时期,他有许多脍炙人口的杰作,例如《格列佛游记》、《一只桶的故事》、《一个温和的建议》等等。1745年10月19日,斯威夫特辞世,终年78岁,葬于圣帕特里克大教堂。

作品及导读

作品 1

A Modest Proposal

导 读

Jonathan gained great reputation in English literature by his artistic irony, vivid language and simple style. *A Modest Proposal* was first published anonymously in Berlin. Later on, it was reprinted in London. Several reprinting witnesses its popularity among the readers.

In the 16 th century, Ireland became a dependency of England. In the 18th century, though Ireland established its congress, it was still under the strict control of England. Irish people are exploited and oppressed by both English businessmen and Irish big landlords. The situation worsened when Swift wrote the prose. In 1729, Ireland was greatly stricken by natural disasters. Irish people suffered a lot and many of them became beggars in the street. However, the ruling class showed no sympathy to the poor. Instead, they came up with all kinds of "proposals" to solve the overpopulation problem. In essence, these "proposals" made the Irish poor people in worse situation. These "advisers" tried to save the country by loftily proposing "suggestions". Swift hated this group of cruel "advisers." In *A Modest Proposal*, he employed the tone of "advisers" to solve the overpopulation problem by suggesting eating children from poor families. In the prose, Swift showed the serious situation of Irish children. Then he calculated the number of children who were a "burden" to their parents or country. After logical analysis of the problem, he finally made "a modest proposal"—the best solution to the problem that Ireland faced.

Swift revealed Ireland's social problems, and blamed the exploitation by English rulers and the oppression by Irish landlords. His sympathy to the poor in Ireland was showed through.

Jonathan Swift's *A Modest Proposal* is considered as a perfect model of irony in which he is against tyranny and for liberty. Swift once wrote a poem to comment on his life: "Fair LIBERTY was all his cry, for her he stood prepared to die." *A Modest Proposal*, as a masterpiece of irony in English literature, has become a classic. As time goes on, it will still attract the attention of future generations from all over the world.

乔纳森的讽刺艺术,语言生动,风格简单,在英国文学中赢得了极大的声誉。《一个温和的建议》首次于柏林匿名发表。后来,在伦敦又被反复重印,且重印版在读者群体中大受欢迎。

16世纪,爱尔兰成为英格兰的殖民地。18世纪,尽管爱尔兰国会成立,它仍然处于英国的严格控制下。爱尔兰人长期饱受英国商人和爱尔兰大地主的压迫与摧残。在斯威夫特写这篇文章时,这种局势愈演愈烈。1729年,爱尔兰遭受严重的自然灾害。爱尔兰人民饱受疾苦,许多人开始沿街乞讨。然而,统治阶级并没有对穷人表现出任何的同情心。相反,他们想出了各种各样的"建议",以解决人口过剩问题。本质上,这些"建议",使爱尔兰穷人的处境更糟。这些"建议者"傲慢地提出"建议",试图拯救国家。斯威夫特厌恶这群残酷的"建议者"。在《一个温和的建议》中,他以"建议者"的口吻,通过建议吃掉来自贫困家庭的孩子们去解决人口过剩问题。在散文中,斯威夫特解释了爱尔兰孩子的严峻形势。然后他计算了那些对于他们的父母或国家是"负担"的孩子的数量。在对问题进行逻辑分析之后,他终于做出了"一个温和的建议"——解决爱尔兰面临问题的最佳方案。

斯威夫特披露了爱尔兰的社会问题,并指责英国统治者和爱尔兰地主的压迫与统治。他同情爱尔兰穷人。

乔纳森·斯威夫特的《一个温和的建议》被誉为他反对专制与自由最为完美的讽刺模型。乔纳森·斯威夫特曾作了一首诗来评论他的生活:"公平的自由是他的呐喊,他为她随时准备好牺牲。"作为英国文学讽刺艺术的著作,《一个温和的建议》已成为英国文学史上的经典。随着时间的推移,它仍然会吸引未来全世界的注意。

选 文

It is a melancholy object to those, who walk through this great town, or travel in the country, when they see the streets, the roads and cabin-doors crowded with beggars of the female sex, followed by three, four, or six children, all in rags, and importuning every passenger for alms. These mothers instead of being able to work for their honest livelihood, are forced to employ all their time in strolling to beg sustenance for their helpless infants who, as they grow up, either turn thieves for want of work, or leave their dear native country, to fight for the Pretender in Spain, or sell themselves to the Barbadoes.

I think it is agreed by all parties, that this prodigious number of children in the arms, or on the backs, or at the heels of their mothers, and frequently of their fathers, is in the present deplorable state of the kingdom, a very great additional grievance; and therefore whoever could find out a fair, cheap and easy method of making these children sound and useful members of the common-wealth, would deserve so well of the public, as to have his statue set up for a preserver of the nation.

But my intention is very far from being confined to provide only for the children of professed beggars: it is of a much greater extent, and shall take in the whole number of infants at a certain age, who are born of parents in effect as little able to support them, as those who demand our charity in the streets.

As to my own part, having turned my thoughts for many years, upon this important subject, and maturely weighed the several schemes of our projectors, I have always found them grossly mistaken in their computation. It is true, a child just dropt from its dam, may be supported by her milk, for a solar year, with little other nourishment: at most not above the value of two shillings, which the mother may certainly get, or the value in scraps, by her lawful occupation of begging; and it is exactly at one year old that I propose to provide for them in such a manner, as, instead of being a charge upon their parents, or the parish, or wanting food and raiment for the rest of their lives, they shall, on the contrary, contribute to the feeding, and partly to the clothing of many thousands.

There is likewise another great advantage in my scheme, that it will prevent those voluntary abortions, and that horrid practice of women murdering their bastard children, alas! too frequent among us, sacrificing the poor innocent babes, I doubt, more to avoid the expense than the shame, which would move tears and pity in the most savage and inhuman breast.

The number of souls in this kingdom being usually reckoned one million and a half, of these I calculate there may be about two hundred thousand couple whose wives are breeders; from which number I subtract thirty thousand couple, who are able to maintain their own children, although I apprehend there cannot be so many, under the present distresses of the kingdom but this being granted, there will remain an hundred and seventy thousand breeders. I again subtract fifty thousand, for those women who miscarry, or whose children die by accident or disease within the year. There only remain an hundred and twenty thousand children of poor parents annually born. The question therefore is, how this number shall be reared, and provided for? Which, as I have already said, under the present situation of affairs is utterly impossible by all the methods hitherto proposed, for we can neither employ them in handicraft or agriculture; we neither build houses, (I mean in the country) nor cultivate land: they can very seldom pick up a livelihood by stealing till they arrive at six years old; except where they are of towardly parts, although I confess they learn the rudiments much earlier; during which time they can however be properly looked upon only as probationers: As I have been informed by a principal gentleman in the county of Cavan, who protested to me, that he never knew above one or two instances under the age of six, even in a part of the kingdom so renowned for the quickest proficiency in that art.

I am assured by our merchants, that a boy or a girl before twelve years old, is no salable commodity, and even when they come to this age, they will not yield above three pounds, or three pounds and half a crown at most, on the exchange; which cannot turn to account either to the parents or kingdom, the charge of nutriments and rags having been at least four times that value.

I shall now therefore humbly propose my own thoughts, which I hope will not be liable to the least objection.

I have been assured by a very knowing American of my acquaintance in London, that a young healthy child well nursed, is, at a year old, a most delicious nourishing and wholesome food, whether stewed, roasted, baked, or boiled; and I make no doubt that it will equally serve in a fricassee, or a ragout.

I do therefore humbly offer it to public consideration, that of the hundred and twenty thousand children, already computed, twenty thousand may be reserved for breed, whereof only one fourth part to be males; which is more than we allow to sheep, black cattle, or swine, and my reason is, that these children are seldom the fruits of marriage, a circumstance not much regarded by our savages, therefore, one male will be sufficient to serve four females. That the remaining hundred thousand may, at a year old, be offered in sale to the persons of quality and fortune, through the kingdom, always advising the mother to let them suck plentifully in the last month, so as to render them plump, and fat for a good table. A child will make two dishes at an entertainment for friends, and when the family dines alone, the fore or hind quarter will make a reasonable dish, and seasoned with a little pepper or salt, will be very good boiled on the fourth day, especially in winter.

I have reckoned upon a medium, that a child just born will weigh 12 pounds, and in a solar year, if tolerably nursed increase to 28 pounds.

I grant this food will be somewhat dear and therefore very proper for landlords, who, as they have already devoured most of the parents, seem to have the best title to the children.

Infant's flesh will be in season throughout the year, but more plentiful in March, and a little before and after; for we are told by a grave author, an eminent French physician, that fish being a prolific diet, there are more children born in Roman Catholic countries about nine months after Lent, the markets will be more glutted than usual, because the number of Popish infants, is at least three to one in this kingdom, and therefore it will have one other collateral advantage, by lessening the number of Papists among us.

I have already computed the charge of nursing a beggar's child (in which list I reckon all cottagers, laborers, and four-fifths of the farmers) to be about two shillings per an-um, rags included; and I believe no gentleman would repine to give ten shillings for the carcass of a good fat child, which, as I have said, will make four dishes of excellent nutritive meat, when he hath only some particular friend, or his own family to dine with him. Thus the squire will learn to be a good landlord, and grow popular among his tenants, the mother will have eight shillings neat profit, and be fit for work till she produces another child.

Those who are over thrifty (as I must confess the times require) may flea the carcass; the skin of which, artificially dressed, will make admirable gloves for ladies, and summer boots for fine gentlemen.

As to our City of Dublin, shambles may be appointed for this purpose, in the most convenient parts of it, and butchers we may be assured will not be wanting; although I rather recommend buying the children alive, and dressing them hot from the knife, as we do roasting pigs.

A very worthy person, a true lover of his country, and whose virtues I highly esteem, was lately pleased, in discoursing on this matter, to offer a refinement upon my scheme. He said, that many gentlemen of this kingdom, having of late destroyed their deer, he conceived that the want of venison might be well supplied by the bodies of young lads and maidens, not exceeding fourteen years of age, nor under twelve; so great a number of both sexes in every country being now ready to starve for want of work and service: And these to be disposed of by their parents if alive, or otherwise by their nearest relations. But with due deference to so excellent a friend, and so deserving a patriot, I cannot be altogether in his sentiments; for as to the males, my American acquaintance assured me from frequent experience, that their flesh was generally tough and lean, like that of our school-boys, by continual exercise, and their taste disagreeable, and to fatten them would not answer the charge. Then as to the females, it would, I think, with humble submission, be a loss to the public, because they soon would become breeders themselves: And besides, it is not improbable that some scrupulous people might be apt to censure such a practice, (although indeed very unjustly) as a little bordering upon cruelty, which, I confess, hath always been with me the strongest objection against any project, howsoever intended.

But in order to justify my friend, he confessed, that this expedient was put into his head by the famous Psalmanazar, a native of the island Formosa, who came from thence to London, above twenty years ago, and in conversation told my friend, that in his country, when any young person happened to be put to death, the executioner sold the carcass to persons of quality, as a prime dainty; and that, in his time, the body of a plump girl of fifteen, who was crucified for an attempt to poison the Emperor, was sold to his imperial majesty's prime minister of state, and other great mandarins of the court in joints from the gibbet, at four hundred crowns. Neither indeed can I deny, that if the same use were made of several plump young girls in this town who, without one single groat to their fortunes, cannot stir abroad without a chair, and appear at a play-house and assemblies in foreign fineries which they never will pay for; the kingdom would not be the worse.

Some persons of a desponding spirit are in great concern about that vast number of poor people, who are aged, diseased, or maimed; and I have been desired to employ my thoughts what course may be taken, to ease the nation of so grievous an encumbrance. But I am not in the least pain upon that matter, because it is very well known, that they are every day dying, and rotting, by cold and famine, and filth, and vermin, as fast as can be reasonably expected. And as to the young laborers, they are now in almost as hopeful a condition. They cannot get work, and consequently pine away from want of nourishment, to a degree, that if at any time they are accidentally hired to common labor, they have not strength to perform it, and thus the country and themselves are happily delivered from the evils to come.

I have too long digressed, and therefore shall return to my subject. I think the advantages by the proposal which I have made are obvious and many, as well as of the highest importance.

For first, as I have already observed, it would greatly lessen the number of Papists, with whom we are yearly over-run, being the principal breeders of the nation, as well as our most dangerous enemies, and who stay at home on purpose with a design to deliver the kingdom to the Pretender, hoping to take their advantage by the absence of so many good Protestants, who have chosen rather to leave their country, than stay at home and pay tithes against their conscience to an Episcopal curate.

Secondly, the poorer tenants will have something valuable of their own, which by law may be made liable to distress, and help to pay their landlord's rent, their corn and cattle being already seized, and money a thing unknown.

Thirdly, Whereas the maintenance of an hundred thousand children, from two years old, and upwards, cannot be computed at less than ten shillings a piece per an-um, the nation's stock will be thereby increased fifty thousand pounds per an-um, besides the profit of a new dish, introduced to the tables of all gentlemen of fortune in the kingdom, who have any refinement in taste. And the money will circulate among our selves, the goods being entirely of our own growth and manufacture.

Fourthly, the constant breeders, besides the gain of eight shillings sterling per annum by the sale of their children, will be rid of the charge of maintaining them after the first year.

Fifthly, This food would likewise bring great custom to taverns, where the vintners will certainly be so prudent as to procure the best receipts for dressing it to perfection; and consequently have their houses frequented by all the fine gentlemen, who justly value themselves upon their knowledge in good eating; and a skillful cook, who understands how to oblige his guests, will contrive to make it as expensive as they please.

Sixthly, this would be a great inducement to marriage, which all wise nations have either encouraged by rewards, or enforced by laws and penalties. It would increase the care and tenderness of mothers towards their children, when they were sure of a settlement for life to the poor babes, provided in some sort by the public, to their annual profit instead of expense. We should soon see an honest emulation among the married women, which of them could bring the fattest child to the market. Men would become as fond of their wives, during the time of their pregnancy, as they are now of their mares in foal, their cows in calf, or sow when they are ready to far-row; nor offer to beat or kick them (as is too frequent a practice) for fear of a miscarriage.

Many other advantages might be enumerated. For instance, the addition of some thousand carcasses in our exportation of barreled beef: the propagation of swine's flesh, and improvement in the art of making good bacon, so much wanted among us by the great destruction of pigs, too frequent at our tables; which are no way comparable in taste or magnificence to a well grown, fat yearly child, which roasted whole will make a considerable figure at a Lord Mayor's feast, or any other public entertainment. But this, and many others, I omit, being studious of brevity.

Supposing that one thousand families in this city, would be constant customers for infants flesh, besides others who might have it at merry meetings, particularly at weddings and christenings, I compute that Dublin would take off annually about twenty thousand carcasses; and the rest of the kingdom (where probably they will be sold somewhat cheaper) the remaining eighty thousand.

I can think of no one objection, that will possibly be raised against this proposal, unless it should be urged, that the number of people will be thereby much lessened in the kingdom. This I freely own, and 'twas indeed one principal design in offering it to the world. I desire the reader will observe, that I calculate my remedy for this one individual Kingdom of Ireland, and for no other that ever was, is, or, I think, ever can be upon Earth. Therefore let no man talk to me of other expedients: Of taxing our absentees at five shillings a pound: Of using neither clothes, nor household furniture, except what is of our own growth and manufacture: Of utterly rejecting the materials and instruments that promote foreign luxury: Of curing the expensiveness of pride, vanity, idleness, and gaming in our women: Of introducing a vein of parsimony, prudence and temperance: Of learning to love our country, wherein we differ even from Laplanders, and the inhabitants of Topinamboo: Of quitting our animosities and factions, nor acting any longer like the Jews, who were murdering one another at the very moment their city was taken: Of being a little cautious not to sell our country and consciences for nothing: Of teaching landlords to have at least one degree of mercy towards their tenants. Lastly, of putting a spirit of honesty, industry, and skill into our shop-keepers, who, if a resolution could now be taken to buy only our native goods, would immediately unite to cheat and exact upon us in the price, the measure, and the goodness, nor could ever yet be brought to make one fair proposal of just dealing, though often and earnestly invited to it.

Therefore I repeat, let no man talk to me of these expedients, 'till he hath at least some glimpse of hope, that there will ever be some hearty and sincere attempt to put them into practice.

But, as to my self, having been wearied out for many years with offering vain, idle, visionary thoughts, and at length utterly despairing of success, I fortunately fell upon this proposal, which, as it is wholly new, so it hath something solid and real, of no expense and little trouble, full in our own power, and whereby we can incur no danger in disobliging England. For this kind of commodity will not bear exportation, and flesh being of too tender a consistence, to admit a long continuance in salt, although perhaps I could name a country, which would be glad to eat up our whole nation without it.

After all, I am not so violently bent upon my own opinion, as to reject any offer, proposed by wise men, which shall be found equally innocent, cheap, easy, and effectual. But before something of that kind shall be advanced in contradiction to my scheme, and offering a better, I desire the author or authors will be pleased maturely to consider two points. First, as things stand, how they will be able to find food and raiment for a hundred thousand useless mouths and backs. And secondly, There being a round million of creatures in humane figure throughout this kingdom, whose whole subsistence put into a common stock, would leave them in debt two million of pounds sterling, adding those who are beggars by profession, to the bulk of farmers, cottagers and laborers, with their wives and children, who are beggars in effect; I desire those politicians who dislike my overture, and may perhaps be so bold to attempt an answer, that they will first ask the parents of these mortals, whether they would not at this day think it a great happiness to have been sold for food at a year old, in the manner I prescribe, and thereby have avoided such a perpetual scene of misfortunes, as they have since gone through, by the oppression of landlords, the impossibility of paying rent without money or trade, the want of common sustenance, with neither house nor clothes to cover them from the in-clemencies of the weather, and the most inevitable prospect of entailing the like, or greater miseries, upon their breed for ever.

I profess, in the sincerity of my heart, that I have not the least personal interest in endeavoring to promote this necessary work, having no other motive than the public good of my country, by advancing our trade, providing for infants, relieving the poor, and giving some pleasure to the rich. I have no children, by which I can propose to get a single penny; the youngest being nine years old, and my wife past child-bearing.

Chapter 5 William Wordsworth

作者简介

William Wordsworth was one of the most influential one of England's Romantic poets. He was born on 7 April, 1770 in Cockermouth, Cumberland. Wordsworth's magnum opus is generally considered to be *The Prelude*, a semiautobiographical poem of his early years which he revised and expanded a number of times. *Lyrical Ballads*, *Lines Composed a Few Miles above Tintern Abbey* and *Lucy Poems* are also his masterpieces. Wordsworth was Britain's Poet Laureate from 1843 until his death in 1850. And he, Coleridge and Robert Southey were known as Lake Poets.

His father was a lawyer. Both Wordsworth's parents died before he was 15, and he and his four siblings were left in the care of different relatives. As a young man, Wordsworth developed a love of nature, a theme reflected in many of his poems. Wordsworth made his debut as a writer in 1787 when he published a sonnet in The European Magazine. That same year he began attending St John's College, Cambridge, and received his B. A. degree in 1791. While studying at Cambridge University, Wordsworth spent a summer holiday on a walking tour in Switzerland and France. He became an enthusiast for the ideals of the French Revolution. He began to write poetry while he was at school, but none was published until 1793.

The poet Samuel Taylor Coleridge was an admirer of Wordsworth's work. They collaborated on "Lyrical Ballads", which was published in 1798. In 1799, after a visit to Germany with Coleridge, Wordsworth and his sister Dorothy settled at Dove Cottage in Grasmere in the Lake District. Coleridge lived nearby with his family. Wordsworth's most famous poem, *I Wandered Lonely as a Cloud* was written at Dove Cottage in 1804.

In 1802, Wordsworth married a childhood friend, Mary Hutchinson. The next few years were personally difficult for Wordsworth. Two of his children died. His brother was drowned at sea and Dorothy suffered a mental breakdown. His political views underwent a transformation around the turn of the century, and he became increasingly conservative, disillusioned by events in France culminating in Napoleon Bonaparte taking power.

Wordsworth died on 23 April, 1850 and was buried in Grasmere churchyard.

威廉·华兹华斯是英国最著名的浪漫主义诗人之一。他于1770年生于英国坎伯兰郡的科克茅斯。自传体长诗《序曲》是华兹华斯的著作,这是他的早期作品,后来又进行了反复的修改和添加。《抒情歌谣集》、《丁登寺杂咏》以及组诗《露茜》也是他的代表作。1843后,已是古稀之年的华兹华斯被封为"桂冠诗人"。他和柯勒律治、罗伯特·骚塞被誉为著名的"湖畔诗人"。

华兹华斯的父亲是一名律师,父母都在他15岁前去世。之后,他和兄弟姐妹们就由不同的亲戚照管。年轻时期的华兹华斯对自然无限热爱,这一主题也在他的众多诗歌中得以体现。1787年,华兹华斯第一次以一个写作者的身份在欧洲杂志上发表了一首十四行诗。同年,他进入剑桥大学圣·约翰学院,并且于1791年毕业获得文学学士学位。在剑桥上学期间,华兹华斯于暑假期间在瑞士和法国游历,当时正是法国大革命之际,年轻的华兹华斯对革命产生了深厚的热情。他在上学期间写了很多诗,但直到1793年才出版。

柯勒律治十分欣赏华兹华斯的作品,他们于1798年合作出版了《抒情歌谣集》。1799年,在同柯勒律治游历完德国之后,华兹华斯和妹妹多萝西定居于英国湖区的格拉斯米尔湖,柯勒律治也住在他们家附近。华兹华斯著名的抒情诗《我好似一朵流云独自漫游》于1804年在这里完成。

1802年,华兹华斯和认识多年的朋友玛丽·郝金生结婚。此后几年,对他来说是人生最困难的阶段,两个孩子相继死亡,哥哥溺海,妹妹多萝西也遭受了严重的精神崩溃。他自己也由于政治局势剧变,对法国大革命幻想破灭,政治态度渐趋保守。

1850年4月23日,华兹华斯去世,葬于格拉斯米尔墓地。

作品及导读

作 品 1

The Sparrow's Nest

导 读

The Sparrow's Nest is selected from Wordsworth's *Poems Referring to the Period of Childhood*. This poem describes an interesting story when the author and his sister accidentally discovered a nest of sparrow eggs in the leafy shade of his childhood. The sparrow's nest gleamed like a vision of delight in the children's eyes which shows the children's curiosity, and the language of the poem is full of childlike innocence. Whether it rains or shines, they often go to visit it. They want to near it, but they move carefully for fear of hurting it. This poem shows the children's kindness. Although his sister is young, she knows how to take care of these eggs. Her carefulness and kindness influence the author a lot.

In the poem, "Emmeline" refers to the poet's sister Dorothy. The people who write biography for them have pointed out Dorothy has a more sensitive feeling of the natural scenery than the poet, and her observation is also more detailed, and the experience is more subtle; sometimes, it was under his sister's inspiration and guidance, the poet had a deep understanding and comprehension about something; some excellent poems are also due to her first inspiration. In this poem, the poet says his sister gave him eyes, ears, heart, etc., it means Dorothy made his ears and eyes more sensitive and his mind more clever.

《麻雀窝》选自华兹华斯的《有关童年的诗》。这首诗描写了作者童年时候和妹妹在绿叶浓荫中偶然发现一窝麻雀蛋的趣事。麻雀窝在孩子们的眼中散发着迷人的光彩,展示了孩子们的好奇心,充满了童真童趣。无论晴雨,他们都要跑去麻雀窝看看,想要接近,却小心翼翼地不去伤害它,显示了孩子们善良的天性。妹妹虽然年纪小,但她却懂得爱护这窝鸟蛋。她的细致敏锐从小就给了作者非常大的影响。

这首诗中"艾米兰"是指诗人的妹妹多萝西。为诗人兄妹作传的人们曾指出:多萝西对自然景物和人事的感受比诗人更敏锐,观察更细致,体会也更精微;有时是在她的启发和引导下,诗人才加深了对事物的理解和领悟;一些优秀诗篇的写成,也是首先由她触发了诗人的灵感。在这首诗中,诗人说她的妹妹给他以眼、耳、心等等,就是指多萝西使他耳聪目明,心灵开窍。

选 文

The Sparrow's Nest

Behold, within the leafy shade,
Those bright blue eggs together laid!
On me the chance-discovered sight
Gleamed like a vision of delight.
I started — seeming to espy
the home and sheltered bed,
The Sparrow's dwelling, which, hard by
My Father's house, in wet or dry,
My sister Emmeline and I
Together visited.

She looked at it and seemed to fear it;
Dreading, tho' wishing, to be near it:

Such heart was in her, being then
A little Prattler among men.
The Blessing of my later years
Was with me when a boy:
She gave me eyes, she gave me ears;
And humble cares, and delicate fears;
A heart, the fountain of sweet tears;
And love, and thought, and joy.
(*From Poems Referring to the Period of Childhood*)

作品 2

I Wandered Lonely As a Cloud

导 读

"I Wandered Lonely As a Cloud" is a poem about nature. With his pure and poetic language, Wordsworth brings us into a beautiful world where there are daffodils, trees and breeze. We follow the poet at every turn of his feelings. We share his melancholy when he "wandered lonely as a cloud" and his delight the moment his heart "with pleasure filling". We come to realize the great power of nature that may influence our life deeply as revealed in the poem. He slowes down the tempo in line 4 to keep in accordance with his bated breath the moment he glimpses at a host of golden daffodils, thus conveying to us the poet's intoxication in the face of nature. With all these musical devices, Wordsworth secures a songlike effect of his poem in addition to communicate his emotion and meaning. What's more, Wordsworth goes further to communicate his emotion and meaning by his thoughtful tone. The choosing of the word "lonely" in "I wandered lonely as a cloud" instead of other words like "carefree", "leisure" or "jolly" conveys to us the poet's depression and disconsolateness at the very beginning. But as he catches sight of the daffodils stretching as far as the eyes can see and finds him in the midst of nature, his loneliness turns into relaxation and joy. Thus the shift of the poet's mood from sadness to happiness manifests the theme — the great influence of nature upon human beings.

《我好似一朵流云独自漫游》是一个关于自然的诗。华兹华斯用纯诗意的语言给我们描述了一个有水仙花、树木、微风的美丽世界。诗人带动我们跟随他的每个感情转折点,我们分享他的忧郁,把他"当做一朵孤云",分享他的喜悦,带领我们感受大自然的伟大力量,这是深深影响我们生活的诗。诗歌缓慢的节奏,他瞥向金色水仙花屏住呼吸的时刻传达了诗人在大自然陶醉的状态。这些影响了诗的情感交流和意义。更重要的是,华兹华斯更进一步表达了他的情感。《我好似一朵流云独自漫游》并不是说喜欢无忧无虑,休闲或愉快地向我们传达诗人的忧郁和悲伤。当他瞥见在视线范围内无限蔓延的水仙花,他发现自己徜徉于大自然中,孤独消失了,取而代之的是轻松和快乐。诗人从悲伤到幸福这一情绪的转变地体现了本诗的主题——伟大的自然对人类的影响。

选 文

I Wandered Lonely as a Cloud

I wandered lonely as a cloud
That floats on high o'er vales and hills,
When all at once I saw a crowd,
A host, of golden daffodils.
Beside the lake, beneath the trees,
Fluttering and dancing in the breeze.

Continuous as the stars that shine
And twinkle on the Milky Way,
They stretched in never-ending line
Along the margin of a bay:
Ten thousand saw I at a glance,
Tossing their heads in sprightly dance.

The waves beside them danced; but they
Outdid the sparkling waves in glee;
A poet could not but be gay;
In such a jocund company;
I gazed -and gazed -but little thought
What wealth the show to me had brought:

For oft, when on my couch I lie
In vacant or in pensive mood,
They flash upon that inward eye
Which is the bliss of solitude;
And then my heart with pleasure fills,
And dances with the daffodils.

相关链接

Romanticism was a movement in literature, philosophy, music and art which developed in Europe in the late 18th and early 19th centuries. Starting from the ideas of Rousseau in

France and from the Storm and Stress movement in Germany, they held that classicism, dominant since the 16th century, failed to express man's emotional nature and overlooked his profound inner forces. The term Romantic first appeared in 18th-century English and originally meant "romantique".

Romanticism may be defined as a movement in the history of culture, as an aesthetic style, and as an attitude or spirit. As a movement, romanticism involved a revolt against convention and authority and a search for freedom in personal, political, and artistic life. Romanticism emphasized individual values and aspirations above those of society. As a reaction to the industrial revolution, it looked to the Middle Ages and contacted directly with nature for inspiration. It gave impetus to the national liberation movement in the 19th century Europe. Literature took the full force of Romanticism. It brought forth a full flowering of literary talents. The leading Romantic writers were Blake, Wordsworth, Coleridge, Scott, Byron, Shelley and Keats in England, Hugo and Sand in France, Heine in Germany, Manzoni and Leopardi in Italy, Pushkin in Russia, and Michie-wicz in Poland. Their works, diversified in character and daring in spirit, all depicted men's eager search for individual freedom, pure sentiments and ideal beauty.

浪漫主义运动时是18世纪末19世纪初欧洲的文学、哲学、音乐和艺术的发展的运动。浪漫主义法国卢梭的思想以及德国的暴风骤雨运动,浪漫主义者认为古典风格虽从16世纪以来占主导地位,但未能表达人的情感,并忽视他内在的力量。浪漫这个词最早出现在18世纪英国,最初的意思是"罗曼蒂克"。

浪漫主义可以被定义为一个有关历史文化的运动,也可被定义为一种审美风格和一种态度或精神。作为一个运动,浪漫主义涉及了一个反抗权威的精神,寻找个人自由,政治和艺术的生活。浪漫主义强调了一个个人价值观和愿望之上的社会。它是工业革命的反映,它主张回归中世纪,通过直接接触自然来寻求灵感。推动了19世纪欧洲民族解放运动,是文学浪漫主义的全部力量。主要的浪漫主义作家:英国有布莱克、华兹华斯、柯勒律治、斯科特、拜伦、雪莱和济慈,法国的雨果,德国的海涅,意大利的曼卓尼,俄罗斯的普希金。作品呈现了多元化和无畏的精神,所有都揭示了人类热切寻找个人自由、纯粹的情感和理想的美。

Chapter 6 Samuel Taylor Coleridge

作者简介

Samuel Taylor Coleridge(1772 – 1834), poet and critic, was born in Ottery St. Mary, Devonshire, and the son of a clergy man. He received education at Cambridge but left without a degree. Inspired by the radical thinkers with their idealism, Coleridge joined Robert Southey in a Utopian plan of establishing an ideal democratic community in America, named "Pantisocracy". In the spring of 1797, Coleridge met and began his long friendship with William Wordsworth. The following year, they published a joint volume of poetry, Lyrical Ballads, which become a landmark in English poetry. Coleridge's poem, "The Rime of the Ancient Mariner", was included in the volume.

The years 1797 to 1798 were among the most fruitful of Coleridge's literary Career. In addition to "The Ancient Mariner", he wrote "Kubla Khan", and began writing "Christabel", composed "This Lime-Tree Bower My Prison", "Frost at Midnight", and "The Nightingale", which are considered to be his best "conversational" poems.

In 1798, he traveled with the Wordsworths to Germany. In 1810, Coleridge quarreled seriously with Wordsworth. Although they reconciled with each other later on, their friendship had never reached its former intimacy. In 1813, his tragic drama *Remorse* received popular welcome. In 1816, he wrote his major prose work, "Biographia Literaria". In 1817, he wrote a series of autobiographical notes and dissertations on many subjects, including some brilliantly perceptive literary criticism. His major works are *The Rime of the Ancient Mariner*, *Kubla Khan*, *Christabel*.

His actual achievement as a poet can be divided into two remarkably diverse groups: the demonic & the conversational. The demonic group includes his three masterpieces: "The Rime of the Ancient Mariner", "Christabel" and "Kubla Khan". Strong imagination is the distinctive features of this group. Generally, the conversational group speaks more directly of an allied theme: the desire to go home, not to the past, but to "an improved infancy." Each of these poems bears a kind of purgatorial atonement, in which Coleridge must fail or suffer so that he may succeed or experience joy. In analyzing Shakespeare, Coleridge emphasizes the philosophic implication, going deeper into the inner reality than only caring for the outer form.

塞缪尔·泰勒·柯勒律治(1772—1834),诗人和评论家,出生在奥特里·圣·玛丽德文郡,是一个牧师的儿子。他在剑桥大学接受过教育但未能获得学位。受激进的思想家和他们的理想主义的启发,柯勒律治加入了罗伯特·骚塞关于在美国建立一个理想的民主社会,命名为"大同世界"的乌托邦计划。1797年春天,柯勒律治遇到威廉·华兹华斯并且开始了他们长久的友谊。第二年,他们联合发表的抒情诗集《抒性歌谣集》成为英文诗歌的一个里程碑。柯勒律治的诗歌《古舟子咏》包含在其中。

1797年到1798年是柯勒律治的诗歌生涯中最多产时期。除了《古舟子咏》外,他还写了《忽必烈汗》,并且开始写《克里斯特贝尔》。《监狱之歌》,《霜在午夜》和《夜莺》被认为是他最好的"对话"的诗。

1798年,他与华兹华斯前往德国旅游。1810年,柯勒律治与华兹华斯发生严重争吵。尽管此后他们彼此和好,他们的友谊再也未能达到以前那样亲密。1813年,他的悲剧戏剧《悔恨》受到公众的欢迎。1816年,他写了他主要的散文作品,《文学传记》,1817年他写了一系列的自传笔记和关于许多主题的论文,包括一些精辟的文学批评。他的主要作品包括:《古舟子咏》、《忽必烈汗》、《克里斯塔贝尔》。

作为一名诗人,柯勒律治的贡献主要可以分为两个方面。一方面,他开启了迷幻色彩的时代。另一方面,对话形式较为常见。魔幻色彩的作品包括他的三部伟大的巨作《古舟子咏》、《克里斯塔贝尔》、《忽必烈汗》,大胆的想象是这类作品最明显的特点。通常,对话形式最能阐明主题,如《渴望归来》、《不是过去而是一种出奇的改进》,这类诗承受着一种炼狱的赎罪,在这些诗中柯勒律治必须承受如此的痛苦以便于他日后的成功。在分析莎士比亚时,柯勒律治强调哲学意蕴并且强调应深入事物的内在现实不是只关心外在形式。

作品及导读

作 品 1

Kubla Khan

导 读

Along with *The Rime of the Ancient Mariner*, *Kubla Khan* one of is Coleridge's most famous and enduring poems. The story of its composition is also one of the most famous in the history of English poetry. As the poet explains in the short preface to this poem, he had fallen asleep after taking "an anodyne". Before falling asleep, he had been reading a story in which *Kubla Khan* commanded the building of a new palace; Coleridge claims that while he slept, he had a fantastic vision and composed simultaneously — while sleeping — some two or three hundred lines of poetry rush into his mind.

Waking after about three hours, the poet seized a pen and began writing furiously; however, after copying down the first three stanzas of his poem — the first three stanzas of the current poem as we know it — he was interrupted by a person on business who detained him for an hour. After this interruption, he was unable to recall the rest of the vision or the poetry he had composed in his opium dream. The mysterious person from Porlock is one of the most notorious and enigmatic figures in Coleridge's biography; no one knows who he was or why he disturbed the poet or what he wanted or, indeed, whether any of Coleridge's story is actually true. But the person from Porlock has become a metaphor for the malicious interruptions the world throws in the way of inspiration and genius, and *Kubla Khan*, strange and ambiguous as it is, has become what is perhaps the definitive statement on the obstruction and thwarting of the visionary genius.

The first three stanzas are products of pure imagination: The pleasure-dome of Kubla Khan is not a useful metaphor for anything in particular; however, it is a fantastically prodigious descriptive act. The poem becomes especially evocative when, after the second stanza, the meter suddenly tightens; the resulting lines are terse and solid, almost beating out the sound of the war drums. The fourth stanza states the theme of the poem as a whole. The speaker says that he once had a vision of the damsel singing of Mount Abora; this vision becomes a metaphor for Coleridge's vision of the 300-hundred-line masterpiece he never completed.

继《古舟子咏》后,《忽必烈汗》是柯勒律治又一最为著名、影响长久的诗作之一。本诗的内容也是英文诗史上最具影响力之一的瑰宝。正如本诗引言中所介绍的,他在服用鸦片药剂后入睡,而在睡前,作者阅读过有关《忽必烈汗》征用一处建造新宫殿的文章。柯勒律治说,在他睡着之时他看到过美妙的景色和创作,而这几乎是与此同时的——在睡着的同时——涌现了两三百行的诗作。

三个小时的睡眠后,作者清醒过来,抓起笔便开始奋笔疾书。然而在他誊抄下梦里诗作的前三节时,也就是我们现在所看到的这些,他因公事而被人打断。一个小时的中断后他再也无法想起他吸食鸦片后梦境里的诗句了。那个来自波洛克的神秘人也是柯勒律治自传中最臭名昭著之一的谜一样的人物。没人知道他是谁、为什么打断诗人、他想要干什么,或,甚至准确地说,没人知道那些故事是不是真的。但来自波洛克神秘人成为世上代表恶意中断灵感或天赋精神的暗喻形象;而《忽必烈汗》,一如既往被置于陌生而歧异四起地地位,成为幻想精神的阻挡和障碍。

诗的前三段是出于纯幻想的:忽必烈汗的那座富丽堂皇的安乐殿堂实际上并不是任何事物的暗喻;然而,它的确是一个奇妙而又令人难以置信的描述。整个诗作从第二节开始变为唤出的形势,诗的韵律也极具紧绷,结束句简洁且紧凑结实,甚至表现出了战鼓的声响。第四节诗陈述了整个诗的主题。

选　文

Kubla Khan

In Xanadu did Kubla Khan
A stately pleasure-dome decree:
Where Alph, the sacred river, ran
Through caverns measureless to man
Down to a sunless sea.
So twice five miles of fertile ground
With walls and towers were girdled round:
And there were gardens bright with sinuous rills,
Where blossomed many an incense-bearing tree;
And here were forests ancient as the hills,
Enfolding sunny spots of greenery.

But oh! That deep romantic chasm which slanted
down the green hill athwart a cedarn cover!
A savage place! as holy and enchanted
As e'er beneath a waning moon was haunted
By woman wailing for her demon-lover!
And from this chasm, with ceaseless turmoil seething,
As if this earth in fast thick pants were breathing,
A mighty fountain momently was forced:
Amid whose swift half-intermitted burst
Huge fragments vaulted like rebounding hail,
Or chaffy grain beneath the thresher's flail:
And'mid these dancing rocks at once and ever
It flung up momently the sacred river.
Five miles meandering with a mazy motion
Through wood and dale the sacred river ran,
Then reached the caverns measureless to man,
And sank in tumult to a lifeless ocean:
And'mid this tumult Kubla heard from far
Ancestral voices prophesying war!
The shadow of the dome of pleasure
Floated midway on the waves;
Where was heard the mingled measure

From the fountain and the caves.
It was a miracle of rare device,
A sunny pleasure-dome with caves of ice!

A damsel with a dulcimer.
In a vision once I saw:
It was an Abyssinian maid.
And on her dulcimer she played,
Singing of Mount Abora.
Could I revive within me
Her symphony and song,
To such a deep delight twould win me,
That with music loud and long,
I would build that dome in air,
That sunny dome! those caves of ice!
And all who heard should see them there,
And all should cry. Beware! Beware!
His flashing eyes, his floating hair!
Weave a circle round him thrice,
And close your eyes with holy dread,
For he on honey-dew hath fed,
And drunk the milk of Paradise.

相关链接

Romanticism is a literary and artistic movement, and profound shift in sensibility, which took place in Britain and throughout Europe from 1798 to 1832. The Romantic Age began in 1798 when William Wordsworth and Samuel Taylor Coleridge published *Lyrical Ballads*, and ended in 1832 when Walter Scott (1771 – 1832) died.

Politically it was inspired by the revolutions in America and France and popular wars of independence in Poland, Spain, Greece and elsewhere. Emotionally it expressed an extreme assertion of the self and the value of individual experience (the "egotistical sublime"). Socially it championed progressive causes. It also asserted the unique nature of the individual, the privileged status of emotional outlets, the rejection of civilized corruption and the desire to return to the natural primitivism and the escape from the spiritual destruction of urban life. The works were often set in nature, using the natural imagery and symbolism. Characteristics of romanticism are: imagination, spontaneity, inspiration.

The glory of the age is notably seen in the Poetry of Wordsworth, Coleridge, Byron,

Shelley and Keats, who were grouped into two generations: Passive Romantic poets represented by the Lakers / Lake Poets — Wordsworth, Coleridge, and Southey. Gothic novelists such as Horace Walpole (1717 – 97) and 'Monk' Lewis (1775 – 1818, Matthew Gregory Lewis). Shelley and Keats, who were firm supporters of French Revolution, set themselves against the bourgeois society and the ruling class.

Romanticism expressed an unending revolt against classical form, conservative morality, authoritarian government, personal insincerity, and human moderation. The Romantics saw and felt things brilliantly afresh. They virtually invented certain landscapes — the Lakes, the bays of Italy. They were strenuous walkers, hill-climbers, sea-bathers, or river-lovers. All of them are inclined to love the nature and hate the prosperity of modern urban life. In their critical writings and lectures they described poetry and drama with new elements (the character of *Hamlet*).

浪漫主义，发生在1798—1832年间，波及了当时的整个欧洲，它是一场文学与艺术界的运动，是情感方面的一次大转变。1798年威廉·华兹华斯与塞缪尔·泰勒·柯勒律治出版的《抒情歌谣集》拉开了浪漫主义的帷幕。1832年沃尔特·斯科(1771—1832)的逝世标志着浪漫主义的结束。

政治上，浪漫主义的灵感来源于政治革命，包括美国的独立战争、法国大革命、波兰的独立战争、西班牙、希腊等其他地方的政治革命。情感上，它宣扬一种极端的个人经验价值(自我本位崇高)。社会上，它倡导事业上的奋进。个人上，浪漫主义宣扬了个人的独特，情感的特权地位，拒绝文明社会的腐败，渴望回归自然的原始主义以及倡导逃避都市生活的精神毁灭。浪漫主义的作品经常以自然为基础，使用自然中的一些意象和象征。浪漫主义有三大特征：想象、随意自然以及灵感。

在浪漫主义时期涌现了许多的浪漫主义诗人，如：威廉·华兹华斯，塞缪尔·泰勒·柯勒律治，乔治·戈登·拜伦，波西·比希·雪莱与约翰·济慈。他们被分为两类，一是消极浪漫主义，以湖畔诗人为代表——华兹华斯、柯勒律治、罗伯特·骚塞。另外是哥特式小说家，如霍勒斯·沃波尔、刘易斯。雪莱和济慈是法国革命坚定的继承者，他们反对资本主义社会和统治阶级。

浪漫主义表达了对古典形式、保守的道德、专制政府、个人的不诚实以及人类的节制无休止的反抗。浪漫主义诗人看到和感受到的是事物再度的辉煌，他们凭借自己的想象力去创造了某些景观。他们是奋发的步行者、攀岩者、日光浴者以及湖光山色爱好者，他们喜欢大自然，讨厌现代都市生活。

7 Jane Austen

作者简介

Jane Austen (16 December, 1775 – 18 July, 1817) was an English novelist whose works of romantic fiction set among the gentry have earned her a place as one of the most widely read and most beloved writers in English literature. Among scholars and critics, Austen's realism and biting social commentary have cemented her historical importance as a writer.

Austen lived her entire life as part of a close-knit family located on the lower fringes of the English gentry. She was educated primarily by her father and older brothers as well as through her own reading. The steadfast support of her family was critical to Austen's development as a professional writer. Austen's artistic apprenticeship lasted from her teenage years until she was about thirty-five years old. During this period, she experimented with various literary forms, including the epistolary novel which she tried and then abandoned, and wrote and extensively revised three major novels and began a fourth. During 1811 – 16, with the release of *Sense and Sensibility* (1811), *Pride and Prejudice* (1813), *Mansfield Park* (1814) and *Emma* (1816), she achieved success as a published writer. She wrote two additional novels, *Northanger Abbey* and *Persuasion*, both published posthumously in 1818, and began a third, which was eventually titled *Sanditon*, but died before completing it.

Austen's works critique the novels of sensibility of the second half of the eighteenth century and are part of the transition to nineteenth-century realism. Austen's plots, though fundamentally comic, highlight the dependence of women on marriage to secure social standing and economic security. Like those of Samuel Johnson, one of the strongest influences on her writing, her works are concerned with moral issues.

简·奥斯丁(1775年12月16日—1817年7月18日)是英国著名的小说家。她的作品多是描写乡绅家庭女性的婚姻和生活的浪漫主义小说,这使她成为英国文学史上作品流传最广且深受读者喜爱的作家之一。许多学者和评论家认为,作为一个作家,她的现实主义风格和对社会的嘲讽更凸显了她在历史上的重要性。

　　简·奥斯丁终其一生都生活在封建势力强大的农村地区,她一辈子与家人生活在一起,终身未嫁。她并未进过正规的学校,她所受的教育主要来自父亲、兄长以及自己的阅读。家庭坚定地支持在奥斯丁成为一名专业作家的过程中起着至关重要的作用。奥斯丁的艺术"学徒期"从她青年时期一直持续到了35岁左右。在此期间,她尝试了各种文学类型,包括书信体小说,同时,她创作了三部小说,并且开始了第四部小说的创作。1811年至1816年,她先后出版了《理智与情感》、《傲慢与偏见》、《曼斯菲尔德的庄园》、《爱玛》四部小说,获得了成功。她的另外两部小说《诺桑觉寺》、《劝导》在她去世后,于1818年出版。她生前还曾创作了小说《桑底顿》,但是并未完成。

　　简·奥斯丁的小说出现在19世纪初叶,一扫风行一时的假浪漫主义潮流,继承和发展了英国18世纪的现实主义传统,为19世纪现实主义小说的高潮做了准备。她的作品格调轻松诙谐,往往通过喜剧性的故事,强调已婚女性要获取社会地位和经济上的独立。塞缪尔·约翰逊是对简·奥斯丁产生巨大影响的作家之一。受其影响,她的作品常常涉及道德方面的议题。

作品及导读

作品 1

Pride and Prejudice

导 读

　　Pride and Prejudice is a novel by Jane Austen, first published in 1813. The story follows the main character Elizabeth Bennet as she deals with issues of manners, upbringing, morality, education, and marriage in the society of the landed gentry of early 19th-century England.

　　Mrs. Bennet had no other wish if her five daughters could get married as soon as possible with someone wealthy. At a dancing ball, it is obvious that Mr. Bingley could not help falling in love at the first sight with Miss Jane because of her stunning beauty. Mrs. Bennet was so excited that she could not hold her manner and declared publicly she would have a daughter married soon, which frightened Mr. Bingley away. Mr. Collins, a distance nephew of Mr. Bennet, came to ask a marriage to one of his cousins before Mrs. Bennet was able to get clear why Mr. Bingley left suddenly. After receiving the hint from Mrs. Bennet that Jane already had an admirer, Mr. Collins turned to Elizabeth without wasting a minute and to Miss Charlotte Lucas two days later after refused by Elizabeth. It was difficult for Mrs. Bennet to recover herself as a result of the "deadly stupid" decision made by Elizabeth until she got the news that Lydia finally married Mr. Wickham, though the marriage was built on the basis of ten thousand pounds. Mr. Darcy offered the money and did everything departing from his will just because he loved Elizabeth so much. He could not hide his feelings any more and showed his affection to Elizabeth at last, who, because of a series of misunderstandings towards him, rejected him without hesitation. This plot is the climax of the novel as the prejudice of Elizabeth to Mr. Darcy was exposed and removed since then. And the combination of the two young couples, Jane and Bingley, Elizabeth and Darcy came at last.

《傲慢与偏见》是英国小说家简·奥斯丁的作品,于1813年出版。小说从主人公伊丽莎白·贝内特的视角出发,描述了她在19世纪早期英国地主乡绅贵族的社里会处理关于礼仪、养育、道德、教育和婚姻的问题。

贝内特太太最大的愿望是希望自己的五个女儿尽快嫁入豪门。在一次舞会上,宾利对简一见钟情。贝内特太太欣喜若狂地向公众宣布她的一个女儿即将出嫁的消息,宾利听后吓得逃走了。在贝内特太太仍对宾利的不辞而别感到不解之时,贝内特先生的远房侄子柯林斯前来求婚。在被告知简已有钟情之人后,柯林斯便立马转向简的妹妹伊丽莎白求婚,在遭到拒绝之后他又转向伊丽莎白的好友夏洛特求婚。正当贝内特太太懊恼伊丽莎白这一"愚蠢"决定时接到莉迪亚嫁给威克翰姆的消息,尽管这门婚姻是建立在一万英镑的基础之上。达尔西帮助解决了伊丽莎白家遇到的难题,只因他对伊丽莎白深爱而愿为之改掉自己的傲慢姿态。一连串的误解最终得以解释,伊丽莎白也在此过程中看到了达尔西的改变和对自己的爱。她也渐渐抛开了偏见接受了达尔西的求婚。简和宾利经过一番周折之后也终于言归于好。故事的结局,两对有情人终成眷属。

选 文

Pride and Prejudice
(*Excerpt*)
Chapter 1

It is a truth universally acknowledged, that a single man in possession of a good fortune must be in want of a wife.

However little known the feelings or views of such a man may be on his first entering a neighborhood, this truth is so well fixed in the minds of the surrounding families, that he is considered as the rightful property of some one or other of their daughters.

"My dear Mr. Bennet," said his lady to him one day, "have you heard that Netherfield Park is let at last?"

Mr. Bennet replied that he had not.

"But it is," returned she, "for Mrs. Long has just been here, and she told me all about it."

Mr. Bennet made no answer.

"Do not you want to know who has taken it?" cried his wife impatiently.

"You want to tell me, and I have no objection to hearing it."

This was invitation enough.

"Why, my dear, you must know, Mrs. Long says that Netherfield is taken by a young man of large fortune from the north of England; that he came down on Monday in a chaise and four to see the place, and was so much delighted with it that he agreed with Mr. Morris immediately; that he is to take possession before Michaelmas, and some of his servants are to be in the house by the end of next week."

"What is his name?"

"Bingley."

"Is he married or single?"

"Oh! single, my dear, to be sure! He is a single man with large fortune; four or five thousand a year. What a fine thing for our girls!"

"How so? How can it affect them?"

"My dear Mr. Bennet," replied his wife, "how can you be so tiresome! You must know that I am thinking of his marrying one of them."

"Is that his design in settling here?"

"Design! Nonsense, how can you talk so! But it is very likely that he may fall in love with one of them, and therefore you must visit him as soon as he comes."

"I see no occasion for that. You and the girls may go, or you may send them by themselves, which perhaps will be still better; for, as you are as handsome as any of them, Mr. Bingley might like you the best of the party."

"My dear, you flatter me. I certainly have had my share of beauty, but I do not pretend to be any thing extraordinary now. When a woman has five grown up daughters, she ought to give over thinking of her own beauty."

"In such cases, a woman has not often much beauty to think of."

"But, my dear, you must indeed go and see Mr. Bingley when he comes into the neighborhood."

"It is more than I engage for, I assure you."

"But consider your daughters. Only think what an establishment it would be for one of them. Sir William and Lady Lucas are determined to go, merely on that account, for in general, you know they visit no new comers. Indeed you must go, for it will be impossible for us to visit him, if you do not."

"You are over-scrupulous, surely. I dare say Mr. Bingley will be very glad to see you; and I will send a few lines by you to assure him of my hearty consent to his marrying which ever he chooses of the girls; though I must throw in a good word for my little Lizzy."

"I desire you will do no such thing. Lizzy is not a bit better than the others; and I am sure she is not half so handsome as Jane, nor half so good humored as Lydia. But you are always giving her the preference."

"They have none of them much to recommend them," replied he, "they are all silly and ignorant like other girls; but Lizzy has something more of quickness than her sisters."

"Mr. Bennet, how can you abuse your own children in such way? You take delight in vexing me. You have no compassion on my poor nerves."

"You mistake me, my dear. I have a high respect for your nerves. They are my old friends. I have heard you mention them with consideration these twenty years at least."

"Ah! You do not know what I suffer."

"But I hope you will get over it, and live to see many young men of four thousand a year come into the neighborhood."

"It will be no use to us if twenty such should come, since you will not visit them."

"Depend upon it, my dear, that when there are twenty I will visit them all."

Mr. Bennet was so odd a mixture of quick parts, sarcastic humor, reserve, and caprice, that the experience of three and twenty years had been insufficient to make his wife understand his character. Her mind was less difficult to develope. She was a woman of mean understanding, little information, and uncertain temper. When she was discontented, she fancied herself nervous. The business of her life was to get her daughters married; its solace was visiting and news.

Chapter 60

Elizabeth's spirits soon rising to playfulness again, she wanted Mr. Darcy to account for his having ever fallen in love with her. "How could you begin?" said she. "I can comprehend your going on charmingly, when you had once made a beginning; but what could set you off in the first place?"

"I cannot fix on the hour, or the spot, or the look, or the words, which laid the foundation. It is too long ago. I was in the middle before I knew that I had begun."

"My beauty you had early withstood, and as for my manners — my behaviour to you was at least always bordering on the uncivil, and I never spoke to you without rather wishing to give you pain than not. Now be sincere; did you admire me for my impertinence?"

"For the liveliness of your mind, I did."

"You may as well call it impertinence at once. It was very little less. The fact is, that you were sick of civility, of deference, of officious attention. You were disgusted with the women who were always speaking, and looking, and thinking for your approbation alone. I roused, and interested you, because I was so unlike them. Had you not been really amiable, you would have hated me for it; but in spite of the pains you took to disguise yourself, your feelings were always noble and just; and in your heart, you thoroughly despised the persons who so assiduously courted you. There — I have saved you the trouble of accounting for it; and really, all things considered, I begin to think it perfectly reasonable. To be sure, you knew no actual good of me — but nobody thinks of that when they fall in love."

"Was there no good in your affectionate behaviour to Jane while she was ill at

Netherfield?"

"Dearest Jane! Who could have done less for her? But make a virtue of it by all means. My good qualities are under your protection, and you are to exaggerate them as much as possible; and, in return, it belongs to me to find occasions for teasing and quarreling with you as often as may be; and I shall begin directly by asking you what made you so unwilling to come to the point at last. What made you so shy of me, when you first called, and afterwards dined here? Why, especially, when you called, did you look as if you did not care about me?"

"Because you were grave and silent, and gave me no encouragement."

"But I was embarrassed."

"And so was I."

"You might have talked to me more when you came to dinner."

"A man who had felt less, might."

"How unlucky that you should have a reasonable answer to give, and that I should be so reasonable as to admit it! But I wonder how long you would have gone on, if you had been left to yourself. I wonder when you would have spoken, if I had not asked you! My resolution of thanking you for your kindness to Lydia had certainly great effect. Too much, I am afraid; for what becomes of the moral, if our comfort springs from a breach of promise for I ought not to have mentioned the subject. This will never do."

"You need not distress yourself. The moral will be perfectly fair. Lady Catherine's unjustifiable endeavors to separate us were the means of removing all my doubts. I am not indebted for my present happiness to your eager desire of expressing your gratitude. I was not in a humor to wait for any opening of yours. My aunt's intelligence had given me hope, and I was determined at once to know every thing."

"Lady Catherine has been of infinite use, which ought to make her happy, for she loves to be of use. But tell me, what did you come down to Netherfield for? Was it merely to ride to Longbourn and be embarrassed? Or had you intended any more serious consequence?"

"My real purpose was to see you, and to judge, if I could, whether I might ever hope to make you love me."

"Shall you ever have courage to announce to Lady Catherine what is to befall her?"

"I am more likely to want more time than courage, Elizabeth. But it ought to do, and if you will give me a sheet of paper, it shall be done directly."

"And if I had not a letter to write myself, I might sit by you and admire the evenness of your writing, as another young lady once did. But I have an aunt, too, who must not be longer neglected."

From an unwillingness to confess how much her intimacy with Mr. Darcy had been over-rated, Elizabeth had never yet answered Mrs. Gardiner's long letter; but now, having that to communicate which she knew would be most welcome, she was almost ashamed to find that her uncle and aunt had already lost three days of happiness, and immediately wrote as follows:

"I would have thanked you before, my dear aunt, as I ought to have done, for your long, kind, satisfactory, detail of particulars; but to say the truth; I was too cross to write. You supposed more than really existed. But now suppose as much as you chuse; give a loose to your fancy, indulge your imagination in every possible flight which the subject will afford, and unless you believe me actually married, you cannot greatly err. You must write again very soon, and praise him a great deal more than you did in your last. I thank you, again and again, for not going to the Lakes. How could I be so silly as to wish it! Your idea of the ponies is delightful. We will go round the park every day. I am the happiest creature in the world. Perhaps other people have said so before, but not one with such justice. I am happier even than Jane; she only smiles, I laugh. Mr. Darcy sends you all the love in the world that he can spare from me. You are all to come to pemberley at Christmas. Your's"

Mr. Darcy's letter to Lady Catherine was in a different style; and still different from either was what Mr. Bennet sent to Mr. Collins, in reply to his last.

"DEAR SIR,

I must trouble you once more for congratulations. Elizabeth will soon be the wife of Mr. Darcy. Console Lady Catherine as well as you can. But, if I were you, I would stand by the nephew. He has more to give.

Your's sincerely"

Miss Bingley's congratulations to her brother, on his approaching marriage, were all that was affectionate and insincere. She wrote even to Jane on the occasion, to express her delight, and repeat all her former professions of regard. Jane was not deceived, but she was affected; and though feeling no reliance on her could not help writing her a much kinder answer than she knew was deserved.

The joy which Miss Darcy expressed on receiving similar information was as sincere as her brother's in sending it. Four sides of paper were insufficient to contain all her delight, and all her earnest desire of being loved by her sister.

Before any answer could arrive from Mr. Collins, or any congratulations to Elizabeth from his wife, the Longbourn family heard that the Collins's were come themselves to Lucas lodge. The reason of this sudden removal was soon evident. Lady Catherine had been rendered so exceedingly angry by the contents of her nephew's letter, that Charlotte, really rejoicing in the match, was anxious to get away till the storm was blown over. At such a moment, the arrival of her friend was a sincere pleasure to Elizabeth, though in the course of their meetings she must sometimes think the pleasure dearly bought, when she saw Mr. Darcy exposed to all the parading and obsequious civility of her husband. He bore it, however, with admirable calmness. He could even listen to Sir William Lucas, when he complimented him on carrying away the brightest jewel of the country, and expressed his hopes of their all meeting frequently at St. James's, with very decent composure. If he did shrug his shoulders, it was not till Sir William was out of sight.

Mrs. philips's vulgarity was another, and perhaps a greater, tax on his forbearance; and though Mrs. philips, as well as her sister, stood in too much awe of him to speak with the familiarity which Bingley's good humor encouraged, yet, whenever she did speak, she must be vulgar. Nor was her respect for him, though it made her quieter, at all likely to make her more elegant. Elizabeth did all she could to shield him from the frequent notice of either, and was ever anxious to keep him to herself, and to those of her family with whom he might converse without mortification; and though the uncomfortable feelings arising from all this took from the season of courtship much of its pleasure, it added to the hope of the future; and she looked forward with delight to the time when they should be removed from society so little pleasing to either, to all the comfort and elegance of their family party at pemberley.

Chapter 8 Charles Dickens

作者简介

Charles Dickens (7 February, 1812 – 9 June, 1870) was an English writer and social critic. He created some of the world's most memorable fictional characters in his works and is generally regarded as the greatest novelist of the Victorian period. During his life, his works enjoyed unprecedented fame, and his literary genius was broadly acknowledged by critics and scholars.

At the age of 10 his families were forced to move into debtor's prison. When he was 15 years old, Dickens became an apprentice in a law firm and later a civil court judge clerk and then a newspaper reporter stationed in parliament. He had only a few years of school life, he, however, was a prolific writer created a large number of classical works by his hard work and talent.

Over his career he edited a weekly journal for 20 years, wrote 15 novels, 5 novellas and hundreds of short stories and non-fiction articles, lectured and performed extensively. In 1833, Dickens's first story, *A Dinner at Poplar Walk* was published in London periodical, *Monthly Magazine*. His first novel, *The Pickwick Papers* got a great success in March 1836. In November 1836, as a novelist, Charles Dickens's success continued. He created *Oliver Twist*, *Nicholas Nickleby*, and *The Old Curiosity Shop* and so on. In late November 1851, Dickens moved into Tavistock House, where he would write *Black House*, *Hard Times* and *Little Dorrit*. It was here he indulged in the amateur theatricals. *A Tale of Two Cities* and *Great Expectations* soon followed and would prove resounding successes.

Dickens was known for his literary style. He is good at showing fantastic optimism in his works by using novella picaresque and exaggeration. His writing style is marked by a profuse linguistic creativity. Satire, flourishing in caricature, is his forte. His literary style is also a mixture of fantasy and realism. He criticized bourgeois and their morality by exploration of man's inner conflicts.

Dickens's fame and acclaim stemmed from his novels, novellas, and short stories. He was regarded as the literary colossus of his age in both English literature and the whole world literature.

查尔斯·狄更斯（1812年2月7日—1870年6月9日），英国作家，也是一位社会评论家。在他的作品中，他塑造出众多令人难忘的虚拟人物形象，而他本人被认为是维多利亚时期最伟大的小说家。在他的创作生涯中，他的作品为他赢得了空前的声誉。他的文学天赋曾受到各界评论家和学者们的广泛认同。

狄更斯10岁时全家被迫迁入负债者监狱。15岁时，他曾当过律师事务所学徒，随后，还曾是民事诉讼法庭的记录员。狄更斯虽只上过几年学，但凭着刻苦和天赋创作出了一大批经典著作，成为一位高产作家。

在他的一生中，他作为周刊的编辑长达20年，写过15部长篇小说、5部中篇小说、上百部短篇故事及一些得到广泛演讲和表演的非小说类文学作品。1833年，狄更斯的第一个故事《在白杨城共进晚餐》在伦敦的期刊《月刊》上发表。1836年3月，他的第一部小说《匹克威克外传》获得巨大成功。1836年11月，作为小说家的狄更斯继续成功前行，他创作出了《雾都孤儿》、《尼古拉斯·尼克贝尔》和《老古玩店》等作品。狄更斯在1851年11月下旬搬进塔维斯托克楼，在那里他创作了《荒凉山庄》、《艰难时世》和《小杜丽》。正是在这里，他沉迷于业余戏剧演出。《双城记》和《远大前程》紧随其后，它们则成为令人瞩目的成功之作。

狄更斯因他的文体风格而出名。在他的作品中，他擅长以"流浪汉"小说的结构模式和夸张的艺术手法展现其充满幻想的乐观精神。他的写作风格总能显示出其丰富的语言创作力。运用讽刺手法创作讽刺文学是他的优点。他的文体风格也是幻想主义和现实主义的混合体。他通过尖锐的矛盾主导情节设计，表达了对于资本家及其道德的批判。

狄更斯的名望和赞誉来源于他的长、中篇小说和短篇故事。在他那个时代，他不仅被认为是英国文坛，更是整个世界文学界的文学巨匠。

作品及导读

作品 1

Great Expectations

导 读

Great Expectations is Charles Dickens's thirteenth novel. It is his second novel, after David Copperfield, to be fully narrated in the first person. *Great Expectations* is a bildungsroman, or a coming-of-age novel, and it is a classic work of Victorian literature. It depicts the growth and personal development of an orphan named Pip. The story is divided into three phases of Pips' expectations. The first "expectations" is allotted 19 charpters, and the other two 20 chapters each in the 59-chapter work.

Time passes, and Pip is now twenty-three. One night, during a midnight thunderstorm, he hears heavy footsteps trudging up his stairs. An old sailor enters Pip's apartment, and Pip treats him nervously and haughtily before recognizing him. It is a convict, who was relieved in the cemetery by Pip when he was a little boy.

Horrified, Pip learns the truth of his situation: the convict went to Australia, where he worked in sheep ranching and earned a huge fortune. Moved by Pip's kindness to him on the marsh, he arranged to use his wealth to make Pip a gentleman. The convict, not Miss Havisham, is Pip's secret benefactor. Pip is not meant to marry Estella at all.

With a crestfallen heart, Pip hears that the convict is even now on the run from the law, and that if he is caught, he could be put to death. Pip realizes that though the convict's story has plunged him into despair, it is his duty to help his benefactor. He feeds him and gives him Herbert's bed for the night, since Herbert is away. Terrified of his new situation, Pip looks in on the convict, who is sleeping with a pistol on his pillow, and then locks the doors and falls asleep. He awakes at five o'clock in the morning to a dark sky tormented by wind and rain.

《远大前程》是狄更斯的第13部小说。它是继《大卫·科波菲尔》后第二部完全采用第一人称进行叙述的小说。《远大前程》是一部教育小说,或者说是一部成人礼小说,它也是维多利亚文化下的一部古典作品。它刻画了一个叫皮普的孤儿的成长和个人发展历程。小说将皮普的"远大前程"划分为3个阶段。第一个"远大前程"涉及19章,剩下的两个"远大前程"在59章中各自占据了20章。

时光流逝,皮普此时已经23岁。在一个风雨交加的夜晚,他听见一阵拖沓上楼的沉重脚步声。一位老水手进入皮普住处,在未判断出来者何人前,皮普一直提心吊胆地以一种傲慢的态度相对。原来来者是一名逃犯,当皮普还是一位小男孩的时候,曾在墓地救济过他。

惊恐中,皮普了解到了他此时的处境:这名逃犯曾去过澳大利亚,在那里的牧场劳动并积蓄了大量的财富。他被当初皮普的善良所感动,于是决定用自己的钱将皮普培养成一位绅士。皮普的秘密捐助者是这名逃犯而不是哈维莎姆小姐。皮普根本不可能与埃丝特拉结婚。

得知那名逃犯仍未逃脱法律的制裁时,皮普非常痛苦,因为他一旦被抓住,就会被判处死刑。皮普知道即使逃犯让他倍感绝望,但是帮助他的恩人是他的责任,于是他给逃犯吃的,并在赫伯特不在的时候腾出床供他休息。皮普对自己的现状感到很害怕,看到逃犯时,他的枕头旁边还有一把手枪,把逃犯反锁在房间后,皮普才睡去。当他早上5点醒来时,黑暗的天空风雨交加。

选 文

Great Expectations
(Chapter 39)

I was three and twenty years of age. Not another word had I heard to enlighten me on the subject of my expectations, and my twenty third birthdays was a week gone. We had left Barnard's Inn more than a year, and lived in the Temple. Our chambers were in Garden court, down by the river. Mr Pocket and I had for some time parted company as to our original relations, though we continued on the best terms. Notwithstanding my inability to settle to anything — which I hope arose out of the restless and incomplete tenure on which I held my means — I had a taste for reading, and read regularly so many hours a day. That matter of Herbert's was still progressing, and everything with me was as I have brought it down to the close of the last preceding chapter.

Business had taken Herbert on a journey to Marseilles. I was alone, and had a dull sense of being alone. Dispirited and anxious, long hoping that tomorrow or next week would clear my way, and long disappointed, I sadly missed the cheerful face and ready response of my friend.

It was wretched weather; stormy and wet, stormy and wet; and mud, mud, mud, deep in all the streets. Day after day, a vast heavy veil had been driving over London from the East, and it drove still, as if in the East there were an Eternity of cloud and wind. So furious had been the gusts, that high buildings in town had had the lead stripped off their roofs; and in the country, trees had been torn up, and sails of windmills carried away; and gloomy accounts had come in from the coast, of shipwreck and death. Violent blasts of rain had accompanied these rages of wind, and the day just closed as I sat down to read had been the worst of all.

Alterations have been made in that part of the Temple since that time, and it has not now so lonely a character as it had then, nor is it so exposed to the river. We lived at the top of the last house, and the wind rushing up the river shook the house that night, like discharges of cannon, or breakings of a sea. When the rain came with it and dashed against the windows, I thought, raising my eyes to them as they rocked, that I might have fancied myself in a storm beaten light house. Occasionally, the smoke came rolling down the chimney as though it could not bear to go out into such a night; and when I set the doors open and looked down the staircase, the staircase lamps were blown out; and when I shaded my face with my hands and looked through the black windows (opening them ever so little, was out of the question in the teeth of such wind and rain) I saw that the lamps in the court were blown out, and that the lamps on the bridges and the shore were shuddering, and that the coal fires in barges on the river were being carried away before the wind like red hot splashes in the rain.

I read with my watch upon the table, purposing to close my book at eleven o'clock. As I shut it, Saint Paul's, and all the many church clocks in the City — some leading, some accompanying, some following — struck that hour. The sound was curiously flawed by the wind; and I was listening, and thinking how the wind assailed and tore it, when I heard a footstep on the stair.

What nervous folly made me start, and awfully connect it with the footstep of my dead sister, matters not. It was past in a moment, and I listened again, and heard the footstep stumble in coming on. Remembering then, that the staircase lights were blown out, I took up my reading lamp and went out to the stair head. Whoever was below had stopped on seeing my lamp, for all was quiet.

"There is some one down there, is there not?" I called out, looking down.

"Yes," said a voice from the darkness beneath.

"What floor do you want?"

"The top. Mr. Pip."

"That is my name. — There is nothing the matter?"

"Nothing the matter," returned the voice. And the man came on.

I stood with my lamp held out over the stair-rail, and he came slowly within its light. It was a shaded lamp, to shine upon a book, and its circle of light was very contracted; so that he was in it for a mere instant, and then out of it. In the instant, I had seen a face that was strange to me, looking up with an incomprehensible air of being touched and pleased by the sight of me.

Moving the lamp as the man moved, I made out that he was substantially dressed, but roughly; like a voyager by sea. That he had long iron grey hair. That his age was about sixty. That he was a muscular man, strong on his legs, and that he was browned and hardened by exposure to weather. As he ascended the last stair or two, and the light of my lamp included us both, I saw, with a stupid kind of amazement, that he was holding out both his hands to me.

"Pray what is your business?" I asked him.

"My business?" he repeated, pausing. "Ah! Yes. I will explain my business, by your leave."

"Do you wish to come in?"

"Yes," he replied; "I wish to come in, Master."

I had asked him the question inhospitably enough, for I resented the sort of bright and gratified recognition that still shone in his face. I resented it, because it seemed to imply that he expected me to respond to it. But, I took him into the room I had just left, and, having set the lamp on the table, asked him as civilly as I could, to explain himself.

He looked about him with the strangest air an air of wondering pleasure, as if he had some part in the things he admired and he pulled off a rough outer coat, and his hat. Then, I saw that his head was furrowed and bald, and that the long iron grey hair grew only on its sides. But, I saw nothing that in the least explained him. On the contrary, I saw him next moment, once more holding out both his hands to me.

"What do you mean?" said I, half suspecting him to be mad.

He stopped in his looking at me, and slowly rubbed his right hand over his head. "It's disapinting to a man," he said, in a coarse broken voice, "arter having looked for'ard so distant, and come so fur; but you're not to blame for that — neither on us is to blame for that. I'll speak in half a minute. Give me half a minute, please."

He sat down on a chair that stood before the fire, and covered his forehead with his large brown veinous hands. I looked at him attentively then, and recoiled a little from him; but I did not know him.

"There's no one nigh," said he, looking over his shoulder; "is there?"

"Why do you, a stranger coming into my rooms at this time of the night, ask that question?" said I.

"You're a game one," he returned, shaking his head at me with a deliberate affection, at once most unintelligible and most exasperating; "I'm glad you've grow'd up, a game one! But don't catch hold of me. You'd be sorry afterwards to have done it."

I relinquished the intention he had detected, for I knew him! Even yet, I could not recall a single feature, but I knew him! If the wind and the rain had driven away the intervening years, had scattered all the intervening objects, had swept us to the churchyard where we first stood face to face on such different levels, I could not have known my convict more distinctly than I knew him now as he sat in the chair before the fire. No need to take a file from his pocket and show it to me; no need to take the handkerchief from his neck and twist it round his head; no need to hug himself with both his arms, and take a shivering turn across the room, looking back at me for recognition. I knew him before he gave me one of those aids, though, a moment before, I had not been conscious of remotely suspecting his identity.

He came back to where I stood, and again held out both his hands. Not knowing what to do — for, in my astonishment I had lost my self possession — I reluctantly gave him my hands. He grasped them heartily, raised them to his lips, kissed them, and still held them.

"You acted noble, my boy," said he. "Noble, Pip! And I have never forgot it!"

At a change in his manner as if he were even going to embrace me, I laid a hand upon his breast and put him away.

"Stay!" said I. "Keep off! If you are grateful to me for what I did when I was a little child, I hope you have shown your gratitude by mending your way of life. If you have come here to thank me, it was not necessary. Still, however you have found me out, there must be something good in the feeling that has brought you here, and I will not repulse you; but surely you must understand that I —"

My attention was so attracted by the singularity of his fixed look at me, that the words died away on my tongue.

"You was a saying," he observed, when we had confronted one another in silence, "that surely I must understand. What, surely must I understand?"

"That I cannot wish to renew that chance intercourse with you of long ago, under these different circumstances. I am glad to believe you have repented and recovered yourself. I am glad to tell you so. I am glad that, thinking I deserve to be thanked, you have come to thank me. But our ways are different ways, none the less. You are wet, and you look weary. Will you drink something before you go?"

He had replaced his neckerchief loosely, and had stood, keenly observant of me, biting a long end of it. "I think" he answered, still with the end at his mouth and still observant of me, "that I will drink (I thank you) afore I go."

There was a tray ready on a side table. I brought it to the table near the fire, and asked him what he would have? He touched one of the bottles without looking at it or speaking, and I made him some hot rum and water. I tried to keep my hand steady while I did so, but his look at me as he leaned back in his chair with the long draggled end of his neckerchief between his teeth — evidently forgotten — made my hand very difficult to master. When at last I put the glass to him, I saw with amazement that his eyes were full of tears.

Up to this time I had remained standing, not to disguise that I wished him gone. But I was softened by the softened aspect of the man, and felt a touch of reproach. "I hope," said I, hurriedly putting something into a glass for myself, and drawing a chair to the table, "that you will not think I spoke harshly to you just now. I had no intention of doing it, and I am sorry for it if I did. I wish you well, and happy!"

As I put my glass to my lips, he glanced with surprise at the end of his neckerchief, dropping from his mouth when he opened it, and stretched out his hand. I gave him mine, and then he drank, and drew his sleeve across his eyes and forehead.

"How are you living?" I asked him.

"I've been a sheep-farmer, stock breeder, other trades besides, away in the new world," said he: "many a thousand mile of stormy water off from this."

"I hope you have done well."

"I've done wonderfully well. There's others went out alonger me as has done well too, but no man has done nigh as well as me. I'm famous for it."

"I am glad to hear it."

"I hope to hear you say so, my dear boy."

Without stopping to try to understand those words or the tone in which they were spoken, I turned off to a point that had just come into my mind.

"Have you ever seen a messenger you once sent to me," I inquired, "since he undertook that trust?"

"Never set eyes upon him. I warn't likely to it."

"He came faithfully, and he brought me the two one pound notes. I was a poor boy then, as you know, and to a poor boy they were a little fortune. But, like you, I have done well since, and you must let me pay them back. You can put them to some other poor boy's use." I took out my purse.

He watched me as I laid my purse upon the table and opened it, and he watched me as I separated two one pound notes from its contents. They were clean and new, and I spread them out and handed them over to him. Still watching me, he laid them one upon the other, folded them long wise, gave them a twist, set fire to them at the lamp, and dropped the ashes into the tray.

"May I make so bold," he said then, with a smile that was like a frown, and with a frown that was like a smile, "as ask you how you have done well, since you and me was out on them lone shivering marshes?"

"How?"

"Ah!"

He emptied his glass, got up, and stood at the side of the fire, with his heavy brown hand on the mantelshelf. He put a foot up to the bars, to dry and warm it, and the wet boot began to steam; but, he neither looked at it, nor at the fire, but steadily looked at me. It was only now that I began to tremble.

When my lips had parted, and had shaped some words that were without sound, I forced myself to tell him (though I could not do it distinctly), that I had been chosen to succeed to some property.

"Might a mere warmint ask what property?" said he.

I faltered, "I don't know."

"Might a mere warmint ask whose property?" said he.

I faltered again, "I don't know."

"Could I make a guess, I wonder," said the Convict, "at your income since you come of age! As to the first figure now, Five?"

With my heart beating like a heavy hammer of disordered action, I rose out of my chair, and stood with my hand upon the back of it, looking wildly at him.

"Concerning a guardian," he went on. "There ought to have been some guardian, or such like, whiles you was a minor. Some lawyer, maybe. As to the first letter of that lawyer's name now, would it be J?"

All the truth of my position came flashing on me; and its disappointments, dangers, disgraces, consequences of all kinds, rushed in in such a multitude that I was borne down by them and had to struggle for every breath I drew.

"Put it," he resumed, "as the employer of that lawyer whose name begun with a J, and might be Jaggers — put it as he had come over sea to Portsmouth, and had landed there, and had wanted to come on to you. "However, you have found me out," you say just now. Well! However, did I find you out? Why, I wrote from Portsmouth to a person in London, for particulars of your address. Is that person's name? Why, Wemmick."

I could not have spoken one word, though it had been to save my life. I stood, with a hand on the chair back and a hand on my breast, where I seemed to be suffocating — I stood so, looking wildly at him, until I grasped at the chair, when the room began to surge and turn. He caught me, drew me to the sofa, put me up against the cushions, and bent on one knee before me: bringing the face that I now well remembered, and that I shuddered at, very near to mine.

"Yes, Pip, dear boy, I've made a gentleman on you! It's me wot has done it! I swore that time, sure as ever I earned a guinea, that guinea should go to you. I swore arterwards, sure as ever I spec'lated and got rich, you should get rich. I lived rough, that you should live smooth; I worked hard, that you should be above work. What odds, dear boy? Do I tell it fur you to feel a obligation? Not a bit. I tell it, fur you to know as that there hunted dunghill dog wot you kep life in, got his head so high that he could make a gentleman — and, Pip, you're him!"

The abhorrence in which I held the man, the dread I had of him, the repugnance with which I shrank from him, could not have been exceeded if he had been some terrible beast.

"Look'ee here, Pip. I'm your second father. You're neither my son — more to me nor any son. I've put away money, only for you to spend. When I was a hired out shepherd in a solitary hut, not seeing no faces but faces of sheep till I half forgot wot men's and women's faces wos like, I see yourn. I drops my knife many a time in that hut when I was a eating my dinner or my supper, and I says, "Here's the boy again, a looking at me whiles I eats and drinks!" I see you there a many times, as plain as ever I see you on them misty marshes. "Lord strikes me dead!" I say each time-and I go out in the air to say it under the open heavens —"but wot, if I get liberty and money, I'll make that boy a gentleman!" And I did it. Why, look at you, dear boy! Look at these here lodgings o'yourn, fit for a lord! A lord? Ah! You shall show money with lords for wagers, and beat' em!"

In his heat and triumph, and in his knowledge that I had been nearly fainting, he did not remark on my reception of all this. It was the one grain of relief I had.

"Look'ee here!" he went on, taking my watch out of my pocket, and turning towards him a ring on my finger, while I recoiled from his touch as if he had been a snake, "a gold 'un and a beauty: that's a gentleman's, I hope! A diamond all set round with rubies; that's a gentleman's, I hope! Look at your linen; fine and beautiful! Look at your clothes; better ain't to be got! And your books too," turning his eyes round the room, "mounting up, on their shelves, by hundreds! And you read'em; don't you? I see you'd been a reading of'em when I come in. Ha, ha, ha! You shall read'em to me, dear boy! And if they're in foreign languages wot I don't understand, I shall be just as proud as if I did."

Again he took both my hands and put them to his lips, while my blood ran cold within me.

"Don't you mind talking, Pip," said he, after again drawing his sleeve over his eyes and forehead, as the click came in his throat which I well remembered — and he was all the more horrible to me that he was so much in earnest; "you can't do better nor keep quiet, dear boy. You ain't looked slowly forward to this as I have; you wosn't prepared for this, as I wos. But didn't you ever think it might be me?"

"O no, no, no," I returned, "Never never!"

"Well, you see it wos me, and single handed. Never a soul in it but my own self and Mr Jaggers."

"Was there no one else?" I asked.

"No," said he, with a glance of surprise: "who else should there be? And, dear boy, how good looking you have growed! There are bright eyes somewheres — eh? Isn't there bright eyes somewheres, wot you love the thoughts on?"

O Estella, Estella!

"They shall be yourn, dear boy, if money can buy'em. Not that a gentleman like you, so well set up as you, can't win 'em off of his own game; but money shall back you! Let me finish wot I was a telling you, dear boy. From that there hut and that there hiringout, I got money left me by my master (which died, and had been the same as me), and got my liberty and went for myself. In every single thing I went for, I went for you. "Lord Strikes a blight upon it," I say, wotever it was I went for, 'if it ain't for him!' It all prospered wonderful. As I giv' you to understand just now, I'm famous for it. It was the money left me, and the gains of the first few year wot I sent home to Mr Jaggers — all for you — when he first come arter you, agreeable to my letter."

O, that he had never come! That he had left me at the forge — far from contented, yet, by comparison happy!

"And then, dear boy, it was recompense to me, look'ee here, to know in secret that I was making a gentleman. The blood horses of them colonists might fling up the dust over me as I was walking; what do I say? I say to myself, 'I'm making a better gentleman nor ever you'll be!' When one of 'em says to another, 'He was a convict, a few year ago, and is a ignorant common fellow now, for all he's lucky,' what do I say? I says to myself, 'If I ain't a gentleman, nor yet ain't got no learning, I'm the owner of such. All on you owns stock and land; which on you owns a brought up London gentleman?' This was I kep myself a going. And this way I held steady afore my mind that I would for certain come one day and see my boy, and make myself known to him, on his own ground."

He laid his hand on my shoulder. I shuddered at the thought that for anything I knew, his hand might be stained with blood.

"It warn't easy, Pip, for me to leave them parts, nor yet it wasn't safe. But I held to it, and the harder it was, the stronger I held, for I was determined, and my mind firm made up. At last I did it. Dear boy, I done it!"

I tried to collect my thoughts, but I was stunned. Throughout, I had seemed to myself to attend more to the wind and the rain than to him; even now, I could not separate his voice from those voices, though those were loud and his was silent.

"Where will you put me?" he asked, presently. "I must be put somewheres, dear boy."

"To sleep?" said I.

"Yes. And to sleep long and sound," he answered; "for I've been sea tossed and sea washed, months and months."

"My friend and companion," said I, rising from the sofa, "is absent; you must have his room."

"He won't come back to-morrow; will he?"

"No," said I, answering almost mechanically, in spite of my utmost efforts; "not to-morrow."

"Because, look'ee here, dear boy," he said, dropping his voice, and laying a long finger on my breast in an impressive manner, "caution is necessary."

"How do you mean? Caution?"

"By G—, it's Death!"

"What's death?"

"I was sent for life. It's death to come back. There's been overmuch coming back of late years, and I should of a certainty be hanged if took."

Nothing was needed but this; the wretched man, after loading wretched me with his gold and silver chains for years, had risked his life to come to me, and I held it there in my keeping! If I had loved him instead of abhorring him; if I had been attracted to him by the strongest admiration and affection, instead of shrinking from him with the strongest repugnance; it could have been no worse. On the contrary, it would have been better, for his preservation would then have naturally and tenderly addressed my heart.

My first care was to close the shutters, so that no light might be seen from without, and then to close and make fast the doors. While I did so, he stood at the table drinking rum and eating biscuit; and when I saw him thus engaged, I saw my convict on the marshes at his meal again. It almost seemed to me as if he must stoop down presently, to file at his leg.

When I had gone into Herbert's room, and had shut off any other communication between it and the staircase than through the room in which our conversation had been held, I asked him if he would go to bed? He said yes, but asked me for some of my "gentleman's linen" to put on in the morning. I brought it out, and laid it ready for him, and my blood again ran cold when he again took me by both hands to give me good night.

I got away from him, without knowing how I did it, and mended the fire in the room where we had been together, and sat down by it, afraid to go to bed. For an hour or more, I remained too stunned to think; and it was not until I began to think, that I began fully to know how wrecked I was, and how the ship in which I had sailed was gone to pieces.

Miss Havisham's intentions towards me, all a mere dream; Estella not designed for me; I only suffered in Satis House as a convenience, a sting for the greedy relations, a model with a mechanical heart to practise on when no other practice was at hand; those were the first smarts I had. But, sharpest and deepest pain of all — it was for the convict, guilty of I knew not what crimes, and liable to be taken out of those rooms where I sat thinking, and hanged at the Old Bailey door, that I had deserted Joe.

I would not have gone back to Joe now, I would not have gone back to Biddy now, for any consideration: simply, I suppose, because my sense of my own worthless conduct to them was greater than every consideration. No wisdom on earth could have given me the comfort that I should have derived from their simplicity and fidelity; but I could never, never, undo what I had done.

In every rage of wind and rush of rain, I heard pursuers. Twice, I could have sworn there was a knocking and whispering at the outer door. With these fears upon me, I began either to imagine or recall that I had had mysterious warnings of this man's approach. That, these likenesses had grown more numerous, as he, coming over the sea, had drawn nearer. That, his wicked spirit had somehow sent these messengers to mine, and that now on this stormy night he was as good as his word, and with me.

Crowding up with these reflections came the reflection that I had seen him with my childish eyes to be a desperately violent man; that I had heard that other convict reiterate that he had tried to murder him; that I had seen him down in the ditch tearing and fighting like a wild beast. Out of such remembrances I brought into the light of fire, a half formed terror that it might not be safe to be shut up there with him in the dead of the wild solitary night. This dilated until it filled the room, and impelled me to take a candle and go in and look at my dreadful burden.

He had rolled a handkerchief round his head, and his face was set and lowering in his sleep. But he was asleep, and quietly too, though he had a pistol lying on the pillow. Assured of this, I softly removed the key to the outside of his door, and turned it on him before I again sat down by the fire. Gradually I slipped from the chair and lay on the floor. When I awoke, without having parted in my sleep with the perception of my wretchedness, the clocks of the Eastward churches were striking five, the candles were wasted out, the fire was dead, and the wind and rain intensified the thick black darkness.

THIS IS THE END OF THE SECOND STAGE OF PIP'S EXPECTATIONS. (1860)

Critical Realism:

In the mid and late 19th century, a new literary trend — critical realism appeared.

English critical realism of the 19th century flourished in the forties and in the early fifties. The critical realists described with much vividness and artistic skill the chief traits (characteristics) of the English society and criticized the capitalist system from a democratic viewpoint. It found its expressions in the form of novel. The greatest English realist of the time was Charles Dickens. With striking force and truthfulness, he creates pictures of bourgeois civilization, showing the misery and sufferings of the common people. Others are Bronte sisters, Elizabeth Gaskell, George Eliot, and Thomas Hardy. The novelists exposed and criticized the corrupted society mercilessly. They are generally known as critical realists.

The English critical realists of the 19th century not only gave a satirical portrayal of the bourgeoisie and all the ruling classes, but also showed profound sympathy for the common people. In their best works, the greed and hypocrisy of the upper classes are contrasted with the honesty and good-heartedness of the obscure "simple people" of the lower classes. Hence humor and satire abound in the English realistic novels of the 19th century. The humor is often used to stress the fine qualities of the positive characters. At the same time, bitter satire and grotesque is used to expose the seamy side of the bourgeois society. Critical realism reveals the corrupting influence of the rule of cash upon human nature. Here lies essentially democratic and humanistic character of critical realism. Their works do not point to revolution but rather evolution or reformism. They often start with a powerful exposure of the ugliness of the bourgeois world in their works, but their novels usually have happy endings or an impotent compromise in the end.

The major contribution made by the 19th century critical realists is their perfection of the novel. Like the realists of the 18th century, the 19th century critical realists made use of the form of novel for full and detailed representations of social and political events, and of the fate of individuals and of whole social classes.

批判现实主义：

在19世纪中后期，出现了一种新型文学潮流——批判现实主义。英国批判现实主义在19世纪40年代到50年代初期蓬勃发展起来。批判现实主义者们用足够生动并且充满艺术感的手法来描述英国社会的主要特征，并从民主的角度批判资本主义制度。这一批判以小说的形式实现。当时最为出色的英国批判家是查尔斯·狄更斯。他凭借显著的批判力度和真诚，绘制了资产阶级文明的画面，展现出普通民众的疾苦。其他还有像勃朗特三姐妹、伊丽莎白·加斯科尔、乔治·埃利奥特和托马斯·哈代等，这些小说家们无情地揭露批判腐败堕落的社会。他们均被称为批判现实主义小说家。

19世纪的英国批判现实主义作家不仅嘲讽地描绘出资产阶级和所有统治阶级的面貌，而且对普通民众表现出极大的同情。在他们最出色的作品中，上层阶级的贪婪和伪善与下层阶级人民的诚实和善良形成了强烈对比。自此幽默和讽刺频繁出现于19世纪的批判现实主义文学作品中。幽默主要用来强调正面人物的美好品质。同时，尖锐的讽刺用来揭露资产阶级的阴暗面。批判现实主义展现了金钱主义对人本性的腐化影响，这蕴含了批判现实主义的民主主义和人文主义这两个根本特征。他们的作品没有指出要进行革命而是要变革或者改革。他们通常以对资产阶级世界的丑恶嘴脸进行强有力的揭露为开始，但小说通常拥有一个幸福的结尾或是以无力的妥协收场。

19世纪批判现实主义作家所做的主要贡献是对于小说的完善。和18世纪的现实主义者的做法类似,19世纪的批判现实主义作家们以小说的形式针砭时弊,对社会及政治事件和个人及整个社会的命运进行了全面详细的展示。

Chapter 9 Alfred Tennyson

作者简介

Alfred Tennyson (1809 – 92) was one of the greatest representative poets of the Victorian Age. His poetry was full of musicality and expression in the language. Tennyson was born at an ordinary family in Somersby, Lincolnshire in 1809. His initial education was conducted largely by his father. The boy showed an early interest and talent in poetic composition. By the time he was 15, Tennyson had produced several blank-verse plays and an epic. In 1827, his boyhood poetry *Poems by Two Brothers* was published in collaboration with his brother.

In 1828 Tennyson entered Trinity College, University of Cambridge, where he got acquainted with Arthur Henry Hallam who became his closest friend. While there he wrote a blank-verse poem, *Timbuctoo* in 1829, for which he received a prize, and published his first book on his own, *Poems, Chiefly Lyrical* in 1830, which includes *Mariana*. Tennyson also wrote some notable poems including *Idylls of the King*, *Ulysses*, and *Tithonus*. In the spring of 1831, Tennyson's father died, requiring him to leave Cambridge before taking his degree. In 1833 Tennyson published his second book of poetry, which included his well-known poem, *The Lady of Shalott*. The volume met heavy criticism, adding the sudden death of his friend Hallam in the same year produced in Tennyson a profound spiritual depression, which so discouraged Tennyson that he did not publish again for ten years, although he did continue to write.

In 1842 while living modestly in London, Tennyson published two volumes of *Poems*, of which the first included works already published and the second was made up almost entirely of new poems. They met with immediate success. Poems from this collection, such as *Locksley Hall*, *The Princess* and *Ulysses* have met enduring fame. It was in 1850 that Tennyson reached the pinnacle of his career, finally publishing his masterpiece, *In Memoriam A. H. H.*, which was written over a period of 17 years and it is widely considered to be one of the greatest poems of the 19th century. Later the same year he was appointed Poet Laureate succeeding William Wordsworth.

阿尔弗雷德·丁尼生（1809—1892）是维多利亚时期最具代表性的诗人之一。他的诗歌语言极富音乐感和表现力。丁尼生生于林肯郡的萨默斯比的一个普通家庭,他的启蒙教育大多来自他的父亲。丁尼生在很小时就表现出对诗作的兴趣与天赋。到15岁时,他已经创造出不少的无韵诗和一部史诗。1827年,丁尼生与其兄共同出版了他们共同创作的童年诗集《两兄弟诗集》。

1828年,丁尼生进入剑桥大学三一学院学习,并在那里结识了他的挚友哈勒姆。次年他写了一篇无韵诗《延巴克图》,并获得金奖,在1830年他又出版了他个人的第一部《抒情诗集》,其中包括《马里亚纳》。丁尼生后期也创作了其他一些备受瞩目的无韵诗,如:《国王之歌》、《尤利西斯》和《提托诺斯》等。1831年,因父亲逝世,他未取得学位就离开了剑桥。1833年,他出版了他的第二部诗集,这其中包括了他很有名的诗《夏洛特夫人》。他的诗集遭到负面评价,加之在同一年,好朋友哈勒姆的突然死亡使他深受打击,此后10年,尽管消沉的丁尼生一直在写诗,但这期间从未发表过诗作。

1842年,低调地在伦敦居住的丁尼生出版了两部诗,其中包括一部已经发表过的作品,第二部几乎完全是新诗,这些作品立即取得了成功。这个诗集中包括《洛克斯利厅》、《公主》与《尤利西斯》,这些都获得了持久的名誉。在1850年,丁尼生达到了职业生涯的巅峰,他终于出版了他的杰作《悼念》,这个创作历时17年,它被广泛认为是19世纪最伟大的诗歌之一。在同年不久,他被任命为继威廉·华兹华斯之后的又一桂冠诗人。

作品及导读

作品 1

Ulysses

导 读

"Ulysses" is a poem in blank verse by the Victorian poet Alfred Lord Tennyson (1809 - 92), written in 1833 and published in 1842 in his well-received second volume of poetry. An oft-quoted poem, it is popularly used to illustrate the dramatic monologue form. "Ulysses" describes, to an unspecified audience, his discontent and restlessness upon returning to his kingdom, Ithaca, after his far-ranging travels. Facing old age, Ulysses yearns to explore again, despite his reunion with his wife Penelope and son Telemachus.

The character of Ulysses (in Greek, Odysseus) has been explored widely in literature. The adventures of Odysseus were first recorded in Homer's *Iliad* and *Odyssey* (c. 800 – 700 BC), and Tennyson draws on Homer's narrative in the poem. Most critics, however, find that Tennyson's "Ulysses" recalls Dante's Ulisse in his "Inferno" (c. 1320). In Dante's retelling, Ulisse is condemned to hell among the false counsellors, both for his pursuit of knowledge beyond human bounds and for his adventures in disregard of his family.

For much of this poem's history, readers viewed Ulysses as resolute and heroic, admiring him for his determination "To strive, to seek, to find, and not to yield." The view that Tennyson intended a heroic character is supported by his statements about the poem, and by the events in his life — the death of his closest friend — that prompted him to write it. In the twentieth century, some new interpretations of "Ulysses" highlighted potential ironies in the poem. They argued, for example, that Ulysses wishes to selfishly abandon his kingdom and family, and they questioned more positive assessments of Ulysses' character by demonstrating how he resembles flawed protagonists in earlier literature.

《尤利西斯》是一首无韵诗,由维多利亚时代的诗人阿尔弗雷德·丁尼生勋爵(1809-1892)所著,写于1833年,并于1842年在他广受欢迎的第二个诗歌集中出版。《尤利西斯》是一首经常被引用的诗。尤其在说明戏剧独白的形式这方面很受欢迎。尤利西斯向一位不知名的听众描述了自己在一段长距离的旅程之后,回到伊萨卡王国时的不满与躁动。年龄越来越老,尤利西斯渴望再次去探索,尽管他与妻子佩内洛普和儿子特勒马库斯此刻已经团聚。

尤利西斯(希腊语中为奥德修斯)的人物性格在文学方面被广泛研究探索。奥德修斯的冒险首先被记录在荷马的《伊利亚特》和《奥德赛》(公元前800—700)中。丁尼生借鉴了荷马的叙事诗。然而多数评论家发现,丁尼生的尤利西斯对应了但丁《地狱》(约1320)里的尤利西斯。在但丁的讲述中,尤利西斯被虚伪的参赞打入地狱,罪名是他的追求超越了人类知识的界限,还有他不顾家人的冒险。

对于这首诗的历史,读者认为尤利西斯是果敢而又英勇的,仰慕他"去奋头、去探索、去发现、永不屈服"的决心。不管是丁尼生本人对这首诗的描述还是他生活中遭遇的变故都表明他意在塑造一位英雄人物。挚友的离世极大程度上促使了这首诗的创作。在20世纪,对《尤利西斯》的一些新的诠释强调它是一首潜在的讽刺诗。例如,他们认为,尤利西斯想自私地放弃他的国家和家人,通过展示在早期文献中主角的缺陷,他们质疑一些关于尤利西斯积极的评价。

选 文

Ulysses

It little profits that an idle king,
By this still hearth, among these barren crags,
Matched with an aged wife, I mete and dole
Unequal laws unto a savage race,
That hoard, and sleep, and feed, and know not me.

◄ ◄ ◄ ◄ THE BRITISH PART

I cannot rest from travel; I will drink
Life to the lees. All times I have enjoyed
Greatly, have suffered greatly, both with those
That loved me, and alone; on shore, and when
Through scudding drifts the rainy Hyades
Vexed the dim sea. I am become a name;
For always roaming with a hungry heart
Much have I seen and known, cities of men
And manners, climates, councils, governments,
Myself not least, but honoured of them all,
And drunk delight of battle with my peers,
Far on the ringing plains of windy Troy.
I am part of all that I have met,
Yet all experience is an arch wherethrough
Gleams that untravelled world whose margin fades
Forever and forever when I move.
How dull it is to pause, to make an end,
To rust unburnished, not to shine in use!
As though to breath were life. Life piled on life
Were all to little, and of one to me
Little remains; but every hour is saved
From that eternal silence, something more,
A bringer of new things; and vile it were
For some three suns to store and hoard myself,
And this gray spirit yearning in desire
To follow knowledge like a sinking star,
Beyond the utmost bound of human thought.

This is my son, mine own Telemachus,
To whom I leave the scepter and the isle —
Well-loved of me, discerning to fulfill
This labour, by slow prudence to make mild
A rugged people, and through soft degrees
Subdue them to the useful and the good.
Most blameless is he, centered in the sphere
Of common duties, decent not to fail
In offices of tenderness, and pay
Meet adoration to my household gods,
When I am gone. He works his work, I mine.

There lies the port; the vessel puffs her sail:
There gloom the dark, broad seas. My mariners,
Souls that have toiled, and wrought, and thought with me —
That ever with a frolic welcome took
The thunder and the sunshine, and opposed
Free hearts, free foreheads — you and I are old;
Old age had yet his honour and his toil.
Death closes all: but something ere the end,
Some work of noble note, may yet be done,
Not unbecoming men that strove with Gods.
The lights begin to twinkle from the rocks;
The long day wanes; the slow moon climbs; the deep
Moans round with many voices. Come, my friends,
'Tis not too late to seek a newer world.
Push off, and sitting well in order smite
The sounding furrows; for my purpose holds
To sail beyond the sunset, and the baths
Of all the western stars, until I die.
It may be that the gulfs will wash us down;
It may be we shall touch the Happy Isles,
And see the great Achilles, whom we knew.

Though much is taken, much abides; and though
We are not now that strength which in the old days
Moved earth and heaven, that which we are, we are,
One equal temper of heroic hearts,
Made weak by time and fate, but strong in will
To strive, to seek, to find, and not to yield.

Chapter 10 Thomas Hardy

作者简介

Thomas Hardy, a famous English novelist and poet, was born in Dorset, England in 1840. His father Thomas worked as a stonemason and local builder, while his mother Jemima was well-read and educated Thomas until he went to his first school at the age of eight. However, Hardy's family lacked the means for a university education, and his formal education ended at the age of sixteen when he became apprenticed to James Hicks, a local architect. He was trained as an architect and worked in London and Dorset for ten years.

Hardy never felt at home in London. He was acutely conscious of class divisions and his social inferiority. However, he was interested in social reform and was familiar with the works of John Stuart Mill. During this period he was introduced by his Dorset friend Horace Moule to the works of Charles Fourier and Auguste Comte. Five years later, concerned about his health, he returned to Dorset and decided to dedicate him to writing. Hardy began his writing career as a novelist, publishing *Desperate Remedies* in 1871, and was soon successful enough to leave the field of architecture for writing. His novels *Tess of the D'Urbervilles* (1891) and *Jude the Obscure* (1895), which are considered literary classics today, received negative reviews upon publication and Hardy was criticized for being too pessimistic and preoccupied with sex. He left fiction writing for poetry, and published eight collections, including *Wessex Poems* (1898) and *Satires of Circumstance* (1912).

Hardy's poetry explores a fatalist outlook against the dark, rugged landscape of his native Dorset. He rejected the Victorian belief in a benevolent God, and much of his poetry reads as a sardonic lament on the bleakness of the human condition.

Hardy also found happiness in his personal life. His first wife, Emma, died in 1912. Although their marriage had not been happy, Hardy grieved at her sudden death. In 1914, he married Florence Dugale, and she was extremely devoted to him. After his death, Florence published Hardy's autobiography in two parts under her own name.

After a long and highly successful life, Thomas Hardy died on January 11, 1928, at the age of 87. His ashes were buried in Poets' Corner at Westminster Abbey. Hardy's work was admired by many writers of a younger generation including D. H. Lawrence, John Cowper Powys, and Virginia Woolf.

1840年,英国著名小说家、诗人托马斯·哈代出生于英格兰多赛特。他的父亲是一名石匠,也是当地的建筑工人,而他的母亲受过良好教育,一直教育他直到他8岁入学。然而,哈代的家庭却无力负担起他的大学教育。他接受正式教育的阶段也随着他16岁成为当地建筑师詹姆斯·希克斯的学徒时正式宣告结束。他被训练为一名建筑师并且在伦敦和多赛特工作了整整10年。

哈代在伦敦从未有过家的感觉,他强烈地意识到阶级分化和社会劣势。然而他对社会改革很感兴趣,并且熟知约翰·穆勒的作品。在此期间,他曾被多赛特的好朋友贺拉斯·穆勒引进到查尔斯·博里以及奥古斯特·孔德的作品当中。5年后,因为担心自己的健康状况,哈代回到了多塞特,决定要专心写作。他以写小说开始了自己的作家生涯,1871年发表了《绝望的补救措施》,并且迅速取得足够的成功得以离开建筑领域而专心致力于写作。他的小说《德伯家的苔丝》(1891年)以及《无名的裘德》(1895年)在发表之后被视为当今文学的经典之作,但在当时却收到了负面的评论。哈代因为过于悲观和风流成性而遭到批判。他放弃了小说而创作诗歌,并发表了8部诗集,其中包括《韦塞克斯诗集》(1898年)、《环境的讽刺》(1912年)。

哈代的诗歌从一个宿命论者的角度对多赛特黑暗、崎岖的景观进行了探索。他拒绝维多利亚时代仁慈上帝的信仰,而且他的大部分诗歌被解读为对人类生存条件苍凉的讽刺与悲哀。

哈代在私人生活中也发现了他的幸福。他的第一任妻子,艾玛,死于1912年。虽然他们的婚姻不是多么幸福,但哈代仍为妻子的突然离世而悲痛不已。1914年,他与他的秘书佛罗伦萨·达格代尔结婚,她为他奉献了太多。在哈代死后,佛罗伦萨以自己的名义通过两部分发表了他的自传。

经历了长期成功的生活,托马斯·哈代于1928年1月11日逝世,享年87岁。他的骨灰被埋葬在威斯敏斯特大教堂的诗人角。哈代的作品被许多新一代作家所敬仰,其中包括D·H·劳伦斯、约翰·库伯·波伊斯以及弗吉尼亚·伍尔夫。

THE BRITISH PART

作品及导读

作品 1

Tess of the D'Urbervilles

导 读

  This novel is generally regarded as Hardy's finest. A brilliant tale of seduction, love, betrayal, and murder, *Tess of the D'Urbervilles* yields to narrative convention by punishing Tess's sin, but boldly exposes this standard denouement of unforgiving morality and the injustice of society. Throughout, Hardy's most lyrical and atmospheric language frames his shattering narrative. The novel centers around a young woman who struggles to find her place in society. When it is discovered that the low-class Durbeyfield family is in reality the d'Urbervilles, the last of a famous bloodline that dates back hundreds of years, the mother sends her eldest daughter, Tess, to beg money from relations with the obvious desire that Tess wed the rich Mr. D'Urbervilles. Thus begins a tale of woe in which a wealthy man cruelly mistreats a poor girl. Tess is taken advantage of by Mr. D'Urbervilles and leaves his house, returning home to have their child, who subsequently dies. Throughout the rest of this fascinating novel, Tess is tormented by guilt at the thought of her impurity and vows to never marry. She is tested when she meets Angel, the clever son of a priest, and falls in love with him. After days of pleading, Tess gives in to Angel and consents to marry him. Angel deserts Tess when he finds the innocent country girl he fell in love with is not so pure.

  This part is selected from 35th chapter which mainly tells that Tess finally decides to open her heart to Clare about her wretched lot with the hope of being forgiven, but Clare's respond is not what she expected before because he cares too much about her concealment and impurity.

  《德伯家的苔丝》这本小说被普遍认为是哈代最出色的作品,讲述了一个精彩的关于诱惑、爱情、背叛和谋杀的故事。这部作品并没有循规蹈矩地批判苔丝的罪恶,而是大胆地揭露了无情的道德标准和社会的不公。自始至终,哈代用浪漫抒情、极具感染力的语言为读者讲述了一个令人震撼的故事。小说以一个努力寻找自己社会地位的年轻女性为中心。当低阶层家庭的德比得知自己实际是贵族德伯家族的后代,其血统可以追溯到数百年前,他的妻子也就是孩子的母亲便将她的大女儿苔丝送去德伯家想靠这层关系能得到一笔钱,并希望她嫁给有钱人德伯维尔先生。因此,悲剧开始了,一个富人家的男主人残忍地诱奸了这个可怜的女孩。苔丝被占了便宜,离开了德伯维尔家,回家发现自己怀孕,孩子生下来却夭折了。在这本引人入胜的小说的其余部分,苔丝被深深的内疚所折磨,她觉得自己已不纯洁,并发誓永不结婚。直到她遇见安吉尔,她爱上了一个牧师的儿子安吉尔·克莱尔,他聪明、美好。经过一些日子的考验,她终于决定嫁给安吉尔。然而,这个男人还是无情地抛弃了她,因为他发现自己爱的这个单纯乡下姑娘并非他想象的那么纯洁。

本段选文选自小说的第35章,讲述了苔丝在新婚之夜鼓起勇气告诉了克莱尔他曾经悲惨的遭遇,她本以为克莱尔会宽恕她,然而克莱尔却对她的隐瞒和不纯洁耿耿于怀。

选 文

Tess of the D'Urbervilles
(Chapter 7)

Her narrative ended; even its re-assertions and secondary explanations were done. Tess's voice throughout had hardly risen higher than its opening tone; there had been no exculpatory phrase of any kind, and she had not wept.

But the complexion even of external things seemed to suffer transmutation as her announcement progressed. The fire in the grate looked impish — demoniacally funny, as if it did not care in the least about her strait. The fender grinned idly, as if it too did not care. The light from the water-bottle was merely engaged in a chromatic problem. All material objects around announced their irresponsibility with terrible iteration. And yet nothing had changed since the moments when he had been kissing her; or rather, nothing in the substance of things. But the essence of things had changed.

When she ceased the auricular impressions from their previous endearments seemed to hustle away into the corner of their brains, repeating themselves as echoes from a time of supremely purblind foolishness.

Clare performed the irrelevant act of stirring the fire; the intelligence had not even yet got to the bottom of him. After stirring the embers he rose to his feet; all the force of her disclosure had imparted itself now. His face had withered. In the strenuousness of his concentration he treaded fitfully on the floor. He could not, by any contrivance, think closely enough; that was the meaning of his vague movement. When he spoke it was in the most inadequate, commonplace voice of the many varied tones she had heard from him.

"Tess!"

"Yes, dearest."

"Am I to believe this? From your manner I am to take it as true. O you cannot be out of your mind! You ought to be! Yet you are not.... My wife, my Tess — nothing in you warrants such a supposition as that?"

"I am not out of my mind," she said.

"And yet —" He looked vacantly at her, to resume with dazed senses: "Why didn't you tell me before? Ah, yes, you would have told me, in a way — but I hindered you, I remember!"

These and other of his words were nothing but the perfunctory babble of the surface while the depths remained paralyzed. He turned away, and bent over a chair. Tess followed him to the middle of the room where he was, and stood there staring at him with eyes that did not weep. Presently she slid down upon her knees beside his foot, and from this position she crouched in a heap.

"In the name of our love, forgive me!" she whispered with a dry mouth. "I have forgiven you for the same!"

And, as he did not answer, she said again —

"Forgive me as you are forgiven! I forgive you, Angel."

"You — yes, you do."

"But you do not forgive me?"

"O Tess, forgiveness does not apply to the case! You were one person; now you are another. My God — how can forgiveness meet such a grotesque — prestidigitation as that!"

He paused, contemplating this definition; then suddenly broke into horrible laughter — as unnatural and ghastly as a laugh in hell.

"Don't — don't! It kills me quite, that!" she shrieked. "O have mercy upon me — have mercy!"

He did not answer; and, sickly white, she jumped up.

"Angel, Angel! What do you mean by that laugh?" she cried out. "Do you know what this is to me?"

He shook his head.

"I have been hoping, longing, praying, to make you happy! I have thought what joy it will be to do it, what an unworthy wife I shall be if I do not! That's what I have felt, Angel!"

"I know that."

"I thought, Angel, that you loved me — me, my very self! If it is I you do love, O how can it be that you look and speak so? It frightens me! Having begun to love you, I love you for ever — in all changes, in all disgraces, because you are yourself. I ask no more. Then how can you, O my own husband, stop loving me?"

"I repeat, the woman I have loved is not you."

"But who?"

"Another woman in your shape."

She perceived in his words the realization of her own apprehensive foreboding in former times. He looked upon her as a species of imposter; a guilty woman in the guise of an innocent one. Terror was upon her white face as she saw it; her cheek was flaccid, and her mouth had almost the aspect of a round little hole. The horrible sense of his view of her so deadened her that she staggered; and he stepped forward, thinking she was going to fall.

"Sit down, sit down," he said gently. "You are ill; and it is natural that you should be."

She did sit down, without knowing where she was, that strained look still upon her face, and her eyes such as to make his flesh creep.

"I don't belong to you any more, then; do I, Angel?" she asked helplessly. "It is not me, but another woman like me that he loved, he says."

The image raised caused her to take pity upon herself as one who was ill-used. Her eyes filled as she regarded her position further; she turned round and burst into a flood of self-sympathetic tears.

Clare was relieved at this change, for the effect on her of what had happened was beginning to be a trouble to him only less than the woe of the disclosure itself. He waited patiently, apathetically, till the violence of her grief had worn itself out, and her rush of weeping had lessened to a catching gasp at intervals.

"Angel," she said suddenly, in her natural tones, the insane, dry voice of terror having left her now. "Angel, am I too wicked for you and me to live together?"

"I have not been able to think what we can do."

"I shan't ask you to let me live with you, Angel, because I have no right to! I shall not write to mother and sisters to say we be married, as I said I would do; and I shan't finish the good-hussif' I cut out and meant to make while we were in lodgings."

"Shan't you?"

"No, I shan't do anything, unless you order me to; and if you go away from me I shall not follow 'ee; and if you never speak to me any more I shall not ask why, unless you tell me I may."

"And if I order you to do anything?"

"I will obey you like your wretched slave, even if it is to lie down and die."

"You are very good. But it strikes me that there is a want of harmony between your present mood of self-sacrifice and your past mood of self-preservation."

These were the first words of antagonism. To fling elaborate sarcasms at Tess, however, was much like flinging them at a dog or cat. The charms of their subtlety passed by her unappreciated, and she only received them as inimical sounds which meant that anger ruled. She remained mute, not knowing that he was smothering his affection for her. She hardly observed that a tear descended slowly upon his cheek, a tear so large that it magnified the pores of the skin over which it rolled, like the object lens of a microscope. Meanwhile reillumination as to the terrible and total change that her confession had wrought in his life, in his universe, returned to him, and he tried desperately to advance among the new conditions in which he stood. Some consequent action was necessary; yet what?

"Tess," he said, as gently as he could speak, "I cannot stay — in this room — just now. I will walk out a little way."

He quietly left the room, and the two glasses of wine that he had poured out for their supper — one for her, one for him — remained on the table untasted. This was what their agape had come to. At tea, two or three hours earlier, they had, in the freakishness of affection, drunk from one cup.

The closing of the door behind him, gently as it had been pulled to, roused Tess from her stupor. He was gone; she could not stay. Hastily flinging her cloak around her she opened the door and followed, putting out the candles as if she were never coming back. The rain was over and the night was now clear.

She was soon close at his heels, for Clare walked slowly and without purpose. His form beside her light gray figure looked black, sinister, and forbidding, and she felt as sarcasm the touch of the jewels of which she had been momentarily so proud. Clare turned at hearing her footsteps, but his recognition of her presence seemed to make no difference to him, and he went on over the five yawning arches of the great bridge in front of the house.

The cow and horse tracks in the road were full of water, and rain having been enough to charge them, but not enough to wash them away. Across these minute pools the reflected stars flitted in a quick transit as she passed; she would not have known they were shining overhead if she had not seen them there — the vastest things of the universe imaged in objects so mean.

The place to which they had travelled today was in the same valley as Talbothays, but some miles lower down the river; and the surroundings being open she kept easily in sight of him. Away from the house the road wound through the meads, and along these she followed Clare without any attempt to come up with him or to attract him, but with dumb and vacant fidelity.

At last, however, her listless walk brought her up alongside him, and still he said nothing. The cruelty of fooled honesty is often great after enlightenment, and it was mighty in Clare now. The outdoor air had apparently taken away from him all tendencies to act on impulse; she knew that he saw her without irradiation — in all her bareness; that Time was chanting his satiric psalm at her then —

Behold, when thy face is made bare, he that loved thee shall hate; Thy face shall be no more fair at the fall of thy fate. For thy life shall fall as a leaf and be shed as the rain; And the veil of thine head shall be grief, and the crown shall be pain.

He was still intently thinking, and her companionship had now insufficient power to break or divert the strain of thought. What a weak thing her presence must have become to him! She could not help addressing Clare.

"What have I done — what have I done! I have not told of anything that interferes with or belies my love for you. You don't think I planned it, do you? It is in your own mind what you are angry at, Angel; it is not in me. O, it is not in me, and I am not that deceitful woman you think me!"

"H'm — well. Not deceitful, my wife; but not the same. No, not the same. But do not make me reproach you. I have sworn that I will not; and I will do everything to avoid it."

But she went on pleading in her distraction; and perhaps said things that would have been better left to silence.

"Angel! — Angel! I was a child — a child when it happened! I knew nothing of men."

"You were more sinned against than sinning, that I admit."

"Then will you not forgive me?"

"I do forgive you, but forgiveness is not all."

"And love me?"

To this question he did not answer.

"O Angel — my mother says that it sometimes happens so! — she knows several cases where they were worse than I, and the husband has not minded it much — has got over it at least. And yet the woman had not loved him as I do you!"

"Don't, Tess; don't argue. Different societies, different manners. You almost make me say you are an unapprehending peasant woman, who has never been initiated into the proportions of social things. You don't know what you say."

"I am only a peasant by position, not by nature!"

She spoke with an impulse to anger, but it went as it came.

"So much the worse for you. I think that parson who unearthed your pedigree would have done better if he had held his tongue. I cannot help associating your decline as a family with this other fact — of your want of firmness. Decrepit families imply decrepit wills decrepit conduct. Heaven, why did you give me a handle for despising you more by informing me of your descent! Here was I thinking you a new-sprung child of nature; there were you, the belated seedling of an effete aristocracy!"

"Lots of families are as bad as mine in that! Retty's family was once large landowners, and so were Dairyman Billett's. And the Debby houses, who now are carters, were once the De Bayeux family. You find such as I everywhere; 'tis a feature of our county, and I can't help it."

"So much the worse for the county."

She took these reproaches in their bulk simply, not in their particulars; he did not love her as he had loved her hitherto, and to all else she was indifferent.

They wandered on again in silence. It was said afterwards that a cottager of Wellbridge, who went out late that night for a doctor, met two lovers in the pastures, walking very slowly, without converse, one behind the other, as in a funeral procession, and the glimpse that he obtained of their faces seemed to denote that they were anxious and sad. Returning later, he passed them again in the same field, progressing just as slowly, and as regardless of the hour and of the cheerless night as before. It was only on account of his preoccupation with his own affairs, and the illness in his house, that he did not bear in mind the curious incident, which, however, he recalled a long while after.

During the interval of the cottager's going and coming, she had said to her husband —

"I don't see how I can help being the cause of much misery to you all your life. The river is down there. I can put an end to myself in it. I am not afraid."

"I don't wish to add murder to my other follies," he said.

"I will leave something to show that I did it myself — on account of my shame. They will not blame you then."

"Don't speak so absurdly — I wish not to hear it. It is nonsense to have such thoughts in this kind of case, which is rather one for satirical laughter than for tragedy. You don't in the least understand the quality of the mishap. It would be viewed in the light of a joke by nine-tenths of the world if it were known. Please oblige me by returning to the house, and going to bed."

"I will," said she dutifully.

They had rambled round by a road which led to the well-known ruins of the Cistercian abbey behind the mill, the latter having, in centuries past, been attached to the monastic establishment. The mill still worked on, food being a perennial necessity; the abbey had perished, creeds being transient. One continually sees the ministration of the temporary outlasting the ministration of the eternal. Their walk having been circuitous they were still not far from the house, and in obeying his direction she only had to reach the large stone bridge across the main river, and follow the road for a few yards. When she got back everything remained as she had left it, the fire being still burning. She did not stay downstairs for more than a minute, but proceeded to her chamber, whither the luggage had been taken. Here she sat down on the edge of the bed, looking blankly around and presently began to undress. In removing the light towards the bedstead its rays fell upon the tester of white dimity; something was hanging beneath it, and she lifted the candle to see what it was. A bough of mistletoe. Angel had put it there; she knew that in an instant. This was the explanation of that mysterious parcel which it had been so difficult to pack and bring; whose contents he would not explain to her, saying that time would soon show her the purpose thereof. In his zest and his gaiety he had hung it there. How foolish and inopportune that mistletoe looked now.

Having nothing more to fear, having scarce anything to hope, for that he would relent there seemed no promise whatever, she lay down dully. When sorrow ceases to be speculative sleep sees her opportunity. Among so many happier moods which forbid repose this was a mood which welcomed it, and in a few minutes the lonely Tess forgot existence, surrounded by the aromatic stillness of the chamber that had once, possibly, been the bride-chamber of her own ancestry.

Later on that night Clare also retraced his steps to the house. Entering softly to the sitting-room he obtained a light, and with the manner of one who had considered his course he spread his rugs upon the old horse-hair sofa which stood there, and roughly shaped it to a sleeping-couch. Before lying down he crept shoeless upstairs, and listened at the door of her apartment. Her measured breathing told that she was sleeping profoundly.

"Thank God!" murmured Clare; and yet he was conscious of a pang of bitterness at the thought — approximately true, though not wholly so — that having shifted the burden of her life to his shoulders she was now reposing without care.

He turned away to descend; then, irresolute, faced round to her door again. In the act he caught sight of one of the D'Urbervilles dames, whose portrait was immediately over the entrance to Tess's bedchamber. In the candlelight the painting was more than unpleasant. Sinister design lurked in the woman's features, a concentrated purpose of revenge on the other sex — so it seemed to him then. The Caroline bodice of the portrait was low — precisely as Tess's had been when he tucked it in to show the necklace; and again he experienced the distressing sensation of a resemblance between them.

The check was sufficient. He resumed his retreat and descended.

His air remained calm and cold, his small compressed mouth indexing his powers of self-control; his face wearing still that terrible sterile expression which had spread thereon since her disclosure. It was the face of a man who was no longer passion's slave, yet who found no advantage in his enfranchisement. He was simply regarding the harrowing contingencies of human experience, the unexpectedness of things. Nothing so pure, so sweet, so virginal as Tess had seemed possible all the long while that he had adored her, up to an hour ago; but

The little less, and what worlds away!

He argued erroneously when he said to himself that her heart was not indexed in the honest freshness of her face; but Tess had no advocate to set him right. Could it be possible, he continued, that eyes which as they gazed never expressed any divergence from what the tongue was telling, were yet ever seeing another world behind her ostensible one, discordant and contrasting?

He reclined on his couch in the sitting-room, and extinguished the light. The night came in, and took up its place there, unconcerned and indifferent; the night which had already swallowed up his happiness, and was now digesting it listlessly; and was ready to swallow up the happiness of a thousand other people with as little disturbance or change of mien.

11 George Bernard Shaw

作者简介

George Bernard Shaw was born on 26 July, 1856 in Dublin, Ireland, and died on November, 1950 (1950-11-02) at ninety-four years old. He was an Irish playwright, critic, and political activist, as well as the co-founder of the London School of Economics. He is the only person to have been awarded both a Nobel Prize in Literature (1925) and an Oscar (1938), for his contributions to literature and for his work on the film *Pygmalion* (adaptation of his play of the same name), respectively. He was the son of a civil servant. His education was irregular, due to his dislike of any organized training. After working in an estate agent's office for a while he moved to London as a young man (1876), where he established himself as a leading music and theatre critic in the eighties and nineties and became a prominent member of the Fabian Society, for which he composed many pamphlets. Although his first profitable writing was music and literary criticism, in which capacity he wrote many highly articulate pieces of journalism, his main talent was for drama, and he wrote more than 60 plays. He was also an essayist, novelist and short story writer. Nearly all his writings address prevailing social problems, but have a vein of comedy which makes their stark themes more palatable. Issues which engaged Shaw's attention included education, marriage, religion, government, health care and class privilege. His main works are *Widowers' Houses*, *Saint Joan*, *Pygmalion*, *The Devil's Disciple*, *Man and Superman*, *Heartbreak House*, *Ms Warren's Profession*, *Major Barbara*, *The Apple Cart*, *The Doctor's Dilemma*.

萧伯纳,1856年7月出生于爱尔兰的都柏林,死于1950年11月,享年94岁。他被认为是一位爱尔兰的戏剧作家、批评家和积极的政治活动家,也是伦敦经济院系的创建人。他于1925年因对文学事业的贡献获得诺贝尔文学奖,1938年凭借以他的同名小说《茶花女》改编的电影获奥斯卡奖项。他是唯一荣获这两种奖项的人。他出生于一个小公务员家里。从小接受的教育也不是很正规,因为他不喜欢这种组织式的学习。当他年轻时,在一个机构工作了一段时间之后,搬家到伦敦。在那里,他成为19世纪80、90年代享誉声名的音乐和戏剧评论家。后来加入费边社,并为该组织创作了很多小册子。虽然他最初是因为音乐与批判性的作品被大家所熟知,然而他是极具戏剧天赋的,他写了60多部戏剧作品。他同时也是一位散文家、小说家和短篇故事的作家。他所有的作品都与社会问题有关,但是在他的作品中总以喜剧形式开始,这样就使他作品的主题为人们所接受。他作品中反映的社会问题包括教育、婚姻、宗教、政府、健康以及等级歧视。他的主要作品有《鳏夫的房产》、《圣女贞德》、《卖花女》、《魔鬼的门徒》、《人与超人》、《伤心之家》、《华伦夫人的职业》、《巴巴拉少校》、《苹果车》与《医生的两难选择》。

作品及导读

作品 1

Pygmalion

导 读

Pygmalion is a play by George Bernard Shaw, named after a Greek mythological character. It was first presented on stage in 1912.

Professor of phonetics Henry Higgins makes a bet that he can train a bedraggled Cockney flower girl, Eliza Doolittle, to pass for a duchess at an ambassador's garden party by teaching her to assume a veneer of gentility, the most important element of which, he believes, is impeccable speech. The play is a sharp lampoon of the rigid British class system of the day and a commentary on women's independence.

In ancient Greek mythology, Pygmalion fell in love with one of his sculptures, which then came to life. The general idea of that myth was a popular subject for Victorian era English playwrights, including one of Shaw's influences, W. S. Gilbert, who wrote a successful play based on the story called *Pygmalion and Galatea* first presented in 1871. Shaw also would have been familiar with the burlesque version, *Galatea*, or *Pygmalion Reversed*. Shaw's play has been adapted for numerous times, most notably the musical *My Fair Lady* and the film of that name.

Shaw mentions that the character of Professor Henry Higgins was inspired by several British professors of phonetics: Alexander, Alexander J. Ellis, Tito Pagliardini, but above all, the cantankerous Henry Sweet.

《卖花女》(又名《皮格马利翁》)是萧伯纳的一部戏剧,以希腊神话命名。它于1912年第一次向公众呈现在舞台上。

　　语言学教授亨利·希金斯下了一个赌注,即他可以训练一个纯伦敦腔的卖花女,并让她出现在公爵夫人的游园会上,他认为其中最重要的一个因素是无可挑剔的、完美的言辞。这部戏剧是对刚性的英国等级制度和妇女独立的一篇尖锐讽刺。

　　古希腊神话中,皮格马利翁要上了他的雕塑,后来雕塑复活。这一神话的总体思想在维多利亚时代的剧作家中间非常流行。根据这个故事,W. S. 吉尔伯特创作了戏剧《皮格巴利翁和加拉迪亚》并大获成功。吉尔伯特给萧伯纳带来了不小的影响。此外萧伯纳很可能也对滑稽版《加拉迪亚》(《皮格马利翁归来》)有所熟悉。萧伯纳的《皮格马利翁》问世后也经过了数次改编。最著名的不外乎音乐剧《窈窕淑女》以及其同名电影。

　　萧伯纳指出,亨利·希金斯教授角色的灵感来源于几个英国的语音学教授,其中印象最为深刻的是脾气古怪的亨利·斯威特教授。

选　文

Pygmalion

(Act 1)

Cab whistles blowing frantically in all directions. Pedestrians running for shelter into the market and under the portico of St. Paul's Church, where there are already several people, among them a lady and her daughter in evening dress. They are all peering out gloomily at the rain, except one man with his back turned to the rest, who seems wholly preoccupied with a notebook in which he is writing busily. The church clock strikes the first quarter.

The Daughter: [*in the space between the central pillars, close to the one at her left*] I'm getting chilled to the bone. What can Freddy are doing all his time? He's been gone twenty minutes.

The Mother: [*on her daughter's right*] Not so long. But he ought to have got us a cab by this.

A Bystander: [*on the lady's right*] He won't get no cab not until half-past either, missus, when they come back after dropping their theatre fares.

The Mother: But we must have a cab. We can't stand here until half-past eleven. It's too bad.

The Bystander: Well, it ain't my fault, missus.

The Daughter: If Freddy had a bit of gumption, he would have got one at the theater door.

The Mother: What could he have done, poor boy?

The Daughter: Other people got cabs. Why couldn't he?

　　[*Freddy rush in out of the rain from the Southampton Street side, and comes between them closing a dripping umbrella. He is a young man of twenty, in evening dress, very wet round the ankles.*]

The Daughter: Well, haven't you got a cab?

Freddy: There's not one to be had for love or money.

The Mother: Oh, Freddy, there must be one. You can't have tried.

The Daughter: It's too tiresome. Do you expect us to go and get one ourselves?

Freddy: I tell you they're all engaged. The rain was so sudden, nobody was prepared, and everybody had to take a cab. I've been to Charing Cross one way and nearly to Ludgate Circus the other, and they were all engaged.

The Mother: Did you try Trafalgar Square?

Freddy: There wasn't one at Trafalgar Square.

The Daughter: Did you try?

Freddy: I tried as far as Charing Cross Station. Did you expect me to walk to Hammersmith?

The Daughter: You haven't tried at all.

The Mother: You really are very helpless, Freddy. Go again, and don't come back until you have found a cab.

Freddy: I shall simply get soaked for nothing.

The Daughter: And what about us? And we stay here all night in this draught, with next to nothing on. You selfish pig —

Freddy: oh, very well, I'll go, I'll go. [*He opens his umbrella and dashes off strand wards, but comes into collision with a flower girl, who is hurrying in for shelter, knocking her basket out of her hands. A blinding flash of lightning, followed instantly by a rattling peal of a thunder, orchestrates in the incident.*]

The flower girl: Nah then, Freddy, look why gown, deah.

Freddy: Sorry. [*He rushes off.*]

The flower girl: [*picking up her scattered flowers and replacing them in the basket.*] There's manners f'yer! Te-oo banches o voyiets trod into the mad. [*She sits down on the plinth of the column, sorting her flowers, on the lady's right. She is not at all an attractive person. She is perhaps eighteen, perhaps twenty, hardly older. she wears a litter sailor hat of black straw that has long been exposed to the dust and soot of London and has seldom if ever been brushed. Her hair needs washing rather badly; its mousy color can hardly be natural. She wears a shoddy black coat that reaches nearly to her knees and is shaped to her waist. She has a brown skirt with a coarse apron. Her boots are much the worse for wear. She is no doubt as clean as she can afford to be; but compared to the lady, she is very dirty. Her features are no worse than theirs; but their condition leaves something to be desired; and she needs the services of a dentist.*]

The Mother: How do you know that my son's name is Freddy, Prey?

The Flower Girl: Ow, eez ye-ooa san, is e? Wal, fewd dan y'deooty bawmz a mather should, eed now bettern to spawl a pore gel's flahrzn than ran awy athaht pyin, will ye-oo py me f'them?

The Daughter: Do nothing of the sort, mother, and the idea!

The Mother: please allow me, Clara. Have you any pennies?

The Daughter: No, I've nothing smaller than sixpence.

The Flower Girl: [*Hopefully*] I can give you change for a tanner, kind lady.

The Mother: [*to Clara*] give it to me. [*Clara parts reluctantly.*] Now [*to a girl*] this is for your flowers.

The Flower Girl: Thank you kindly, lady.

The Daughter: Make her give you the change. These things are only a penny a bunch.

The Mother: Do hold your tongue, Clare. [*To the girl*] You can keep the change.

The Flower Girl: Oh, thank you, lady.

The Mother: Now tell me how you know that young gentleman's name.

The Flower Girl: I didn't.

The Mother: I heard you call him by it. Don't try to deceive me.

The Flower Girl: [*protesting*] who's trying to deceive you? I called him Freddy or Charlie same as you might yourself if you was talking to a stranger and wished to be pleasant.

The Daughter: Sixpence thrown away! Really, mamma, you might have spared Freddy that [*She retreats in disgust behind the pillar.*]

An elderly gentleman of the amiable military type rushes into shelter, and closes a dripping umbrella. He is in the same plight as Freddy, very wet about the ankles. He is in evening dress, with a light overcoat. He takes the place left vacant by the daughter's retirement.

The Gentleman: Phew!

The Mother: [*to the gentleman*] oh, sir, is there any sigh of its stopping?

The Gentleman: I'm afraid not. It started worse than ever about two minutes ago. [*He goes to the plinth beside the flower girl; puts up his foot on it; and stops to turn down his trouser ends.*]

The Mother: Oh, dear! [*She retires sadly and joins her daughter.*]

The Flower Girl: [*taking advantage of the military gentleman's proximity to establish friendly relations with him*] If it's worse, it's a sign it's nearly over. So cheer up, Captain, and buy a flower off a poor girl.

The Gentleman: I'm sorry. I haven't any change.

The Flower Girl: I can give you change, Captain.

The Gentleman: For a sovereign? I've nothing less.

The Flower Girl: Oh do buy a flower off me, Captain! I can change half-a-crown. Take this for upended.

The Gentleman: Now don't be troublesome; there is a good girl. [*trying his pockets*) I really haven't any change-Stop: here's three halfpence, if that's any use to you. [*He retreats to the other pillar.*]

The Flower Girl: [*disappointed, but thinking three halfpence better than nothing*] Thank you, sir.

The Bystander: [*to the girl*] you be careful: give him a flower for it. There is a bloke here behind taking down every blessed word your saying. [*All turn to the man who is taking notes.*]

Flower Girl: [*Springing up terrified*] I ain't done anything wrong by speaking to the gentleman. I've a right to sell flowers if I keep off the cab. I'm a respectable girl: so help me, I never spoke to him except to ask him to buy a flower off me. [*General hubbub, mostly sympathetic to the flower girl, but deprecating her excessive sensibility. Cries of* don't start holler. Who's hurting you? Nobody is going to touch you. What's the good of fussing? Steady on. Easy, *etc., come from the elderly staid spectators, who pat her comfortingly. Less patient ones bid her shut her head, or ask her roughly what is wrong with her. A remoter group, not knowing what the matter is, crowd in and increase the noise with question and answer:* What's the row? What she do? Where is he? Took money off the gentleman, *etc. The flower girl, distraught and mobbed, breaks through them to the gentleman, crying wildly*] Oh, sir, don't let him charge me. You don't want it means to me. They will take away my character and drive me on the streets for speaking to gentleman. They —

The Note Taker: [*coming forward on her right, the rest crowing after him*] There, there, there, there! Who's hurting you, you silly girl? What do you take me for?

The Bystander: It's all right: he is a gentleman: look at his boots. [*explaining to the note taker*] She thought you was a copper's nark, sir.

The Note Taker: [*with quick interest*] What's a copper nark?

The Bystander: [*inapt at definition*] It's a — well, it's a copper's nark, as you might say. What else would you call it? A sort of informer.

The Flower Girl: [*still hysterical*] I take my Bible oath I never said a word —

The Note Taker: [*overbearing but good-humored*] Oh, shut up, shut up. Do I look like a policeman?

The Flower Girl: [*far from reassured*] Then what did you take down my words for? How do I know whether you took me down right? You just shew me what you've wrote about me. [*The note taker opens his book and holds it steadily under her nose, though the pressure of the mob trying to read it over his shoulder would upset a weaker man.*] What's that? That aint proper writing. I can't read that.

The Note Taker: I can. [*reads, reproducing her pronunciation exactly*] "Cheer up, Captain."

The Flower Girl: [*much distressed*] It's because I called him Captain. I meant no harm. [*to the gentleman*] Oh, Sir, don't let him lay a charge agen me for a word like that. You —

The Gentleman: Charge! I make no charge. [*to the note taker*] Really, sir, if you are a detective, you need not begin protecting me against molestation by young women until I ask you. Anybody could see that the girl meant no harm.

Bystanders Generally: [*demonstrating against police espionage*] Course they could. What business is it of yours? You mind your own affairs. He wants promotion, he does.

► ► ► ► **THE BRITISH PART**

Taking down people's words! Girl never said a word to him. What harm if she did? Nice thing a girl can't shelter from the rain without being insulted etc. [*She is conducted by the more sympathetic demonstrators back to her plinth, where she resumes her seat and struggles with her emotions.*]

The Bystander: He's a blooming busybody, that's what he is. I tell you, look at his boots.

The Note Taker: [*turning on him genially*] And how are all your people down at Selsey?

The Bystander: [*suspiciously*] Who told you my people come from Selsey?

The Note Taker: Never you mind. They did. [*to the girl*] How do you come to be up so far east? You were born in Lisson Grove.

The Flower Girl: [*appalled*] Oh, what harm is there in my leaving Lisson Grove? It wasn't fit for a pig to live in; and I had to pay four-and-six a week. [*In tears*] Oh, boo — hoo — oo

The Note Taker: Live where you like; but stop that noise.

The Gentleman: [*to the girl*] Come, come! He can't touch you; you have a right to live where you please.

A Sarcastic Bystander: [*thrusting himself between the note taker and the gentleman*] Park Lane, for instance. I'd like to go into the Housing Question with you, I would.

The Flower Girl: [*subsiding into a brooding melancholy over her basket, and talk very low-spiritedly to herself*] I am a good girl, mam.

The Sarcastic Bystander: [*not attending to her*] Do you know where I come from?

The Note Taker: [*promptly*] Hoxton.

Tittering. Popular interest in the note taker's performance increases.

The Sarcastic One: [*amazed*] Well, who said I didn't? bly me! You know everything, you do.

The Flower Girl: [*still nursing her sense of injury*] Aint no call to meddle with me, he aint.

The Bystanders: [*encouraged by this seeming point of law*] Yes, where is your warrant?

The Flower Girl: Let him say what he likes. I don't want to have no truck with him.

The Bystander: You take us for dirt under your feet, don't you? Catch you tacking liberties with a gentleman!

The Sarcastic Bystander: Yes, tell him where he comes from if you want to go fortune-telling.

The Note Taker: Cheltenham, Harrow, Cambridge, and India.

The Gentleman: Quite right. [*Great laughter. Reaction in the note taker's favor. Exclamation of he knows all about it. Told him proper. Hear him tell the toff where he come from? Etc.*] May I ask, sir, do you do this for living at a music hall?

The Note Taker: I've thought go that. Perhaps I shall some day. [*The rain has stopped, and the people on the outside of the crowd begin to drop off.*]

The Flower Girl: [*resenting the reaction*] He is no gentleman, he aint, to interfere with a poor girl.

The Daughter: [*out of patience, pursing her way rudely to the front and displacing the*

gentleman, who politely retires to the other side of the pillar] What on earth is Freddy doing? Shall get pneumonia if I say in this draught any longer.

The Note Taker: [*to himself, hastily making a note of her pronunciation of "monia"*] Earlscourt.

The Daughter: [*violently*] Will you please keep your impertinent remarks to yourself?

The Note Taker: Did I say that out loud? I didn't mean to. I beg your pardon. Your mother's Epsom, unmistakably.

The Mother: [*advancing between her daughter and the note taker*] How very curious! I was brought up in Largelady Park, near Epsom.

The Note Taker: [*uproariously amused*] Ha! Ha! What a devil of a name! Excuse me, [*to the daughter*] You want a cab, do you?

The Daughter: Don't dare speak to me.

The Mother: Oh, please, Clara. [*Her daughter repudiates her with an angry shrug and retires haughtily.*] We should be going grateful to you, sir, if you found us a cab. [*The note taker produces a whistle.*] Oh, thank you. [*She joins her daughter.*] [*The note taker blows a piercing blast.*]

The Sarcastic Bystander: There! I know he was a plain-clothes copper.

The Bystander: That aint a police whistle: that's a sporting whistle.

The Flower Girl: [*preoccupied with her wounded feelings*] He's no right to take away my character. My character is the same to me as any lady's.

The Note Taker: I don't know whether you have noticed it; but the rain stopped about two minutes ago.

The Bystander: So it has. Why didn't you say so before? And us losing our time listening to your silliness! [*He walks off towards the Strand.*]

The Sarcastic Bystander: I can tell where you come from. You come from Anwell. Go back there.

The Note Taker: [*hopefully*] Hanwell.

The Sarcastic Bystander: [*affecting great distinction of speech*] Thank you, teacher. Haw! So long. [*He touches his hat with mock respect and strolls off.*]

The Flower Girl: Frightening people like that! How would he like it himself?

The Mother: It's quite fine now, Clara. We can walk to a motor bus. Come. [*She gathers her skirts above her ankles and hurries off towards the Strand.*]

The Daughter: But the cub —[*her mother is out of hearing.*] Oh, how tiresome! [*She follows angrily.*]

All the rest have gone except the note take, the gentleman, and the flower girl, who sits arranging her basket, and still pitying herself in murmurs.

The Flower Girl: Poor girl! Hard enough tor her to live without being worried and chivied.

The Gentleman: [*returning to his former place on the note taker's left*] How do you do it, if I may ask?

The Note Taker: Simply phonetics. The science of speech, that's my profession, also my hobby. Happy is the man who can make a living by his hobby! You can spot an Irisman or a Yorkshieman by his brogue. I can place any man with six miles. I can place him with two miles in London. Sometimes within two streets.

The Flower Girl: Ought to be ashamed of himself, unmanly coward!

The Gentleman: But is there a living in that?

The Note Taker: Oh, yes, quite a fat one. This is an age of upstarts. Men begin in Kentish Town with 80 a year, and end in Park Lane with a hundred thousand. They want to drop Kentish Town, but they give themselves away every time they open their mouths. Now I can teach them.

The Flower Girl: Let him mind his own business and leave a poor girl.

The Note Taker: [*explosively*] Woman, ceases this detestable boohooing instantly, or else seek the shelter of some other, same as you.

The Note Taker: A woman who utters such depressing and disgusting sounds has no right to be anywhere — no right to live. Remember that you are a human being with a soul and the divine gift or articulate speech: that your native language is the language of Shakespeare and Milton and The Bible: and don't sit there crooning like a bilious pigeon.

The Flower Girl: [*quite overwhelmed, looking up at him in mingled wonder and deprecation without daring to raise her head*] Ah-ah-ah-ow-ow-oo!

The Note Taker: [*whipping out his book*] Heavens! What a sound! [*He writes, then holds out the book and reads, reproducing her vowels exactly*] Ah-ah-ah-ow-ow-ow-oo!

The Flower Girl: [*tickled by the performance, and laughing in spite of herself*] Gam!

The Note Taker: You see this creature with her curbstone English: the English that will keep her in the gutter to the end of her days. Well, sir, in three months I could pass that girl off as a duchess at ambassador's garden party. I could even get her a place as lady's maid or shop assistant, which requires better English. That's the sort of thing I do for commercial millionaires. And on the profits of it I do genuine scientific work in phonetics, and a little as a poet on Miltonic lines. The Gentleman: I am myself a student of Indian dialects; and —

The Note Taker: Henry Higgins, author of Higgins's Universal Alphabet.

Pickering: [*with enthusiasm*] I came from India to meet you.

Higgins: I was going to India to meet you.

Pickering: Where do you live?

Higgins: 27A Wimpole Street. Come and see me tomorrow.

Pickering: I am at the Carton. Come with me now and let's have a jaw over some supper.

Higgins: Right you are.

The Flower Girl: [*to Pickering, as he passes her*] Buy a flower, kind gentleman. I'm short for my lodging.

Pickering: I really haven't any change. I'm sorry. [*He goes away.*]

Higgins: [*shocked at the girl's mendacity*] Liar, you said you could change half-a-crown.

The Flower Girl: [*rising in desperation*] You ought to be stuffed with nails, you ought. [*Flinging the basket at his feet*] Take the whole blooming basket for sixpence. [*The church clocks strike the second quarter.*]

Higgins: [*hearing in it the voice of God, rebuking him fir his Pharisaic want of charity to the poor girl*] A reminder. [*He raises his hat solemnly; then throws a handful of money into the basket and follows Pickering.*]

The Flower Girl: [*Picking up a half-crown*] Ah-ow-ooh! [*Picking up a couple of florins*] Aaah-ow-ooh! [*Picking up several coins*] Aaaaaah-ow - ooh! [*Picking up a half-sovereign*] Aaaaaaaaah-ow-ooh!!!

Freddy: [*springing out of a taxicab*] Got one at last. Hallo! [*to the girl*] Where are the two ladies that were here?

The Flower Girl: They walked to the bus when the rain stopped.

Freddy: And left me with a cab on my hands! Damnation!

The Flower Girl: [*with grandeur*] never you mind, young man. I am going home in a taxi. [*She sails off to the cub. The driver puts his hand behind him and holds the door firmly shut against her. Quite understanding his mistrust, she shews him her handful of money.*] Eight pence aint no object to me, Charlie. [*He grins and opens the door.*] Angel Court, Drury Lane, round the corner, of Micklejohn's oil shop. Let's see how fast you can make her hop it. [*She gets in and pulls the door to with a slam as the taxicab starts.*]

Freddy: Well, I am dashed!

Chapter 12 Joseph Conrad

作者简介

Joseph Conrad (3 December, 1857 – 3 August, 1924) was a Polish author who wrote in English after settling in England. He was granted British nationality in 1886, but always considered himself a Pole. Conrad is regarded as one of the greatest novelists in English, though he did not speak the language fluently until he was in his twenties (and always with a marked accent). He wrote stories and novels, often with a nautical setting, that depicts trials of the human spirit in the midst of an indifferent universe. He was a master prose stylist who brought a distinctly non-English tragic sensibility into English literature.

While some of his works have a strain of romanticism, his works are viewed as modernist literature. His narrative style and anti-heroic characters have influenced many authors, including D. H. Lawrence, F. Scott Fitzgerald, William Faulkner, Ernest Hemingway, George Orwell and so on. Films have been adapted from or inspired by Conrad *Almayer's Folly*, *An Outcast of the Islands*, *Heart of Darkness*, *Lord Jim*, *Nostromo*, *The Secret Agent*, *The Duel*, *Victory*, *The Shadow Line*, and *The Rover*. Writing in the heyday of the British Empire, Conrad drew on his native Poland's national experiences and on his personal experiences in the French and British merchant navies, to create short stories and novels that reflect aspects of a European-dominated world, while plumbing the depths of the human soul. Appreciated early on by literary *cognoscenti*, his fiction and nonfiction have gained an almost prophetic cachet in the light of subsequent national and international disasters of the 20th and 21st centuries.

约瑟夫·康拉德(1857年12月3日—1924年8月3日),定居英国后,是一位用英语创作的波兰作家。在1886年,他被授予英国国籍,却始终认为自己是波兰人。尽管到20多岁(还总是带着明显的口音)时英文还不是很流利,但康拉德却被认为是最伟大的英文小说家之一。他写的故事和小说,经常以航海为背景,描绘了冷漠世界中对人类精神的考验。他是以英语散文文体写作的大师,把明显的非英国式的悲惨情感带给英国文学。

虽然作品中有带有浪漫主义，但他的作品被视为现代主义文学。他的叙事风格和反英雄人物的写作特点影响了许多作家，包括 D·H·劳伦斯、斯科特·菲茨杰拉德、威廉·福克纳、欧内斯特·海明威、乔治·奥威尔等。许多电影由康拉德的作品改编或受到他的作品的启发，如《艾拉梅尔的愚蠢》、《离岛的弃儿》、《黑暗之心》、《吉姆老爷》、《诺斯托罗莫》、《特务》、《决斗》、《胜利》、《阴影线》和《流动站》。康拉德通过描绘了他在祖国波兰的经历和当法国商人的自身经历以及当英国海军的亲身经历，在大英帝国的全盛时期创作了许多短篇小说和长篇小说，反映了一个以欧洲为主导的世界，同时探究人类灵魂的深处。由于早期的文学鉴赏家的赞赏，在随后的 20 世纪和 21 世纪，他的小说和其他作品获得了预料中的声望。

作品及导读

作 品 1

The Lagoon

导 读

The Lagoon is a short story by Joseph Conrad composed in 1896 and first published in *Cornhill Magazine* in 1897. The story is about a white man, referred to as "Tuan" (the equivalent of "Lord" or "Sir"), who is travelling through an Indonesian rainforest and is forced to stop for the night with a distant Malay friend named Arsat. Upon arriving, he finds Arsat distraught, for his lover is dying. Arsat tells the distant and rather silent white man a story of his past.

The story that Arsat tells Tuan is about sadness and betrayal. Arsat tells of the time when he and his brother kidnapped Diamelen (his lover, who was previously a servant of the Rajah's wife). They all fled in a boat at night and travelled until they were exhausted. They stopped on a bit of land jutting out into the water to rest. Soon however, they spotted a large boat of the Rajah's men coming to find them. Arsat's brother told Diamelen and Arsat to flee to the other side, where there was a fisherman's hut. He instructed them to take the fisherman's boat and then stayed back, telling them to wait for him while he dealt with the pursuers. However, Arsat did everything but wait for his brother. As he pushed the boat from shore, he saw his brother running down the path, being chased by the pursuers. Arsat's brother tripped and the enemy was upon him. His brother called out to him three times, but Arsat never looked back; he had betrayed his brother for the woman he loved.

Towards the end of the story, symbolically, the sun rises and Diamelen dies. Arsat has nothing now; not a brother nor a wife. He has lost everything. He plans to return to his home village to avenge his brother's death, but dies in the process. The story concludes with "Tuan's" simply leaving, and Arsat's staring dejectedly into the sun and "a world of illusion".

《礁湖》是约瑟夫·康拉德于1896年完成的一个短篇小说,并于1897年首次发表在《康希尔》杂志。故事讲述的是一个白人男子,被称为"团"(相当于"主教"或"先生"),他在印尼的热带雨林旅游,被迫和一个来自遥远马来的朋友阿萨特留宿一晚。抵达后,他发现阿萨特悲痛欲绝,他的爱人奄奄一息。阿萨特向这个来自远方的而且极其沉默不语的白人男子讲述了他过去的故事。

阿萨特告诉"团"的故事是关于悲伤和背叛的。阿萨特讲述了他和他的哥哥绑架戴美伦(他的爱人,以前王爷妻子的仆人)的事。他们在夜间都逃到了船上,并且航行到他们筋疲力尽。他们停在一小片水中凸出的土地上休息。然而不久,他们发现王爷的人来找他们的大船。阿萨特的哥哥告诉戴美伦和阿萨特,逃到有渔夫居住的小屋。他指示他们划渔民的船逃走,然后再返回来,同时告诉他们他应付那些追兵,让阿萨特和戴美伦等他。然而,阿萨特并没有按照指示等待哥哥。当他从岸上推船时,他看见他的哥哥逃跑的路径,而且被追兵追逐。阿萨特的哥哥绊倒,追兵抓住了阿萨特的哥哥。他的哥哥叫了他三次,但阿萨特再也没有回头,他为他所爱的女人背叛了自己的哥哥。在故事的结尾具有象征意义,太阳升起和戴美伦死亡。阿萨特现在什么也没有,既没有哥哥,也没有妻子。他已经失去了一切。他打算回到自己的家乡,为他的哥哥的报仇,但是在这一过程中,他失败了。这个故事的以"团"的离开,阿萨特沮丧地盯着太阳,进入了幻想世界作为结尾。

选 文

The Lagoon

The white man, leaning with both arms over the roof of the little house in the stern of the boat, said to the steersman —

"We will pass the night in Arsat's clearing. It is late."

The Malay only grunted, and went on looking fixedly at the river. The white man rested his chin on his crossed arms and gazed at the wake of the boat. At the end of the straight avenue of forests cut by the intense glitter of the river, the sun appeared unclouded and dazzling, poised low over the water that shone smoothly like a band of metal. The forests, somber and dull, stood motionless and silent on each side of the broad stream. At the foot of big, towering trees, trunkless nipa palms rose from the mud of the bank, in bunches of leaves enormous and heavy, that hung unstring over the brown swirl of eddies. In the stillness of the air every tree, every leaf, every bough, every tendril of creeper and every petal of minute blossoms seemed to have been bewitched into immobility perfect and final. Nothing moved on the river but the eight paddles that rose flashing regularly, dipped together with a single splash; while the steersman swept right and left with a periodic and sudden flourish of his blade describing a glinting semicircle above his head. The churnedup water frothed alongside with a confused murmur. And the white man's canoe, advancing up stream in the short-lived disturbance of its own making, seemed to enter the portals of a land from which the very memory of motion had for ever departed.

The white man, turning his back upon the setting sun, looked along the empty and broad expanse of the sea-reach. For the last three miles of its course the wandering, hesitating river, as if enticed irresistibly by the freedom of an open horizon, flows straight into the sea, flows straight to the east — to the east that harbors both light and darkness. Astern of the boat the repeated call of some bird, a cry discordant and feeble, skipped along over the smooth water and lost itself, before it could reach the other shore, in the breathless silence of the world.

The steersman dug his paddle into the stream, and held hard with stiffened arms, his body thrown forward. The water gurgled aloud; and suddenly the long straight reach seemed to pivot on its center, the forests swung in a semicircle, and the slanting beams of sunset touched the broadside of the canoe with a fiery glow, throwing the slender and distorted shadows of its crew upon the streaked glitter of the river. The white man turned to look ahead. The course of the boat had been altered at right-angles to the stream, and the carved dragon-head of its prow was pointing now at a gap in the fringing bushes of the bank. It glided through, brushing the overhanging twigs, and disappeared from the river like some slim and amphibious creature leaving the water for its lair in the forests.

The narrow creek was like a ditch: tortuous, fabulously deep; filled with gloom under the thin strip of pure and shining blue of the heaven. Immense trees soared up, invisible behind the festooned draperies of creepers. Here and there, near the glistening blackness of the water, a twisted root of some tall tree showed amongst the tracery of small ferns, black and dull, writhing and motionless, like an arrested snake. The short words of the paddlers reverberated loudly between the thick and somber walls of vegetation. Darkness oozed out from between the trees, through the tangled maze of the creepers, from behind the great fantastic and unstring leaves; the darkness, mysterious and invincible; the darkness scented and poisonous of impenetrable forests.

The men poled in the shoaling water. The creek broadened, opening out into a wide sweep of a stagnant lagoon. The forests receded from the marshy bank, leaving a level strip of bright-green, reedy grass to frame the reflected blueness of the sky. A fleecy pink cloud drifted high above, trailing the delicate coloring of its image under the floating leaves and the silvery blossoms of the lotus. A little house, perched on high piles, appeared black in the distance. Near it, two tall nibong palms, that seemed to have come out of the forests in the background, leaned slightly over the ragged roof, with a suggestion of sad tenderness and care in the droop of their leafy and soaring heads.

The steersman, pointing with his paddle, said, "Arsat is there. I see his canoe fast between the piles."

The polers ran along the sides of the boat glancing over their shoulders at the end of the day's journey. They would have preferred to spend the night somewhere else than on this lagoon of weird aspect and ghostly reputation. Moreover, they disliked Arsat, first as a stranger, and also because he who repairs a ruined house, and dwells in it, proclaims that he is not afraid to live amongst the spirits that haunt the places abandoned by mankind. Such a man can disturb the course of fate by glances or words; while his familiar ghosts are not easy to propitiate by casual wayfarers upon whom they long to wreak the malice of their human master. White men care not for such things, being unbelievers and in league with the Father of Evil, who leads them unharmed through the invisible dangers of this world. To the warnings of the righteous they oppose an offensive pretence of disbelief. What is there to be done?

So they thought, throwing their weight on the end of their long poles. The big canoe glided on swiftly, noiselessly and smoothly, towards Arsat's clearing, till, in a great rattling of poles thrown down, and the loud murmurs of "Allah be praised!" it came with a gentle knock against the crooked piles below the house.

The boatmen with uplifted faces shouted discordantly, "Arsat! O Arsat!" Nobody came. The white man began to climb the rude ladder giving access to the bamboo platform before the house. The juragan of the boat said sulkily, "We will cook in the sampan, and sleep on the water."

"Pass my blankets and the basket," said the white man curtly.

He knelt on the edge of the platform to receive the bundle. Then the boat shoved off, and the white man, standing up, confronted Arsat, who had come out through the low door of his hut. He was a man young, powerful, with a broad chest and muscular arms. He had nothing on but his sarong. His head was bare. His big, soft eyes stared eagerly at the white man, but his voice and demeanor were composed as he asked, without any words of greeting —

"Have you medicine, Tuan?"

"No," said the visitor in a startled tone. "No. Why? Is there sickness in the house?"

"Enter and see," replied Arsat, in the same calm manner, and turning short round, passed again through the small doorway. The white man, dropping his bundles, followed.

In the dim light of the dwelling he made out on a couch of bamboos a woman stretched on her back under a broad sheet of red cotton cloth. She lay still, as if dead; but her big eyes, wide open, glittered in the gloom, staring upwards at the slender rafters, motionless and unseeing. She was in a high fever, and evidently unconscious. Her cheeks were sunk slightly, her lips were partly open, and on the young face there was the ominous and fixed expression — the absorbed, contemplating expression of the unconscious that are going to die. The two men stood looking down at her in silence.

"Has she been long ill?" asked the traveler.

"I have not slept for five nights," answered the Malay, in a deliberate tone. "At first she heard voices calling her from the water and struggled against me who held her. But since the sun of to-day rose she hears nothing — she hears not me. She sees nothing. She sees not me — me!"

He remained silent for a minute, then asked softly —

"Tuan, will she die?"

"I fear so," said the white man sorrowfully. He had known Arsat years ago, in a far country in times of trouble and danger, when no friendship is to be despised. And since his Malay friend had come unexpectedly to dwell in the hut on the lagoon with a strange woman, he had slept many times there, in his journeys up or down the river. He liked the man who knew how to keep faith in council and how to fight without fear by the side of his white friend. He liked him - not so much perhaps as a man likes his favorite dog — but still he liked him well enough to help and ask no questions, to think sometimes vaguely and hazily in the midst of his own pursuits, about the lonely man and the long-haired woman with audacious face and triumphant eyes, who lived together hidden by the forests — alone and feared.

The white man came out of the hut in time to see the enormous conflagration of sunset put out by the swift and stealthy shadows that, rising like a black and impalpable vapor above the tree-tops, spread over the heaven, extinguishing the crimson glow of floating clouds and the red brilliance of departing daylight. In a few moments all the stars came out above the intense blackness of the earth, and the great lagoon gleaming suddenly with reflected lights resembled an oval patch of night-sky flung down into the hopeless and abysmal night of the wilderness. The white man had some supper out of the basket, then collecting a few sticks that lay about the platform, made up a small fire, not for warmth, but for the sake of the smoke, which would keep off the mosquito. He wrapped himself in his blankets and sat with his back against the reed wall of the house, smoking thoughtfully.

Arsat came through the doorway with noiseless steps and squatted down by the fire. The white man moved his outstretched legs a little.

"She breathes," said Arsat in a low voice, anticipating the expected question. "She breathes and burns as if with a great fire. She speaks not; she hears not — and burns!"

He paused for a moment, then asked in a quiet, incurious tone —

"Tuan ... will she die?"

The white man moved his shoulders uneasily, and muttered in a hesitating manner —

"If such is her fate."

"No, Tuan," said Arsat calmly. "If such is my fate. I hear, I see, I wait. I remember ... Tuan, do you remember the old days? Do you remember my brother?"

"Yes," said the white man. The Malay rose suddenly and went in. The other, sitting still outside, could hear the voice in the hut. Arsat said: "Hear me! Speak!" His words were succeeded by a complete silence. "O! Diamelen!" he cried suddenly. After that cry there was a deep sigh. Arsat came out and sank down again in his old place.

They sat in silence before the fire. There was no sound within the house, there was no sound near them; but far away on the lagoon they could hear the voices of the boatmen ringing fitful and distinct on the calm water. The fire in the bows of the sampan shone faintly in the distance with a hazy red glow. Then it died out. The voices ceased. The land and the water slept invisible, unstring and mute. It was as though there had been nothing left in the world but the glitter of stars streaming, ceaseless and vain, through the black stillness of the night.

The white man gazed straight before him into the darkness with wide-open eyes. The fear and fascination, the inspiration and the wonder of death — of death near, unavoidable and unseen, soothed the unrest of his race and stirred the most indistinct, the most intimate of his thoughts. The ever-ready suspicion of evil, the gnawing suspicion that lurks in our hearts, flowed out into the stillness round him — into the stillness profound and dumb, and made it appear untrustworthy and infamous, like the placid and impenetrable mask of an unjustifiable violence. In that fleeting and powerful disturbance of his being the earth enfolded in the starlight peace became a shadowy country of inhuman strife, a battle-field of phantoms terrible and charming, august or ignoble, struggling ardently for the possession of our helpless hearts. An unquiet and mysterious country of inextinguishable desires and fears.

A plaintive murmur rose in the night; a murmur saddening and startling, as if the great solitudes of surrounding woods had tried to whisper into his ear the wisdom of their immense and lofty indifference. Sounds hesitating and vague floated in the air round him, shaped themselves slowly into words; and at last flowed on gently in a murmuring stream of soft and monotonous sentences. He stirred like a man waking up and changed his position slightly. Arsat, motionless and shadowy, sitting with bowed head under the stars, was speaking in a low and dreamy tone.

"... for where can we lay down the heaviness of our trouble but in a friend's heart? A man must speak of war and of love. You, Tuan, know what war is, and you have seen me in time of danger seek death as other men seek life! A writing may be lost; a lie may be written; but what the eye has seen is truth and remains in the mind!"

"I remember," said the white man quietly. Arsat went on with mournful composure.

"Therefore I shall speak to you of love. Speak in the night. Speak before both night and love are gone - and the eye of day looks upon my sorrow and my shame; upon my blackened face; upon my burnt-up heart."

A sigh, short and faint, marked an almost imperceptible pause, and then his words flowed on, without a stir, without a gesture.

"After the time of trouble and war was over and you went away from my country in the pursuit of your desires, which we, men of the islands, cannot understand, I and my brother became again, as we had been before, the sword-bearers of the Ruler. You know we were men of family, belonging to a ruling race, and more fit than any to carry on our right shoulder the emblem of power. And in the time of prosperity Si Dendring showed us favor, as we, in time of sorrow, had showed to him the faithfulness of our courage. It was a time of peace. A time of deer-hunts and cock-fights; of idle talks and foolish squabbles between men whose bellies are full and weapons are rusty. But the sower watched the young rice-shoots grow up without fear, and the traders came and went, departed lean and returned fat into the river of peace. They brought news too. Brought lies and truth mixed together, so that no man knew when to rejoice and when to be sorry. We heard from them about you also. They had seen you here and had seen you there. And I was glad to hear, for I remembered the stirring times, and I always remembered you, Tuan, till the time came when my eyes could see nothing in the past, because they had looked upon the one who is dying there — in the house."

He stopped to exclaim in an intense whisper, "O Mara Bahia! O Calamity!" then went on speaking a little louder.

"There's no worse enemy and no better friend than a brother, Tuan, for one brother knows another, and in perfect knowledge is strength for good or evil. I loved my brother. I went to him and told him that I could see nothing but one face, hear nothing but one voice. He told me: "Open your heart so that she can see what is in it — and wait. Patience is wisdom. Inchi Midah may die or our Ruler may throw off his fear of a woman!" ... I waited! ... You remember the lady with the veiled face, Tuan, and the fear of our Ruler before her cunning and temper. And if she wanted her servant, what could I do? But I fed the hunger of my heart on short glances and stealthy words. I loitered on the path to the bath-houses in the daytime, and when the sun had fallen behind the forest I crept along the jasmine hedges of the women's courtyard. Unseeing, we spoke to one another through the scent of flowers, through the veil of leaves, through the blades of long grass that stood still before our lips: so great was our prudence, so faint was the murmur of our great longing. The time passed swiftly ... and there were whispers amongst women — and our enemies watched — my brother was gloomy, and I began to think of killing and of a fierce death .... We are of a people who take what they want — like you whites. There is a time when a man should forget loyalty and respect. Might and authority are given to rulers, but to all men is given love and strength and courage. My brother said, "You shall take her from their midst. We are two who are like one." And I answered, "Let it be soon, for I find no warmth in sunlight that does not shine upon her." Our time came when the Ruler and all the great people went to the mouth of the river to fish by torchlight. There were hundreds of boats, and on the white sand, between the water and the forests, dwellings of leaves were built for the households of the Rajahs. The smoke of cooking-fires was like a blue mist of the evening, and many voices rang in it joyfully. While they were making the boats ready to beat up the fish, my brother came to me and said, "To-night!" I made ready my weapons, and when the time came our canoe took its place in the circle of boats carrying the torches. The lights blazed on the water, but behind the boats there was darkness. When the shouting began and the excitement made them like mad we dropped out. The water swallowed our fire, and we floated back to the shore that was dark with only here and there the glimmer of embers. We could hear the talk of slave girls amongst the sheds. Then we found a place deserted and silent. We waited there. She came. She came running along the shore, rapid and leaving no trace, like a leaf driven by the wind into the sea. My brother said gloomily, "Go and take her; carry her into our boat." I lifted her in my arms. She panted. Her heart was beating against my breast. I said, "I take you from those people. You came to the cry of my heart, but my arms take you into my boat against the will of the great!" "It is right," said my brother. "We are men who take what we want and can hold it against many. We should have taken her in daylight." I said, "Let us be off;" for since she was in my boat I began to think of our Ruler's many men. "Yes. Let us be off," said my brother. "We are cast out and this boat is our country now — and the sea is our refuge." He lingered with his foot on the shore, and I entreated him to hasten, for I remembered the strokes of her heart against my breast and thought that two men cannot withstand a hundred. We left, paddling downstream close to the bank; and as we passed by the creek where they were fishing, the great shouting had ceased, but the murmur of voices was loud like the humming of insects flying at noonday. The boats floated, clustered together, in the red light of torches, under a black roof of smoke; and men talked of their sport. Men that boasted, and praised, and jeered — men that would have been our friends in the morning, but on that night were already our enemies. We paddled swiftly past. We had no more friends in the country of our birth. She sat in the middle of the canoe with covered face; silent as she is now; unseeing as she is now — and I had no regret at what I was leaving because I could hear her breathing close to me — as I can hear her now."

He paused, listened with his ear turned to the doorway, then shook his head and went on.

"My brother wanted to shout the cry of challenge — one cry only — to let the people know we were freeborn robbers that trusted our arms and the great sea. And again I begged him in the name of our love to be silent. Could I not hear her breathing close to me? I knew the pursuit would come quick enough. My brother loved me. He dipped his paddle without a splash. He only said, "There is half a man in you now — the other half is in that woman. I can wait. When you are a whole man again, you will come back with me here to shout defiance. We are sons of the same mother." I made no answer. All my strength and all my spirit were in my hands that held the paddle — for I longed to be with her in a safe place beyond the reach of men's anger and of women's spite. My love was so great, that I thought it could guide me to a country where death was unknown, if I could only escape from Inchi Midah's spite and from our Ruler's sword. We paddled with fury, breathing through our teeth. The blades bit deep into the smooth water. We passed out of the river; we flew in clear channels amongst the shallows. We skirted the black coast; we skirted the sand beaches where the sea speaks in whispers to the land; and the gleam of white sand flashed back past our boat, so swiftly she ran upon the water. We spoke not. Only once I said, "Sleep, Diamelen, for soon you may want all your strength." I heard the sweetness of her voice, but I never turned my head. The sun rose and still we went on. Water fell from my face like rain from a cloud. We flew in the light and heat. I never looked back, but I knew that my brother's eyes, behind me, were looking steadily ahead, for the boat went as straight as a bushman's dart, when it leaves the end of the sump tan. There was no better paddler, no better steersman than my brother. Many times, together, we had won races in that canoe. But we never had put out our strength as we did then — then, when for the last time we paddled together! There was no braver or stronger man in our country than my brother. I could not spare the strength to turn my head and look at him, but every moment I heard the hiss of his breath getting louder behind me. Still he did not speak. The sun was high. The heat clung to my back like a flame of fire. My ribs were ready to burst, but I could no longer get enough air into my chest. And then I felt I must cry out with my last breath, "Let us rest!" "Good!" he answered; and his voice was firm. He was strong. He was brave. He knew not fear and no fatigue ... My brother!"

A rumor powerful and gentle, a rumor vast and faint; the rumor of trembling leaves, of stirring boughs, ran through the tangled depths of the forests, ran over the starry smoothness of the lagoon, and the water between the piles lapped the slimy timber once with a sudden splash. A breath of warm air touched the two men's faces and passed on with a mournful sound — a breath loud and short like an uneasy sigh of the dreaming earth.

Arsat went on in an even, low voice.

"We ran our canoe on the white beach of a little bay close to a long tongue of land that seemed to bar our road; a long wooded cape going far into the sea. My brother knew that place. Beyond the cape a river has its entrance. Through the jungle of that land there is a narrow path. We made a fire and cooked rice. Then we slept on the soft sand in the shade of our canoe, while she watched. No sooner had I closed my eyes than I heard her cry of alarm. We leaped up. The sun was halfway down the sky already, and coming in sight in the opening of the bay we saw a pray manned by many paddlers. We knew it at once; it was one of our Rajah's prays. They were watching the shore, and saw us. They beat the gong, and turned the head of the pray into the bay. I felt my heart become weak within my breast. Diamelen sat on the sand and covered her face. There was no escape by sea. My brother laughed. He had the gun you had given him, Tuan, before you went away, but there was only a handful of powder. He spoke to me quickly: "Run with her along the path. I shall keep them back, for they have no firearms, and landing in the face of a man with a gun is certain death for some. Run with her. On the other side of that wood there is a fisherman's house — and a canoe. When I have fired all the shots I will follow. I am a great runner, and before they can come up we shall be gone. I will hold out as long as I can, for she is but a woman — that can neither run nor fight, but she has your heart in her weak hands." He dropped behind the canoe. The prau was coming. She and I ran, and as we rushed along the path I heard shots. My brother fired — once — twice — and the booming of the gong ceased. There was silence behind us. That neck of land is narrow. Before I heard my brother fire the third shot I saw the shelving shore, and I saw the water again: the mouth of a broad river. We crossed a grassy glade. We ran down to the water. I saw a low hut above the black mud, and a small canoe hauled up. I heard another shot behind me. I thought, "That is his last charge." We rushed down to the canoe; a man came running from the hut, but I leaped on him, and we rolled together in the mud. Then I got up, and he lay still at my feet. I don't know whether I had killed him or not. I and Diamelen pushed the canoe afloat. I heard yells behind me, and I saw my brother run across the glade. Many men were bounding after him. I took her in my arms and threw her into the boat, then leaped in myself. When I looked back I saw that my brother had fallen. He fell and was up again, but the men were closing round him. He shouted, "I am coming!" The men were close to him. I looked. Then I looked at her. Tuan, I pushed the canoe! I pushed it into deep water. She was kneeling forward looking at me, and I said, "Take your paddle," while I struck the water with mine. Tuan, I heard him cry. I heard him cry my name twice; and I heard voices shouting, "Kill! Strike!" I never turned back. I heard him calling my name again with a great shriek, as when life is going out together with the voice — and I never turned my head. My own name! ... My brother! Three times he called — but I was not afraid of life. Was she not there in that canoe? And could I not with her find a country where death is forgotten — where death is unknown?"

The white man sat up. Arsat rose and stood an indistinct and silent figure above the dying embers of the fire. Over the lagoon a mist drifting and low had crept, erasing slowly the glittering images of the stars. And now a great expanse of white vapor covered the land: flowed cold and gray in the darkness, eddied in noiseless whirls round the tree-trunks and about the platform of the house, which seemed to float upon a restless and impalpable illusion of a sea; seemed the only thing surviving the destruction of the world by that undulating and voiceless phantom of a flood. Only far away the tops of the trees stood outlined on the twinkle of heaven, like a somber and forbidding shore — a coast deceptive, pitiless and black.

Arsat's voice vibrated loudly in the profound peace.

"I had her there! I had her! To get her I would have faced all mankind. But I had her — and —"

His words went out ringing into the empty distances. He paused, and seemed to listen to them dying away very far — beyond help and beyond recall. Then he said quietly —

"Tuan, I loved my brother."

A breath of wind made him shiver. High above his head, high above the silent sea of mist the drooping leaves of the palms rattled together with a mournful and expiring sound. The white man stretched his legs. His chin rested on his chest, and he murmured sadly without lifting his head —

"We all love our brothers."

Arsat burst out with an intense whispering violence —

"What did I care who died? I wanted peace in my own heart."

He seemed to hear a stir in the house — listened — then stepped in noiselessly. The white man stood up. A breeze was coming in fitful puffs. The stars shone paler as if they had retreated into the frozen depths of immense space. After a chill gust of wind there were a few seconds of perfect calm and absolute silence. Then from behind the black and wavy line of the forests a column of golden light shot up into the heavens and spread over the semicircle of the eastern horizon. The sun had risen. The mist lifted, broke into drifting patches, vanished into thin flying wreaths; and the unveiled lagoon lay, polished and black, in the heavy shadows at the foot of the wall of trees. A white eagle rose over it with a slanting and ponderous flight, reached the clear sunshine and appeared dazzlingly brilliant for a moment, then soaring higher, became a dark and motionless speck before it vanished into the blue as if it had left the earth for ever. The white man, standing gazing upwards before the doorway, heard in the hut a confused and broken murmur of distracted words ending with a loud groan. Suddenly Arsat stumbled out with outstretched hands, shivered, and stood still for some time with fixed eyes. Then he said —

"She burns no more."

Before his face the sun showed its edge above the tree-tops, rising steadily. The breeze freshened; a great brilliance burst upon the lagoon, sparkled on the rippling water. The forests came out of the clear shadows of the morning, became distinct, as if they had rushed nearer — to stop short in a great stir of leaves, of nodding boughs, of swaying branches. In the merciless sunshine the whisper of unconscious life grew louder, speaking in an incomprehensible voice round the dumb darkness of that human sorrow. Arsat's eyes wandered slowly, then stared at the rising sun.

"I can see nothing," he said half aloud to himself.

"There is nothing," said the white man, moving to the edge of the platform and waving his hand to his boat. A shout came faintly over the lagoon and the sampan began to glide towards the abode of the friend of ghosts.

"If you want to come with me, I will wait all the morning," said the white man, looking away upon the water.

"No, Tuan," said Arsat softly. "I shall not eat or sleep in this house, but I must first see my road. Now I can see nothing — see nothing! There is no light and no peace in the world; but there is death — death for many. We were sons of the same mother — and I left him in the midst of enemies; but I am going back now."

He drew a long breath and went on in a dreamy tone.

"In a little while I shall see clear enough to strike — to strike. But she has died, and ... now ... darkness."

He flung his arms wide open, let them fall along his body, and then stood still with unmoved face and stony eyes, staring at the sun. The white man got down into his canoe.

The polers ran smartly along the sides of the boat, looking over their shoulders at the beginning of a weary journey. High in the stern, his head muffled up in white rags, the juragan sat moody, letting his paddle trail in the water. The white man, leaning with both arms over the grass roof of the little cabin, looked back at the shining ripple of the boat's wake. Before the sampan passed out of the lagoon into the creek he lifted his eyes. Arsat had not moved. In the searching clearness of crude sunshine he was still standing before the house, he was still looking through the great light of a cloudless day into the hopeless darkness of the world.

13 E. M. Forster

作者简介

  Born in London, **E. M. Forster** (1879 – 1970), was a famous English writer in the 20th century. During all his life time he published six long novels, two short story collections, several biographies and some essays, which, because of mirroring the fact of class difference and hypocrisy in British society, arouse great attention, thus lead him to be even considered by some critics as likely the greatest writer following Thomas Hardy if he continued his writing after his last, also his greatest work *A Passage to India* published in 1942.

  E. M. Forster was a child of an architect's family. When he was young, he attended the notable public school, Tonbridge School in Kent. In 1897, he studied at Cambridge and became a member of the Apostles, whose members later went on to constitute what known as the Bloomsbury Group. After leaving university, he travelled in continental Europe. In 1905 he published his first novel *Where Angels Fear to Tread*. After that, he continually published the others, including *The Longest Journey* (1907), *A Room with a view* (1908), *Howard End* (1910), *A Passage to India* (1924), etc. Forster achieved his greatest success with *A Passage to India* (1924). The novel took as its subject the relationship between East and West, seen through the lens of India in the later days of the British Raj. Forster connected personal relationships with the politics of colonialism through the story of the English woman Adela Quested, the Indian Dr. Aziz, and the question of what did or did not happen between them in the Marabar Caves.

  Forster passed away at home on July 7th, 1970.

  爱华德·摩根·福斯特出生于伦敦,是20世纪著名的英国作家。福斯特一生共发表6篇长篇小说、2篇短篇小说、几部传记和若干评论文章。这些作品反映了当时英国社会存在的阶级差异和虚伪现象,正因为如此,它们在当时引起了不小的关注,甚至有评论家这样认为:如果福斯特没有在1942年发表了最后一篇、也是其著名的小说后就停止创作,他很有可能是继托马斯·哈代后最伟大的小说家。

  爱华德·摩根·福斯特出生于一个建筑师家庭。小时候,他就读于肯特郡唐布利奇学校。后来在 1897 年,他来到剑桥大学学习,并加入了门徒社,该社社员后来继续发展,组成了"布鲁斯布里集团"。离开大学后,福斯特游历于欧洲大陆。1905 年他发表了第一部小说《天使不敢驻足的地方》。此后,他继续创作、发表作品。这其中包括 1907 年的《最漫长的路程》、1908 年的《看得见风景的房间》、1910 年的《霍华德庄园》以及 1924 年的《印度之旅》等等。福斯特在其 1924 年的作品《印度之旅》上达到创作巅峰。该小说抓住了东西方关系,透析了在英国统治的最后岁月下的印度。福斯特通过发生在英国女人阿苔拉和印度人阿齐兹之间的故事以及关于"在岩洞中他们俩之间到底了发生什么"这一问题,和当时政治上的殖民主义联系到了一起。

  福斯特于 1970 年 7 月 7 日在家中去世。

作品及导读

作 品 1

A Passage to India

导 读

  A Passage to India (1924) is a novel by E. M. Forster set against the backdrop of the British Raj and the Indian independence movement in the 1920s. By telling the story of two British Women in India, the book showcases the unbridgable gap between Britain and its colory India. Chapter XVI is the most exciting chapter, The British-Indian conflict is raised to the extreme, and Adela Quest accused Tide Aziz the doctor attempting in a cave in Maraba her sexual abuse.

  Adela, suddenly realizing that she does not love Ronny, asks Adela whether he has more than one wife — a question he considers offensive. Aziz storms off into a cave, and when he returns, Adela is gone. Aziz scolds the guide for losing Adela, and heads down the hill. Back at the picnic site, Aziz finds Fielding waiting for him. Aziz is unconcerned to learn that Adela has hastily taken a car back to Chandrapore, as he is overjoyed to see Fielding.

  《印度之旅》(1924)是一部 E·M·福斯特在 20 世纪 20 年代反对英国统治和印度独立运动的背景下写成的小说。全书通过两个英国女人来到印度后所发生的一系列事情,展示英国与其殖民地印度两个民族间不可逾越的鸿沟。第 16 章是全书最精彩的章节,英国人与印度人的矛盾冲突被引发到了极致,阿德拉·奎斯提德指控阿齐兹医生企图在马拉巴的一个山洞里对她实施性侵害。

阿德拉突然意识到她不爱罗尼了,她问阿齐兹他是不是有好几个妻子,这个问题在阿齐兹看来是很唐突无礼的。阿齐兹快步躲进一个山洞,他回来时阿德拉已经不见了。他指责导游让阿德拉走散了,导游便也跑开了。阿齐兹发现了阿德拉那个摔坏了的双筒望远镜,于是他朝山下走去。回到野餐地后,阿齐兹发现菲尔丁在等他。见到了菲尔丁,阿齐兹过于高兴,因而当得知阿德拉已经驾车匆匆返回钱德拉波尔时,阿齐兹并未感到焦虑。

选 文

A Passage to India
(*Chapter* 26)

He waited in his cave a minute and lit a cigarette, so that he could remark on rejoining her, "I bolted in to get out of the draught," or something of the sort. When he returned, he found the guide, alone, with his head on one side. He had heard a noise, he said and then Aziz heard it too: the noise of a motor-car. They were now on the outer shoulder of the Kawa Dol and by scrambling twenty yards they got a glimpse of the plain. A car was coming towards the hills down the Chandrapore road. But they could not get a good view of it, because the precipitous bastion curved at the top, so that the base was not easily seen and the car disappeared as it came nearer. No doubt it would stop almost exactly beneath them, at the place where the pukka road degenerated into a path and the elephant had turned to sidle into the hills.

He ran back to tell the strange news to his guest.

The guide explained that she had gone into a cave.

"Which cave?"

He indicated the group vaguely.

"You should have kept her in sight, it was your duty," said Aziz severely. "Here are twelve caves at least. How am I to know which contains my guest? Which is the cave I was in myself?"

The same vague gesture. And Aziz, looking again, could not even be sure he had returned to the same group. Caves appeared in every direction it seemed their original spawning place and the orifices were always the same size. He thought, "Merciful Heavens, Miss Quested is lost," then pulled himself together and began to look for her calmly.

"Shout!" he commanded.

When they had done this for awhile, the guide explained that to shout is useless, because a Marabar cave can hear no sound but its own. Aziz wiped his head and sweat began to stream inside his clothes. The place was so confusing; it was partly a terrace, partly a zigzag and full of grooves that led this way and that like snake tracks. He tried to go into every one, but he never knew where he had started. Caves got behind caves or confabulated in pairs and some were at the entrance of a gully.

"Come here!" he called gently and when the guide was in reach, he struck him in the face for a punishment. The man fled and he was left alone. He thought, "This is the end of my career, my guest is lost." And then he discovered the simple and sufficient explanation of the mystery.

Miss Quested wasn't lost. She had joined the people in the car friends of hers, no doubt, Mr. Heaslop perhaps. He had a sudden glimpse of her, far down the gully only a glimpse, but there she was quite plain, framed between rocks and speaking to another lady. He was so relieved that he did not think her conduct odd. Accustomed to sudden changes of plan, he supposed that she had run down the Kawa Do! Impulsively, in the hope of a little drive. He started back alone towards his camp and almost at once caught sight of something which would have disquieted him very much a moment before: Miss Quested's field glasses. They were lying at the verge of a cave, half-way down an entrance tunnel. He tried to hang them over his shoulder, but the leather strap had broken, so he put them into his pocket instead. When he had gone a few steps, he thought she might have dropped something else, so he went back to look. But the previous difficulty recurred: he couldn't identify the cave. Down in the plain he heard the car starting; however, he couldn't catch a second glimpse of that. So he scrambled down the valley-face of the hill towards Mrs. Moore and here he was more successful: the color and confusion of his little camp soon appeared and in the midst of it he saw an Englishman's topi and beneath it oh, joy! Smiled not Mr. Heaslop, but Fielding.

"Fielding! Oh, I have so wanted you!" he cried, dropping the "Mr." for the first time.

And his friend ran to meet him, all so pleasant and jolly, no dignity, shouting explanations and apologies about the train. Fielding had come in the newly arrived car Miss Derek's car that other lady was Miss Derek. Excellent Miss Derek! She had met Fielding by chance at the post-office; said, "Why haven't you gone to the Marabar?" heard how he missed the train, offered to run him there and then. Another nice English lady. Where was she? Car couldn't get up no, of course not hundreds of people must go down to escort Miss Derek and show her the way. The elephant in person....

"Aziz, can I have a drink?"

"Certainly not." He flew to get one.

"Mr. Fielding!" called Mrs. Moore, from her patch of shade; they had not spoken yet, because his arrival had coincided with the torrent from the hill.

"Good morning again!" he cried, relieved to find all well.

"Mr. Fielding, have you seen Miss Quested?"

"But I've only just arrived. Where is she?"

"I do not know."

"Aziz! Where have you put Miss Quested to?"

Aziz, who was returning with a drink in his hand, had to think for a moment. His heart was full of new happiness. The picnic, after a nasty shock or two, had developed into something beyond his dreams, for Fielding had not only come, but brought an uninvited guest. "Oh, she's all right," he said; "she went down to see Miss Derek. Well, here's luck! Chin-chin!"

"Here's luck, but chin-chin I do refuse," laughed Fielding, who detested the phrase. "Here's to India!"

"Here's luck and here's to England!"

Miss Derek's chauffeur stopped the cavalcade which was starting to escort his mistress up and informed it that she had gone back with the other young lady to Chandrapore; she had sent him to say so. She was driving herself.

"Oh yes, that's quite likely," said Aziz. "I knew they'd gone for a spin."

"Chandrapore? The man's made a mistake," Fielding exclaimed.

"Oh no, why?" He was disappointed, but made light of it; no doubt the two young ladies were great friends. He would prefer to give breakfast to all four; still, guests must do as they wish, or they become prisoners. He went away cheerfully to inspect the porridge and the ice.

"What's happened?" asked Fielding, who felt at once that something had gone queer. All the way out

Miss Derek had chattered about the picnic, called it an unexpected treat and said that she preferred Indians who didn't invite her to their entertainments to those who did it. Mrs. Moore sat swinging her foot and appeared sulky and stupid. She said: "Miss Derek is most unsatisfactory and restless, always in a hurry, always wanting something new; she will do anything in the world except go back to the Indian lady who pays her."

Fielding, who didn't dislike Miss Derek, replied: "She wasn't in a hurry when I left her. There was no question of returning to Chandrapore. It looks to me as if Miss Quested's in the hurry."

"Adela? She's never been in a hurry in her life," said the old lady sharply.

"I say it'll prove to be Miss Quested's wish, in fact I know it is," persisted the schoolmaster. He was annoyed chiefly with himself. He had begun by missing a train a sin he was never guilty of and now that he did arrive it was to upset Aziz' arrangements for the second time. He wanted someone to share the blame and frowned at Mrs. Moore rather magisterially. "Aziz is a charming fellow," he announced.

"I know," she answered, with a yawn.

"He has taken endless trouble to make a success of our picnic."

They knew one another very little and felt rather awkward at being drawn together by an Indian. The racial problem can take subtle forms. In their case it had induced a sort of jealousy, a mutual suspicion. He tried to goad her enthusiasm; she scarcely spoke. Aziz fetched them to breakfast.

"It is quite natural about Miss Quested," he remarked, for he had been working the incident a little in his mind, to get rid of its roughness. "We were having an interesting talk with our guide and then the car was seen, so she decided to go down to her friend."

Incurably inaccurate, he already thought that this was what had occurred. He was inaccurate because he was sensitive. He did not like to remember Miss Quested's remark about polygamy, because it was unworthy of a guest, so he put it from his mind and with it the knowledge that he had bolted into a cave to get away from her. He was inaccurate because he desired to honor her and facts being entangled he had to arrange them in her vicinity, as one tidies the ground after extracting a weed. Before breakfast was over, he had told a good many lies. "She ran to her friend, I to mine," he went on, smiling. "And now I am with my friends and they are with me and each other, which is happiness."

Loving them both, he expected them to love each other. They didn't want to. Fielding thought with hostility, "I knew these women would make trouble," and Mrs. Moore thought, "This man, having missed the train, tries to blame us"; but her thoughts were feeble; since her faintness in the cave she was sunk in apathy and cynicism. The wonderful India of her opening weeks, with its cool nights and acceptable hints of infinity, had vanished.

Fielding ran up to see one cave. He wasn't impressed. Then they got on the elephant and the picnic began to unwind out of the corridor and escaped under the precipice towards the railway station, pursued bystabs of hot air. They came to the place where he had quitted the car. A disagreeable thought now struck him and he said: "Aziz, exactly where and how did you leave Miss Quested?"

"Up there." He indicated the Kawa Dol cheerfully.

"But how —" A gully, or rather a crease, showed among the rocks at this place; it was scurfy with cactuses. "I suppose the guide helped her."

"Oh, rather, most helpful."

"Is there a path off the top?"

"Millions of paths, my dear fellow."

Fielding could see nothing but the crease. Everywhere else the glaring granite plunged into the earth.

"But you saw them get down safe?"

"Yes, yes, she and Miss Derek and go off in the car."

"Then the guide came back to you?"

"Exactly. Got a cigarette?"

"I hope she wasn't ill," pursued the Englishman. The crease continued as a nullah across the plain, the water draining off this way towards the Ganges.

"She would have wanted me, if she was ill, to attend her."

"Yes, that sounds sense."

"I see you're worrying, let's talk of other things," he said kindly. "Miss Quested was always to do what she wished, it was our arrangement. I see you are worrying on my account, but really I don't mind, I never notice trifles."

"I do worry on your account. I consider they have been impolite!" said Fielding, lowering his voice.

"She had no right to dash away from your party and Miss Derek had no right to abet her."

So touchy as a rule, Aziz was unassailable. The wings that uplifted him did not falter, because he was a Mogul emperor who had done his duty. Perched on his elephant, he watched the Marabar Hills recede and saw again, as provinces of his kingdom, the grim untidy plain, the frantic and feeble movements of the buckets, the white shrines, the shallow graves, the suave sky, the snake that looked like a tree. He had given his guests as good a time as he could and if they came late or left early that was not his affair. Mrs. Moore slept, swaying against the rods of the howdah; Mohammed Latif embraced her with efficiency and respect and by his own side sat Fielding, whom he began to think of as "Cyril."

"Aziz, have you figured out what this picnic will cost you?"

"Shh! my dear chap, don't mention that part. Hundreds and hundreds of rupees. The completed account will be too awful; my friends' servants have robbed me right and left and as for an elephant, she apparently eats gold. I can trust you not to repeat this. And ML please employ initials, he listens is far the worst of all."

"I told you he's no good."

"He is plenty of good for himself; his dishonesty will ruin me."

"Aziz, how monstrous!"

"I am delighted with him really, he has made my guests comfortable; besides, it is my duty to employ him, he is my cousin. If money goes, money comes. If money stays, death comes. Did you ever hear that useful Urdu proverb? Probably not, for I have just invented it."

"My proverbs are: A penny saved is a penny earned; A stitch in time saves nine; Look before you leap; and the British Empire rests on them. You will never kick us out, you know, until you cease employing ML's and such."

"Oh, kick you out? Why should I trouble over that dirty job? Leave it to the politicians. No, when I was a student I got excited over your damned countrymen, certainly; but if they'll let me get on with my profession and not be too rude to me officially, I really don't ask for more."

"But you do; you take them to a picnic."

"This picnic is nothing to do with English or Indian; it is an expedition of friends."

So the cavalcade ended, partly pleasant, partly not; the Brahman cook was picked up, the train arrived, pushing its burning throat over the plain and the twentieth century took over from the sixteenth. Mrs. Moore entered her carriage; the three men went to theirs, adjusted the shutters, turned on the electric fan and tried to get some sleep. In the twilight, all resembled corpses and the train itself seemed dead though it moved a coffin from the scientific north which troubled the scenery four times a day. As it left the Marabars, their nasty little cosmos disappeared and gave place to the Marabars seen from a distance, finite and rather romantic. The train halted once under a pump, to drench the stock of coal in its tender. Then it caught sight of the main line in the distance, took courage and bumped forward, rounded the civil station, surmounted the level-crossing (the rails were scorching now) and clanked to a standstill. Chandrapore, Chandrapore! The expedition was over.

And as it ended, as they sat up in the gloom and prepared to enter ordinary life, suddenly the long drawn strangeness of the morning snapped. Mr. Haq, the Inspector of Police, flung open the door of their carriage and said in shrill tones: "Dr. Aziz, it is my highly painful duty to arrest you."

"Hullo, some mistake," said Fielding, at once taking charge of the situation.

"Sir, they are my instructions. I know nothing."

"On what charge do you arrest him?"

"I am under instructions not to say."

"Don't answer me like that. Produce your warrant."

"Sir, excuse me, no warrant is required under these particular circumstances. Refer to Mr. McBryde."

"Very well, so we will. Come along, Aziz, old man; nothing to fuss about, some blunder."

"Dr. Aziz, will you kindly come? A closed conveyance stands in readiness."

The young man sobbed his first sound and tried to escape out of the opposite door on to the line.

"That will compel me to use force," Mr. Haq wailed.

"Oh, for God's sake" cried Fielding, his own nerves breaking under the contagion and pulled him back before a scandal started and shook him like a baby. A second later and he would have been out, whistles blowing, a man-hunt .... "Dear fellow, we're coming to McBryde together and enquire what's gone wrong he's a decent fellow, it's all unintentional ... he'll apologize. Never, never act the criminal."

"My children and my name!" he gasped, his wings broken.

"Nothing of the sort. Put your hat straight and take my arm. I'll see you through."

"Ah, thank God, he comes," the Inspector exclaimed.

They emerged into the midday heat, arm in arm. The station was seething. Passengers and porters rushed out of every recess, many Government servants and more police. Ronny escorted Mrs. Moore. Mohammed Latif began wailing. And before they could make their way through the chaos, Fielding was called off by the authoritative tones of Mr. Turton and Aziz went on to prison alone.

14 Thomas Stearns Eliot

作者简介

Thomas Stearns Eliot (26 September, 1888 - 4 January, 1965) was a poet, playwright, literary and social critic and one of the founders of the New Criticism. He was born in St. Louis, Missouri in the United States, and moved to the United Kingdom in 1914 (at age 25) and was naturalized as a British subject in 1927 at age 39. His father was a businessman and his mother was a very talented poet. In 1906, Eliot studied philosophy and English-French literature at Harvard University. During this period, he was exposed to Sanskrit and eastern culture. He had strong interests in the philosophers from Hagel School, and also was influenced by the French Symbolism. In 1914, he traveled to London for studying Greek philosophy at the Oxford University. He got married later and resided in the UK. He had worked as teacher, bank staff and magazine editor. His first important poetry and also one of his masterpieces — *The Love Song of J. Alfred Prufrock* was published in 1915 and Eliot started to be recognized since then. In 1922 Eliot founded the literature critical magazine *Standard* and served as the chief editor until 1939. Eliot considered himself as a royalist in politics, British catholic in religion and classicist in literature. In 1922, his poetry the *Waste Land* was published and won him global recognition. It is considered as the most influential poetry in the 20th century and a milestone of modern western poetry by the criticisms. In 1927 Eliot was naturalized as a British subject. In 1943, the *Four Quartets* was published and won him the 1948 Nobel Prize in Literature. It also made him the greatest English poet and writer alive. Eliot was dedicated to play writing in his late years and *Murder in the Cathedral* is one of his major plays. Eliot died in 1956 in London.

托马斯·史登斯·艾略特(Thomas Stearns Eliot,1888 — 1965)英美诗人、剧作家、批评家和英美新批评派的奠基人之一。1888年出生于美国密苏里州圣路易斯。父亲经商,母亲是诗人,博学多才。1906年艾略特曾在哈佛大学学习哲学和英法文学,接触过梵文和东方文化,对黑格尔派的哲学家颇感兴趣，也曾受到法国象征主义文学的影响。1914 年，他赴伦敦进入牛津大学学习希腊哲学。不久即成婚并定居英国，先后当过教师、银行职员、杂志编辑。1922 年艾略特创办文学评论季刊《标准》，任主编至 1939 年。艾略特认为自己在政治上是保皇党，宗教上是英国天主教徒，文学上是古典主义者。1915 年他发表的诗作 *The Love Song of J. Alfred Prufrock* 是他的第一部具有影响力的诗作，为他赢得了广泛的关注。1922 年发表的《荒原》为他赢得了国际声誉，被评论界看作是 20 世纪最有影响力的一部诗作，被认为是英美现代诗歌的里程碑。1927 年，艾略特加入英国国籍。1943 年结集出版的《四个四重奏》使他获得了 1948 年度诺贝尔文学奖并确立了当时在世的最伟大英语诗人和作家的地位。晚年致力于诗剧创作，主要作品有《大教堂中的谋杀》等。1965 年艾略特在伦敦逝世。

作品及导读

作品 1

The Waste Land

导读

The Waste Land is a long poem written by T. S. Eliot. It is widely regarded as "one of the most important poems of the 20th century" and a central text in Modernist poetry. Published in 1922, the 434-line poem first appeared in the U. K. in the October issue of *The Criterion* and in the U. S. in the November issue of *The Dial*. It was published in book form in December 1922. Among its famous phrases are "April is the cruelest month", "I will show you fear in a handful of dust", and the mantra in the Sanskrit language "Shantih shantih shantih".

Eliot's poem loosely follows the legend of the Holy Grail and the Fisher King combined with vignettes of the contemporary social condition in British society. Eliot employs many literary and cultural allusions from the Western canon and from Buddhism and the Hindu Upanishads. Because of this, critics and scholars regard the poem as obscure. The poem shifts between voices of satire and prophecy featuring abrupt and unannounced changes of speaker, location and time and conjuring of a vast and dissonant range of cultures and literatures.

The poem is preceded by a Latin and Greek epigraph from *The Satyricon of Petronius*. In English, it reads: "I saw with my own eyes the Sibyl of Cumae hanging in a jar, and when the boys said to her, *Sibyl, what do you want?* She replied *I want to die.*"

The five parts of *The Waste Land* are titled:
1. *The Burial of the Dead*
2. *A Game of Chess*
3. *The Fire Sermon*
4. *Death by Water*
5. *What the Thunder Said*

The first section, titled *The Burial of the Dead* introduces the diverse themes of disillusionment and despair. The second, titled A Game of Chess employs vignettes of several characters — alternating narrations — that address those themes experientially. *The Fire Sermon*, the third section, offers a philosophical meditation in relation to the imagery of death and views of self-denial in juxtaposition influenced by Augustine and eastern religions. After a fourth section that includes a brief lyrical petition, the culminating fifth section, *What the Thunder Said* concludes with an image of judgment.

《荒原》是托马斯写的一首长诗。它被广泛认为是"20世纪最重要的诗之一"和现代主义诗歌的支柱。这首发表于1922年的434行诗最早出现在英国《标准》的十月期和美国《日晷》的十一月期。并在1922年出版成书。其中的名句包括"四月是最残忍的一个月","我将向你展示尘灰中的恐惧"以及在梵文中的口头语"和平 和平 和平"。

艾略特的诗遵循圣杯及费舍尔国王的传说也结合了英国社会当代社会状况。艾略特从西方经典和佛教及印度教中借鉴了许多文学和文化典故。正因为如此,评论家和学者认为这首诗很晦涩。这首诗在讽刺的声音和意外的预知和说话者、场地、时间没有宣告改变和一个重要的祈求和文化与文学不和谐的范围内转变的。

这首诗先于拉丁文和希腊文的铭文《萨迪利空的佩特罗尼乌斯》。在英语中,它写道:"我亲眼看到了库迈的女巫被挂在一个罐子里,当一个男孩问她,女巫,你想要什么?她回答道 我想死。"

《荒原》的这5个部分分别为:
1. 死者的葬礼
2. 一局棋戏
3. 火的说教
4. 水里的死亡
5. 雷的说话

第一部分"死者的葬礼"介绍了幻灭和绝望的不同主题。第二部分"一局棋戏"讲述了几种小人物的角色之间交替的陈述并且讲到了经验上的主题。"火的说教"是第三部分,提供了一个哲学的沉思在死亡的想象和自我否定观点中受到奥古斯丁和东方宗教影响的关系。在包含了一个简短的抒情请愿书的第四部分后,最后的第五部分"雷的说话"提出了判断的概念。

选文

The Waste Land

Ⅰ. The Burial of the Dead

APRIL is the cruelest month, breeding
Lilacs out of the dead land, mixing
Memory and desire, stirring
Dull roots with spring rain
Winter kept us warm, covering
Earth in forgetful snow, feeding
A little life with dried tubers.
Summer surprised us, coming over the Starnbergersee
With a shower of rain; we stopped in the colonnade,
And went on in sunlight, into the Hofgarten
And drank coffee, and talked for an hour.
Bin gar keine Russin, stamm' aus Litauen, echt deutsch.
And when we were children, staying at the arch-duke's,
My cousin's, he took me out on a sled,
And I was frightened. He said, Marie,
Marie, hold on tight. And down we went.
In the mountains, there you feel free.
I read, much of the night, and go south in the winter.
What are the roots that clutch, what branches grow
Out of this stony rubbish? Son of man,
You cannot say, or guess, for you know only
A heap of broken images, where the sun beats,
And the dead tree gives no shelter, the cricket no relief,
And the dry stone no sound of water. Only
There is shadow under this red rock,
(Come in under the shadow of this red rock),
And I will show you something different from either
Your shadow at morning striding behind you
Or your shadow at evening rising to meet you;
I will show you fear in a handful of dust.
       Frisch weht der Wind
       Der Heimat zu
       Mein Irisch Kind,
       Wo weilest du?
'You gave me hyacinths first a year ago;

They called me the hyacinth girl.'
— Yet when we came back, late, from the Hyacinth garden,
Your arms full, and your hair wet, I could not
Speak, and my eyes failed, I was neither
Living nor dead, and I knew nothing,
Looking into the heart of light, the silence
Od' und leer das Meer.
Madame Sosostris, famous clairvoyante,
Had a bad cold, nevertheless
Is known to be the wisest woman in Europe,
With a wicked pack of cards. Here, said she,
Is your card, the drowned Phoenician Sailor
(Those are pearls that were his eyes. Look!)
Here is Belladonna, the Lady of the Rocks,
The lady of situations
Here is the man with three staves, and here the Wheel,
And here is the one-eyed merchant, and this card,
Which is blank, is something he carries on his back,
Which I am forbidden to see. I do not find
The Hanged Man. Fear death by water
I see crowds of people, walking round in a ring.
Thank you. If you see dear Mrs. Equitone,
Tell her I bring the horoscope myself:
One must be so careful these days.
Unreal City,
Under the brown fog of a winter dawn,
A crowd flowed over London Bridge, so many,
I had not thought death had undone so many.
Sighs, short and infrequent, were exhaled,
And each man fixed his eyes before his feet.
Flowed up the hill and down King William Street,
To where Saint Mary Woolnoth kept the hours
With a dead sound on the final stroke of nine
There I saw one I knew, and stopped him, crying: 'Stetson!
'You who were with me in the ships at Mylae!
'That corpse you planted last year in your garden,
'Has it begun to sprout? Will it bloom this year?
'Or has the sudden frost disturbed its bed?
'Oh keep the Dog far hence, that's friend to men,

'Or with his nails he'll dig it up again!
'You! Hypocrite lecteur! — Mon semblable,— Mon frère!'

II. A Game of Chess
THE Chair she sat in, like a burnished throne,
Glowed on the marble, where the glass
Held up by standards wrought with fruited vines
From which a golden Cupidon peeped out
(Another hid his eyes behind his wing)
Doubled the flames of seven-branched candelabra
Reflecting light upon the table as
The glitter of her jewels rose to meet it,
From satin cases poured in rich profusion.
In vials of ivory and coloured glass
Unstoppered, lurked her strange synthetic perfume
Unguent, powdered, or liquid — troubled, confused
And drowned the sense in odors; stirred by the air
That freshened from the window, these ascended
In fattening the prolonged candle-flames,
Flung their smoke into the laquearia,
Stirring the pattern on the coffered ceiling.
Huge sea-wood fed with copper
Burned green and orange, framed by the coloured stone
In which sad light a carved dolphin swam
Above the antique mantel was displayed
As though a window gave upon the sylvan scene
The change of Philomel, by the barbarous king
So rudely forced; yet there the nightingale
Filled all the desert with inviolable voice
And still she cried, and still the world pursues,
'Jug Jug' to dirty ears.
And other withered stumps of time
Were told upon the walls; staring forms
Leaned out, leaning, and hushing the room enclosed.
Footsteps shuffled on the stair.
Under the firelight, under the brush, her hair
Spread out in fiery points
Glowed into words, and then would be savagely still.
'My nerves are bad to-night. Yes, bad. Stay with me

'Speak to me. Why do you never speak? Speak.
'What are you thinking of? What thinking? What?
'I never know what you are thinking. Think.'

I think we are in rat's alley
Where the dead men lost their bones
'What is that noise?'
The wind under the door
'What is that noise now? What is the wind doing?'
Nothing again nothing
'DoYou know nothing? Do you see nothing? Do you remember?'
Nothing?
I remember
Those are pearls that were his eyes.
'Are you alive, or not? Is there nothing in your head?'
But
O O O O that Shakespeherian Rag —
It's so elegant
So intelligent
'What shall I do now? What shall I do?'
'I shall rush out as I am, and walk the street
With my hair down, so. What shall we do to-morrow?
'What shall we ever do?'
The hot water at ten.
And if it rains, a closed car at four.
And we shall play a game of chess,
Pressing lidless eyes and waiting for a knock upon the door.
When Lil's husband got demobbed, I said —
I didn't mince my words, I said to her myself,
HURRY UP PLEASE IT'S TIME
Now Albert's coming back, make yourself a bit smart.
He'll want to know what you done with that money he gave you
To get yourself some teeth. He did, I was there.
You have them all out, Lil, and get a nice set,
He said, I swear, I can't bear to look at you.
And no more can't I, I said, and think of poor Albert,
He's been in the army four years; he wants a good time,
And if you don't give it him, there's others will, I said.
Oh is there, she said. Something o' that, I said.

Then I'll know who to thank, she said, and give me a straight look.
HURRY UP PLEASE IT'S TIME
If you don't like it you can get on with it, I said.
Others can pick and choose if you can't.
But if Albert makes off, it won't be for lack of telling.
You ought to be ashamed, I said, to look so antique.
(And her only thirty-one)
I can't help it, she said, pulling a long face,
It's them pills I took, to bring it off, she said.
(She's had five already and nearly died of young George.)
The chemist said it would be alright, but I've never been the same.
You are a proper fool, I said.
Well, if Albert won't leave you alone, there it is, I said,
What you get married for if you don't want children?
HURRY UP PLEASE IT'S TIME
Well, that Sunday Albert was home, they had a hot gammon,
And they asked me in to dinner, to get the beauty of it hot —
HURRY UP PLEASE IT'S TIME
HURRY UP PLEASE IT'S TIME
Goonight Bill. Goonight Lou. Goonight May. Goonight
Ta ta. Goonight. Goonight
Good night, ladies, good night, sweet ladies, good night, good night.

15 James Joyce

作者简介

James Joyce (2 February, 1882 – 13 January, 1941) was an Irish novelist and poet, who is considered to be one of the most influential writers in the modernist avant-garde of the early 20th century. Joyce is best known for *Ulysses* (1922), a landmark work in which the episodes of *Homer's Odyssey* are paralleled in an array of contrasting literary styles, and perhaps the most prominent among these is the stream of consciousness technique he perfected in his works. The other major works consist of the short-story collection *Dubliners* (1914), and the long novel *A Portrait of the Artist as a Young Man* (1916) and *Finnegans Wake* (1939). His complete oeuvre also includes three books of poetry, a play, some occasional journalism, and his published letters.

Joyce was born in a middle class family in Dublin, where he excelled as a student at the Jesuit schools Clongowes and Belvedere, then at University College Dublin. In his early twenties he immigrated permanently to continental Europe, living in Trieste, Paris and Zurich. Even though most of his adult life was spent abroad, Joyce's fictional universe does not extend far beyond Dublin, and is populated largely by characters that closely resemble the family members, enemies and friends from his time there. *Ulysses* in particular is set with precision in the streets and alleyways of the city. Shortly after the publication of *Ulysses* he elucidated this preoccupation somewhat, saying, "For myself, I always write about Dublin, because if I can get to the heart of Dublin I can get to the heart of all the cities of the world. In the particular is contained the universal."

詹姆斯·奥古斯丁·阿洛伊修斯·乔伊斯(1882年2月2日—1941年1月13日),是一位爱尔兰作家和诗人。他是20世纪早期中众多颇具影响力的现代主义先锋派作家的一位典型。乔伊斯最出名的一部小说是其《尤利西斯》(1922)。这是一部里程碑式的作品,其每一章都和《荷马史诗》之《奥德赛》的一个章节相对应,而且他把意识流的写作手法在此发挥得炉火纯青。其他一些主要作品还包括其短篇小说集《都柏林人》(1914),长篇小说《一个青年艺术家的画像》(1916),以及《芬尼根的苏醒》(1939)。他的作品还包括三部诗集、一部戏剧,偶尔的新闻评论以及其他一些已经出版的文学作品。

乔伊斯出生在都柏林一个中产阶级家庭,他先后就读于基督教兄弟会学校和贝尔维德中学,表现十分出色,后来进入都柏林大学继续学习。在他20几岁时,他移民到欧洲大陆,先后生活在的里雅斯特,巴黎和苏黎世。但是,尽管他大部分时间都生活在国外,他的小说里的世界从未延伸到都柏林之外。而且,书里的主人公都是以其生活中的家人,敌人和朋友为原型。特别是《尤利西斯》这部作品,其整个故事都发生在这个城市的街道和小巷。在《尤利西斯》出版后,他从某种程度上解释了这一点。他说:"我自己总是写关于都柏林的故事,因为如果我能触及都柏林的核心,那么我就可以触及这个世界上所有城市的核心。它们都有共性。"

作品及导读

作品 1

Araby

导 读

Considered one of Joyce's best known short stories, *Araby* is the third story in his short fiction collection, *Dubliners*, which was published in 1914. It is perceived as a prime example of Joyce's use of epiphany — a sudden revelation of truth about life inspired by a seemingly trivial incident — as the young narrator realizes his disillusionment with his concept of ideal love when he attempts to buy a token of affection for a young girl. As the third story, *Araby* is often viewed as an important step between the first two stories — *The Sisters* and *An Encounter* — and the rest of the collection.

The narrator of *Araby* is a young boy living with his aunt and uncle in a dark, untidy home in Dublin that was once the residence of a priest, now deceased. The boy is infatuated with his friend's older sister, and often follows her to school, never having the courage to talk to her. Finally she speaks to him, asking him if he is going to attend a visiting bazaar, known as the *Araby*. When she indicates that she cannot attend, he offers to bring her something from the bazaar, hoping to impress her. On the night he is to attend, his uncle is late coming home from work. By the time the young boy borrows money from his uncle and makes his way to the bazaar, most of the people have left and many of the stalls are closed. As he looks for something to buy his friend's sister, he overhears a banal young salesgirl flirt with two young men. When the disinterested salesgirl asks him if he needs help, he declines, and he walks through the dark, empty halls, disillusioned with himself and the world around him.

《阿拉比》是乔伊斯最著名的短篇小说,也是他发表于1914年的短篇小说集《都柏林人》中的第三篇小说。它是乔伊斯运用顿悟的一个特例,这种顿悟是由看似琐碎的事激发起来的真实生活的突然显露,正如年轻的叙述者要尝试为一个年轻女孩投入大量感情时,意识到他对理想的爱情的幻灭。《阿拉比》作为第三篇小说,经常被认为是前两篇小说《姐妹》《冲突》和其余小说之间的重要一步。

《阿拉比》的叙述者是一个小男孩,他和叔叔阿姨一起住在黑暗肮脏的在都柏林的房子里,那里曾经是已故的牧师的家。这个男孩迷恋上了他朋友的姐姐,经常跟踪她去学校,但从没勇气和她说话。有一天他终于与他交谈,问他是否要去阿拉比集市。当她说她不能去时,他承诺从市场给她带东西希望可以打动她。晚上临去前,他的叔叔因工作回家晚了,男孩向他叔叔借了钱,随后离开了。大多数赶集的人早已离去,许多摊点也已收摊。当他要给朋友的姐姐买东西时,他听到女售货员和两个男人调情的乏味声音,女售货员问他是否需要帮助,他拒绝了,并且失望地走向黑暗无人的大厅。

选 文

Araby

North Richmond Street, being blind, was a quiet street except at the hour when the Christmas Brother's School set the boys free. An uninhabited house of two stories stood at the blind end, detached from its neighbors in a square ground. The other houses of the street, conscious of decent lives within them, gazed at one another with brown imperturbable faces.

The former tenant of our house, a priest, had died in the back drawing-room Air, musty from having been long enclosed, hung in all the rooms, and the waste room behind the kitchen was littered with old useless papers. Among these I found a few paper-covered books, the pages of which were curled and damp: *The Abbot*, by Walter Scott, *The Devout Communicant* and *The Memoirs of Vedocq*. I liked the last best because its leaves were yellow. The wild garden behind the house contained a central apple-tree and a few straggling bushes, under one of which I found the late tenant's rusty bicycle-pump. He had been a very charitable priest; in his will he had left all his money to institutions and the furniture of his house to his sister.

When the short days of winter came dusk fell before we had well eaten our dinners. When we met in the street the houses had grown somber. The space of sky above us was the color of ever-changing violet and towards it the lamps of the street lifted their feeble lanterns. The cold air stung us and we played till our bodies glowed. Our shouts echoed in the silent street. The career of our play brought us through the dark muddy lanes behind the houses where we ran the gauntlet of the rough tribes from the cottages, to the back doors of the dark dripping gardens where odors arose from ash pits, to the dark odorous stables where a coachman smoothed and combed the horse or shook music from the buckled harness. When we returned to the street, light from the kitchen windows had filled the areas. If my uncle was seen turning the corner we hid in the shadow until we had seen him safely housed. Or if Mangan's sister came out on the doorstep to call her brother in to his tea we watched her from our shadow peer up and down the street. We waited to see whether she would remain or go in and, if she remained, we left our shadow and walked up to Mangan's steps resignedly. She was waiting for us, her figure deceased by the light from the half-opened door. Her brother always teased her before he obeyed and I stood by the railings looking at her. Her dress swung as she moved her body and the soft rope her hair tossed from side to side.

Every morning I lay on the floor in the front parlor watching her door. The blind was pulled down to within an inch of the sash so that I could not be seen. When she came out on the doorstep my heart leaped. I ran to the hall, seized my books and followed her. I kept her brown figure always in my eye and, when we came hear the point at which our ways diverged, I quickened my pace and passed her. This happened morning after morning. I had never spoken to her, except for a few casual words, and yet her name was like a summons to all my foolish blood.

Her image accompanied me even in places the most hostile to romance. On Saturday evenings when my aunt went marketing I had to go to carry some of the parcels. We walked through the flaring streets, jostled by drunken men and bargaining women, amid the curses of laborers, the shrill litanies of shop-boys who stood on guard by the barrels of pigs' cheeks, the nasal chanting of street-singers, who sang a come-all-you about O'Donovan Rosa, or a ballad about sensation of life for me: I imagined that I bore my chalice safely through a throng of foes. Her name sprang to my lips at moments in strange prayers and praises which I myself did not understand. My eyes were often full of tears (I could not tell why) and at times a flood from my heart seemed to pour itself out into my bosom. I thought little of the future. I did not know whether I would ever tell her of my confused adoration. But my body was like a harp and her words and gestures were like fingers running upon the wires.

One evening I went into the back drawing-room in which the priest had died. It was a dark rainy evening and there was no sound in the house. Through one of the broken panes I heard the rain impinge upon the earth, the fine incessant needles of water playing in the sodden beds. Some distant lamp or lighted window gleamed below me. I was thankful that I could see so little. All my senses seemed to desire to veil themselves and, feeling that I was about t slip from them, I pressed the palms of my hands together until they trembled, murmuring: "O love! O Love!" many times.

At last she spoke to me. When she addressed the first words to me I was so confused that I did not know what to answer. She asked me whether I was going to Araby. I forgot whether I answered yes or no. it would be a splendid bazaar, she said she would love to go.

"And why can't you?" I asked.

While she spoke she turned a silver bracelet round and round her wrist. She could not go, she said, because there would be a retreat that week in her convent. Her brother and two other boys were fighting for their caps and I was alone at the railings. She held one of the spikes, bowing her head towards me. The light from the lamp opposite our door caught the white curve of her neck, lit up her hair that rested there and, falling, lit up the hand upon the railing. It fell over one side of her dress and caught the white border of a petticoat, just visible as she stood at ease.

"It's well for you," she said.

"If I go," I said, "I will bring you something."

What innumerable follies laid waste my waking and sleeping thoughts after that evening! I wished to annihilate the tedious intervening days. I chafed against the work of school. At night in my bedroom and by day in the classroom her image came between me and the page I strove to read. The syllables of the word *Araby* were called to me through the silence in which my soul luxuriated and cast an Eastern enchantment over me. I asked for leave to go to the bazaar on Saturday night. My aunt was surprised and hoped it was not some Freemason affair. I answered few questions in class. I watched my master's face pass from amiability to sternness; he hoped I was not beginning to idle. I could not call my wandering thoughts together. I had hardly any patience with the serious work of life which, now that it stood between me and my desire, seemed to me child's play, ugly monotonous child's play.

On Saturday morning I reminded my uncle that I wished to go to the bazaar in the evening. He was fussing at the hallstand, looking for the hat-brush, and answered me curtly:

"Yes, boy, I know."

As he was in the hall I could not go into the front parlor and lie at the window. I left the house in bad humor and walked slowly towards the school. The air was pitilessly raw and already my heart misgave me.

When I came home to dinner my uncle had not yet been home. Still it was early. I sat staring at the clock for some time and, when its ticking began to irritate me, I left the room. I mounted the staircase and gained the upper part of the house. The high cold empty gloomy rooms liberated me and I went from room to room singing. From the front window I saw my companions playing below in the street. Their cries reached me weakened and indistinct and, leaning my forehead against the cool glass, I looked over at the dark house where she lived. I may have stood there for an hour, seeing nothing but the brown-clad figure cast by my imagination, touched discreetly by the lamplight at the curved neck, at the hand upon the railings and at the border below the dress.

When I came downstairs again I found Mrs. Mercer sitting at the fire. She was an old garrulous woman, a pawnbroker's widow, who collected used stamps for some pious purpose. I had to endure the gossip of the tea-table. The meal was prolonged beyond an hour and still my uncle did not come. Mrs. Mercer stood up to go: she was sorry she couldn't wait any longer, but it was after eight o'clock and she did not like to be out late, as the night air was bad for her. When she had gone I began to walk up and down the room, cleaning my fists. My aunt said:

"I'm afraid you may put off your bazaar for this night of Our Lord."

At nine o'clock I heard my uncle's latchkey in the hall door. I heard him talking to himself and heard the hallstand rocking when it had received the weight of his overcoat. I could interpret these signs. When he was midway through his dinner I asked him to give me the money to go the bazaar. He had forgotten.

"The people are in bed and after their first sleep now," he said.

I did not smile. My aunt said to him energetically:

"Can't you give him the money and let him go? You've kept him late enough as it is."

My uncle said he was very sorry he had forgotten. He said he believed in the old saying: "All work and no play make Jack a dull boy." He asked me where I was going and, when I had told him a second time he asked me did I know The Arab's Farewell to His Steed. When I left the kitchen, he was about to recite the opening lines of the piece to my aunt.

I held a florin tightly in my hand as I strode down Buckingham Street towards the station. The sight of the trees thronged with buyers and glaring with gas recalled to me the purpose of my journey. I took my seat I a third-class carriage of a deserted train. After an intolerable delay the train moved out of the station slowly. It crept onward among ruinous houses and the twinkling river. At Westland Row Station a crowd of people pressed to the carriage doors; but the porters moved them back, saying that it was a special train for the bazaar. I remained alone in the bare carriage. In a few minutes the train drew up beside an improvised wooden platform. I passed out on to the road and saw by the lighted dial of a clock that it was ten minutes to ten. In front of me was a large building which displayed the magical name.

I could not find any sixpenny entrance and, fearing that the bazaar would be closed, I passed in quickly through a turnstile, handing a shilling to a weary-looking man. I found myself in a big hall girdled at half its height by gallery. Nearly all the stalls were closed and the greater part of the hall was in darkness. I recognized a silence like that which pervades a church after a service. I walked into the center of the bazaar timidly. A few people were gathered about the stalls which were still open. Before a curtain, over which the words Café Chantant were written in colored lamps, two men were counting money on a salver. I listened to the fall of the coins.

Remembering with difficulty why I had come I went over to one of the stalls and examined porcelain vases and flowered tea-sets. At the door of the stall a young lady was talking and laughing with two young gentlemen. I remarked their English accents and listened vaguely to their conversation.

"O, I never said such a thing!"

"O, but you did!"

"O, but I didn't!"

"Didn't she say that?"

"Yes. I heard her."

"O, there's a... fib!"

Observing me the young lady came over and asked me did I wish to buy anything. The tone of her voice was not encouraging; she seemed to have spoken to me out of a sense of duty. I looked humbly at the great jars that stood like eastern guards at either side of the dark entrance to the stall and murmured:

"No, thank you."

The young lady changed the position of one of the vases and went back to the two young men. They began to talk of the same subject. Once or twice the young lady glanced at me over her shoulder.

I lingered before her stall, though I knew my stay was useless, to make my interest in her wares seem the more real. Then I turned away slowly and walked down the middle of the bazaar. I allowed the two pennies to fall against the sixpence in my pocket. I heard a voice call from one end of the gallery that the light was out. The upper part of the hall was now completely dark.

Gazing up into the darkness I saw myself as a creature driven and derided by vanity; and my eyes burned with anguish and anger.

相关链接

Stream of consciousness is a form of narrative technique in novel which is used to "render the flow of myriad impressions — visual, auditory, physical, associative, and subliminal — that impinge on the consciousness of an individual and form part of his awareness along with the trend of his rational thoughts". In literature, this technique that records the multifarious thoughts and feelings of a character lacks of logical argument or narrative sequence. The writer attempts to reflect all the forces, external and internal by the stream of consciousness, influencing the psychology of a character at a single moment. The phrase "stream of consciousness" was first used by William James in *Principles of Psychology* (1890). The technique was subsequently used by such notable writers as James Joyce, Virginia Woolf.

意识流是小说写作的一种叙事技巧，常用内心独白的形式展现连续不断的印象：视觉的、听觉的、触觉的、联想的、下意识的等，这些印象影响着个人的思想，也伴随着他理性的想法形成了其意识的一部分。文学作品中，这种技巧展现的人物情感的印象缺乏逻辑联系、充满矛盾，作者通过这种形式集中刻画"人物本身"，展现内在、外在的在某一时刻影响人物意识的各种因素。"意识流"一词首先出现在美国心理学家威廉·詹姆斯的《心理学原理》一书中。随后这种技巧被用于詹姆斯·乔伊斯和弗吉尼亚·伍尔夫等名家的作品中。

Chapter 16 D. H. Lawrence

作者简介

D. H. Lawrence (1885 – 1930), born on September 11, 1885 in Eastwood, was an English novelist, poet, playwright, literary critic and painter. He was the fourth child of a struggling coal miner who was a heavy drinker. His mother was a teacher, greatly superior in education to her husband. Lawrence's childhood was dominated by poverty and friction between his parents. He was educated at Nottingham High School, to which he had won a scholarship. He worked as a clerk in a surgical appliance factory and then for four years as a pupil-teacher. After studies at Nottingham University, Lawrence briefly pursued a teaching career. Lawrence's mother died in 1910. It was said that she had been ill with cancer. The young man was devastated and he described the next few months as his "sick year." It is clear that Lawrence had an extremely close relationship with his mother and his grief following her death became a major turning point in his life, just as the death of Mrs. Morel forms a major turning point in his autobiographical novel *Sons and Lovers*, a work that draws upon much of the writer's provincial upbringing. In 1909, a number of Lawrence's poems were published by Ford Max Ford in the *English Review*. The appearance of his first novel, *The White Peacock* (1911), launched Lawrence into a writing career. In 1912 he met Frieda and fell in love with her, thus she left her husband and three children, and they eloped to Bavaria. In 1913 Lawrence's novel *Sons and Lovers* which was based on his childhood was published. In 1914 Lawrence married Frieda, and traveled with her in several countries. During the First World War Lawrence and his wife were unable to obtain passports and were targets of constant harassment from the authorities. They were accused of spying for the Germans and officially expelled from Cornwall in 1917. The Lawrences were not permitted to emigrate until 1919, when their years of wandering began.

On March 2, 1930 D. H. Lawrence died in Vence, France because of lung disease. But he gained posthumous renown for his expressionistic paintings completed in the 1920s. And Lawrence, in the view of many people, is a intelligent and also controversial person.

His famous works include novels *The White Peacock* (1911), *Sons and Lovers* (1913), *The Rainbow* (1915), *Women in Love* (1920), and short stories *Love Poems and Others* (1913), *Look! We have come through!* (1917), and *The Widowing of Mrs Holroyd* (1914), *A Collier's Friday Night* (1934). Lawrence's best known work is *Lady Chatterley's Lover*, first published privately in Florence in 1928.

戴维·赫伯特·劳伦斯,出生于1885年,死于1930年,英国著名小说家,评论家,诗人以及画家,他是20世纪英国文坛最伟大的人物之一。他是家里的第四个孩子,父亲是一名矿工,酗酒成性,母亲是一名教师,受教育水平远远高于她的丈夫。劳伦斯的童年是在贫困和父母的争吵声中渡过的。他在诺丁汉高中就读并获得奖学金,毕业后在手术器械厂当过职员,之后的4年中,他当过小学教师。从汉诺丁大学毕业后,他曾短暂地追求过教师生涯。他的母亲死于1910年。有传闻说他母亲得了癌症,劳伦斯为了减轻母亲病重的痛苦而故意加大她服药的剂量。劳伦斯和他的母亲关系非常亲密,他最著名的作品之一《儿子与情人》(1913)曾引发西方评论界关于"恋母情结"的巨大争议。母亲的去世是劳伦斯人生中的重大转折点。1909年,劳伦斯的许多诗被Ford Max Ford发表在《英国评论》上。他的第一部小说——《白孔雀》(1911)的出现开启了他的写作生涯。1913年,小说《儿子与情人》出版,这部小说以他的童年经历为基础。在1914年,劳伦斯与Frieda结婚并与她一起在多国旅行。一战期间,劳伦斯和他的妻子无法获得护照,因而成为有关当局骚扰的对象,他们被指控为德国的间谍。1917年,他们被驱逐出康沃尔。直到1919年,他们才获得移民别国的权利。随后,夫妻俩便开始了他们的旅居生活。

1930年3月2日,D·H·劳伦斯由于肺病死于法国的旺斯。由于他在20世纪20年代表现主义的绘画,在死后他也获得了名望。总的来说,劳伦斯是一位富有才华却广受争议的人。

他的著名长篇小说有《白孔雀》、《儿子与情人》、《恋爱中的女人》、《彩虹》;短篇小说《普鲁士军官》,劳伦斯最著名的小说作品是《查特莱夫人的情人》。

作品及导读

作品 1

Sons and Lovers

导读

Mrs. Morel (Paul's mother)'s doctor tells Paul that Baxter Dawes is in hospital for fever. Paul asks him to tell Dawes he will visit. The doctor reports that he will. Even though Dawes seemed angry at first, Paul still leaves some money before going.

Paul informs Clara (Dawes's wife) about Dawes's illness. She is shocked, feeling guilty for having treated Dawes badly, and feels that he loved and respected her more than Paul does. She visits Dawes and tries to make up, but there is too great a distance between them. Soon after, Paul visits Dawes and makes the first mention of Clara, revealing that their romance is fading.

Mrs. Morel gets sicker, and Paul is deeply affected. He and his sister decide to give her sleeping pills to speed up her death. He puts it in her milk, and she sleeps heavily through the night, and dies in the morning. Paul looks at her dead body at night; it seems youthful to him. He kisses her lips and strokes her hair, but sadly knows that she will never return. Morel avoids looking at his dead wife's body.

Paul's relationship with Clara remains distanced. Dawes heals slowly and stays with Paul for a few days at the seaside, their friendship much stronger now. Paul suggests that Clara wants Dawes and belongs to him, and suggests they reunite. Clara comes the next day, and Paul says he is leaving that afternoon. Clara says she will join him later. She does not, however, and begs Dawes to take her back, which he does.

莫瑞尔太太(保罗妈妈)的医生告诉保罗说道斯也在医院,保罗就让医生带话说自己会去看他。一开始,道斯看起来很生气,但保罗还是在临走前给他留下了一些钱。

保罗告诉克拉拉(道斯的妻子)道斯生病了,她惊呆了,而且她对于之前对道斯的做法感到愧疚。她去看望道斯,希望能修复他们的关系,但他们之间已经相距太远。

莫瑞尔太太的病越来越严重,而保罗也因此深受打击。他和姐姐决定给他妈妈服大量的安眠药,让她快点结束痛苦。他把药放到牛奶里,第二天早上她就去世了。他很伤心,不停亲吻他妈妈,抚摸她的头发,但他知道她不会再回来了。而他爸爸却不想去看她死去妻子的尸体。

保罗和克拉拉之间的距离越来越大,他就给道斯说其实克拉拉想要的是道斯,而且她的心一直都属于道斯,他希望他们能复合。第二天克拉拉来找道斯,之后他们就在一起了。

选 文

Sons and Lovers

(*Excerpt*)

December came, and some snow. He stayed at home all the while now. They could not afford a nurse. Annie came to look after her mother; the parish nurse, whom they loved, came in morning and evening. Paul shared the nursing with Annie. Often, in the evenings, when friends were in the kitchen with them, they all laughed together and shook with laughter. It was reaction. Paul was so comical, Annie was so quaint. The whole party laughed till they cried, trying to subdue the sound. And Mrs. Morel, lying alone in the darkness heard them, and among her bitterness was a feeling of relief.

Then Paul would go upstairs gingerly, guiltily, to see if she had heard.

"Shall I give you some milk?" he asked.

"A little," she replied plaintively.

And he would put some water with it, so that it should not nourish her. Yet he loved her more than his own life.

She had sleeping pills every night, and her heart got fitful. Annie slept beside her. Paul would go in the early morning, when his sister got up. Darker and darker grew her eyes, all pupils, with the torture. In the mornings the weariness and ache were too much to bear. Yet she could not — would not — weep, or even complain much.

"You slept a bit later this morning, little one," he would say to her.

"Did I?" she answered, with fretful weariness.

"Yes; it's nearly eight o'clock."

He stood looking out of the window. The whole country was bleak and pallid under the snow. Then he felt her pulse. There was a strong stroke and a weak one, like a sound and its echo. That was supposed to betoken the end. She let him feel her wrist, knowing what he wanted.

Sometimes they looked in each other's eyes. Then they almost seemed to make an agreement. It was almost as if he were agreeing to die also. But she did not consent to die; she would not. Her body was wasted to a fragment of ash. Her eyes were dark and full of torture.

"Can't you give her something to put an end to it?" he asked the doctor at last.

But the doctor shook his head.

"She can't last many days now, Mr. Morel," he said.

Paul went indoors.

"I can't bear it much longer; we shall all go mad," said Annie.

The two sat down to breakfast.

"Go and sit with her while we have breakfast, Minnie," said Annie. But the girl was frightened.

Paul went through the country, through the woods, over the snow. He saw the marks of rabbits and birds in the white snow. He wandered miles and miles. A smoky red sunset came on slowly, painfully, lingering. He thought she would die that day. There was a donkey that came up to him over the snow by the wood's edge, and put its head against him, and walked with him alongside. He put his arms round the donkey's neck, and stroked his cheeks against his ears.

His mother, silent, was still alive, with her hard mouth gripped grimly, her eyes of dark torture only living.

It was nearing Christmas; there was more snow. Annie and he felt as if they could go on no more. Still her dark eyes were alive. Sometimes he would go into the sick-room and look at her. Then he backed out, bewildered.

She kept her hold on life still. The miners had been out on strike, and returned a fortnight or so before Christmas.

Minnie went upstairs with the feeding-cup. It was two days after the men had been in.

"Have the men been saying their hands are sore, Minnie?" she asked, in the faint, querulous voice that would not give in. Minnie stood surprised.

"Not as I know of, Mrs. Morel," she answered.

"But I'll bet they are sore," said the dying woman, as she moved her head with a sigh of weariness. "But, at any rate, there'll be something to buy in with this week."

Not a thing did she let slip.

"Your father's pit things will want well airing, Annie," she said, when the men were going back to work.

"Don't you bother about that, my dear," said Annie.

One night Annie and Paul were alone. Nurse was upstairs.

"She'll live over Christmas," said Annie. They were both full of horror. "She won't, "he replied grimly."

"All that came from Sheffield," said Paul.

"Ay — do!" said Annie.

The next day he was painting in the bedroom. She seemed to be asleep. He stepped softly backwards and forwards at his painting. Suddenly her small voice wailed:

"Don't walk about, Paul."

He looked round. Her eyes, like dark bubbles in her face, were looking at him.

"No, my dear," he said gently.

"What are you doing?" said Annie.

Then they both laughed together like two conspiring children. On top of all their horror flicked this little sanity.

Nurse did not come that night to settle Mrs. Morel down. Paul went up with the hot milk in a feeding-cup. It was nine o'clock.

She was reared up in bed, and he put the feeding-cup between her lips that he would have died to save from any hurt. She took a sip, then put the spout of the cup away and looked at him with her dark, wondering eyes. He looked at her.

"Oh, it IS bitter, Paul!" she said, making a little grimace.

"It's a new sleeping draught the doctor gave me for you," he said. "He thought it would leave you in such a state in the morning."

"And I hope it won't," she said, like a child.

She drank some more of the milk.

"But it IS horrid!" she said.

He saw her frail fingers over the cup, her lips making a little move.

"I know — I tasted it," he said. "But I'll give you some clean milk afterwards."

"I think so," she said, and she went on with the draught. She was obedient to him like a child. He wondered if she knew. He saw her poor wasted throat moving as she drank with difficulty. Then he ran downstairs for more milk.

There were no grains in the bottom of the cup.

"Has she had it?" whispered Annie.

"Yes — and she said it was bitter."

"Oh!" laughed Annie, putting her under lip between her teeth.

"And I told her it was a new draught. Where's that milk?"

They both went upstairs.

"I wonder why nurse didn't come to settle me down?" complained the mother, like a child, wistfully.

"She said she was going to a concert, my love," replied Annie.

"Did she?"

They were silent a minute. Mrs. Morel gulped the little clean milk.

"Annie, that draught WAS horrid!" she said plaintively.

"Was it, my love? Well, never mind."

The mother sighed again with weariness. Her pulse was very irregular.

"Let US settle you down," said Annie. "Perhaps nurse will be so late."

"Ay," said the mother — "try."

They turned the clothes back. Paul saw his mother like a girl curled up in her flannel nightdress. Quickly they made one half of the bed, moved her, made the other, straightened her nightgown over her small feet, and covered her up.

"There," said Paul, stroking her softly. "There! — now you'll sleep."

"Yes," she said. "I didn't think you could do the bed so nicely," she added, almost gaily. Then she curled up, with her cheek on her hand. Paul put the long thin plait of grey hair over her shoulder and kissed her.

"You'll sleep, my love," he said.

"Yes," she answered trustfully. "Good night."

They put out the light, and it was still.

Morel was in bed. Nurse did not come. Annie and Paul came to look at her at about eleven. She seemed to be sleeping as usual after her draught. Her mouth had come a bit open.

"Shall we sit up?" said Paul.

"I still lie with her as I always do," said Annie. "She might wake up."

"Yes."

They lingered before the bedroom fire, feeling the night big and black and snowy outside, their two selves alone in the world. At last he went into the next room and went to bed.

He slept almost immediately, but kept waking every now and again. Then he went sound asleep. He started awake at Annie's whispered, "Paul, Paul!" He saw his sister in her white nightdress, with her long plait of hair down her back, standing in the darkness.

"Yes?" he whispered, sitting up.

"Come and look at her."

He slipped out of bed. A bud of gas was burning in the sick chamber. His mother lay with her cheek on her hand, curled up as she had gone to sleep. But her mouth had fallen open, and she breathed with great, hoarse breaths, like snoring, and there were long intervals between.

"She's going!" he whispered.

"Yes," said Annie.

"How long has she been like it?"

"I only just woke up."

There was a space — a long space. Then they started. The great, snoring breath was taken again. He bent close down and looked at her.

"Isn't it awful!" whispered Annie.

He nodded. They sat down again helplessly.

Again it was given back, long and harsh. The sound, so irregular, at such wide intervals, sounded through the house. Morel, in his room, slept on. Paul and Annie sat crouched, huddled, and motionless. The great snoring sound began again — there was a painful pause while the breath was held — back came the rasping breath. Minute after minute passed. Paul looked at her again, bending low over her.

"She may last like this," he said.

They were both silent. He looked out of the window, and could faintly discern the snow on the garden.

"You go to my bed," he said to Annie. "I'll sit up."

"No," she said, "I'll stop with you."

"I'd rather you didn't," he said.

At last Annie crept out of the room, and he was alone. He hugged himself in his brown blanket, crouched in front of his mother, watching. She looked dreadful, with the bottom jaw fallen back. He watched. Sometimes he thought the great breath would never begin again. He could not bear it — the waiting. He mended the fire again, noiselessly. She must not be disturbed. The minutes went by. The night was going, breath by breath. Each time the sound came he felt it wring him, till at last he could not feel so much.

His father got up. Paul heard the miner drawing his stockings on, yawning. Then Morel, in shirt and stockings, entered.

"Hush!" said Paul.

Morel stood watching. Then he looked at his son, helplessly, and in horror.

"Had I better stop a-whom?" he whispered.

"No. Go to work. She'll last through tomorrow."

"I don't think so."

"Yes. Go to work."

The miner looked at her again, in fear, and went obediently out of the room. Paul saw the tape of his garters swinging against his legs.

After another half-hour Paul went downstairs and drank a cup of tea, then returned. Morel, dressed for the pit, came upstairs again.

"Am I to go?" he said.

"Yes."

And in a few minutes Paul heard his father's heavy steps go thudding over the deadening snow. Miners called in the streets as they tramped in gangs to work. The terrible, long-drawn breaths continued — heave — heave — heave; then a long pause — then — ah-h-h-h-h! as it came back. One after another they crowed and boomed, some small and far away, some near, the blowers of the collieries and the other works. Then there was silence. He mended the fire. The great breaths broke the silence — she looked just the same. He put back the blind and peered out. Still it was dark. Perhaps there was a lighter tinge. Perhaps the snow was bluer. He drew up the blind and got dressed. Then, shuddering, he drank brandy from the bottle on the wash-stand. The snow WAS growing blue. He heard a cart clanking down the street. Yes, it was seven o'clock, and it was coming a little bit light. He heard some people calling. The world was waking. A grey, deathly dawn crept over the snow. Yes, he could see the houses. He put out the gas. It seemed very dark.

The breathing came still, but he was almost used to it. He could see her. She was just the same. He wondered if he piled heavy clothes on top of her it would stop. He looked at her. That was not her — not her a bit. If he piled the blanket and heavy coats on her —

Suddenly the door opened, and Annie entered. She looked at him questioningly.

"Just the same," he said calmly.

They whispered together a minute, then he went downstairs to get breakfast. It was twenty to eight. Soon Annie came down.

"If she looks like that!" said Annie.

"Drink some tea," he said.

They went upstairs again.

It went on just the same. She lay with her cheek in her hand, her mouth fallen open, and the great, ghastly snores came and went.

At ten o'clock nurse came. She looked strange and woebegone.

"Nurse," cried Paul, "she'll last like this for days?"

"She can't, Mr. Morel," said nurse. "She can't."

There was a silence.

"Isn't it dreadful!" wailed the nurse. "Who would have thought she could stand it? Go down now, Mr. Morel, go down."

Nurse and Arthur were upstairs. Paul sat with his head in his hand. Suddenly Annie came flying across the yard crying, half mad: "Paul — Paul — she's gone!"

In a second he was back in his own house and upstairs. She lay curled up and still, with her face on her hand, and nurse was wiping her mouth. They all stood back. He kneeled down, and put his face to hers and his arms round her: "My love — my love — oh, my love!" he whispered again and again.

Then he heard the nurse behind him, crying, and saying: "She's better, Mr. Morel, she's better."

When he took his face up from his warm, dead mother he went straight downstairs and began blacking his boots.

There was a good deal to do, letters to write, and so on. The doctor came and glanced at her, and sighed.

The father came home from work at about four o'clock. He dragged silently into the house and sat down. Minnie bustled to give him his dinner. Tired, he laid his black arms on the table. Paul wondered if he knew. It was some time, and nobody had spoken. At last the son said: "You noticed the blinds were down?"

Morel looked up.

"No," he said. "Why — has she gone?"

"Yes."

The miner sat still for a moment, then began his dinner. It was as if nothing had happened. He ate his turnips in silence. Afterwards he washed and went upstairs to dress. The door of her room was shut.

"Have you seen her?" Annie asked of him when he came down.

"No," he said.

In a little while he went out. Annie went away, and Paul called on the undertaker, the clergyman, the doctor, the registrar. It was a long business. He got back at nearly eight o'clock. The undertaker was coming soon to measure for the coffin. The house was empty except for her. He took a candle and went upstairs.

The room was cold, that had been warm for so long. Flowers, bottles, plates, all sick-room litter was taken away; everything was harsh and austere. She lay like a maiden asleep. With his candle in his hand, he bent over her. She lay like a girl asleep and dreaming of her love. The mouth was a little open as if wondering from the suffering, but her face was young, her brow clear and white as if life had never touched it. He looked again at the eyebrows, at the small, winsome nose a bit on one side. She was young again. Only the hair as it arched so beautifully from her temples was mixed with silver, and the two simple plaits that lay on her shoulders were filigree of silver and brown. She would wake up. She would lift her eyelids. She was with him still. He bent and kissed her passionately. But there was coldness against his mouth. He bit his lips with horror. Looking at her, he felt he could never, never let her go. No! He stroked the hair from her temples. That, too, was cold. He saw the mouth so dumb and wondering at the hurt. Then he crouched on the floor, whispering to her: "Mother, mother!"

He was still with her when the undertakers came, young men who had been to school with him. They touched her reverently, and in a quiet, businesslike fashion. They did not look at her. He watched jealously. He and Annie guarded her fiercely. After a while Paul went out of the house, and played cards at a friend's. It was midnight when he got back. His father rose from the couch as he entered.

"I didn't think you'd sit up," said Paul.

"I forgot you'd be alone, father," he said.

"Dost want to eat?" asked Morel.

"No."

Paul drank it.

After a while Morel went to bed. He hurried past the closed door, and left his own door open. Soon the son came upstairs also. He went in to kiss her good-night, as usual. It was cold and dark. He wished they had kept her fire burning. Still she dreamed her young dream. But she would be cold.

"My dear!" he whispered.

And he did not kiss her, for fear she should be cold and strange to him. It eased him she slept so beautifully. He shut her door softly, not to wake her, and went to bed.

In the morning Morel summoned his courage, hearing Annie downstairs and Paul coughing in the room across the landing. He opened her door, and went into the darkened room. He saw the white uplifted form in the twilight, but her he dared not see. Bewildered, too frightened to possess any of his faculties, he got out of the room again and left her. He never looked at her again. He had not seen her for months, because he had not dared to look. And she looked like his young wife again.

"Have you seen her?" Annie asked of him sharply after breakfast.

"Yes," he said.

"And don't you think she looks nice?"

"Yes."

He went out of the house soon after. And all the time He seemed to be creeping aside to avoid it.

Paul went about from place to place, doing the business of the death. He met Clara in Nottingham, and they had tea together in a café, when they were quite jolly again. She was infinitely relieved to find he did not take it tragically.

Later, when the relatives began to come for the funeral, the affair became public, and the children became social beings. They put themselves aside. They buried her in a furious storm of rain and wind. Annie gripped his arm and leaned forward. Down below she saw a dark corner of William's coffin. The oak box sank steadily. She was gone. The rain poured in the grave. The procession of black, with its umbrellas glistening, turned away. The cemetery was deserted under the drenching cold rain.

Paul went home and busied himself supplying the guests with drinks. His father sat in the kitchen with Mrs. Morel's relatives, "superior" people, and wept, and said what a good lass she'd been, and how he'd tried to do everything he could for her — everything. He had done all his life to do what he could for her, and he'd nothing to reproach himself with. She was gone, but he'd done his best for her. He wiped his eyes with his white handkerchief. He'd nothing to reproach himself for, he repeated. All his life he'd done his best for her.

And that was how he tried to dismiss her. He never thought of her personally. Everything deep in him he denied.

"I have been dreaming of thy mother," he said in a small voice.

"Have you, father? When I dream of her it's always just as she was when she was well. I dream of her often, but it seems quite nice and natural, as if nothing had altered."

But Morel crouched in front of the fire in terror.

Paul went restless from place to place. For some months, since his mother had been worse, he had not made love to Clara. She was, as it were, dumb to him, rather distant. Dawes saw her very occasionally, but the two could not get an inch across the great distance between them. The three of them were drifting forward.

Dawes mended very slowly. His father was with Annie in Sheffield. Dawes came to Paul's lodgings. His time in the home was up. Dawes depended on Morel now. He knew Paul and Clara had practically separated. Two days after Christmas Paul was to go back to Nottingham. "You know Clara's coming down for the day tomorrow?" he said.

The other man glanced at him.

"Yes, you told me," he replied.

Paul drank the remainder of his glass of whisky.

"I told the landlady your wife was coming," he said.

"Did you?" said Dawes, shrinking, but almost leaving himself in the other's hands. He got up rather stiffly, and reached for Morel's glass.

"Let me fill you up," he said.

Paul jumped up.

"You sit still," he said.

But Dawes, with rather shaky hand, continued to mix the drink.

"Say when," he said.

"Thanks!" replied the other. "But you've no business to get up."

"It does me good, lad," replied Dawes. "I begin to think I'm right again, then."

"You are about right, you know."

"I am, certainly I am," said Dawes, nodding to him.

"And Len says he can get you on in Sheffield."

Dawes glanced at him again, with dark eyes that agreed with everything the other would say, perhaps a trifle dominated by him.

"It's funny," said Paul, "starting again. I feel in a lot bigger mess than you."

I don't know. I don't know. It's as if I was in a tangled sort of hole, rather dark and dreary, and no road anywhere."

"I know — I understand it," Dawes said, nodding. "But you'll find it'll come all right."

He spoke caressingly.

"I suppose so," said Paul.

Dawes knocked his pipe in a hopeless fashion.

"You've not done for yourself like I have," he said.

Morel saw the wrist and the white hand of the other man gripping the stem of the pipe and knocking out the ash, as if he had given up.

"How old are you?" Paul asked.

"Thirty-nine," replied Dawes, glancing at him.

"You'll just be in your prime," said Morel. "You don't look as if much life had gone out of you."

The brown eyes of the other flashed suddenly.

"It hasn't," he said. "The go is there."

Paul looked up and laughed.

"We've both got plenty of life in us yet to make things fly," he said.

The eyes of the two men met. They exchanged one look. Having recognised the stress of passion each in the other, they both drank their whisky.

"Yes, begod!" said Dawes, breathless.

There was a pause.

"And I don't see," said Paul, "why you shouldn't go on where you left off."

"What —" said Dawes, suggestively.

"Yes — fit your old home together again."

Dawes hid his face and shook his head.

"Couldn't be done," he said, and looked up with an ironic smile.

"Why? Because you don't want?"

"Perhaps."

They smoked in silence. Dawes showed his teeth as he bit his pipe stem.

"You mean you don't want her?" asked Paul.

Dawes stared up at the picture with a caustic expression on his face.

"I hardly know," he said.

The smoke floated softly up.

"I believe she wants you," said Paul.

"Do you?" replied the other, soft, satirical, abstract.

"Yes. She never really hitched on to me — you were always there in the background. That's why she wouldn't get a divorce."

Dawes continued to stare in a satirical fashion at the picture over the mantelpiece.

"That's how women are with me," said Paul. "They want me like mad, but they don't want to belong to me. And she belonged to you all the time. I knew."

The triumphant male came up in Dawes. He showed his teeth more distinctly.

"Perhaps I was a fool," he said.

"You were a big fool," said Morel.

"But perhaps even then you were a bigger fool," said Dawes.

There was a touch of triumph and malice in it.

"Do you think so?" said Paul.

They were silent for some time.

"At any rate, I'm clearing out tomorrow," said Morel.

"I see," answered Dawes.

Then they did not talk any more. The instinct to murder each other had returned. They almost avoided each other.

They shared the same bedroom. When they retired Dawes seemed abstract, thinking of something. He sat on the side of the bed in his shirt, looking at his legs.

"Aren't you getting cold?" asked Morel.

"I was looking at these legs," replied the other.

"What's up with them? They look all right," replied Paul, from his bed.

"They look all right. But there's some water in them yet."

"And what's about it?"

"Come and look."

Paul reluctantly got out of bed and went to look at the rather handsome legs of the other man that were covered with glistening, dark gold hair.

"Look here," said Dawes, pointing to his shin. "Look at the water under here."

"Where?" said Paul.

The man pressed in his finger-tips. They left little dents that filled up slowly.

"It's nothing," said Paul.

"You feel," said Dawes.

Paul tried with his fingers. It made little dents.

"H'm!" he said.

"Rotten, isn't it?" said Dawes.

"Why? It's nothing much."

"You're not much of a man with water in your legs."

"I can't see as it makes any difference," said Morel. "I've got a weak chest."

He returned to his own bed.

"I suppose the rest of me's all right," said Dawes, and he put out the light.

In the morning it was raining. Morel packed his bag. The sea was grey and shaggy and dismal. He seemed to be cutting himself off from life more and more. It gave him a wicked pleasure to do it.

The two men were at the station. Clara stepped out of the train, and came along the platform, very erect and coldly composed. She wore a long coat and a tweed hat. Both men hated her for her composure. Paul shook hands with her at the barrier. Dawes was leaning against the bookstall, watching. His black overcoat was buttoned up to the chin because of the rain. He was pale, with almost a touch of nobility in his quietness. He came forward, limping slightly.

"You ought to look better than this," she said.

"Oh, I'm all right now."

The three stood at a loss. She kept the two men hesitating near her.

"Shall we go to the lodging straight off," said Paul, "or somewhere else?"

"We may as well go home," said Dawes.

Paul walked on the outside of the pavement, then Dawes, then Clara. They made polite conversation. The sitting-room faced the sea, whose tide, grey and shaggy, hissed not far off.

Morel swung up the big arm-chair.

"Sit down, Jack," he said.

"I don't want that chair," said Dawes.

"Sit down!" Morel repeated.

Clara took off her things and laid them on the couch. She had a slight air of resentment. Lifting her hair with her fingers, she sat down, rather aloof and composed. Paul ran downstairs to speak to the landlady.

"I should think you're cold," said Dawes to his wife. "Come nearer to the fire."

"Thank you, I'm quite warm," she answered.

She looked out of the window at the rain and at the sea.

"When are you going back?" she asked.

"Well, the rooms are taken until tomorrow, so he wants me to stop. He's going back tonight."

"And then you're thinking of going to Sheffield?"

"Yes."

"Are you fit to start work?"

"I'm going to start."

"You've really got a place?"

"Yes — begin on Monday."

"You don't look fit."

"Why don't I?"

She looked again out of the window instead of answering.

"And have you got lodgings in Sheffield?"

"Yes."

Again she looked away out of the window. The panes were blurred with streaming rain.

"And can you manage all right?" she asked.

They were silent when Morel returned.

"I shall go by the four-twenty," he said as he entered.

Nobody answered.

"I wish you'd take your boots off," he said to Clara.

"There's a pair of slippers of mine."

"Thank you," she said. "They aren't wet."

He put the slippers near her feet. She left them there.

Morel sat down. Both the men seemed helpless, and each of them had a rather hunted look. Clara thought she had never seen him look so small and mean. He was as if trying to get himself into the smallest possible compass.

And as he went about arranging, and as he sat talking, there seemed something false about him and out of tune. Watching him unknown, she said to herself there was no stability about him. He was fine in his way, passionate, and able to give her drinks of pure life when he was in one mood. And now he looked paltry and insignificant. There was nothing stable about him. Her husband had more manly dignity. At any rate he did not worry about with any wind. There was something evanescent about Morel, she thought, something shifting and false. He would never make sure ground for any woman to stand on. She despised him rather for his shrinking together, getting smaller. Her husband at least was manly, and when he was beaten gave in. But this other would never own to being beaten. He would shift round and round, prowl, get smaller. She despised him. And yet she watched him rather than Dawes, and it seemed as if their three fates lay in his hands. She hated him for it.

She seemed to understand better now about men, and what they could or would do. She was less afraid of them, more sure of herself. That they were not the small egoists she had imagined them made her more comfortable.

She had learned a good deal — almost as much as she wanted to learn. Her cup had been full. It was still as full as she could carry. On the whole, she would not be sorry when he was gone.

They had dinner, and sat eating nuts and drinking by the fire. Not a serious word had been spoken. He was a mean fellow, after all, to take what he wanted and then give her back. She did not remember that she herself had had what she wanted, and really, at the bottom of her heart, wished to be given back.

Paul felt crumpled up and lonely. His mother had really supported his life. He had loved her; they two had, in fact, faced the world together. Now she was gone, and forever behind him was the gap in life, the tear in the veil, through which his life seemed to drift slowly, as if he were drawn towards death. He wanted someone of their own free initiative to help him. The lesser things he began to let go from him, for fear of this big thing, the lapse towards death, following in the wake of his beloved. Clara could not stand for him to hold on to. She wanted him, but not to understand him. He felt she wanted the man on top, not the real him that was in trouble.

That would be too much trouble to her; he dared not give it her. She could not cope with him. It made him ashamed. So, secretly ashamed because he was in such a mess, because his own hold on life was so unsure, because nobody held him, feeling unsubstantial, shadowy, as if he did not count for much in this concrete world, he drew himself together smaller and smaller. He did not want to die; he would not give in. But he was not afraid of death. If nobody would help, he would go on alone.

Dawes had been driven to the extremity of life, until he was afraid. He could go to the brink of death, he could lie on the edge and look in. Then, cowed, afraid, he had to crawl back, and like a beggar take what offered. There was certain nobility in it. As Clara saw, he owned himself beaten, and he wanted to be taken back whether or not. That she could do for him. It was three o'clock.

"I am going by the four-twenty," said Paul again to Clara. "Are you coming then or later?"

"I don't know," she said.

"I'm meeting my father in Nottingham at seven-fifteen," he said.

"Then," she answered, "I'll come later."

Dawes jerked suddenly, as if he had been held on a strain. He looked out over the sea, but he saw nothing.

"There are one or two books in the corner," said Morel. "I've done with them."

At about four o'clock he went.

"I shall see you both later," he said, as he shook hands.

"I suppose so," said Dawes. "An' perhaps — one day — I will be able to pay you back the money as —"

"I shall come for it, you'll see," laughed Paul. "I will be on the rocks before I'm very much older."

"Ay — well —" said Dawes.

"Good-bye," he said to Clara.

"Good-bye," she said, giving him her hand. Then she glanced at him for the last time, dumb and humble.

He was gone. Dawes and his wife sat down again.

"It's a nasty day for travelling," said the man.

"Yes," she answered.

They talked in a desultory fashion until it grew dark. The landlady brought in the tea. Dawes drew up his chair to the table without being invited, like a husband. Then he sat humbly waiting for his cup.

After tea, as it drew near to six o'clock, he went to the window. All was dark outside. The sea was roaring.

"It's raining yet," he said.

"Is it?" she answered.

"You won't go tonight, shall you?" he said, hesitating.

She did not answer. He waited.

"I shouldn't go in this rain," he said.

"Do you want me to stay?" she asked.

His hand as he held the dark curtain trembled.

"Yes," he said.

He remained with his back to her. She rose and went slowly to him. He let go the curtain, turned, hesitating, towards her. She stood with her hands behind her back, looking up at him in a heavy, inscrutable fashion.

"Do you want me, Baxter?" she asked.

His voice was hoarse as he answered: "Do you want to come back to me?"

She made a moaning noise, lifted her arms, and put them round his neck, drawing him to her. He hid his face on her shoulder, holding her clasped.

"Take me back!" she whispered, ecstatic. "Take me back, take me back!" And she put her fingers through his fine, thin dark hair, as if she were only semi-conscious. He tightened his grasp on her.

"Do you want me again?" he murmured, broken.

17 William Golding

作者简介

William Golding grew up at his family home in Marlborough, Wiltshire, where his father was a headmaster and a science master at Marlborough Grammar School. His father was a socialist with a strong commitment to scientific rationalism. The young Golding and his elder brother Joseph attended the school where his father taught. In 1930 Golding went to Oxford University as an undergraduate at Brasenose College, where he read Natural Sciences for two years before transferring to English Literature. Golding's father set a great example to him and he was fond of literature since he was very young. He was familiar with all fairy tales from ancient Greek to modern society. Golding took his Second Class in the summer of 1934, and later that year his first book, *Poems*, was published in London with the help of his Oxford friend, the anthroposophist Adam Brittlestar. It was a poetry collection including twenty-four poems, which showed his great talent in poem writing. After his graduation, he took part in a lot of jobs including writer, performer, director, and screenwriter and so on. During World War II, Golding fought in the Royal Navy and was briefly involved in the pursuit and sinking of Germany's mightiest battleship, the Bismarck. He also participated in the invasion of Normandy on D-Day, commanding a landing ship that fired salves of rockets onto the beaches, and then in a naval action at Walcheren in which 23 out of 24 assault craft were sunk. At the war's end he returned to teaching and writing. After the war, he totally changed his opinion to human beings. His later novels include *Darkness Visible* (1979), *The Paper Men* (1984), and the comic-historical sea trilogy *To the Ends of the Earth* (BBC TV 2005), comprising the Booker Prize-winning *Rites of Passage* (1980), *Close Quarters* (1987), and *Fire down Below* (1989).

威廉·戈尔丁,出生于英格兰西南角康沃尔郡一个知识分子家庭,父亲是当地学校的校长,也是一位学者,痴迷于求知和探索。其父对政治有极大的热情,相信科学。戈尔丁继承了父亲开明、理智的秉性,自小爱好文学。他熟读所有儿童文学,包括古希腊至现代的一切童话故事。戈尔丁的家后来搬到马尔波罗,他就在马尔波罗的语言学校就学。1930年遵父命入牛津大学布拉西诺斯学院学习自然科学,两年之后,转而攻读英国文学。1934年,在毕业的前一年,戈尔丁出版了处女作——题为《诗集》的包括24首小诗的小册子,展示了他的写作才华。毕业后,他做了4年社会工作,从事包括写作、表演、导演和编剧等各种工作。1940年戈尔丁加入了英国皇家海军,作为战舰的指挥官,他亲身经历了许多难忘的战斗,他参加了击沉德军战列舰俾斯麦号的战役。随后他又参加了诺曼底登陆。战争结束后,戈尔丁于1945年退役,他重又回到该教会学校执教,教授英国文学,并坚持业余写作。经过战争,他对人类的看法完全改变了。以后他就开始了小说创作,从《蝇王》到《纸人》,展现了人的本质是罪恶的观念。此后他陆续出版了《继承者》、《平彻·马丁》、《赢得自由》、《塔尖》、《金字塔》等作品。

作品及导读

作 品 1

Lord of the Flies

导 读

Lord of the Flies is a dystopian novel by Nobel Prize-winning English author William Golding about a group of British boys stuck on an uninhabited island who try to govern themselves with disastrous results. Its stances on the already controversial subjects of human nature and individual welfare versus the common good earned it position 68 on the American Library Association's list of the 100 most frequently challenged books of 1990 - 1999. The book indicates that it takes place in the midst of an unspecified nuclear war. Some of the marooned characters are ordinary students, while others arrive as a musical choir under an established leader. Most (with the exception of the choirboys) appear never to have encountered one another before. The book portrays their descent into savagery; left to themselves in a paradisiacal country, far from modern civilization, the well-educated children regress to a primitive state. At an allegorical level, the central theme is the conflicting human impulses toward civilization — living by rules, peacefully and in harmony — and toward the will to power. Themes include the tension between groupthink and individuality, between rational and emotional reactions, and between morality and immorality. How these play out, and how different people feel the influences of these, form a major subtext of *Lord of the Flies*. And in the Lord of the Flies, the chapter called "The Sound of the Shell" tell us that Piggy and Ralph meet up with each other after escaping from their shot-down plane. And it is because of the event of this time, a large scar was made in the untouched jungle, symbolizing the first of man's destruction on the island. But as a matter of fact, a war is going on in the outside world. Seemingly, it is lucky for the rest of the people in the book in that everyone will be isolated from it and put into their "world." There Piggy spots a conch shell, and tells Ralph how to use it to make a noise. Ralph does so, and calls all of the other boys on the island that crashed down with the plane. Jack and his Choir, Simon, Sam and Eric, and many other characters join in an assembly (including the littl'uns, which is the youngest kids at about 6 or 7 years old). Rules are set down, and Ralph is to be chief. There is no one else on the island but the young boys, so Jack decides to take his choir out to hunt for wild pigs. However, he is unsuccessful in killing a small pig with his knife. And the significance lies in that chapter is that while Jack's first attempt to kill the pig failed, his quote "next time..." foreshadowed his future of savage and cruel hunting.

《蝇王》是英国作家、诺贝尔和平奖获得者威廉·戈尔丁所撰写的反乌托邦的小说。作品讲述了一群英国男孩被困在一座荒岛上，试图掌控自我却引来了灾难性的结局。小说立足于已备受争议的人性主题以及个人福利与公共利益的对抗，使其赢得了从1990—1999年100部最具挑战性的书籍中，在美国图书馆协会名列第68的地位。这本书讲述的故事发生于一次不明的核战争中，小说中被遗弃的角色有一些是普通学生，其他则是有"领袖"领导的合唱团成员。大多数（除了唱诗班男孩）在之前互不相识。这本书描绘了他们堕入野蛮、被遗弃于一个"天堂"的国度、远离现代文明、受过良好教育的儿童回归到原始状态的事迹。从寓言层面而言，中心主题是冲突的人类对文明的冲动——依靠规则、平静并和谐地活着——过渡到对权利的渴望。小说的主题包括集体思维和个性思维之间的差异，理性与感性、道德和非道德的关系。而这些如何演绎出来，以及不同的人对这些影响的感受，构成了《蝇王》的主题。《蝇王》一书中，"海螺的声音"这一章告诉我们：在从被击落的飞机逃离后，小猪仔和雷尔夫相遇。也正是由于此次事故，一个巨大的"伤疤"出现在了这片未开发的丛林中，这象征着人类在岛上的首次破坏。但事实上在外部世界，战争仍在持续。此时书中的其他人似乎很幸运，因为他们将与外界隔绝、建立自己的"世界"。在小岛上，小猪仔发现了一枚海螺，并告诉雷尔夫如何利用它发出声音。雷尔夫照做了，且召集了岛上所有遭遇飞机失事的男孩。杰克和他的唱诗班、赛门、山姆和艾力克，以及其他许多人（包括"比较小的小朋友"，这位年纪最小的孩子有六七岁）也参加了集会。规则制定了下来，雷尔夫将成为领导者。但是因为小岛上除了男孩子之外，并无其他人的存在，所以杰克决定带领他的唱诗班外出狩猎野猪，然而，杰克却并未成功用刀子杀死一头小野猪。这一章节的意义在于：尽管杰克首次杀死野猪的尝试无疾而终，但他的话"下一次……"却预示其未来野蛮且残酷的猎杀。

选 文

Lord of Flies

(*Chapter* 1)

The Sound of the Shell

The boy with fair hair lowered himself down the last few feet of rock and began to pick his way toward the lagoon. Though he had taken off his school sweater and trailed it now from one hand, his grey shirt stuck to him and his hair was plastered to his forehead. All round him the long scar smashed into the jungle was a bath of heat. He was clambering heavily among the creepers and broken trunks when a bird, a vision of red and yellow, flashed upwards with a witch-like cry; and this cry was echoed by another.

"Hi!" it said. "Wait a minute!"

The undergrowth at the side of the scar was shaken and a multitude of raindrops fell pattering.

"Wait a minute," the voice said. "I got caught up."

The fair boy stopped and jerked his stockings with an automatic gesture that made the jungle seem for a moment like the Home Counties.

The voice spoke again.

"I can't hardly move with all these creeper things."

The owner of the voice came backing out of the undergrowth so that twigs scratched on a greasy wind-breaker. The naked crooks of his knees were plump, caught and scratched by thorns. He bent down, removed the thorns carefully, and turned round. He was shorter than the fair boy and very fat. He came forward, searching out safe lodgments for his feet, and then looked up through thick spectacles.

"Where's the man with the megaphone?"

The fair boy shook his head.

"This is an island. At least I think it's an island. That's a reef out in the sea. Perhaps there aren't any grownups anywhere."

The fat boy looked startled.

"There was that pilot. But he wasn't in the passenger cabin, he was up in front."

The fair boy was peering at the reef through screwed-up eyes.

"All them other lads," the fat boy went on. "Some of them must have got out. They must have, mustn't they?"

The fair boy began to pick his way as casually as possible toward the water. He tried to be offhand and not too obviously uninterested, but the fat boy hurried after him.

"Aren't there any grownups at all?"

"I don't think so."

The fair boy said this solemnly; but then the delight of a realized ambition overcame him. In the middle of the scar he stood on his head and grinned at the reversed fat boy.

"No grownups!"

The fat boy thought for a moment.

"That pilot."

The fair boy allowed his feet to come down and sat on the steamy earth.

"He must have flown off after he dropped us. He couldn't land here. Not in a plane with wheels."

"We were attacked!"

"He'll be back all right."

The fat boy shook his head.

"When wewere coming down I looked through one of them windows. I saw the other part of the plane. There were flames coming out of it."

He looked up and down the scar.

"And this is what the cabin done."

The fair boy reached out and touched the jagged end of a trunk. For a moment he looked interested.

"What happened to it?" he asked. "Where's it got to now?"

"That storm dragged it out to sea. It wasn't half dangerous with all them tree trunks falling. There must have been some kids still in it."

He hesitated for a moment, and then spoke again.

"What's your name?"

"Ralph."

The fat boy waited to be asked his name in turn but this proffer of acquaintance was not made; the fair boy called Ralph smiled vaguely, stood up, and began to make las way once more toward the lagoon. The fat boy hung steadily at his shoulder.

"I expect there's a lot more of us scattered about. You haven't seen any others, have you?"

Ralph shook his head and increased his speed. Then he tripped over a branch and came down with a crash. The fat boy stood by him, breathing hard.

"My auntie told me not to run," he explained, "on account of my asthma."

"Ass-mar?"

"That's right. Can't catch my breath? I was the only boy in our school what had asthma," said the fat boy with a touch of pride. "And I've been wearing specs since I was three."

He took off his glasses and held them out to Ralph, blinking and smiling, and then started to wipe them against his grubby wind-breaker. An expression of pain and inward concentration altered the pale contours of his face. He smeared the sweat from his cheeks and quickly adjusted the spectacles on his nose.

"Them fruit."

He glanced round the scar.

"Them fruit," he said, "I expect —"

He put on his glasses, waded away from Ralph, and crouched down among the tangled foliage.

"I'll be out again in just a minute —"

Ralph disentangled himself cautiously and stole away through the branches. In a few seconds the fat boy's grunts were behind him and he was hurrying toward the screen that still lay between him and the lagoon. He climbed over a broken trunk and was out of the jungle. The shore was fledged with palm trees. These stood or leaned or reclined against the light and their green feathers were a hundred feet up in the air. The ground beneath them was a bank covered with coarse grass, torn everywhere by the upheavals of fallen trees, scattered with decaying coconuts and palm saplings. Behind this was the darkness of the forest proper and the open space of the scar. Ralph stood, one hand against a grey trunk, and screwed up his eyes against the shimmering water. Out there, perhaps a mile away, the white surf flinked on a coral reef, and beyond that the open sea was dark blue. Within the irregular arc of coral the lagoon was still as a mountain lake — blue of all shades and shadowy green and purple. The beach between the palm terrace and the water was a thin stick, endless apparently, for to Ralph's left the perspectives of palm and beach and water drew to a point at infinity; and always, almost visible, was the heat.

He jumped down from the terrace. The sand was thick over his black shoes and the heat hit him. He became conscious of the weight of clothes, kicked his shoes off fiercely and ripped off each stocking with its elastic garter in a single movement Then he leapt back on the terrace, pulled off his shirt, and stood there among the skull-like coconuts with green shadows from the palms and the forest sliding over his skin. He undid the snake-clasp of his belt, lugged off his shorts and pants, and stood there naked, looking at the dazzling beach and the water.

He was old enough, twelve years and a few months, to have lost the prominent tummy of childhood; and not yet old enough for adolescence to have made him awkward. You could see now that he might make a boxer, as far as width and heaviness of shoulders went, but there was a mildness about his mouth and eyes that proclaimed no devil. He patted the palm trunk softly, and, forced at last to believe in the reality of the island, laughed delightedly again and stood on his head. He turned neatly on to his feet, jumped down to the beach, knelt and swept a double armful of sand into a pile against his chest. Then he sat back and looked at the water with bright, excited eyes.

"Ralph —"

The fat boy lowered himself over the terrace and sat down carefully, using the edge as a seat.

"I'm sorry I been such a time. Them fruit —"

He wiped his glasses and adjusted them on his button nose. The frame had made a deep, pink "V" on the bridge. He looked critically at Ralph's golden body and then down at his own clothes. He laid a hand on the end of a zipper that extended down his chest.

"My auntie —"

Then he opened the zipper with decision and pulled the whole wind-breaker over his head.

"There!"

Ralph looked at him sidelong and said nothing.

"I expect we'll want to know all their names," said the fat boy, "and make a list. We ought to have a meeting."

Ralph did not take the hint so the fat boy was forced to continue.

"I don't care what they call me," he said confidentially, "so long as they don't call me what they used to call me at school."

Ralph was faintly interested.

"What was that?"

The fat boy glanced over his shoulder, and then leaned toward Ralph.

He whispered.

"They used to call me 'Piggy.'"

Ralph shrieked with laughter. He jumped up.

"Piggy! Piggy!"

"Ralph — please!"

Piggy clasped his hands in apprehension.

"I said I didn't want —"

"Piggy! Piggy!"

Ralph danced out into the hot air of the beach and then returned as a fighter-plane, with wings swept back, and machinegunned Piggy.

"Sche-aa-ow!"

He dived in the sand at Piggy's feet and lay there laughing.

"Piggy!"

Piggy grinned reluctantly, pleased despite himself at even this much recognition.

"So long as you don't tell the others —"

Ralph giggled into the sand. The expression of pain and concentration returned to Piggy's face.

"Half a second."

He hastened back into the forest. Ralph stood up and trotted along to the right.

Here the beach was interrupted abruptly by the square motif of the landscape; a great platform of pink granite thrust up uncompromisingly through forest and terrace and sand and lagoon to make a raised jetty four feet high. The top of this was covered with a thin layer of soil and coarse grass and shaded with young palm trees. There was not enough soil for them to grow to any height and when they reached perhaps twenty feet they fell and dried, forming a criss-cross pattern of trunks, very convenient to sit on. The palms that still stood made a green roof, covered on the underside with a quivering tangle of reflections from the lagoon. Ralph hauled himself onto this platform, noted the coolness and shade, shut one eye, and decided that the shadows on his body were really green. He picked his way to the seaward edge of the platform and stood looking down into the water. It was clear to the bottom and bright with the efflorescence of tropical weed and coral. A school of tiny, glittering fish flicked hither and thither. Ralph spoke to himself, sounding the bass strings of delight.

"Whizzoh!"

Beyond the platform there was more enchantment. Some act of God — a typhoon perhaps, or the storm that had accompanied his own arrival — had banked sand inside the lagoon so that there was a long, deep pool in the beach with a high ledge of pink granite at the further end. Ralph had been deceived before now by the specious appearance of depth in a beach pool and he approached this one preparing to be disappointed. But the island ran true to form and the incredible pool, which clearly was only invaded by the sea at high tide, was so deep at one end as to be dark green. Ralph inspected the whole thirty yards carefully and then plunged in. The water was warmer than his blood and he might have been swimming in a huge bath.

Piggy appeared again, sat on the rocky ledge, and watched Ralph's green and white body enviously.

"You can't half swim."

"Piggy."

Piggy took off his shoes and socks, ranged them carefully on the ledge, and tested the water with one toe.

"It's hot!"

"What did you expect?"

"I didn't expect anything. My auntie —"

"Sucks to your auntie!"

Ralph did a surface dive and swam under water with his eyes open; the sandy edge of the pool loomed up like a hillside. He turned over, holding his nose, and a golden light danced and shattered just over his face. Piggy was looking determined and began to take off his shorts. Presently he was palely and fatly naked. He tiptoed down the sandy side of the pool, and sat there up to his neck in water smiling proudly at Ralph.

"Aren't you going to swim?"

Piggy shook his head.

"I can't swim. I wasn't allowed. My asthma —"

"Sucks to your ass-mar!"

Piggy bore this with a sort of humble patience.

"You can't half swim well."

Ralph paddled backwards down the slope, immersed his mouth and blew a jet of water into the air. Then he lifted his chin and spoke.

"I could swim when I was five. Daddy taught me. He's a commander in the Navy. When he gets leave hell come and rescue us. What's your father?"

Piggy flushed suddenly.

"My dad's dead," he said quickly, "and my mum —"

He took off his glasses and looked vainly for something with which to clean them.

"I used to live with my auntie. She kept a candy store. I used to get ever so many candies. As many as I liked. When'll your dad rescue us?"

"Soon as he can."

Piggy rose dripping from the water and stood naked, cleaning his glasses with a sock. The only sound that reached them now through the heat of the morning was the long, grinding roar of the breakers on the reef.

"How does he know we're here?"

Ralph lolled in the water. Sleep enveloped him like the swathing mirages that were wrestling with the brilliance of the lagoon.

"How does he know we're here?"

Because, thought Ralph, because, because. The roar from the reef became very distant.

"They'd tell him at the airport."

Piggy shook his head, put on his flashing glasses and looked down at Ralph.

"Not them. Didn't you hear what the pilot said? About the atom bomb? They're all dead."

Ralph pulled himself out of the water, stood facing Piggy, and considered this unusual problem.

Piggy persisted.

"This is an island, isn't it?"

"I climbed a rock," said Ralph slowly, "and I think this is an island."

"They're all dead," said Piggy, "and this is an island. Nobody don't know we're here. Your dad don't know, nobody don't know —"

His lips quivered and the spectacles were dimmed with mist.

"We may stay here till we die."

With that word the heat seemed to increase till it became a threatening weight and the lagoon attacked them with a blinding effulgence.

"Get my clothes," muttered Ralph. "Along there."

He trotted through the sand, enduring the sun's enmity, crossed the platform and found his scattered clothes. To put on a grey shirt once more was strangely pleasing. Then he climbed the edge of the platform and sat in the green shade on a convenient trunk. Piggy hauled himself up, carrying most of his clothes under his arms. Then he sat carefully on a fallen trunk near the little cliff that fronted the lagoon; and the tangled reflections quivered over him.

Presently he spoke.

"We got to find the others. We got to do something."

Ralph said nothing. Here was a coral island. Protected from the sun, ignoring Piggy's ill-omened talk, he dreamed pleasantly.

Piggy insisted.

"How many of us are there?"

Ralph came forward and stood by Piggy.

"I don't know."

Here and there, little breezes crept over the polished waters beneath the haze of heat. When these breezes reached the platform the palm fronds would whisper, so that spots of blurred sunlight slid over their bodies or moved like bright, winged things in the shade.

Piggy looked up at Ralph. All the shadows on Ralph's face were reversed; green above, bright below from the lagoon. A blur of sunlight was crawling across his hair.

"We got to do something."

Ralph looked through him. Here at last was the imagined out never fully realized place leaping into real life. Ralph's lips parted in a delighted smile and Piggy, taking this smile to himself as a mark of recognition, laughed with pleasure.

"If it really is an island —"

"What's that?"

Ralph had stopped smiling and was pointing into the lagoon. Something creamy lay among the ferny weeds.

"A stone."

"No. A shell"

Suddenly Piggy was a bubble with decorous excitement

"S'right. It's a shell! I see one like that before. On someone's back wall A conch he called it. He used to blow it and then his mum would come. It's ever so valuable —"

Near to Ralph's elbow a palm sapling leaned out over the lagoon. Indeed, the weight was already pulling a lump from the poor soil and soon it would fall. He tore out the stem and began to poke about in the water, while the brilliant fish flicked away on this side and that. Piggy leaned dangerously.

"Careful! You'll break it —"

"Shut up."

Ralph spoke absently. The shell was interesting and pretty and a worthy plaything; but the vivid phantoms of his day-dream still interposed between him and Piggy, who in this context was an irrelevance. The palm sapling, bending, pushed the shell across the weeds. Ralph used one hand as a fulcrum and pressed down with the other till the shell rose, dripping, and Piggy could make a grab.

Now the shell was no longer a thing seen but not to be touched. Ralph too became excited. Piggy babbled: "— a conch; ever so expensive. I bet if you wanted to buy one, you'd have to pay pounds and pounds and pounds — he had it on his garden wall, and my auntie —"

Ralph took the shell from Piggy and a little water ran down his arm. In color the shell was deep cream, touched here and there with fading pink. Between the point, worn away into a little hole, and the pink lips of the mouth, lay eighteen inches of shell with a slight spiral twist and covered with a delicate, embossed pattern. Ralph shook sand out of the deep tube.

"— mooed like a cow," he said. "He had some white stones too, an' a bird cage with a green parrot. He didn't blow the white stones, of course, an' he said —"

Piggy paused for breath and stroked the glistening thing that lay in Ralph's hands.

"Ralph!"

Ralph looked up.

"We can use this to call the others. Have a meeting. They'll come when they hear us —"

He beamed at Ralph.

"That was what you meant, didn't you? That's why you got the conch out of the water?"

Ralph pushed back his fair hair.

"How did your friend blow the conch?"

"He kind of spat," said Piggy. "My auntie wouldn't let me blow on account of my asthma. He said you blew from down here." Piggy laid a hand on his jutting abdomen. "You try, Ralph. You'll call the others."

Doubtfully, Ralph laid the small end of the shell against his mouth and blew. There came a rushing sound from its mouth but nothing more. Ralph wiped the salt water off his lips and tried again, but the shell remained silent.

"He kind of spat."

Ralph pursed his lips and squirted air into the shell, which emitted a low, farting noise. This amused both boys so much that Ralph went on squirting for some minutes, between bouts of laughter.

"He blew from down here."

Ralph grasped the idea and hit the shell with air from his diaphragm. Immediately the thing sounded. A deep, harsh note boomed under the palms, spread through the intricacies of the forest and echoed back from the pink granite of the mountain. Clouds of birds rose from the tree-tops, and something squealed and ran in the undergrowth.

Ralph took the shell away from his lips.

"Gosh!"

His ordinary voice sounded like a whisper after the harsh note of the conch. He laid the conch against his lips, took a deep breath and blew once more. The note Doomed again; and then at his firmer pressure, the note, fluking up an octave, became a strident blare more penetrating than before. Piggy was shouting something, his face pleased, his glasses flashing. The birds cried, and small animals scuttered. Ralph's breath failed; the note dropped the octave, became a low wubber, and was a rush of air.

The conch was silent, a gleaming tusk; Ralph's face was dark with breathlessness and the air over the island was full of beclamor and echoes ringing.

"I bet you can hear that for miles."

Ralph found his breath and blew a series of short blasts.

Piggy exclaimed: "There's one!"

A child had appeared among the palms, about a hundred yards along the beach. He was a boy of perhaps six years, sturdy and fair, his clothes torn, his face covered with a sticky mess of fruit. His trousers had been lowered for an obvious purpose and had only been pulled back half-way. He jumped off the palm terrace into the sand and his trousers fell about his ankles; he stepped out of them and trotted to the platform. Piggy helped him up. Meanwhile Ralph continued to blow till voices shouted in the forest The small boy squatted in front of Ralph, looking up brightly and vertically. As he received the reassurance of something purposeful being done he began to look satisfied, and his only clean digit, a pink thumb, slid into his mouth.

Piggy leaned down to him.

"What's yer name?"

"Johnny."

Piggy muttered the name to him and then shouted it to Ralph, who was not interested because he was still blowing. His face was dark with the violent pleasure of making this stupendous noise, and his heart was making the stretched shirt shake. The shouting in the forest was nearer.

Signs of life were visible now on the beach. The sand, trembling beneath the heat haze, concealed many figures in its miles of length; boys were making their way toward the platform through the hot, dumb sand. Three small children, no older than Johnny, appeared from startlingly dose at hand where they had been gorging fruit in the forest A dark little boy, not much younger than Piggy, parted a tangle of undergrowth, walked on to the platform, and smiled cheerfully at everybody. More and more of them came. Taking their cue from the innocent Johnny, they sat down on the fallen palm trunks and waited. Ralph continued to blow short, penetrating blasts. Piggy moved among the crowd, asking names and frowning to remember them. The children gave him the same simple obedience that they had given to the men with megaphones. Some were naked and carrying their clothes; others half-naked, or more or less dressed, in school uniforms, grey, blue, fawn, jacketed or jerseyed. There were badges, mottoes even, stripes of color in stockings and pullovers. Their heads clustered above the trunks in the green shade; heads brown, fair, black, chestnut, sandy, and mouse-colored; heads muttering, whispering, heads full of eyes that watched Ralph and speculated. Something was being done.

The children who came along the beach, singly or in twos, leapt into visibility when they crossed the line from heat haze to nearer sand. Here, the eye was first attracted to a black, bat-like creature that danced on the sand, and only later perceived the body above it. The bat was the child's shadow, shrunk by the vertical sun to a patch between the hurrying feet. Even while he blew, Ralph noticed the last pair of bodies that reached the platform above a fluttering patch of Hack. The two boys, bulletheaded and with hair like tow, flung themselves down and lay grinning and panting at Ralph like dogs. They were twins, and the eye was shocked and incredulous at such cheery duplication. They breathed together, they grinned together, and they were chunky and vital. They raised wet lips at Ralph, for they seemed provided with not quite enough skin; so that their profiles were blurred and their mouths pulled open. Piggy bent his flashing glasses to them and could be heard between the blasts, repeating their names.

"Sam, Eric, Sam, Eric."

Then he got muddled; the twins shook their heads and pointed at each other and the crowd laughed.

At last Ralph ceased to blow and sat there, the conch trailing from one hand, his head bowed on his knees. As the echoes died away so did the laughter, and there was silence.

Within the diamond haze of the beach something dark was fumbling along. Ralph saw it first and watched till the intentness of his gaze drew all eyes that way. Then the creature stepped from mirage on to clear sand, and they saw that the darkness was not all shadows but mostly clothing. The creature was a party of boys, marching approximately in step in two parallel lines and dressed in strangely eccentric clothing. Shorts, shirts, and different garments they carried in their hands; but each boy wore asquare black cap with a silver badge on it. Their bodies, from throat to ankle, were hidden by black cloaks which bore a long silver cross on the left breast and each neck was finished off with a hambone frill. The heat of the tropics, the descent, the search for food, and now this sweaty march along the blazing beach had given them the complexions of newly washed plums. The boy who controlled them was dressed in the same way though his cap badge was golden. When his party was about ten yards from the platform he shouted an order and they halted, gasping, sweating, and swaying in the fierce light. The boy himself came forward, vaulted on to the platform with his cloak flying, and peered into what to him was almost complete darkness.

"Where's the man with the trumpet?"

Ralph, sensing his sun-blindness, answered him.

"There's no man with a trumpet. Only me."

The boy came close and peered down at Ralph, screwing up his face as he did so. What he saw of the fair-haired boy with the creamy shell on his knees did not seem to satisfy him. He turned quickly, his black cloak circling.

"Isn't there a ship, then?"

Inside the floating cloak he was tall, thin, and bony: and his hair was red beneath the black cap. His face was crumpled and freckled, and ugly without silliness. Out of this face stared two light blue eyes, frustrated now, and turning, or ready to turn, to anger.

"Isn't there a man here?" Ralph spoke to his back.

"No. We're having a meeting. Come and join in."

THE BRITISH PART

The group of cloaked boys began to scatter from close line. The tall boy shouted at them.

"Choir! Stand still!"

Wearily obedient, the choir huddled into line and stood there swaying in the sun. None the less, some began to protest faintly.

"But, Merridew. Please, Merridew . . . can't we?"

Then one of the boys flopped on his face in the sand and the line broke up. They heaved the fallen boy to the platform and let him be. Merridew, his eyes staring, made the best of a bad job.

"All right then. Sit down. Let him alone."

"But Merridew."

"He's always throwing a faint," said Merridew. "He did in Gib.; and Addis; and at matins over the precentor."

This last piece of shop brought sniggers from the choir, who perched like black birds on the criss-cross trunks and examined Ralph with interest. Piggy asked no names. He was intimidated by this uniformed superiority and the offhand authority in Merridew's voice. He shrank to the other side of Ralph and busied himself with his glasses. Merridew turned to Ralph.

"Aren't there any grownups?"

"No."

Merridew sat down on a trunk and looked round the circle.

"Then well have to look after ourselves."

Secure on the other side of Ralph, Piggy spoke timidly.

"That's why Ralph made a meeting. So as we can decide what to do. We've heard names. That's Johnny. Those two — they're twins, Sam 'n Eric. Which is Eric? — You? No — you're Sam —"

"I'm Sam —"

"'n I'm Eric."

"We'd better all have names," said Ralph, "so I'm Ralph."

"We got most names," said Piggy. "Got 'em just now."

"Kidsv names," said Merridew. Why should I be Jack? I'm Merridew.

Ralph turned to him quickly. This was the voice of one who knew his own mind.

"Then," went on Piggy, "that boy — I forget —"

"You're talking too much," said Jack Merridew. "Shut up, Fatty."

Laughter arose.

"He's not Fatty," cried Ralph, "his real name's Piggy!"

"Piggy!" "Piggy!"

"Oh, Piggy!"

A storm of laughter arose and even the tiniest child joined in. For the moment the boys

163

were a closed circuit of sympathy with Piggy outside; he went very pink, bowed his head and cleaned his glasses again.

Finally the laughter died away and the naming continued. There was Maurice, next in size among the choir boys to Jack, but broad and grinning all the time. There was a slight, furtive boy whom no one knew, who kept to himself with an inner intensity of avoidance and secrecy. He muttered that his name was Roger and was silent again. Bill, Robert, Harold, Henry; the choir boy who had fainted sat up against a palm trunk, smiled pallidly at Ralph and said that his name was Simon.

Jack spoke.

"We've got to decide about being rescued."

There was a buzz. One of the small boys, Henry, said that he wanted to go home.

"Shut up," said Ralph absently. He lifted the conch. "Seems to me we ought to have a chief to decide things."

"A chief! A chief!"

"I ought to be chief," said Jack with simple arrogance, "because I'm chapter chorister and head boy. I can sing C sharp."

Another buzz.

"Well then," said Jack, "I —"

He hesitated. The dark boy, Roger, stirred at last and spoke up.

"Let's have a vote."

"Yes!"

"Vote for chief!"

"Let's vote —"

This toy of voting was almost as pleasing as the conch. Jack started to protest but the clamor changed from the general wish for a chief to an election by acclaim of Ralph himself. None of the boys could have found good reason for this; what intelligence had been shown was traceable to Piggy while the most obvious leader was Jack. But there was stillness about Ralph as he sat that marked him out; there was his size, and attractive appearance; and most obscurely, yet most powerfully, there was the conch. The being that had blown that, had sat waiting for them on the platform with the delicate thing balanced on his knees, was set apart.

"Him with the shell." "Ralph! Ralph!"

"Let him be chief with the trumpet-thing."

Ralph raised a hand for silence.

"All right. Who wants Jack for chief?"

With dreary obedience the choir raised their hands.

"Who wants me?"

Every hand outside the choir except Piggy's was raised immediately. Then Piggy, too, raised his hand grudgingly into the air.

Ralph counted. "I'm chief then." The circle of boys broke into applause. Even the choir applauded; and the freckles on Jack's face disappeared under a blush of mortification. He started up, then changed his mind and sat down again while the air rang.

Ralph looked at him, eager to offer something.

"The choir belongs to you, of course."

"They could be the army —"

"Or hunters —"

"They could be —"

The suffusion drained away from Jack's face. Ralph waved again for silence.

"Jack's in charge of the choir. They can be — what do you want them to be?"

"Hunters."

Jack and Ralph smiled at each other with shy liking. The rest began to talk eagerly.

Jack stood up.

"All right, choir. Take off your togs."

As if released from class, the choir boys stood up, chattered, piled their black cloaks on the grass. Jack laid his on the trunk by Ralph. His grey shorts were sticking to him with sweat. Ralph glanced at them admiringly, and when Jack saw his glance he explained.

"I tried to get over that hill to see if there was water all round. But your shell called us."

Ralph smiled and held up the conch for silence.

"Listen, everybody. I've got to have time to think things out I can't decide what to do straight off. If this isn't an island we might be rescued straight away. So we've got to decide if this is an island. Everybody must stay round here and wait and not go away. Three of us — if we take more we'd get all mixed, and lose each other — three of us will go on an expedition and find out. I'll go, and Jack, and, and . . . ."

He looked round the circle of eager faces. There was no lack of boys to choose from.

"And Simon."

The boys round Simon giggled, and he stood up, laughing a little. Now that the pallor of his faint was over, he was a skinny, vivid little boy, with a glance coming up from under a hut of straight hair that hung down, black and coarse.

He nodded at Ralph.

"I'll come."

"And I —"

Jack snatched from behind him a sizable sheath-knife and clouted it into a trunk. The buzz rose and died away.

Piggy stirred, "I'll come."

Ralph turned to him. "You're no good on a job like this."

"All the same —"

"We don't want you," said Jack, flatly.

"Three's enough."

Piggy's glasses flashed.

"I was with him when he found the conch. I was with him before anyone else was."

Jack and the others paid no attention. There was a general dispersal. Ralph, Jack and Simon jumped off the platform and walked along the sand past the bathing pool. Piggy hung bumbling behind them.

"If Simon walks in the middle of us," said Ralph, "then we could talk over his head."

The three of them fell into step. This meant that every now and then Simon had to do a double shuffle to eaten up with the others. Presently Ralph stopped and turned back to Piggy.

"Look."

Jack and Simon pretended to notice nothing. They walked on.

"You can't come."

Piggy's glasses were misted again — this time with humiliation.

"You told 'em. After what I said."

His face flushed, his mouth trembled. "After I said I didn't want —"

"What on earth are you talking about?"

"About being called Piggy. I said I didn't care as long as they didn't call me Piggy; and I said not to tell and then you went an' said straight out —"

Stillness descended on them. Ralph, looking with more understanding at Piggy, saw that he was hurt and crushed. He hovered between the two courses of apology or further insult.

"Better Piggy than Fatty," he said at last, with the directness of genuine leadership, "and anyway, I'm sorry if you feel like that. Now go back, Piggy, and take names. That's your job. So long."

He turned and raced after the other two. Piggy stood and the rose of indignation faded slowly from his cheeks. He went back to the platform.

Chapter 18 Doris Lessing

作者简介

Doris Lessing (22 October, 1919 – 17 November, 2013) was a well-known British novelist, poet, playwright, librettist, biographer and short story writer. She first sold stories to magazines at the age of 15, in South Africa. Her first novel, *The Grass is Singing*, was published in 1950. And her breakthrough work, *The Golden Notebook*, was written in 1962. By the time of her death, more than 50 of her novels had been published. Her novels include *The Grass is Singing* (1950), the sequence of five novels collectively called *Children of Violence* (1952 – 69), *Big Women* (1999), *The Good Terrorist* (1985), and five novels collectively known as *Canopus in Argos*, etc. During the late 1990s, Lessing suffered a mini-stroke which stopped her from traveling during her later years. She was still able to attend the theatre and opera. She began to focus her mind on death, for example, asking herself if she would have time to finish a new book. She died on 17 November, 2013, aged 94, at her home in London, predeceased by her two sons, but survived by her daughter, Jean, who lives in South Africa. In 2001, Lessing was awarded the David Cohen Prize for a lifetime's great achievement in British literature. Lessing was also awarded the 2007 Nobel Prize in Literature. In awarding the prize, the Swedish Academy described her as "that epicist of the female experience, who with Scepticism, Fire and Visionary power has subjected a divided civilization to scrutiny." Lessing was the eleventh woman and the oldest person ever to receive the Nobel Prize in Literature. In 2008, *The Times* ranked her fifth on a list of the 50 greatest British writers since 1945. A number of girls and women who read her works have regarded her as their ideal expecting to become excellent like her.

多丽丝·莱辛(1919年10月22日—2013年11月17日)是一位众所周知的英国小说家、诗人、剧作家、歌词作者、生物学家以及短篇小说作家。在南非时,15岁的她首次把小说卖给了杂志社。她的第一部小说《青草在唱歌》于1950年出版。而她的代表作《金色笔记》创作于1962年。她一生一共出版了五十多部小说,包括《青草在唱歌》(1950),五部曲《暴力的孩子们》(1952—1969),《大女人》(1999),《好恐怖分子》(1985),《南船座中的老人星座》等等。在 20 世纪 90 年代期间,莱辛患上了小中风,这阻止了她晚年的旅行。但她仍能够坚持去电影院和剧院。她开始把心思放在死亡这件事上,比如,自己问自己是否还有时间去完成一部新书。她于 2013 年 11 月 17 日逝世在伦敦家中,享年 94 岁,死在她的两个儿子之后,但她现居南非的女儿仍然在世。2001 年,由于她在英国文学终身做出的巨大成就,莱辛被授予大卫科恩奖。2007 年又被授予诺贝尔文学家。颁奖的时候,瑞典皇家科学院把她称为"女性中的史诗作家,凭借怀疑精神,热情和无穷的想象力使一种分离的文明服从于仔细审查"。她是第 11 个且是迄今为止最年长的女性诺贝尔获奖者。2008 年,《时代》杂志把她列为自 1945 年以来 50 位最伟大的英国作家名单中的第五名。许多读过她的作品的女孩和妇女都把她当作她们的偶像,希望成为像她那样优秀的人。

作品及导读

作 品 1

A Woman on a Roof

导 读

A Woman on a Roof is one of the most famous works of Doris Lessing. The story happened in London where a woman wore a red scarf tied around her breasts and brief red bikini pants on the roof to have a sunbath. And three men on the roof were seduced. They tried any method to draw the woman's attention, but the woman responded indifferently and coldly, which made the three men very angry and anguished. This anger and agony come from a deep desire of control to women when it suffers the destruction of "the refusal from the roof woman. "Eternal woman" literally satisfies the men's desire of control, such as possession, conquest, reign, etc. In the texture, the desire of control exists in men's charm to fascinate women. The novel uses the common words to describe the life of common people, to reflect their common behavior and to express their common interest in beautiful woman. In the texture, three men are indeed tempted by this stuning roof woman, only the whistle appearing 7 times in the texture, especially from Stanley. His whistle or yells or stamping or swearing never gains the active response from the woman. The Woman's remote and cool eyesight injury his self-esteem that he was confident at his appearance and assured no woman could resist his charm. His irritation reveals that under the condition of male worship and social preference, men's proper pride increases rapidly. In this sense, they take it for granted that they can handle all the situations. But the surrounding has changed. Women said NO. When refused by the roof woman, he turned to flirt with Mrs. Pritchett who helped him recovered his pride again. Then look at Harry, an old man, always smiled tolerantly to Stanley as if he experienced the same case. His indulgence shows his dread about the pass of youth, uncontrollable present and uncertain future.

《屋顶丽人》是多丽丝·莱辛一部比较有名的作品。作品中的故事发生在伦敦,一个女人在屋顶晒日光浴,引起3个附近修房工人的注意。他们想方设法要与她搭讪,但无论吹口哨、跺脚、谩骂,她都置之不理,无动于衷,并且显得很冷漠。这使得3个男人都很生气。这种生气使得男人更想控制女人,尤其是当他们遭到女人的拒绝。永恒的女人满足了男人这种控制欲望,比如,拥有、征服、得到等等。在这篇小说中,男性的控制欲就是想去吸引女性。小说用了很平实的语言讲了普通人的共同反应,他们都会对美女产生极大兴趣。在故事中,3个男人都深深地被屋顶上拥有健康肤色的女人所吸引,仅仅口哨都吹了7次,尤其是斯坦利。他吹口哨、喊叫、跺脚或者咒骂都没引起那个女人的任何注意。他本来对自己的外表是很自信的,他觉得没人能抵制他的魅力,但是那个屋顶女性的冷酷眼神却深深地伤了他的自尊。他的恼怒反映了在男性主义下,男人的骄傲在逐渐上升。在这种情形下,他们理所当然地认为他们能够处理所有的事,但是事实已经改变了,女性敢于说不。当遭到屋顶丽人拒绝后,他又转向普利切特太太,这给他挽回了自尊。再看看那个老男人哈利,总是深有同感似的对着斯坦利傻笑。斯坦利的沉迷显示了他对青春的逝去、难以控制的现状和无法确定的未来的一种恐惧。

选 文

It was during the week of hot sun, that June.

Three men were at work on the roof, where the leads got so hot they had the idea of throwing water on to cool them. But the water steamed, then sizzled; and they make jokes about getting an egg from some woman in the flats under the flats under them, to poach it for their dinner. By two it was not possible to touch the guttering they were replacing, and they speculated about what workmen did in regularly hot countries. Perhaps they should borrow kitchen gloves with the egg? They were all a bit dizzy, not used to the heat; and they shed their coats and stood side by side squeezing themselves into a foot wide patch of shade against a chimney, careful to keep their feet in the thick socks and boots out of the sun. There was a fine view across several acres of roofs. Not far off a man sat in a deck chair reading the newspapers. Then they saw her, between chimneys, about fifty yards away. She lay face down on a brown blanket. They could see the top part of her: black hair, a flushed solid back, arms spread out.

"She's stark naked," said Stanley, sounding annoyed.

Harry, the oldest, a man of about forty-five, said: "Looks like it."

Young Tom, seventeen, said nothing, but he was excited and grinning.

Stanley said: "Someone will report her if she doesn't watch out."

"She thinks no one can see," said Tom, craning his head all ways to see more.

At this point the woman, still lying prone, brought her two hands up behind her shoulders with the ends of a scarf in them, tied it behind her back, and sat up. She wore a red scarf tied around her breasts and brief red bikini pants. This being the first day of the sun she was white, flushing red. She sat smoking, and did not look up when Stanley let out a wolf whistle. Harry said: "Small things amuse small minds," leading the way back to their part of the roof, but it was scorching. Harry said: "Wait, I'm going to rig up some shade," and disappeared down the skylight into the building. Now that he'd gone, Stanley and Tom went to the farthest point they could to peer at the woman. She had moved, and all they could see were two pink legs stretched on the blanket. They whistled and shouted but the legs did not move. Harry came back with a blanket and shouted: "Come on, then." He sounded irritated with them. They clambered back to him and he said to Stanley: "What about your missus?" Stanley was newly married, about three months. Stanley said, jeering: "What about my missus?" — preserving his independence. Tom said nothing, but his mind was full of the nearly naked woman. Harry slung the blanket, which he had borrowed from a friendly woman downstairs, from the stem of a television aerial to a row of chimney-pots. This shade fell across the piece of gutter they had to replace. But the shade kept moving, they had to adjust the blanket, and not much progress was made. At last some of the heat left the roof, and they worked fast, making up for lost time. First Stanley, then Tom, made a trip to the end of the roof to see the woman. "She's on her back," Stanley said, adding a jest which made Tom snicker, and the older man smile tolerantly. Tom's report was that she hadn't moved, but it was a lie. He wanted to keep what he had seen to himself: he had caught her in the act of rolling down the little red pants over her hips, till they were no more than a small triangle. She was on her back, fully visible, glistening with oil.

Next morning, as soon as they came up, they went to look. She was already there, face down, arms spread out, naked except for the little red pants. She had turned brown in the night. Yesterday she was a scarlet-and-white woman, today she was a brown woman. Stanley let out a whistle. She lifted her head, startled, as if she'd been asleep, and looked straight over at them. The sun was in her eyes, she blinked and stared, then she dropped her head again. At this gesture of indifference, they all three, Stanley, Tom and old Harry, let out whistles and yells. Harry was doing it in parody of the younger men, making fun of them, but he was also angry. They were all angry because of her utter indifference to the three men watching her.

"Bitch," said Stanley.

"She should ask us over," said Tom, snickering.

Harry recovered himself and reminded Stanley: "If she's married, her old man wouldn't like that."

"Christ," said Stanley virtuously, "if my wife lay about like that, for everyone to see, I'd soon stop her."

Harry said, smiling: "How do you know, perhaps she's sunning herself at this very moment?"

"Not a chance, not on our roof." The safety of his wife put Stanley into a good humor, and they went to work. But today it was hotter than yesterday; and several times one or the other suggested they should tell Matthew, the foreman, and ask to leave the roof until the heat wave was over. But they didn't. There was work to be done in the basement of the big block of flats, but up here they felt free, on a different level from ordinary humanity shut in the streets or the buildings. A lot more people came out on to the roofs that day, for an hour at midday. Some married couples sat side by side in deck chairs, the women's legs stocking less and scarlet, the men in vests with reddening shoulders.

The woman stayed on her blanket, turning herself over and over. She ignored them, no matter what they did. When Harry went off to fetch more screws, Stanley said: "Come on." Her roof belonged to a different system of roofs, separated from theirs at one point by about twenty feet. It meant a scrambling climb from one level to another, edging along parapets, clinging to chimneys, while their big boots slipped and hared slithered, but at last they stood on a small square projecting roof looking straight down at her, close. She sat smoking, reading a book. Tom thought she looked like a poster, or a magazine cover, with the blue sky behind her and her legs stretched out. Behind her a great crane at work on a new building in Oxford Street swung its black arm across roofs in a great arc. Tom imagined himself at work on the crane, adjusting the arm to swing over and pick her up and swing her back across the sky to drop her near him.

They whistled. She looked up at them, cool and remote, then went on reading. Again, they were furious. Or, rather, Stanley was. His sun-heated face was screwed into a rage as he whistled again and again, trying to make her look up. Young Tom stopped whistling. He stood beside Stanley, excited, grinning; but he felt as if he were saying to the woman: Don't associate me with him, for his grin was apologetic. Last night he had thought of the unknown woman before he slept, and she had been tender with him. This tenderness he was remembering as he shifted his feet by the jeering, whistling Stanley, and watched the indifferent, healthy brown woman a few feet off, with the gap that plunged to the street between them. Tom thought it was romantic, it was like being high on two hilltops. But there was a shout from Harry, and they clambered back. Stanley's face was hard, really angry. The boy kept looking at him and wondered why he hated the woman so much, for by now he loved her.

They played their little games with the blanket, trying to trap shade to work under; but again it was not until nearly four that they could work seriously, and they were exhausted, all three of them. They were grumbling about the weather by now. Stanley was in a thoroughly bad humor. When they made their routine trip to see the woman before they packed up for the day, she was apparently asleep, face down, her back all naked save for the scarlet triangle on her buttocks. "I've got a good mind to report her to the police," said Stanley, and Harry said: "What's eating you? What harm's she doing?"

"I tell you, if she was my wife!"

"But she isn't, is she?" Tom knew that Harry, like himself, was uneasy at Stanley's reaction. He was normally a sharp young man, quick at his work, making a lot of jokes, good company.

"Perhaps it will be cooler tomorrow," said Harry.

"But it wasn't; it was hotter, if anything, and the weather forecast said the good weather would last. As soon as they were on the roof, Harry went over to see if the woman was there, and Tom knew it was to prevent Stanley going, to put off his bad humor. Harry had grownup children, a boy the same age as Tom, and the youth trusted and looked up to him.

Harry came back and said: "She's not there."

"I bet her old man has put his foot down," said Stanley, and Harry and Tom caught each other's eyes and smiled behind the young married man's back.

Harry suggested they should get permission to work in the basement, and they did, that day. But before packing up Stanley said: "Let's have a breath of fresh air." Again Harry and Tom smiled at each other as they followed Stanley up to the roof, Tom in the devout conviction that he was there to protect the woman from Stanley. It was about five-thirty, and a calm, full sunlight lay over the roofs. The great crane still swung its black arm from Oxford Street to above their heads. She was not there. Then there was a flutter of white from behind a parapet, and she stood up, in a belted, white dressing-gown. She had been there all day, probably, but on a different patch of roof, to hide from them. Stanley did not whistle; he said nothing, but watched the woman bend to collect papers, books, cigarettes, then fold the blanket over her arm. Tom was thinking: If they weren't here, I'd go over and say ... What? But he knew from his nightly dreams of her that she was kind and friendly. Perhaps she would ask him down to her flat? Perhaps ... He stood watching her disappear down the skylight. As she went, Stanley let out a shrill derisive yell; she started, and it seemed as if she nearly fell. She clutched to save herself, they could hear things falling. She looked straight at them, angry. Harry said, facetiously : "Better be careful on those slippery ladders, love." Tom knew he said it to save her from Stanley, but she could not know it. She vanished, frowning. Tom was full of a secret delight, because he knew her anger was for the others, not for him.

"Roll on some rain," said Stanley, bitter, looking at the blue evening sky.

Next day was cloudless, and they decided to finish the work in the basement. They felt excluded, shut in the grey cement basement fitting pipes, from the holiday atmosphere of London in a heat wave. At lunchtime they came up for some air, but while the married couples, and the men in shirt-sleeves or vests, were there, she was not there, either on her usual patch of roof or where she had been yesterday. They all, even Harry, clambered about, between chimney-pots, over parapets, the hot leads stinging their fingers. There was not a sign of her. They took off their shirts and vests and exposed their chests, feeling their feet sweaty and hot. They did not mention the woman. But Tom felt alone again. Last night she had him into her flat; it was big and had fitted white carpets and a bed with a padded white leather head-board. She wore a black filmy negligee and her kindness to Tom thickened his throat as he remembered it. He felt she had betrayed him by not being there.

And again after work they climbed up, but still there was nothing to be seen of her. Stanley kept repeating that if it was as hot as this tomorrow he wasn't going to work and that's all there was to it. But they were all there next day. By ten the temperature was in the middle seventies, and it was eighty long before noon. Harry went to the foreman to say it was impossible to work on the leads in that heat; but the foreman said there was nothing else he could put them on, and they'd have to. At midday they stood, silent, watching the skylight on her roof open, and then she slowly emerged in her white gown, holding a bundle of blanket. She looked at them, gravely, then went to the part of the roof where she was hidden from them. Tom was pleased. He felt she was more his when the other men couldn't see her. They had taken off their shirts and vests, but now they put them back again, for they felt the sun bruising their flesh. "She must have the hide of a rhino," said Stanley, tugging at guttering and swearing. They stopped work, and sat in the shade, moving around behind chimney stacks. A woman came to water a yellow window box opposite them. She was middle-aged, wearing a flowered summer dress. Stanley said to her: "We need a drink more than them." She smiled and said: "Better drop down to the pub quick, it'll be closing in a minute." They exchanged pleasantries, and she left them with a smile and a wave.

"Not like Lady Godiva," said Stanley. " She can give us a bit of a chat and a smile. "

"You didn't whistle at her," said Tom, reproving.

"Listen to him," said Stanley, "you didn't whistle, then?"

But the boy felt as if he hadn't whistled, as if only Harry and Stanley had. He was making plans, when it was time to knock off work, to get left behind and somehow make his way over to the woman. The weather report said the hot spell was due to break, so he had to move quickly. But there was no chance of being left. The other two decided to knock off work at four, because they were exhausted. As they went down, Tom quickly climbed a parapet and hoisted himself higher by pulling his weight up a chimney. He caught a glimpse of her lying on her back, her knees up, eyes closed, a brown woman lolling in the sun. He slipped and clattered down, as Stanley looked for information: "She's gone down," he said. He felt as if he had protected her from Stanley, and that she must be grateful to him. He could feel the bond between the woman and himself.

Next day, they stood around on the landing below the roof, reluctant to climb up into the heat. The woman who had lent Harry the blanket came out and offered them a cup of tea. They accepted gratefully, and sat around Mrs. Pritchett's kitchen an hour or so, chatting. She was married to an airline pilot. A smart blonde, of about thirty, she had an eye for the handsome sharp-faced Stanley; and the two teased each other while Harry sat in a corner, watching, indulgent, though his expression reminded Stanley that he was married. And young Tom felt envious of Stanley's ease in badinage; felt, too, that Stanley's getting off with Mrs. Pritchett left his romance with the woman on the roof safe and intact.

"I thought they said the heat waved break," said Stanley, sullen, as the time approached when they really would have to climb up into the sunlight.

"You don't like it, then?" Mrs. Pritchett asked.

"All right for some," said Stanley. "Nothing to do but lie about it was as if a beach up there. Do you ever go up?"

"Went up once," said Mrs. Pritchett. "But it's a dirty place up there, and it's too hot."

"Quite right too," said Stanley.

Then they went up, leaving the cool neat little flat and the friendly Mrs. Pritchett. As soon as they were up they saw her. The three men looked at her, resentful at her ease in this punishing sun. Then Harry said, because of the expression on Stanley's face: "Come on, we've got to pretend to work, at least."

They had to wrench another length of guttering that ran beside a parapet out of its bed, so that they could replace it. Stanley took it in his two hands, tugged, swore, stood up. "Fuck it," he said, and sat down under a chimney. He lit a cigarette. "Fuck them," he said. "What do they think we are, lizards? I've got blisters all over my hands." Then he jumped up and climbed over the roofs and stood with his back to them. He put his fingers either side of his mouth and let out a shrill whistle. Tom and Harry squatted, not looking at each other, watching him. They could just see the woman's head, the beginnings of her brown shoulders. Stanley whistled again. Then he began stamping with his feet, and whistled and yelled and screamed at the woman, his face getting scarlet. He seemed quite mad, as he stamped and whistled, while the woman did not move, she did not move a muscle.

"Barmy," said Tom.

"Yes," said Harry, disapproving.

Suddenly the older man came to a decision. It was, Tom knew, to save some sort of scandal or real trouble over the woman. Harry stood up and began packing tools into a length of oily cloth. "Stanley," he said, commanding. At first Stanley took no notice, but Harry said: "Stanley, we're packing it in, I'll tell Matthew."

Stanley came back, cheeks mottled, eyes glaring.

"Can't go on like this," said Harry. "It'll break in a day or so. I'm going to tell Matthew we've got sunstroke, and if he doesn't like it, it's too bad." Even Harry sounded aggrieved, Tom noted. The small, competent man, the family man with his grey hair, who was never at a loss, sounded really off balance. "Come on," he said, angry. He fitted himself into the open square in the roof, and went down, watching his feet on the ladder. Then Stanley went, with not a glance at the woman. Then Tom, who, his throat beating with excitement, silently promised her on a backward glance: Wait for me, wait, I'm coming.

On the pavement Stanley said: "I'm going home." He looked white now, so perhaps he really did have sunstroke. Harry went off to find the foreman, who was at work on the plumbing of some flats down the street. Tom slipped back, not into the building they had been working on, but the building on whose roof the woman lay. He went straight up, no one stopping him. The skylight stood open, with an iron ladder leading up. He emerged on to the roof a couple of yards from her. She sat up, pushing back hair with both hands. The scarf across her breasts bound them tight, and brown flesh bulged around it. Her legs were brown and smooth. She stared at him in silence. The boy stood grinning, foolish, claiming the tenderness he expected from her.

"What do you want?" she asked.

"I ... I came to ... make your acquaintance," he stammered, grinning, pleading with her.

They looked at each other, the slight, scarlet-faced excited boy, and the serious, nearly naked woman. Then, without a word, she lay down on her brown blanket, ignoring him.

"You like the sun, do you?" he enquired of her glistening back.

Not a word. He felt panic, thinking of how she had held him in her arms, stroked his hair, brought him where he sat, lordly, in her bed, a glass of some exhilarating liquor he had never tasted in life. He felt that if he knelt down, stroked her shoulders, her hair, she would turn and clasp him in her arms.

He said: "The sun's all right for you, isn't it?"

She raised her head, set her chin on two small fists, "Go away," she said. He did not move. "Listen," she said, in a slow reasonable voice, where anger was kept in check, though with difficulty; looking at him, her face weary with anger, "if you get a kick out of seeing women in bikinis, why don't you take a sixpenny bus ride to the Lido? You'd see dozens of them, without all this mountaineering."

She hadn't understood him. He felt her unfairness pale him. He stammered: "But I like you, I've been watching you and ..."

"Thanks," she said, and dropped her face again, turned away from him.

She lay there. He stood there. She said nothing. She had simply shut him out. He stood, saying nothing at all, for some minutes. He thought: She'll have to say something if I stay. But the minutes went past, with no sign of them in her, except in the tension of her back, her thighs, her arms — the tension of waiting for him to go.

He looked up at the sky, where the sun seemed to spin in heat; and over the roofs where he and his mates had been earlier. He could see the heat quivering where they had worked. And they expect us to work in these conditions! he thought, filled with righteous indignation. The woman hadn't moved. A bit of hot wind blew her black hair softly; it shone, and was iridescent. He remembered how he had stroked it last night.

Resentment of her at last moved him off and away down the ladder, through the building, into the street. He got drunk then, in hatred of her.

Next day when he woke the sky was grey. He looked at the wet grey and thought, vicious: Well, that's fixed you, hasn't it now? That's fixed you good and proper.

The three men were at work early on the cool leads, surrounded by damp drizzling roofs where no one came to sun themselves, black roofs, slimy with rain. Because it was cool now, they would finish the job that day, if they hurried.

19 Vidiadhar Surajprasad Naipaul

作者简介

V. S. Naipaul, considered as the leading novelist of the English-speaking Caribbean, won the Nobel Prize in literature 2001. Naipaul's writings dealt with the cultural confusion of the Third World and the problem of an outsider, a feature of his own experience as an Indian in the West Indies, a West Indian in England, and a nomadic intellectual in a postcolonial world. Naipaul has also arisen much controversy because of his politically incorrect views of the "half-made societies". He has constantly refused to avoid unwelcome topics, characterizing his role as a writer "to look and to look again, to re-look and rethink".

V. S. Naipaul was born in a small town in Trinidad into a family of Indian Brahmin origin. His father, Seepersad Naipaul, was a correspondent for the *Trinidad Guardian*. He also published short stories. When Naipaul was six, the family moved to Port of Spain, the capital. Seepersad Naipaul died of a heart attack in 1953 without witnessing the success of his son as a writer. He had encouraged Naipaul in his writing aspirations, telling him in a letter: "Don't be scared of being an artist. D. H. Lawrence was an artist through and through; and, for the time being at any rate, you should think as Lawrence. Remember what he used to say, 'Art for my sake'." At the age of 18 he had written his first novel which was rejected by the publisher.

Naipaul was educated at Queen's Royal College, Port of Spain, and in 1950 he won a scholarship to Oxford. In 1949, after having some pictures of himself taken for his application to the university, Naipaul wrote to his elder sister: "I never knew my face was fat. The picture said so. I looked at the Asiatic on the paper and thought that an Indian from India could look no more Indian than I did... I had hoped to send up a striking intellectual pose to the University people, but look what they have got." After a nervous breakdown he tried to commit suicide, but luckily the gas meter ran out.

While at Oxford he met Patricia Hale; they married in 1955. She died in 1996 and Naipaul married Nadira Alvi, a divorced Pakistani journalist.

Naipaul started his career as a freelance writer after graduation. During this period Naipaul felt himself rootless, but found his voice as a writer in the mid-1950s, when he started to examine his own Trinidadian background. From 1954 to 1956 Naipaul was a broadcaster for the BBC's Caribbean Voices, and between the years 1957 and 1961 he was a regular fiction reviewer for the *New Statesman*.

维·苏·奈保尔是加勒比英语区最重要的小说家,也是2001年诺贝尔文学奖的获得者。奈保尔的作品一半涉及第三世界国家的文化混乱问题以及他作为一个生活在西方国家的印度局外人的问题,除此以外,还涉及后殖民地时期流浪的知识分子问题。奈保尔也引起了很多争议,政治上,他信奉错误的"半成品社会"观点。他一直拒绝和避免不受欢迎的话题,描述他作为一个作家的角色,反复检查,反复思考。维·苏·奈保尔(1932—)年生于中美洲的特立尼达和多巴哥的一个印度婆罗门家庭。他的父亲,西帕瑟德·奈保尔,是《特立尼达卫报》的记者,他还发表短篇小说。当奈保尔六岁时,全家搬到西班牙港。西帕瑟德·奈保尔,1953年死于心脏病发作,他没有看到他的儿子作为一个作家的成功。奈保尔的父亲鼓励奈保尔,在信中告诉他:"不要害怕成为一个艺术家。劳伦斯是一个彻头彻尾的艺术家;而且,目前无论如何,你应该像劳伦斯一样思考。记得他曾说过,"艺术为我"。18岁时,奈保尔写了他的第一部小说但被出版商拒绝了。

奈保尔曾在西班牙港皇家女王学院受过教育。1950年,他获得奖学金到牛津。1949年,申请大学的时候他拍了几张照片,奈保尔写信给他的姐姐:"我从来不知道我的脸很胖,但这些照片说明了这一点。我看着纸上的亚洲人,想到,一个来自印度的印度人比我看上去更像一个印度人。"他试图自杀,但幸运的是,气表泄露。在牛津时他遇到了帕特里夏·黑尔,他们于1955年结婚,她死于1996年。奈保尔又与一个离婚的巴基斯坦记者结婚。

毕业后,奈保尔开始他作为一个自由撰稿人的职业生涯。在此期间,奈保尔感到自己无所寄托,但当他开始审视自己在特立尼达的经历时,又寻找到了自己作为20世纪50年代文坛一名作家的声音。从1954年到1956年,奈保尔是英国广播公司的一名播音员,1957年和1961年之间,他是《新政治家》的一名常驻小说评论员。

THE BRITISH PART

作品及导读

作品 1

A Bend in the River

导 读

Salim, the narrator of *A Bend in the River*, is a young man from an Indian family of traders long resident on the coast of Central Africa, perhaps in what is now known as Zaire. The young man's placement in the world is part of the dramatic structure and vision of the novel.

"Africa was my home, had been the home of my family for centuries. But we came from the east coast and that made a difference. The coast was not truly Africa. It was an Arab-Indian-Persian-Portuguese place, and we who lived there were really people of the Indian Ocean." At the first chapter of the novel, Salim has left the coast to make his way in the interior, there to take on a small trading shop of this and that, Sundries, sold to the natives. The place is "a bend in the river"; it is Africa. There are other Indian families in the town, but the displacement of Salim is to some degree a part of the displacement of the country.

The time of Salim is post-colonial, the time of Independence. The Europeans have withdrawn or been forced to withdraw, and the scene is one of chaos, violent change, warring tribes, ignorance, isolation, poverty, and a lack of preparation for the modern world they have entered, or partially assumed as a sort of decoration. The blind assurance of the colonial administration, with its rules, its commercial exploitation of the available resources, its avenues and handsome houses and clubs for the pleasure of the foreign settlers, has given way to the blinding conflagrations in so many of the newly independent states. Here the power is currently in the hands of the President, a tribal warrior threatened by the ambitions of other warriors of other tribes. But in reality, the town that Salim entered is dirty and poor. After countless wars, the bend has been destroyed totally, where buildings become ruins, and rubbish is everywhere. Zabeth is his fomilar customer. She has lived well at this place because she knows how to cover up herself. The bad smell from her is her mask. Only in this way can she lives well at the place where people are livedpoor.

《河湾》的主人公——年轻的萨林姆——来自于印度一个经商家庭,长期居住在非洲中部的海岸,大概在现在的扎伊尔地区。这个年轻人所处的位置是小说戏剧结构和布局的一部分。

"非洲是我的家,我的家人的家,但是我们来自东海岸,这让我们与别人不同。东海岸并不是真正的非洲,它是阿拉伯人、印度人、波斯人以及葡萄牙人的地方,我们这些住在那里的人才

179

是真正来自印度洋。"小说第一章中提到,萨林姆离开了海岸去内地发展,他从那扎努丁手中低价得到一个小店。这个地方是河湾,是真正的非洲。在这个小镇上还有其他的印度家庭,但是萨林姆的游离失所在某种程度上可以说是整个国家一部分的游离失所。

斯林姆游离失所的时间是后殖民,即独立的时期。欧洲人已经撤退或是被强迫撤退,现场一片混乱,暴力改变、敌对部落、无知、隔离、贫穷以及他们缺乏进入现代世界的准备,或者被称作一种装饰。殖民政府的盲目保证炫目地爆发在许多新的独立国家中,包括它的法规、商业可利用资源、漂亮的房子俱乐部以及外国移民者的快乐,但是现实中萨林姆进入的小镇却是一个脏乱、贫穷的地方。经过战乱的洗劫,这个河湾小镇已经面目全非。他的小店坐落于赃乱环境中,扎贝思是他的常客。这个被称为女魔法师的非洲健壮女人用难闻的气味掩饰自己,也许只有这样才能在那片大陆上生存下去。

选 文

A Bend in the River
(Chapter 1)

The world is what it is; men who are nothing, who allow themselves to become nothing, have no place in it.

Nazruddin, who had sold me the shop cheap, didn't think I would have it easy when I took over. The country, like others in Africa, had had its troubles after independence. The town in the interior, at the bend in the great river, had almost ceased to exist; and Nazruddin said I would have to start from the beginning.

I drove up from the coast in my Peugeot. That isn't the kind of drive you can do nowadays in Africa — from the east coast right through to the centre. Too many of the places on the way have closed down or are full of blood. And even at that time, when the roads were more or less open, the drive took me over a week.

It wasn't only the sand drifts and the mud and the narrow, winding, broken roads up in the mountains. There was all that business at the frontier posts, all that haggling in the forest outside wooden huts that flew strange flags. I had to talk myself and my Peugeot past the men with guns — just to drive through bush and more bush. And then I had to talk even harder, and shed a few more bank notes and give away more of my tinned food, to get myself — and the Peugeot — out of the places I had talked us into.

Some of these palavers could take half a day. The top man would ask for something quite ridiculous — two or three thousand dollars. I would say no. He would go into his hut, as though there was nothing more to say; I would hang around outside, because there was nothing else for me to do. Then after an hour or two I would go inside the hut, or he would come outside, and we would settle for two or three dollars. It was as Nazruddin had said when I asked him about visas and he had said that bank notes were better. "You can always get into those places. What is hard is to get out. That is a private fight. Everybody has to find his own way." As I got deeper into Africa — the scrub, the desert, the rocky climb up to the mountains, the lakes, the rain in the afternoons, the mud, and then, on the other, wetter side of the mountains, the fern forests and the gorilla forests — as I got deeper I thought: But this is madness. I am going in the wrong direction. There can't be a new life at the end of this.

But I drove on. Each day's drive was like an achievement; each day's achievement made it harder for me to turn back. And I couldn't help thinking that that was how it was in the old days with the slaves. They had made the same journey, but of course on foot and in the opposite direction, from the centre of the continent to the east coast. The further away they got from the centre and their tribal area, the less likely they were to cut loose from the caravans and run back home, the more nervous they became of the strange Africans they saw about them, until at the end, on the coast, they were no trouble at all, and were positively anxious to step into the boats and be taken to safe homes across the sea. Like the slave far from home, I became anxious only to arrive.

The greater the discouragements of the journey, the keener I was to press on and embrace my new life.

When I arrived I found that Nazruddin hadn't lied. The place had had its troubles: the town at the bend in the river was more than half destroyed. What had been the European suburb near the rapids had been burnt down, and bush had grown over the ruins; it was hard to distinguish what had been gardens from what had been streets. The official and commercial area near the dock and customs house survived, and some residential streets in the centre. But there wasn't much else.

Even the African cités were inhabited only in corners, and in decay elsewhere, with many of the low, box-like concrete houses in pale blue or pale green abandoned, hung with quick-growing,

quick-dying tropical vines, mattings of brown and green.

Nazruddin's shop was in a market square in the commercial area. It smelt of rats and was fall of dung, but it was intact. I had bought Nazruddin's stock — but there was none of that. I had also bought the goodwill — but that was meaningless, because so many of the Africans had gone back to the bush, to the safety of their villages, which lay up hidden and difficult creeks.

After my anxiety to arrive, there was little for me to do. But I was not alone. There were other traders, other foreigners; some of them had been there right through the troubles. I waited with them. The peace held. People began coming back to the town; the cite yards filled up. People began needing the goods which we could supply. And slowly business started up again.

Zabeth was among the earliest of my regular customers. She was a marchande — not a market woman, but a retailer in a small way. She belonged to a fishing community, almost a little tribe, and every month or so she came from her village to the town to buy her goods wholesale.

From me she bought pencils and copybooks, razor blades, syringes, soap and toothpaste and toothbrushes, cloth, plastic toys, iron pots and aluminum pans, enamel plates and basins. These were some of the simple things Zabeth's fisherfolk needed from the outside world, and had been doing without during the troubles. Not essentials, not luxuries; but things that made ordinary life easier. The people here had many skills; they could get by on their own. They tanned leather, wove cloth, worked iron; they hollowed out large tree trunks into boats and smaller ones into kitchen mortars. But to people looking for a large vessel that wouldn't taint water and food, and wouldn't leak, imagine what a blessing an enamel basin was!

Zabeth knew exactly what the people of her village needed and how much they would be able or willing to pay for it. Traders on the coast (including my own father) used to say — especiallywhen they were consoling themselves for some bad purchase — that everything eventually had its buyer. That wasn't so here. People were interested in new things — like the syringes, which were a surprise to me — and even modern things; but their tastes had set around the first examples of these things that they had accepted. They trusted a particular design, a particular trademark. It was useless for me to try to "sell" anything to Zabeth; I had to stick as far as possible to familiar stock. It made for dull business, but it avoided complications. And it helped to make Zabeth the good and direct businesswoman that, unusually for an African, she was.

She didn't know how to read and write. She carried her complicated shopping list in her head and she remembered what she had paid for things on previous occasions. She never asked for credit — she hated the idea. She paid in cash, taking the money out from the vanity case she brought to town with her. Every trader knew about Zabeth's vanity case. It wasn't that she distrusted banks; she didn't understand them.

I would say to her, in that mixed river language we used, "One day, Beth, somebody will snatch your case. It isn't safe to travel about with money like that."

"The day that happens, Mis' Salim, I will know the time has come to stay home."

It was a strange way of thinking. But she was a strange woman. "Mis'," as used by Zabeth and others, was short for "mister." I was mister because I was a foreigner, someone from the far-off coast, and an English-speaker; and I was mister in order to be distinguished from the other resident foreigners, who were monsieur. That was, of course, before the Big Man came along and made us all citoyens and citoyennes. Which was all right for a while, until the lies he started making us all live made the people confused and frightened, and when a fetish stronger than his was found, made them decide to put an end to it all and go back again to the beginning.

Zabeth's village was only about sixty miles away. But it was some distance off the road, which was little more than a track; and it was some miles in from the main river. By land or by water it was a difficult journey, and took two days. By land during the rainy season it could take three. In the beginning Zabeth came by the land way, trekking with her women assistants to the road and waiting there for a van or truck or bus. When the steamers started up again, Zabeth always used the river; and that wasn't much easier.

The secret channels from the villages were shallow, full of snags, humming with mosquitoes. Down these channels Zabeth and her women poled and often pushed their dugouts to the main river. There, close to the bank, they waited for the steamer, the dugouts full of goods — usually food — to be sold to people on the steamer and the barge the steamer towed. The food was mainly fish or monkey, fresh or boucané — smoked in the way of the country, with a thick black crust.

Sometimes there was a smoked snake or a smoked small crocodile, a black hunk barely recognizable for what it had been — but with white or pale pink flesh below the charred crust.

When the steamer appeared, with its passenger barge in tow, Zabeth and her women poled or paddled out to the middle of the river and stood at the edge of the steamer channel, drifting down with the current. The steamer passed; the dugouts rocked in the swell; and then came the critical moment when the dugouts and the barge came close together. Zabeth and her women threw ropes onto the lower steel deck of the barge, where there were always hands to grab the ropes and tie them to some bulkhead; and the dugouts, from drifting downstream and against the side of the barge, began moving in the other direction, while people on the barge threw down pieces of paper or cloth on the fish or the monkey they wanted to buy. This attaching of dugouts to the moving steamer or barge was a recognized river practice, but it was dangerous. Almost every trip the steamer made there was a report of a dugout being overturned somewhere along the thousand-mile route and of people being drowned. But the risk was worth taking: afterwards, without labour, as a marchande selling goods, Zabeth was towed up the river to the very edge of the town, uncoupling her dugouts by the ruins of the cathedral, a little before the docks, to avoid the officials there, who were always anxious to claim some tax. What a journey! Such trouble and danger to sell simple village things, and to take other goods back to the people of her village.

For a day or two before the steamer came there was a market and a camp in the open space outside the dock gate. Zabeth became part of this camp while she was in the town. If it rained she slept in the verandah of a grocery or a bar; at a later date she put up in an African lodging house, but in the beginning such places didn't exist. When she came to the shop there was nothing in her appearance that spoke of her difficult journey or her nights in the open. She was formally dressed, wrapped in her cotton in the African style that by folds and drapes emphasized the bigness of her bottom. She wore a turban — a piece of downriver style; and she had her vanity case with the creased notes she had got from people in her village and people on the steamer and barge. She shopped, she paid; and some hours before the steamer sailed again her women — thin, short, bald-looking, and in ragged working clothes — came to take the goods away.

This was a quicker journey, downriver. But it was just as dangerous, with the same coupling and uncoupling of the dugouts and the barge. In those days the steamer left the town at four in the afternoon; so it was deep night when Zabeth and her women came to where they had to cast off from the steamer. Zabeth took care then not to give away the entrance to her village. She cast off; she waited for the steamer and the barge and the lights to disappear. Then she and her women poled back up or drifted down to their secret channel, and their nighttime labour of poling and pushing below the overhanging trees.

Going home at night! It wasn't often that I was on the river at night. I never liked it. I never felt in control. In the darkness of river and forest you could be sure only of what you could see — and even on a moonlight night you couldn't see much When you made a noise — dipped a paddle in the water — you heard yourself as though you were another person. The river and the forest were like presences, and much more powerful than you. You felt unprotected, an intruder.

In the daylight — though the colours could be very pale and ghostly, with the heat mist at times suggesting a colder climate — you could imagine the town being rebuilt and spreading. You could imagine the forests being uprooted, the roads being laid across creeks and swamps. You could imagine the land being made part of the present: that was how the Big Man put it later, offering us the vision of a two-hundred-mile "industrial park" along the river. (But he didn't mean it really; it was only his wish to appear a greater magician than any the place had ever known.) In daylight, though, you could believe in that vision of the future. You could imagine the land being made ordinary, fit for men like yourself, as small parts of it had been made ordinary for a short while before independence — the very parts that were now in ruins.

But at night, if you were on the river, it was another thing. You felt the land taking you back to something that was familiar, something you had known at some time but had forgotten or ignored, but which was always there. You felt the land taking you back to what was there a hundred years ago, to what had been there always. What journeys Zabeth made! It was as though she came out each time from her hidden place to snatch from the present (or the future) some precious cargo to take back to her people — those razor blades, for instance, to be taken out from their packets and sold one by one, miracles of metal — cargo that became more precious the further she got from the town, the nearer she got to her fishing village, the true, safe world, protected from other men by forest and clogged-up waterways. And protected in other ways as well. Every man here knew that he was watched from above by his ancestors, living forever in a higher sphere, their passage on earth not forgotten, but essentially preserved, part of the presence of the forest. In the deepest forest was the greatest security. That was the security that Zabeth left behind, to get her precious cargo; that was the security to which she returned.

No one liked going outside his territory. But Zabeth travelled without fear; she came and went with her vanity case and no one molested her. She was not an ordinary person. In appearance she was not at all like the people of our region. They were small and slight and very black. Zabeth was a big woman with a coppery complexion; there were times when this copper glow, especially on her cheekbones, looked like a kind of makeup. There was something else about Zabeth. She had a special smell. It was strong and unpleasant, and at first I thought — because she came from a fishing village — that it was an old and deep smell of fish. Then I thought it had to do with her restricted village diet. But the people of Zabeth's tribe whom I met didn't smell like Zabeth.

Africans noticed her smell. If they came into the shop when Zabeth was there they wrinkled their noses and sometimes they went away.

Metty, the half-African boy who had grown up in my family's house on the coast and had come to join me, Metty said that Zabeth's smell was strong enough to keep mosquitoes away. I thought myself that it was this smell that kept men away from Zabeth, in spite of her fleshiness (which the men here liked) and in spite of her vanity case — because Zabeth wasn't married and, so far as I knew, lived with no man.

But the smell was meant to keep people at a distance. It was Metty — learning local customs fast — who told me that Zabeth was a magician, and was known in our region as a magician. Her smell was the smell of her protecting ointments. Other women used perfumes and scents to attract; Zabeth's ointments repelled and warned. She was protected. She knew it, and other people knew it.

I had treated Zabeth so far as a marchande and a good customer. Now that I knew that in our region she was a person of power, a prophetess, I could never forget it. So the charm worked on me as well.

THE AMERICAN PART

Chapter 1 Nathaniel Hawthorne

作者简介

Nathaniel Hawthorne (July 4, 1804 – May 19, 1864) was an American novelist and short story writer. He was born in 1804 in Salem, Massachusetts. His ancestors include John Hawthorne, the only judge involved in the Salem witch trials who never repented of his actions. Nathaniel later added a "w" to make his name "Hawthorne" in order to hide this relation. He entered Bowdoin College in 1821, was elected to Phi Beta Kappa in 1824, and graduated in 1825. Hawthorne published his first work, a novel titled *Fanshawe*, in 1828; he later tried to suppress it, feeling it was not equal to the standard of his later work. He published several short stories in various periodicals which he collected in 1837 as *Twice-Told Tales*. The next year, he became engaged to Sophia Peabody. He worked at a Custom House and joined Brook Farm, a transcendentalist community, before marrying Peabody in 1842. The couple moved to The Old Manse in Concord, Massachusetts, later moving to Salem, the Berkshires, then to The Wayside in Concord. *The Scarlet Letter* was published in 1850, followed by a succession of other novels. Hawthorne died on May 19, 1864, and was survived by his wife and their three children. Much of Hawthorne's writing centers on New England, many works featuring moral allegories with a Puritan inspiration. His fiction works are considered part of the Romantic Movement and, more specifically, Dark romanticism. His themes often center on the inherent evil and sin of humanity, and his works often have moral messages and deep psychological complexity. His published works include novels, short stories, and a biography of his friend Franklin Pierce.

Hawthorne's works belong to romanticism or, more specifically, dark romanticism, cautionary tales that suggest that guilt, sin, and evil are the most inherent natural qualities of humanity. Many of his works are inspired by Puritan New England, combining historical romance loaded with symbolism and deep psychological themes, bordering on surrealism. His depictions of the past are a version of historical fiction used only as a vehicle to express common themes of ancestral sin, guilt and retribution. His later writings also reflect his negative view of the Transcendentalism movement. Hawthorne was predominantly a short story writer in his early career. Upon publishing *Twice-Told Tales*, however, he noted, "I do not think much of them," and he expected little response from the public. His four major romances were written between 1850 and 1860: *The Scarlet Letter* (1850), *The House of the Seven Gables* (1851), *The Blithedale Romance* (1852) and *The Marble Faun* (1860). Hawthorne also wrote nonfiction. In 2008, The Library of America selected Hawthorne's *A Collection of Wax Figures* for inclusion in its two-century retrospective of American True Crime.

纳撒尼尔·霍桑(1804年7月4日—1864年5月19日)是一位美国小说家和短篇小说家。1804年,他出生于马萨诸塞州塞勒姆镇。他的祖辈约翰·哈桑是卷入塞勒姆驱巫案的法官,但是他的祖父从未对自己的罪行表示忏悔。后来,为了隐藏自己的身份,纳撒尼尔在他的名字中加入了"W",成了霍桑。1821年,他进入博多因学院学习并于1825年毕业。1828年,霍桑出版了第一本长篇小说,名为《范肖》;后来,由于他觉得这本书不足以与后来的作品相媲美,他试图废除这本书。霍桑在不同的时期相继出版过一些短篇小说,这些短篇小说在1837年被收录在《重讲一遍的故事》中。第二年,他与索菲娅·皮博迪订婚。在与索菲娅·皮博迪结婚前,1842年他在海关工作并参加了布鲁克农场,一个先验论者组织。婚后,两人搬到了马萨诸塞州,康科德村的老庄园,接着又搬到塞勒姆镇,伯克郡,之后又搬到了康科德村。《红字》出版于1850年,继其之后出版了一系列其他的小说。霍桑死于1864年5月19日,死于妻子和三个孩子之前。霍桑的很多作品以英格兰为中心,以讽喻为特色,灵感来源于清教。他的小说涉及部分的浪漫运动,确切来讲是黑色浪漫主义。作品主题凸显了人性的邪恶和罪恶,同时兼具一些道德伦理的寓言和精神的错综复杂。他的出版作品囊括小说、短篇小说,及其朋友富兰克林·皮尔斯的自传。霍桑的作品属浪漫主义,劝诫性的故事暗含了犯罪、罪恶及邪恶这些人性中天生的特质。大部分作品受到了新英格兰清教的启迪,结合了满载着象征主义的历史爱情,以及深邃的精神主题,接近超现实主义。他对过去的描写是历史小说的版本,仅作为一项工具去表达原罪、犯罪、报应这些常见的主题。他之后的作品也反映了他对超越主义论的消极态度。霍桑在早年职业生涯中是一位卓越的短篇小说家。在出版《旧事重述》期间,他却写道:"我对它们并不寄予很大期望",同时,他预料来自公众的关注会微乎其微。他的4部主要的爱情小说创作于1850年至1860年间,分别是1850年的《红字》、1851年的《带有7个尖角阁的房子》、1852年的《福谷传奇》、和1860年的《大理石牧神》。此外霍桑也写纪实小说,在2008年,美国图书馆精选了一系列霍桑的作品,组成《蜡像集》,包含了对两个世纪美国真正罪恶的回顾。

作品及导读

作 品 1

The Scarlet Letter

导 读

The Scarlet Letter told a story of a puritan woman Hester Prynne who was punished to wear a scarlet A which stood for the crime of adultery. The pretty young lady tried to settle down in Boston with her old and ugly husband Chillingworth, a scholar. But the latter did not appear for years. During this time, Hester committed adultery with a local Minster Dimmesdale, and gave birth to a girl Pearl. Facing the terrible punishment, Hester refused to give her lover's name away to protect him. Years later, the husband Chillingworth came to the town and found out the whole truth, and he operated an horrible revenge on Dimmesdale, with hiding his own true name. Yet, as the story went on, Hester and Dimmesdale became sympathetic figures, while Chillingworth was a devil at last. The first chapter describes that a large group of people gathered in front of a mansion. The land was divided into two parts, cemetery and prison. The wooden-made jail eroded by wind and rain, engraved with a number of stains which seems like the record of the crime without any flashy. To our amazement, in front of the ugly mansion, weeds and roses grow in a mess. Maybe the fragrances of the roses leave the torturous criminals a ray of mercy. Those roses could be thought of a bit of light color in one's miserable life.

《红字》讲了一个美国女清教徒的故事,海斯特·白兰。她因为通奸而被惩罚佩戴一个猩红的 A 字,A 字是通奸单词"adultery"的首字母。这个年轻漂亮的女人和她又老又丑的丈夫齐灵渥斯打算在波士顿定居,但是她丈夫却几年都未曾出现。在这期间,海斯特和当地的牧师戴美斯戴尔通奸并生下了一个女儿珠儿珍珠。为了保护她的情人,海斯特独自接受惩罚也不肯透露他的名字。但是几年后,她的丈夫来到了这个小镇并且发现整个事实,找出了那个情人,于是他展开了恐怖的复仇计划。然而随着故事的发展,海斯特和戴美斯戴尔成了受人同情的角色,而齐灵渥斯最终成了一个恶魔。第一章讲述了一大群人围在一座大厦前,这块土地被划分为两块:坟地和牢狱。木质牢狱久经风雨侵蚀,外面劣迹斑斑,似乎和罪犯记录一样,没有任何光鲜的地方。这样难看的大厦前,还长着乱七八糟的野草和几簇野生的蔷薇花。或许蔷薇花的香气能够给那些受刑的犯人一丝爱怜。那些蔷薇花或许可以看成是一个人悲苦生活中的些微亮色彩。

选 文

The Scarlet Letter

(Chapter 1: The Prison Door)

  A throng of bearded men, in sad-colored garments and gray steeple crowned hats, intermixed with women, some wearing hoods, and others bareheaded, was assembled in front of a wooden edifice, the door of which was heavily timbered with oak, and studded with iron spikes. The founders of a new colony, whatever Utopia of human virtue and happiness they might originally project, have invariably recognised it among their earliest practical necessities to allot a portion of the virgin soil as a cemetery, and another portion as the site of a prison. In accordance with this rule it may safely be assumed that the forefathers of Boston had built the first prison-house somewhere in the Vicinity of Cornhill, almost as seasonably as they marked out the first burial ground, on Isaac Johnson's lot, and round about his grave, which subsequently became the nucleus of all the congregated sepulchers in the old churchyard of King's Chapel. Certain it is that, some fifteen or twenty years after the settlement of the town, the wooden jail was already marked with weather-stains and other indications of age, which gave a yet darker aspect to its beetle-browed and gloomy front. The rust on the ponderous iron-work of its oaken door looked more antique than anything else in the New World. Like all that pertains to crime, it seemed never to have known a youthful era. Before this ugly edifice, and between it and the wheel-track of the street, was a grass-plot, much overgrown with burdock, pig-weed, apple-pern, and such unsightly vegetation, which evidently found something congenial in the soil that had so early borne the black flower of civilized society, a prison. But on one side of the portal, and rooted almost at the threshold, was a wild rose-bush, covered, in this month of June, with its delicate gems, which might be imagined to offer their fragrance and fragile beauty to the prisoner as he went in, and to the condemned criminal as he came forth to his doom, in token that the deep heart of Nature could pity and be kind to him. This rose-bush, by a strange chance, has been kept alive in history; but whether it had merely survived out of the stern old wilderness, so long after the fall of the gigantic pines and oaks that originally overshadowed it, or whether, as there is far authority for believing, it had sprung up under the footsteps of the sainted Ann Hutchinson as she entered the prison-door, we shall not take upon us to determine. Finding it so directly on the threshold of our narrative, which is now about to issue from that inauspicious portal, we could hardly do otherwise than pluck one of its flowers, and present it to the reader. It may serve, let us hope, to symbolize some sweet moral blossom that may be found along the track, or relieve the darkening close of a tale of human frailty and sorrow.

  The grass-plot before the jail, in Prison Lane, on a certain summer morning, not less than two centuries ago, was occupied by a pretty large number of the inhabitants of Boston; all with their eyes intently fastened on the iron-clamped oaken door. Amongst any other population, or at a later period in the history of New England, the grim rigidity that petrified the bearded physiognomies of these good people would have augured some awful business in hand. It could have betokened nothing short of the anticipated execution of some noted culprit, on whom the sentence of a legal tribunal had but confirmed the verdict of public sentiment. But, in that early severity of the Puritan character, an inference of this kind could not so indubitably be drawn. It might be, that a sluggish bond-servant, or an undutiful child, whom his parents had given over to the civil authority, was to be corrected at the whipping-post. It might be, that an Antinomian, a Quaker, or other heterodox religionist, was to be scourged out of the town, or an idle and vagrant Indian, whom the white man's fire-water had made riotous about the streets, was to be driven with stripes into the shadow of the forest. It might be, too, that a witch, like old Mistress Hibbins, the bitter-tempered widow of the magistrate, was to die upon the gallows. In either case, there was very much the same solemnity of demeanour on the part of the spectators; as befitted a people amongst whom religion and law were almost identical, and in whose character both were so thoroughly interfused, that the mildest and the severest acts of public discipline were alike made venerable and awful. Meagre, indeed, and cold, was the sympathy that a transgressor might look for, from such bystanders, at the scaffold. On the other hand, a penalty which, in our days, would infer a degree of mocking infamy and ridicule, might then be invested with almost as stern a dignity as the punishment of death itself.

It was a circumstance to be noted, on the summer morning when our story begins its course, that the women, of whom there were several in the crowd, appeared to take a peculiar interest in whatever penal infliction might be expected to ensue. The age had not so much refinement, that any sense of impropriety restrained the wearers of petticoat and farthingale from stepping forth into the public ways, and wedging their not unsubstantial persons, if occasion were, into the throng nearest to the scaffold at an execution. Morally, as well as materially, there was a coarser fibre in those wives and maidens of old English birth and breeding, than in their fair descendants, separated from them by a series of six or seven generations; for, throughout that chain of ancestry, every successive mother has transmitted to her child a fainter bloom, a more delicate and briefer beauty, and a slighter physical frame, if not a character of less force and solidity, than her own. The women who were now standing about the prison-door stood within less than half a century of the period when the man-like Elizabeth had been the not altogether unsuitable representative of the sex. They were her country-women; and the beef and ale of their native land, with a moral diet not a whit more refined, entered largely into their composition. The bright morning sun, therefore, shone on broad shoulders and well-developed busts, and on round and ruddy cheeks, that had ripened in the far-off island, and had hardly yet grown paler or thinner in the atmosphere of New England. There was, moreover, a boldness and rotundity of speech among these matrons, as most of them seemed to be, that would startle us at the present day, whether in respect to its purport or its volume of tone.

"Goodwives," said a hard-featured dame of fifty, "I'll tell ye a piece of my mind. It would be greatly for the public behoof, if we women, being of mature age and church-members in good repute, should have the handling of such malefactresses as this Hester Prynne. What think ye, gossips? If the hussy stood up for judgment before us five, that are now here in a knot together, would she come off with such a sentence as the worshipful magistrates have awarded? Marry, I trow not!"

"People say," said another, "that the Reverend Master Dimmesdale, her godly pastor, takes it very grievously to heart that such a scandal should have come upon his congregation."

"The magistrates are God-fearing gentlemen, but merciful overmuch-that is a truth," added a third autumnal matron. "At the very least, they should have put the brand of a hot iron on Hester Prynne's forehead. Madam Hester would have winced at that, I warrant me. But she- the naughty baggage- little will she care what they put upon the bodice of her gown! Why, look you, she may cover it with a brooch, or such like heathenish adornment, and so walk the streets as brave as ever!"

"Ah, but," interposed, more softly, a young wife, holding a child by the hand, "Let her cover the mark as she will, the pang of it will be always in her heart."

"What do we talk of marks and brands, whether on the bodice of her gown, or the flesh of her forehead?" cried another female, the ugliest as well as the most pitiless of these self-constituted judges. "This woman has brought shame upon us all, and ought to die. Is there not law for it? Truly there is, both in the Scripture and the statute-book. Then let the magistrates, who have made it of no effect, thank themselves if their own wives and daughters go astray!"

"Mercy on us, goodwife," exclaimed a man in the crowd, "is there no virtue in woman, save what springs from a wholesome fear of the gallows? That is the hardest word yet! Hush, now, gossips! for the lock is turning in the prison-door, and here comes Mistress Prynne herself."

The door of the jail being flung open from within, there appeared, in the first place, like a black shadow emerging into sunshine, the grim and grisly presence of the town-beadle, with a sword by his side, and his staff of office in his hand. This personage prefigured and represented in his aspect the whole dismal severity of the Puritanic code of law, which it was his business to administer in its final and closest application to the offender. Stretching forth the official staff in his left hand, he laid his right upon the shoulder of a young woman, whom he thus drew forward; until, on the threshold of the prison-door, she repelled him, by an action marked with natural dignity and force of character, and stepped into the open air, as if by her own free will. She bore in her arms a child, a baby of some three months old, who winked and turned aside its little face from the too vivid light of day; because its existence, heretofore, had brought it acquainted only with the grey twilight of a dungeon, or other darksome apartment of the prison.

When the young woman — the mother of this child — stood fully revealed before the crowd, it seemed to be her first impulse to clasp the infant closely to her bosom; not so much by an impulse of motherly affection, as that she might thereby conceal a certain token, which was wrought or fastened into her dress. In a moment, however, wisely judging that one token of her shame would but poorly serve to hide another, she took the baby on her arm, and, with a burning blush, and yet a haughty smile, and a glance that would not be abashed, looked around at her townspeople and neighbours. On the breast of her gown, in fine red cloth, surrounded with an elaborate embroidery and fantastic flourishes of gold thread, appeared the letter A. It was so artistically done, and with so much fertility and gorgeous luxuriance of fancy, that it had all the effect of a last and fitting decoration to the apparel which she wore; and which was of a splendour in accordance with the taste of the age, but greatly beyond what was allowed by the sumptuary regulations of the colony.

The young woman was tall, with a figure of perfect elegance on a large scale. She had dark and abundant hair, so glossy that it threw off the sunshine with a gleam, and a face which, besides being beautiful from regularity of feature and richness of complexion, had the impressiveness belonging to a marked brow and deep black eyes. She was ladylike, too, after the manner of the feminine gentility of those days; characterised by a certain state and dignity, rather than by the delicate, evanescent, and indescribable grace, which is now recognised as its indication. And never had Hester Prynne appeared more ladylike, in the antique interpretation of the term, than as she issued from the prison. Those who had before known her, and had expected to behold her dimmed and obscured by a disastrous cloud, were astonished, and even startled, to perceive how her beauty shone out, and made a halo of the misfortune and ignominy in which she was enveloped. It may be true, that, to a sensitive observer, there was something exquisitely painful in it. Her attire, which, indeed, she had wrought for the occasion, in prison, and had modelled much after her own fancy, seemed to express the attitude of her spirit, the desperate recklessness of her mood, by its wild and picturesque peculiarity. But the point which drew all eyes, and, as it were, transfigured the wearer — so that both men and women, who had been familiarly acquainted with Hester Prynne, were now impressed as if they beheld her for the first time — was that SCARLET LETTER, so fantastically embroidered and illuminated upon her bosom. It had the effect of a spell, taking her out of the ordinary relations with humanity, and enclosing her in a sphere by herself.

"She hath good skill at her needle, that's certain," remarked one of her female spectators; "but did ever a woman, before this brazen hussy, contrive such a way of showing it! Why, gossips, what is it but to laugh in the faces of our godly magistrates, and make a pride out of what they, worthy gentlemen, meant for a punishment?"

"It were well," muttered the most iron-visaged of the old dames, "if we stripped Madam Hester's rich gown off her dainty shoulders; and as for the red letter, which she hath stitched so curiously, I'll bestow a rag of mine own rheumatic flannel, to make a fitter one!"

"Oh, peace, neighbours, peace!" whispered their youngest companion; "do not let her hear you! Not a stitch in that embroidered letter, but she has felt it in her heart."

The grim beadle now made a gesture with his staff.

"Make way, good people, make way, in the King's name!" cried he. "Open a passage; and, I promise ye, Mistress Prynne shall be set where man, woman, and child, may have a fair sight of her brave apparel, from this time till an hour past meridian. A blessing on the righteous Colony of the Massachusetts, where iniquity is dragged out into the sunshine! Come along, Madam Hester, and show your scarlet letter in the market-place!"

A lane was forthwith opened through the crowd of spectators. Preceded by the beadle, and attended by an irregular procession of stern-browed men and unkindly-visaged women, Hester Prynne set forth towards the place appointed for her punishment. A crowd of eager and curious schoolboys, understanding little of the matter in hand, except that it gave them a half-holiday, ran before her progress, turning their heads continually to stare into her face, and at the winking baby in her arms, and at the ignominious letter on her breast. It was no great distance, in those days, from the prison-door to the market-place. Measured by the prisoner's experience, however, it might be reckoned a journey of some length; for, haughty as her demeanour was, she perchance underwent an agony from every footstep of those that thronged to see her, as if her heart had been flung into the street for them all to spurn and trample upon. In our nature, however, there is a provision alike marvellous and merciful, that the sufferer should never know the intensity of what he endures by its present torture, but chiefly by the pang that rankles after it. With almost a serene deportment, therefore, Hester Prynne passed through this portion of her ordeal, and came to a sort of scaffold, at the western extremity of the market-place. It stood nearly beneath the eaves of Boston's earliest church, and appeared to be a fixture there.

In fact, this scaffold constituted a portion of a penal machine, which now, for two or three generations past, has been merely historical and traditionary among us, but was held, in the old time, to be as effectual an agent, in the promotion of good citizenship, as ever was the guillotine among the terrorists of France. It was, in short, the platform of the pillory; and above it rose the framework of that instrument of discipline, so fashioned as to confine the human head in its tight grasp, and thus hold it up to the public gaze. The very ideal of ignominy was embodied and made manifest in this contrivance of wood and iron. There can be no outrage, methinks, against our common nature — whatever be the delinquencies of the individual — no outrage more flagrant than to forbid the culprit to hide his face for shame; as it was the essence of this punishment to do. In Hester Prynne's instance, however, as not unfrequently in other cases, her sentence bore, that she should stand a certain time upon the platform, but without undergoing that gripe about the neck and confinement of the head, the proneness to which was the most devilish characteristic of this ugly engine. Knowing well her part, she ascended a flight of wooden steps, and was thus displayed to the surrounding multitude, at about the height of a man's shoulders above the street.

Had there been a papist among the crowd of Puritans, he might have seen in this beautiful woman, so picturesque in her attire and mien, and with the infant at her bosom, an object to remind him of the image of Divine Maternity, which so many illustrious painters have vied with one another to represent; something which should remind him, indeed, but only by contrast, of that sacred image of sinless motherhood, whose infant was to redeem the world. Here, there was the taint of deepest sin in the most sacred quality of human life, working such effect, that the world was only the darker for this woman's beauty, and the more lost for the infant that she had borne.

The scene was not without a mixture of awe, such as must always invest the spectacle of guilt and shame in a fellow-creature, before society shall have grown corrupt enough to smile, instead of shuddering, at it. The witnesses of Hester Prynne's disgrace had not yet passed beyond their simplicity. They were stern enough to look upon her death, had that been the sentence, without a murmur at its severity, but had none of the heartlessness of another social state, which would find only a theme for jest in an exhibition like the present. Even if there had been a disposition to turn the matter into ridicule, it must have been repressed and overpowered by the solemn presence of men no less dignified than the Governor, and several of his counsellors, a judge, a general, and the ministers of the town; all of whom sat or stood in a balcony of the meetinghouse, looking down upon the platform. When such personages could constitute a part of the spectacle, without risking the majesty or reverence of rank and office, it was safely to be inferred that the infliction of a legal sentence would have an earnest and effectual meaning. Accordingly, the crowd was sombre and grave. The unhappy culprit sustained herself as best a woman might, under the heavy weight of a thousand unrelenting eyes, all fastened upon her and concentrated at her bosom. It was almost intolerable to be borne. Of an impulsive and passionate nature, she had fortified herself to encounter the stings and venomous stabs of public contumely, wreaking itself in every variety of insult; but there was a quality so much more terrible in the solemn mood of the popular mind, that she longed rather to behold all those rigid countenances contorted with scornful merriment, and herself the object. Had a roar of laughter burst from the multitude — each man, each woman, each little shrill-voiced child, contributing their individual parts — Hester Prynne might have repaid them all with a bitter and disdainful smile. But, under the leaden infliction which it was her doom to endure, she felt, at moments, as if she must needs shriek out with the full power of her lungs, and cast herself from the scaffold down upon the ground, or else go mad at once.

Yet there were intervals when the whole scene, in which she was the most conspicuous object, seemed to vanish from her eyes, or at least, glimmered indistinctly before them, like a mass of imperfectly shaped and spectral images. Her mind, and especially her memory, was preternaturally active, and kept bringing up other scenes than this roughly hewn street of a little town, on the edge of the Western wilderness; other faces than were lowering upon her from beneath the brims of those steeple-crowned hats. Reminiscences, the most trifling and immaterial, passages of infancy and school-days, sports, childish quarrels, and the little domestic traits of her maiden years, came swarming back upon her, intermingled with recollections of whatever was gravest in her subsequent life; one picture precisely as vivid as another; as if all were of similar importance, or all alike a play. Possibly, it was an instinctive device of her spirit, to relieve itself, by the exhibition of these phantasmagoric forms, from the cruel weight and hardness of the reality.

Be that as it might, the scaffold of the pillory was a point of view that revealed to Hester Prynne the entire track along which she had been treading, since her happy infancy. Standing on that miserable eminence, she saw her native village, in old England, and her paternal home; a decayed house of grey stone, with a poverty-stricken aspect, but retaining a half-obliterated shield of arms over the portal, in token of antique gentility. She saw her father's face, with its bald brow, and reverend white beard, that flowed over the old-fashioned Elizabethan ruff; her mother's, too, with the look of heedful and anxious love which it always wore in her remembrance, and which, even since her death, had so often laid the impediment of a gentle remonstrance in her daughter's pathway. She saw her own face, glowing with girlish beauty, and illuminating all the interior of the dusky mirror in which she had been wont to gaze at it. There she beheld another countenance, of a man well stricken in years, a pale, thin, scholar-like visage, with eyes dim and bleared by the lamplight that had served them to pore over many ponderous books. Yet those same bleared optics had a strange, penetrating power, when it was their owner's purpose to read the human soul. This figure of the study and the cloister, as Hester Prynne's womanly fancy failed not to recall, was slightly deformed, with the left shoulder a trifle higher than the right. Next rose before her, in memory's picture-gallery, the intricate and narrow thoroughfares, the tall grey houses, the huge cathedrals, and the public edifices, ancient in date and quaint in architecture, of a Continental city; where a new life had awaited her, still in connection with the misshapen scholar; a new life, but feeding itself on time-worn materials, like a tuft of green moss on a crumbling wall. Lastly, in lieu of these shifting scenes, came back the rude market-place of the Puritan settlement, with all the townspeople assembled and levelling their stern regards at Hester Prynne — yes, at herself — who stood on the scaffold of the pillory, an infant on her arm, and the letter A, in scarlet, fantastically embroidered with gold thread, upon her bosom!

Could it be true? She clutched the child so fiercely to her breast, that it sent forth a cry; she turned her eyes downward at the scarlet letter, and even touched it with her finger, to assure herself that the infant and the shame were real. Yes! — these were her realities — all else had vanished!

Chapter 2 Walt Whitman

作者简介

Walt Whitman (May 31, 1819 – March 26, 1892) was an American poet, essayist, journalist, and humanist. Proclaimed the "greatest of all American poets" by many foreign observers. Mere four years after his death, he is viewed as the first urban poet. He was a part of the transition between Transcendentalism and Realism, incorporating both views in his works. His works have been translated into more than twenty-five languages. Whitman is among the most influential and controversial poets in the American canon. His work has been described as a "rude shock" and "the most audacious and debatable contribution yet made to American literature". He largely abandoned the metrical structures of European poetry for an expansionist freestyle verse, which represented his philosophical view that America was destined to reinvent the world as emancipator and liberator of the human spirit. Walter Whitman was born on May 31, 1819 in West Hills, Long Island. He was the second of nine children. One of his siblings, born prior to him, did not make it past infancy. His mother was barely literate and of Dutch descent and his father was a Quaker carpenter. In 1823 the family moved to Brooklyn, where for six years Whitman attended public schools. It was the only formal education he ever received. His mother taught him the value of family ties, and Whitman remained devoted to his family throughout his life, becoming, in a real sense, its leader after the death of his father. Whitman inherited the liberal intellectual and political attitudes of a free thinker from his father.

沃尔特·惠特曼(1819年5月31日—1892年3月26日)是美国的诗人、散文家、记者和人文主义者。他去世短短4年后,便被许多外国观察家称为"最伟大的美国诗人",同时也被认为是第一个城市诗人。他介于超现实主义与现实主义之间,在他的作品中结合了这两种观点,他的作品已被翻译成超过25种语言。惠特曼是美国最具影响力和争议性的诗人之一。他的作品已被描述为一个"强有力的冲击"和"对美国文学最大胆的和有争议的贡献。"他基本上放弃了欧洲诗歌的格律结构,采用自由诗体。这代表了他的哲学观点,即美国注定要成为重塑世界的救星和人类精神的解放者。沃尔特·惠特曼于1819年5月31日出生于长岛的西海山庄,他是9个孩子中的老二。他的一个兄长早年夭折。他的母亲是几乎不识字的荷兰人后裔,他的父亲是一个木匠和贵格会信徒。1823年,全家搬到了布鲁克林,在那里惠特曼就读公立学校6年。这是他一生中受到的唯一的正规教育。他的母亲教他家庭关系的价值,惠特曼在他的生活中很关心他的家人,成为他的父亲去世后的一个真正意义上的家庭领导人。惠特曼从他的父亲那里继承了一个自由思想家的自由主义思想和政治态度。

作品及导读

作品 1

Oh Captain! My Captain!

导 读

Rhyme Scheme — aabb xcxc. The opening couplets of the first two stanzas establish a happy mood, which juxtaposed with the shortened succeeding lines, brings out the disappointment experienced by the poet over the captain's death. (Note the progression: Stanza 1 begins with two happy couplets; Stanza 2 begins with two celebrating couplets, but something isn't quite right as demonstrated by the off rhyme of "bells" and "trills." Stanza 3 re-establishes the rhyming couplet pattern, but the message is as clear as the rhyme: the captain is dead.) Meter and Rhyme — there is no fixed meter; there is, however, a pattern of four long lines followed by four short lines in each stanza. The shortened lines emphasize the personal grief experienced by the poet against the backdrop of a broader victory. The poem's rhythm is created by the varying line lengths. Extended Metaphor — The captain is Abraham Lincoln. The fearful trip is the Civil War. The ship is the United States. The prize is the preservation of the union. The repetition of "heart" in line 5 emphasizes the poet's grief at the death of his captain. "Fallen cold and dead" is repeated at the end of each stanza to emphasize the poet's deep loss. Apostrophe — an apostrophe is a form of personification in which an individual addresses someone who is dead, someone who is not there, or an inanimate object. "O Captain! My Captain!" at the start of the first two stanzas are examples of apostrophe, as is "Exult O shores, and ring O bells!" in the third stanza. The poet refers to the fallen captain as "father", representing his deep respect for president Lincoln and Lincoln's role as father of the Union. Word Choice — words and phrases such as "grim and daring", "weathered every rack", "fearful trip", "flag is flung", "bugle trills", "ribboned wreaths" and "swaying mass" cast a shadow over the celebration, much in the same way the dead cast a shadow over any victory in war celebration.

格律:aabb xcxc。前两节开首便建立了一个欢快的基调。与后续的短行并列,又带出由船长的死亡而生出的失望之情。(读者应留意诗歌的进展:第一节开端有两个表欢快的对句,第二节开头是两个表祝的对句,但结尾的"钟声"和"颤音"却蕴含着不祥的征兆。第三节重建了对句的韵律模式,但信息正如格律一样明确:船长已经死了。韵律和节奏:本诗并无固定的的韵律,但每个诗节中的每四个长句都跟了四个短句。短句强调了诗人在这个欢庆的时刻所经历的失去船长的痛苦,不同长度的诗行构成了整首诗的韵律模式。延伸的隐喻:诗中的船长代表亚伯拉罕·林肯,可怕的行程代表美国内战。船代表美国,战利品代表美国。第五行中"心脏"的重复强调了"船长"死后诗人的悲痛之情。"倒下死去,全身冰凉"在每句末尾都得以重复,强调了诗人深深的失落。呼语——拟人的一种是说话者对一个死去的人,不在场的人,或无生命的物体的称呼。前两节首句的"噢,船长!我的船长!",第三节的"啊,岸上钟声齐鸣,啊,人们一片欢腾!"便是诗中的两处呼语。诗人称死去的船长为"父亲",体现了诗人对林肯总统深深的敬意,同时也表明了林肯作为美国国父的地位。选词:"勇敢,坚定"、"历尽风险"、"历经难险"、"旌旗高悬"、"号角长鸣"、"缎带的花圈"、"人潮涌动"表达都给庆祝活动蒙上了一层阴影,呼应了现实中林肯总统的逝去,和美国内战的胜利。

选 文

O Captain! My Captain!

O Captain! My Captain! our fearful trip is done,
The ship has weather'd every rack, the prize we sought is won,
The port is near, the bells I hear, the people all exulting,
While follow eyes the steady keel, the vessel grim and daring;
But O heart! heart! heart!
O the bleeding drops of red!
Where on the deck my Captain lies,
Fallen cold and dead.

O Captain! My Captain! Rise up and hear the bells;
Rise up — for you the flag is flung — for you the bugle trills,
For you bouquets and ribbon'd wreaths — for you the shores a-crowding,
For you they call, the swaying mass, their eager faces turning;
Here Captain! Dear father!
This arm beneath your head!
It is some dream that on the deck
You've fallen cold and dead.

My Captain does not answer, his lips are pale and still,

My father does not feel my arm, he has no pulse or will;
The ship is anchor'd safe and sound, its voyage closed and done,
From fearful trip the victor ship comes in with object won;
Exult O Shores, and ring O bell!
But I, with mournful tread,
Walk the deck my Captain lies,
Fallen cold and dead.

作 品 2

A Noiseless Patient Spider

导 读

"A Noiseless Patient Spider" is a lyric poem. Walt Whitman wrote the poem in the 1860s and published it in the 1871–1872 editions of *Leaves of Grass*. *Leaves of Grass* was a continually growing collection of his work that began with the publication of the first edition in 1855. The version of the poem on this page is from the 1881–1882 editions of Leaves of Grass. "A Noiseless Patient Spider" develops the following themes: The quest, or exploration, for meaning and knowledge in the vastness of the universe. The patience to build a plexus that links one stopping place to the next. The perseverance to carry on until the "gossamer thread" (line 8) connects to a goal. The poem as a Metaphor: the poem compares a spider to a human. Each creature tirelessly constructs bonds to its surroundings. A spider spins silken thread to span a void. A human builds ships, airplanes, bridges. Sometimes he crosses a void with a telescope (as Galileo did) or reaches new plateaus of knowledge with a question (as Socrates did) or a theory (as Einstein did). Structure: The poem contains two five-line stanzas, the first consisting of one long sentence. The subject is the pronoun "I" (line 2), and the main verb is the compound 'mark'd (line 2 and line 3). The second stanza is one long group of words requiring "I marked" to be carried over unstated from the first stanza in order to make the word group a complete sentence. If inserted, "I marked" would occur after "and" (line 6) or "soul" (line 6). The poet achieves a measure of balance between the two stanzas with the words "unreeling" and "speeding" in the first stanza and "musing", "venturing", "throwing", and "seeking" in the second stanza. He also balances "isolated" in the first stanza (line 1) with "detached" in the second stanza (line 2) and "vacant vast surrounding" in the first stanza (line 2) with "measureless oceans of space" in the second stanza (line 2). Format: Free Verse. Whitman wrote *A Noiseless Patient Spider* in free verse — also called vers libre, a French term. Free verse generally has no metrical pattern or end rhyme. However, it may contain patterns of another kind, such as repetition to impart emphasis, balance, and rhythm.

《一只沉默而耐心的蜘蛛》为一首抒情诗。惠特曼作于19世纪60年代,发表于1871—1872年版的《草叶集》中。自1855年初次发行以后,《草叶集》便在不断得以增补完善。本书刊载的版本选自1881—1882年版的《草叶集》。本诗的主题是包括在茫茫宇宙中对生命意义和知识的追寻和探索,不断构建通往成功道路的耐心,坚持不懈,直到"蛛丝"(第8行)连接至最终的目的地。诗中还包含了一个隐喻:把蜘蛛比作人类。每个生物都孜孜不倦地将自身与外部世界联系起来。蜘蛛通过银丝将空白填充。而人类则相应地建造船舶、飞机和桥梁,有时甚至利用望远镜(比如伽利略)跨越距离,通过提出一个问题(比如苏格拉底)或理论(比如爱因斯坦)来到达新的知识领域。结构方面:本诗包含两个诗节,每节均由五行诗组成,每一节即含一个完整的长句,主语为代词"I",动为第2行和第3行的"marked"。第二节中,要想句子意思完整,须在理解时将第一节中的"I marked"搬过来,放在"and"(第6行)或"soul"(第6行)之后。第二节的"musing"、"venturing"、"throwing"和"seeking"与第一节的"unrealing"和"speeding"相互对应,使整首诗达到了一个平衡。达到相同效果的还有第二节的"detached"(第2行)与第一节的"isolated"(第2行),"measurelss oceans of space"与"vacant vast surrounding"。本诗格式为自由诗。没有格律或尾韵。但有些自由诗可能包含其他特殊格律,比如重复,以达到强调、平衡中押韵的效果。

选 文

A Noiseless Patient Spider

A noiseless patient spider,
I marked where on a promontory it stood isolated,
Marked how to explore the vacant vast surrounding,
It launched forth filament, filament, filament, out of itself,
Ever unreeling them, ever tirelessly speeding them.

And you O my soul where you stand,
Surrounded, detached, in measureless oceans of space,
Ceaselessly musing, venturing, throwing, seeking the spheres to connect them,
Till the bridge you will need be formed, till the ductile anchor hold,
Till the gossamer thread you fling catch somewhere, O my soul.

Chapter 3 Emily Elizabeth Dickinson

作者简介

Emily Elizabeth Dickinson (December 10, 1830 – May 15, 1886) was an American poet. Born in Amherst, Massachusetts, to a successful family with strong community ties, she lived a mostly introverted and reclusive life. After she studied at the Amherst Academy for seven years in her youth, she spent a short time at Mount Holyoke Female Seminary before returning to her family's house in Amherst. Thought of as an eccentric by the locals, she became known for her penchant for white clothing and her reluctance to greet guests or, later in life, even leave her room. Most of her friendships were therefore carried out by correspondence. While Dickinson was a prolific private poet, fewer than a dozen of her nearly eighteen hundred poems were published during her lifetime. The work that was published during her lifetime was usually altered significantly by the publishers to fit the conventional poetic rules of the time. Dickinson's poems are unique for the era in which she wrote. Many of her poems deal with themes of death and immortality, two recurring topics in letters to her friends. Although most of her acquaintances were probably aware of Dickinson's writing, it was not until after her death in 1886 — when Lavinia, Emily's younger sister, discovered her cache of poems — that the breadth of Dickinson's work became apparent. Her first collection of poetry was published in 1890 by personal acquaintances Thomas Wentworth Higginson and Mabel Loomis Todd, both of whom heavily edited the content. A complete and mostly unaltered collection of her poetry became available for the first time in 1955 when *The Poems of Emily Dickinson* was published by scholar Thomas H. Johnson. Despite unfavorable reviews and skepticism of her literary prowess during the late 19th and early 20th century, critics now consider Dickinson to be a major American poet.

艾米莉·伊丽莎白·狄更生(1830年12月10日—1886年5月15日),美国诗人,出生于马萨诸塞州艾摩斯特市一个很有名望的家庭,一生大多过着深居简出的生活。幼年时,曾就读于阿姆赫斯特学院,7年后,进入曼荷莲女子学院,但入学不久便回到艾摩斯特家中。狄更生尤其喜爱白色衣服,且不愿接人待客,到了后来,甚至不愿离开自己的房间,因此当地人都认为她是个怪人。她与朋友的友情都是通过书信维持。但狄更生是一位多产的诗人,她一生所作约1 800首诗歌中,只有少数几首在她生前得以发展,且发表的作品也被出版商大肆修改,使其符合当时公认的诗体规则。在那个年代,狄更生的作品是独一无二的。死亡和永生是她的诗歌最常涉及的主题。与朋友的通信中,她也常常提到这两个话题。1886年,狄更生逝世,她的妹妹拉维妮亚整理遗物时才发现她生前所作的大量诗歌,那以后,其诗作才得以大量问世。1890年,狄更生的第一部诗集得以出版,出版人是其生前好友托马斯·文特沃斯·希金森和梅布尔·卢米斯·托德,但两人对诗歌内容进行了大量修改。1955年,托马斯·H·约翰逊出版《艾米莉·狄更生诗集》,才使公众有机会接触最完整、最原始的狄更生作品。19世纪末20世纪初,狄更生诗歌的文学价值受到了广泛的质疑,但如今,她是大家公认的美国最伟大的诗人之一。

作品及导读

作 品 1

Nobody

选 文

Nobody

I'm nobody! Who are you?
Are you nobody, too?
Then there's a pair of us! Don't tell!
They'd advertise you know!

How dreary to be somebody!
How public, like a frog
To tell one's name the livelong day
To an admiring bog!

赏 析

在这首诗里,作者把自己说成是一个不重要的人,实际上是通过对牛蛙的意象化,进而对现实社会中的所谓公众人物进行嘲弄。作者还把公众舆论比喻成人们深陷其中的沼泽地,而不是什么值得敬重的东西。她也暗示了任何谦逊的人都能把自己从沼泽地里解脱出来。"frog""bog"是押韵的,这样描述出了名的人,实际上是一种捉弄。

作 品 2

I Dwell in Possibility

选 文

I Dwell in Possibility

I dwell in Possibility —
A fairer House than Prose —
More numerous of Windows —
Superior — for Doors —

Of Chambers as the Cedars —
Impregnable of Eye —
And for an Everlasting Roof
The Gambrels of the Sky —

Of Visitors — the fairest —
For Occupation — This —
The spreading wide of narrow Hands
To gather Paradise —

赏 析

诗歌,是自我封闭的,但在封闭之中,却又具有无限可能性。诗歌,有着比散文更为凹凸有致的造型美、纯净美。它比散文更具想象力和发散性,比散文更具优雅的难度,它的门槛,更高远。诗歌的内部,不会被轻易"洞穿",它的内在小宇宙,是无边且微妙的。天生贵质的诗歌,有天穹般的广袤与神秘……

诗人们冠冕堂皇地闯入诗歌的领地,反客为主,鸠占鹊巢,看看我在它内部都做了些什么吧:我写下短小朴素的诗行,创造出了一座神奇的人间天堂。

4 Mark Twain

作者简介

Mark Twain (pseudonym of Samuel Langhorne Clemens, 1835 – 1910), was an American writer, journalist and humorist, who won a worldwide audience for his stories of the youthful adventures of *Tom Sawyer* and *Huckleberry Finn*.

Clemens was born on November 30, 1835 in Florida, Missouri, of a Virginian family. He was brought up in Hannial, Missouri. After his father's death in 1847, he was apprenticed to a printer and wrote for his brother's newspaper. He later worked as a licensed Mississippi river-boat pilot. The Civil War put an end to the steamboat traffic and Clemens moved to Virginia City, where he edited the *Territorial Enterprise*.

In 1864, Mark Twain left for California, and worked in San Francisco as a reporter. He visited Hawaii as a correspondent for *The Sacramento Union*, publishing letters on his trip and giving lectures. He set out on a world tour, traveling in France and Italy. His experiences were recorded in 1869 in *The Innocents Abroad*, which gained him wide popularity, and poked fun at both American and European prejudices and manners.

The success as a writer gave Mark Twain enough financial security to marry Olivia Langdon in 1870. They moved next year to Hartford. Twain continued to lecture in the United States and England. Between 1876 and 1884 he published several masterpieces, *Tom Sawyer* (1881) and *The Prince and The Pauper* (1881). *Life on the Mississippi* appeared in 1883 and *Huckleberry Finn* in 1884.

In the 1890s Mark Twain lost most of his earnings in financial speculations and in the failure of his own publishing firm. To recover from the bankruptcy, he started a world lecture tour, during which one of his daughters died. Twain toured New Zealand, Australia, India, and South Africa. He wrote such books as *The Tragedy of Pudd'head Wilson*

(1884), *Personal Recollections of Joan of Arc* (1885), *A Connecticut Yankee in King Arthur's Court* (1889) and the travel book *Following The Equator* (1897). During his long writing career, Mark Twain also produced a considerable number of essays.

The death of his wife and his second daughter darkened the author's later years, which is seen in his posthumously published autobiography (1924). Twain died on April 21, 1910.

马克·吐温(萨缪尔·克莱门斯的笔名,1835—1910年),是一个美国作家,记者和幽默作家,他以他的《年轻的汤姆·索亚历险记》和《哈克贝利·费恩历险记》赢得了全世界读者的赞誉。

克莱门斯于1835年11月30日出生在密苏里的佛罗里达,父母都是弗吉尼亚人。他成长于密苏里州的汉尼拔。1847年父亲死后,他成为一个印刷工的学徒并为他兄弟的报纸写报道。后来,他当了一名密西西比河上的船舶驾驶员。内战阻碍汽船交通的运行,克莱门斯随后搬到维吉尼亚州的城市,在那里他建立了他的企业。

1864年马克·吐温离开加州,到圣弗朗西科称从事记者工作。他以《萨克拉门托工公》报特约记者的身份到达夏威夷,并在那里发表旅行日志,进行各种演讲。他还进行过一次环球旅行,到过法国和意大利。他的经验记录在1869年的《傻子出行》中,使他大受欢迎,开起了在美国和欧洲的偏见和礼仪的玩笑。

作为一个作家的成功给了马克·吐温足够的经济保障,他在1870年与奥利维亚·兰登结婚,第二年他们搬到哈特福德,吐温继续在美国和英国演讲。从1876年到1884年,他发表了杰作《汤姆·索亚历险记》(1881)、《乞丐王子》(1881)、《密西西比河上的生活》(1883)及《哈克贝利·费恩历险记》(1884)。

在19世纪90年代,马克·吐温在金融投机中,失去了他的大部分收入而且自己的出版公司也失利。从破产中恢复过来后,他开始在世界进行巡回演讲,在这期间,他的一个女儿死亡。马克·吐温参观了新西兰、澳大利亚、印度和南非。他写了一些悲剧作品如:《傻瓜威尔逊》(1884),《圣女贞德的个人回忆》(1885),《亚瑟王宫廷上的康州美国佬》(1889)和《赤道后的旅行书》(1897)。在他漫长的写作生涯中,吐温也创作了相当数量的散文。

他妻子和他的第二个女儿的死使作者的晚年昏暗无光,这是在他死后出版的自传(1924)中发现的。马克·吐温于1910年4月21日去世。

作品及导读

作品 1

The Story of the Bad Little Boy

导 读

Mark Twain is a loved writer by readers, spending his childhood in his uncle Han. His witty, humorous funny stories leave people a sense of artistic charm. Mark Twain shaped the form of every character image. Especially the image of children left a deep impression on people. His children's image is not a fixed pattern. It generally can be divided into "good" and "bad boy". In the 19th century, a kind of serious children's fiction is popular among Americans. According to this kind of morality in the novel, the children were marked with "good" and "bad", namely "good boy" always have a good ending, "bad boy," without exception, have no good end. The montonousness and false contents of these works repulsed many American writers, especially the homorists of the west. From the beginning of the 1940s, there appeared in the United States some writers against this kind of Children's fiction. They were for "bad boys". Mark Twain was the most notable one. His macterpieces of this kind include *The Story of the Good Little Story of the Bad Little Boy* and so on.

Good boys are obedient, good luck following them all the way; Bad children play games or cheat, and eventually are punished. But when the serious moral textbooks are confronted with the reality, can you sit so calm? If you've never doubted the stories you heard, if you are stilf seeking in the reality, if you are still immersed in the fairy tale —"good guys go to heaven, bad guys go to hell", then please come and read Mark Twain's story about the bad child Jim. Perhaps from here you can see what is the hypocrisy of doctrines, the fall of morality, the absurdity bo life, and the cruelty of the reality.

在汉尼拔镇叔叔家度过童年生活的马克·吐温是一位深受读者喜爱的作家,他引人发笑的风趣、幽默的故事散发出动人心魄的艺术魅力。马克·吐温塑造了形形色色的人物形象,其中的儿童形象给人留下了深刻印象。他笔下的儿童形象并不拘泥于一种模式,大体上可分为"好孩子"与"坏孩子"。19世纪美国流行一种严肃的儿童小说,在这类道德小说里儿童分别被标上"好"与"坏"的标签,"好孩子"总是有好的结局,"坏孩子"则无一例外地总无好下场。这种千人一面、内容虚假说教的作品引起一些美国作家,特别是西部幽默作家的强烈反感。从40年代开始,在美国出现了与这种儿童小说唱反调的作家,他们替"坏孩子"叫好,其中首推马克·吐温。其中代表作是《好孩子的故事》、《坏孩子的故事》等等。

好孩子规矩听话,一路好运连连;坏孩子捣鬼使坏,最终遭到惩罚。可当一本正经的道德教科书遭遇水深火热的现实"江湖"时,还能这么气定神闲地正襟危坐吗?如果你从没怀疑过自己听过的故事,如果你还在现实中按图索骥,如果你仍沉浸在"好人上天堂,坏人下地狱"的人间童话里做美梦,那就请来看看马克·吐温笔下这个坏孩子的故事吧。也许从这里你会看到什么叫教条的虚伪、道德的倾覆、人生的荒唐和现实的残酷。

选 文

The Story of the Bad Little Boy

Once there was a bad little boy whose name was Jim — though, if you will notice, you will find that bad little boys are nearly always called James in your Sunday-school books. It was strange, but still it was true that this one was called Jim.

He didn't have any sick mother either — a sick mother who was pious and had the consumption, and would be glad to lie down in the grave and be at rest but for the strong love she bore her boy, and the anxiety she felt that the world might be harsh and cold towards him when she was gone. Most bad boys in the Sunday-books are named James, and have sick mothers, who teach them to say, "Now, I lay me down," etc., and sing them to sleep with sweet, plaintive voices, and then kiss them good-night, and kneel down by the bedside and weep. But it was different with this fellow. He was named Jim, and there wasn't anything the matter with his mother — no consumption, nor anything of that kind. She was rather stout than otherwise, and she was not pious; moreover, she was not anxious on Jim's account. She said if he were to break his neck it wouldn't be much loss. She always spanked Jim to sleep, and she never kissed him good-night; on the contrary, she boxed his ears when she was ready to leave him.

Once this little bad boy stole the key of the pantry, and slipped in there and helped himself to some jam, and filled up the vessel with tar, so that his mother would never know the difference; but all at once a terrible feeling didn't come over him, and something didn't seem to whisper to him, "Is it right to disobey my mother? Isn't it sinful to do this? Where do bad little boys go who gobble up their good kind mother's jam?" and then he didn't kneel down all alone and promise never to be wicked any more, and rise up with a light, happy heart, and go and tell his mother all about it, and beg her forgiveness, and be blessed by her with tears of pride and thankfulness in her eyes. No; that is the way with all other bad boys in the books; but it happened otherwise with this Jim, strangely enough. He ate that jam, and said it was bully, in his sinful, vulgar way; and he put in the tar, and said that was bully also, and laughed, and observed "that the old woman would get up and snort" when she found it out; and when she did find it out, he denied knowing anything about it, and she whipped him severely, and he did the crying himself. Everything about this boy was curious — everything turned out differently with him from the way it does to the bad James in the books.

Once he climbed up in Farmer Acorn's apple-tree to steal apples, and the limb didn't break, and he didn't fall and break his arm, and get torn by the farmer's great dog, and then languish on a sick bed for weeks, and repent and become good. Oh! no; he stole as many apples as he wanted and came down all right; and he was all ready for the dog too, and knocked him endways with a brick when he came to tear him. It was very strange — nothing like it ever happened in those mild little books with marbled backs, and with pictures in them of men with swallow-tailed coats and bell-crowned hats, and pantaloons that are short in the legs, and women with the waists of their dresses under their arms, and no hoops on. Nothing like it in any of the Sunday-school books.

Once he stole the teacher's pen-knife, and, when he was afraid it would be found out and he would get whipped, he slipped it into George Wilson's cap — poor Widow Wilson's son, the moral boy, the good little boy of the village, who always obeyed his mother, and never told an untruth, and was fond of his lessons, and infatuated with Sunday-school. And when the knife dropped from the cap, and poor George hung his head and blushed, as if in conscious guilt, and the grieved teacher charged the theft upon him, and was just in the very act of bringing the switch down upon his trembling shoulders, a white-haired, improbable justice of the peace did not suddenly appear in their midst, and strike an attitude and say, "Spare this noble boy — there stands the cowering culprit! I was passing the school-door at recess, and unseen myself, I saw the theft committed!" And then Jim didn't get whaled, and the venerable justice didn't read the tearful school a homily and take George by the hand and say such a boy deserved to be exalted, and then tell him to come and make his home with him, and sweep out the office, and make fires, and run errands, and chop wood, and study law, and help his wife to do household labors, and have all the balance of the time to play, and get forty cents a month, and be happy. No; it would have happened that way in the books, but it didn't happen that way to Jim. No meddling old clam of a justice dropped in to make trouble, and so the model boy George got thrashed, and Jim was glad of it because, you know, Jim hated moral boys. Jim said he was "down on them milk-sops." Such was the coarse language of this bad, neglected boy.

But the strangest thing that ever happened to Jim was the time he went boating on Sunday, and didn't get drowned, and that other time that he got caught out in the storm when he was fishing on Sunday, and didn't get struck by lighting. Why, you might look, and look, all through the Sunday-school books from now till next Christmas, and you would never come across anything like this. Oh no; you would find that all the bad boys who go boating on Sunday invariably get drowned; and all the bad boys who get caught out in storms when they are fishing on Sunday infallibly get struck by lightning. Boats with bad boys in them always upset on Sunday, and it always storms when bad boys go fishing on the Sabbath. How this Jim ever escaped is a mystery to me.

This Jim bore a charmed life — that must have been the way of it. Nothing could hurt him. He even gave the elephant in the menagerie a plug of tobacco, and the elephant didn't knock the top of his head off with his trunk. He browsed around the cupboard after essence of peppermint, and didn't make a mistake and drink aqua fortis. He stole his father's gun and went hunting on the Sabbath, and didn't shoot three or four of his fingers off. He struck his little sister on the temple with his fist when he was angry, and she didn't linger in pain through long summer days, and die with sweet words of forgiveness upon her lips that redoubled the anguish of his breaking heart. No; she got over it. He ran off and went to sea at last, and didn't come back and find himself sad and alone in the world, his loved ones sleeping in the quiet churchyard, and the vine-embowered home of his boyhood tumbled down and gone to decay. Ah! no; he came home as drunk as a piper, and got into the station-house the first thing.

And he grew up and married, and raised a large family, and brained them all with an axe one night, and got wealthy by all manner of cheating and rascality; and now he is the infernality wickedest scoundrel in his native village, and is universally respected, and belongs to the Legislature.

So you see there never was a bad James in the Sunday-school books that had such a streak of luck as this sinful Jim with the charmed life.

Chapter 5 Henry James

作者简介

Henry James (15 April, 1843 – 28 February, 1916) was an American-born British writer, regarded as one of the key figures of 19th-century literary realism. James was born at a wealthy family in New York City. He was the son of Henry James, Sr. who was one of the best-known intellectuals in mid-19th-century America, and the brother of philosopher and psychologist William James and diarist Alice James. In his youth James traveled back and forth between Europe and America. He studied with tutors in Geneva, London, Paris, Bologna, and Bonn. At the age of 19 he attended Harvard Law School, but preferred reading literature to studying law. James published his first short story, *A Tragedy of Error*, at age 21, and devoted himself to literature. In 1866 and 1871 he was a contributor to *The Nation* and *Atlantic Monthly*. From an early age James read the classics of English, American, French and German literature, and Russian classics in translation. His first novel, *Watch and Ward* (1871), was written while traveling through Venice and Paris. After living in Paris, where he was contributor to the *New York Tribune*. James moved to England in 1876, living first in London and then in Rye, Sussex. During his first years in Europe, James wrote novels that portrayed Americans living abroad.

Among James's masterpieces are *Daisy Miller* (1879), in which the eponymous protagonist, the young and innocent American Daisy Miller, finds her values in conflict with European sophistication, and *The Portrait of a Lady* (1881), in which a Lady whose dream did not come true. It is about the contrast between wish and failure, the hope and disillusion. *The Bostonians* (1886) is set in the era of the rising feminist movement. *What Maisie Knew* (1897) depicts a pre-adolescent girl who must choose between her parents and a motherly governess. In *The Wings of the Dove* (1902) an inheritance destroys the love of a young couple. James considered *The Ambassadors* (1903) his most "perfect" work of art. James's most famous novella is *The Turn of the Screw*, a ghost story in which the question of childhood corruption obsesses a governess. Although James is best known for his novels, his essays are now attracting a more general audience.

Between 1906 and 1910 James revised many of his tales and novels for the *New York* edition of his complete works. His autobiography, *A Small Boy and Others*, appeared in 1913 and was continued in *Notes of a Son and Brother* (1914). The third volume, *The Middle Years*, appeared posthumously in 1917. The outbreak of World War I was a shock for James, and on 26 July, 1915, he became a British citizen as a declaration of loyalty to his adopted country and in protest against America's refusal to enter the war. James suffered a stroke on 2 December 1915, and it soon became apparent that his prognosis was not good. The novelist, seriously ill, was awarded the Order of Merit, bestowed on 1 January, 1916. His health continued to decline and he died in London on 28 February 1916. He was cremated at Golders Green Crematorium and his ashes are interred at Cambridge, Massachusetts.

亨利·詹姆斯(1843年4月15日—1916年2月28日)是一位出生在美国的英国作家,是19世纪文学史上最重要的现实主义作家之一。他出生在纽约一个富裕的家庭,是老亨利·詹姆斯的儿子。他的父亲是美国19世纪中期很出名的学者之一。兄长威廉·詹姆斯是知名的哲学家和心理学家,姐姐艾莉丝·詹姆斯是一位日记作家。在他年轻的时候,他游历于欧洲与美国之间。在日内瓦、巴黎、伦敦、博洛尼亚和波恩跟着家教学习。在19岁的时候,他进入了哈佛大学法学院,但是他热衷于阅读文学,学习法律。在21岁的时候,他发表了他的第一篇短篇故事《一个错误的悲剧》,这使他开始致力于文学。在1866年至1871年间,他是《国家》以及《大西洋月刊》的撰稿人。詹姆斯在年轻的时候就开始阅读英国、美国、法国、德国文学的经典名著以及翻译好的俄罗斯名著。他的第一篇小说《日夜守卫》(1871)是在维纳斯和巴黎旅游时写的。在巴黎定居后,他成为《纽约论坛报》的撰稿人。在1876年,先在伦敦居住,后又搬到了苏塞克斯赖伊。在欧洲的第一年,他写了一部小说描绘了居住在国外的美国人。

詹姆斯的杰作包括《黛西·密勒》(1879),这部书中的主人公是一位美国年轻姑娘黛西·米勒,发现她的价值观与欧洲世故相冲突。《贵妇画像》(1886),在这部书中一位女士的梦想没有实现。这是关于梦想与失败,希望与幻灭的小说。《波士顿人》(1886)写于新兴的女权主义运动时期。《梅西的世界》描绘了一个青春期的女孩儿,必须在她的父母和慈爱的家庭女教师之间做出选择。《鸽之翼》(1902),写的是继承财产破坏了一对年轻夫妇的爱。《大使》(1903)是詹姆斯认为自己最"完美"的一部艺术作品。詹姆斯最著名的中篇小说是《螺丝在拧紧》,讲的是一个鬼故事——童年堕落的问题困扰着一位家庭教师。虽然詹姆斯因他的小说而最负盛名,但现在他的随笔也越来越倍受大众的青睐。

1906 年到 1910 年间,詹姆斯修正了他在《纽约时报集》里面的许多故事和小说。他的自传《一个小男孩和其他人》,发表于 1913 年。《一个儿子和兄弟的故事》(1914)是这部自传的续集。第三部是《中年》,在詹姆斯去世后出版于 1917 年。第一次世界大战的爆发对詹姆斯来说很震撼,并且在 1915 年 7 月 26 日,他成为一名英国公民,宣称他会忠于这个养育了他的国家并且反对美国的拒绝加入战争。詹姆斯在 1925 年 12 月 2 日中风,他的病情一直不见好。病得十分严重的詹姆斯于 1916 年 1 月 1 日被赐予一等勋章。他的病情持续恶化,1916 年 2 月 28 日,逝世于伦敦。詹姆斯在格林火葬场火化,骨灰埋在马塞诸塞州的坎布里奇。

作品及导读

作品 1

The Turn of the Screw

导 读

The Turn of the Screw, originally published in 1898, is a ghost story novella written by Henry James. Due to its ambiguous content, it became a favorite text of academics who subscribe to New Criticism. The novella has had differing interpretations, often mutually exclusive. Many critics have tried to determine the exact nature of the evil hinted at by the story. However, others have argued that the true brilliance of the novella comes with its ability to create an intimate confusion and suspense for the reader.

An unnamed narrator listens to Douglas, a friend, read a manuscript written by a former governess whom Douglas claims to have known and who is now dead. The manuscript tells the story of how the young governess is hired by a man who has become responsible for his young nephew and niece after the death of their parents. He lives mainly in London and is not interested in raising the children himself.

The boy, Miles, is attending a boarding school, while his younger sister, Flora, is living at a country estate in Essex. She is currently being cared for by the housekeeper, Mrs. Grosse. The governess's new employer, the uncle of Miles and Flora, gives her full charge of the children and explicitly states that she is not to bother him with communications of any sort. The governess travels to her new employer's country house, Bly, and begins her duties.

Miles soon returns from school for the summer just after a letter arrives from the headmaster stating that he has been expelled. Miles never speaks of the matter, and the governess is hesitant to raise the issue. She fears that there is some horrible secret behind the expulsion, but is too charmed by the adorable young boy to want to press the issue. Soon thereafter, the governess begins to see around the grounds of the estate the figures of a man and woman whom she does not recognize. These figures come and go at will without ever being seen or challenged by other members of the household, and they seem to the governess to be supernatural. She learns from Mrs. Grosse that her predecessor, Miss Jessel, and another employee, Peter Quint, had a sexual relationship. It is also implied that Quint sexually molested Miles and the other members of the household. Prior to their deaths, they spent much of their time with Flora and Miles, and this fact has grim significance for the governess when she becomes convinced that the two children are secretly aware of the presence of the ghosts.

Later, without permission, Flora leaves the house while Miles is playing music for the governess. The governess notices Flora's absence and goes with Mrs. Grosse in search of her. They find her in a clearing in the wood, and the governess is convinced that she has been talking to the ghost of Miss Jessel. When she finally confronts Flora, Flora denies seeing Miss Jessel, and demands never to see the governess again. At the governess's suggestion Mrs. Grosse takes Flora away to her uncle, leaving the governess with Miles. That night, they are finally talking of Miles' expulsion when the ghost of Quint appears to the governess at the window. The governess shields Miles, who attempts to see the ghost. The governess tells him that he is no longer controlled by the ghost, and then finds that Miles has "passed out" in her arms and the ghost has gone.

《螺丝在拧紧》最早发表于1898年,是亨利·詹姆斯的一部恐怖中篇小说,该小说因为其模棱两可的内容成为新批判主义学者最常引用的对象。对该作品的解读往往相差甚大,且互相对立。许多评论家都在努力探寻故事中所提到的魔鬼的天性。同时,也有人指出这部小说的闪光点恰好在于它所创造的困惑,以及给读者造成的悬念。

小说的背景为叙述者听朋友疲乏格拉斯读一篇女家庭教师留下的手稿。道格拉斯称自己认识这位已故的女教师。手稿讲述了这位女教师受雇于一位男士的故事。这位男士因为侄子侄女父母的死去而承担起了对他们的抚养义务。但他本人大都生活在伦敦,并且没有兴趣亲自抚养孩子。

这位男士的侄子迈尔斯就读于一所寄宿学校,而他的妹妹弗罗拉则住在艾塞克斯乡下,暂时由管家格罗斯太太照看。迈尔斯和弗罗拉的叔叔聘用这位女家庭教师全权照管这两个孩子,并特地交代任何事情都不要去打扰他。于是她便到达雇主的府邸布莱府,开始了她的工作。

不久,迈尔斯被学校开除,回到布莱。迈尔斯自己绝口不谈这件事,女教师也不便多问。她担心这次开除事件背后一定隐藏了什么可怕的秘密,但她不想给惹人怜爱的迈尔斯过多压力。后来,女教师经常看见屋子周围有陌生男女的身影。这些人来去自如,也不会被其他家庭成员所察觉,对女教师来说就是超自然的存在。她从格罗斯太太那里得知,这里雇用的前一位家庭教师杰西小组与另一位仆人彼得·昆特有染。格罗斯太太还说昆特曾经对迈尔斯和其他家庭成员进行过性骚扰。杰西和昆特死前经常跟迈尔斯和弗罗拉在一起,这使女教师确信两个孩子知道鬼魂的存在。

有一天,弗罗拉趁哥哥和女教师在弹钢琴溜出了屋子。发现弗罗拉不见之后,女教师和格罗斯太太便四下寻找,在树林里的一片空地找到了她,这件事更是女教师确信弗罗拉之前一定在和杰西的鬼魂交流。最后,女教师终于忍不住质问了弗罗拉萨市,但弗罗拉什么也不承认,还说以后再也不想见到女教师。然后,在女教师的建议下,格罗斯太太把弗罗拉送到了她叔叔那里,屋里便只剩下迈尔斯和女教师两个人。那一夜,二人终于说起了迈尔斯被学校开除的事,正当此时,昆特的鬼魂出现在了女教师的窗外。迈尔斯试图看看鬼魂,但被女教师挡住了。她告诉他以后他再也不会被鬼魂控制,随后,迈尔斯晕倒在她怀里,鬼魂也消失了。

选 文

The Turn of th Screw

"I quite agree — in regard to Griffin's ghost or whatever it was — that it's appearing first to the little boy, at so tender an age, adds a particular touch. But it's not the first occurrence of its charming kind that I know to have involved a child. If the child gives the effect another turn of the screw, what do you say to TWO children —?"

"We say, of course," somebody exclaimed, "that they give two turns! Also we want to hear about them."

I can see Douglas there before the fire, to which he had got up to present his back, looking down at his interlocutor with his hands in his pockets. "Nobody but me, till now, has ever heard. It's quite too horrible." This, naturally, was declared by several voices to give the thing the utmost price, and our friend, with quiet art, prepared his triumph by turning his eyes over the rest of us and going on: "It's beyond everything. Nothing at all that I know touches it."

"For sheer terror?" I remember asking.

He seemed to say it was not as simple as that; to be really at a loss how to qualify it. He passed his hand over his eyes, made a little wincing grimace. "For dreadful — dreadfulness!"

"Oh, how delicious!" cried one of the women.

He took no notice of her; he looked at me, but as if, instead of me, he saw what he spoke of.

"Well then," I said, "just sit right down and begin."

He turned round to the fire, gave a kick to a log, watched it an instant. Then as he faced us again: "I can't begin. I shall have to send to town." There was a unanimous groan at this, and much reproach; after which, in his preoccupied way, he explained. "The story's written. It's in a locked drawer — it has not been out for years. I could write to my man and enclose the key; he could send down the packet as he finds it." It was to me in particular that he appeared to propound this — appeared almost to appeal for aid not to hesitate. He had broken a thickness of ice, the formation of many a winter; had had his reasons for a long silence. The others resented postponement, but it was just his scruples that charmed me. I adjured him to write by the first post and to agree with us for an early hearing; then I asked him if the experience in question had been his own. To this his answer was prompt. "Oh, thank God, no!"

"And is the record yours? You took the thing down?"

"Nothing but the impression. I took that HERE"— he tapped his heart. "I've never lost it."

"Then your manuscript —?"

"Is in old, faded ink, and in the most beautiful hand?" He hung fire again. "A woman's. She has been dead these twenty years. She sent me the pages in question before she died." They were all listening now, and of course there was somebody to be arch, or at any rate to draw the inference. But if he put the inference by without a smile it was also without irritation. "She was a most charming person, but she was ten years older than I. She was my sister's governess," he quietly said. "She was the most agreeable woman I've ever known in her position; she would have been worthy of any whatever. It was long ago, and this episode was long before. I was at Trinity, and I found her at home on my coming down the second summer. I was much there that year — it was a beautiful one; and we had, in her off-hours, some strolls and talks in the garden — talks in which she struck me as awfully clever and nice. Oh yes; don't grin: I liked her extremely and am glad to this day to think she liked me, too. If she hadn't she wouldn't have told me. She had never told anyone. It wasn't simply that she said so, but that I knew she hadn't. I was sure; I could see. You'll easily judge why when you hear."

"Because the thing had been such a scare?"

He continued to fix me. "You'll easily judge," he repeated: "YOU will."

I fixed him, too. "I see. She was in love."

He laughed for the first time. "You ARE acute. Yes, she was in love. That is, she had been. That came out — she couldn't tell her story without its coming out. I saw it, and she saw I saw it; but neither of us spoke of it. I remember the time and the place — the corner of the lawn, the shade of the great beeches and the long, hot summer afternoon. It wasn't a scene for a shudder; but oh —!" He quitted the fire and dropped back into his chair.

"You'll receive the packet Thursday morning?" I inquired.

"Probably not till the second post."

"Well then; after dinner —"

"You'll all meet me here?" He looked us round again. "Isn't anybody going?" It was almost the tone of hope.

"Everybody will stay!"

"I will"— and "I will!" cried the ladies whose departure had been fixed. Mrs. Griffin, however, expressed the need for a little more light. "Who was it she was in love with?"

"The story will tell," I took upon myself to reply.

"Oh, I can't wait for the story!"

"The story WON'T tell," said Douglas; "not in any literal, vulgar way."

"Mores' the pity, then. That's the only way I ever understand."

"Won't YOU tell, Douglas?" somebody else inquired.

He sprang to his feet again. "Yes — tomorrow. Now I must go to bed. Good night." And quickly catching up a candlestick, he left us slightly bewildered. From our end of the great brown hall we heard his step on the stair; whereupon Mrs. Griffin spoke. "Well, if I don't know who she was in love with, I know who HE was."

"She was ten years older," said her husband.

"Raison de plus — at that age! But it's rather nice, his long reticence."

"Forty years!" Griffin put in.

"With this outbreak at last."

"The outbreak," I returned, "will make a tremendous occasion of Thursday night;" and everyone so agreed with me that, in the light of it, we lost all attention for everything else. The last story, however incomplete and like the mere opening of a serial, had been told; we hand shook and "candle stuck," as somebody said, and went to bed.

I knew the next day that a letter containing the key had, by the first post, gone off to his London apartments; but in spite of — or perhaps just on account of — the eventual diffusion of this knowledge we quite let him alone till after dinner, till such an hour of the evening, in fact, as might best accord with the kind of emotion on which our hopes were fixed. Then he became as communicative as we could desire and indeed gave us his best reason for being so. We had it from him again before the fire in the hall, as we had had our mild wonders of the previous night. It appeared that the narrative he had promised to read us really required for a proper intelligence a few words of prologue. Let me say here distinctly, to have done with it, that this narrative, from an exact transcript of my own made much later, is what I shall presently give. Poor Douglas, before his death — when it was in sight — committed to me the manuscript that reached him on the third of these days and that, on the same spot, with immense effect, he began to read to our hushed little circle on the night of the fourth. The departing ladies who had said they would stay didn't, of course, thank heaven, stay: they departed, in consequence of arrangements made, in a rage of curiosity, as they professed, produced by the touches with which he had already worked us up. But that only made his little final auditory more compact and select, kept it, round the hearth, subject to a common thrill.

The first of these touches conveyed that the written statement took up the tale at a point after it had, in a manner, begun. The fact to be in possession of was therefore that his old friend, the youngest of several daughters of a poor country parson, had, at the age of twenty, on taking service for the first time in the schoolroom, come up to London, in trepidation, to answer in person an advertisement that had already placed her in brief correspondence with the advertiser. This person proved, on her presenting herself, for judgment, at a house in Harley Street, that impressed her as vast and imposing — this prospective patron proved a gentleman, a bachelor in the prime of life, such a figure as had never risen, save in a dream or an old novel, before a fluttered, anxious girl out of a Hampshire vicarage. One could easily fix his type; it never, happily, dies out. He was handsome and bold and pleasant, offhand and gay and kind. He struck her, inevitably, as gallant and splendid, but what took her most of all and gave her the courage she afterward showed was that he put the whole thing to her as a kind of favor, an obligation he should gratefully incur. She conceived him as rich, but as fearfully extravagant — saw him all in a glow of high fashion, of good looks, of expensive habits, of charming ways with women. He had for his own town residence a big house filled with the spoils of travel and the trophies of the chase; but it was to his country home, an old family place in Essex, that he wished her immediately to proceed.

He had been left, by the death of their parents in India, guardian to a small nephew and a small niece, children of a younger, a military brother, whom he had lost two years before. These children were, by the strangest of chances for a man in his position — a lone man without the right sort of experience or a grain of patience — very heavily on his hands. It had all been a great worry and, on his own part doubtless, a series of blunders, but he immensely pitied the poor chicks and had done all he could; had in particular sent them down to his other house, the proper place for them being of course the country, and kept them there, from the first, with the best people he could find to look after them, parting even with his own servants to wait on them and going down himself, whenever he might, to see how they were doing. The awkward thing was that they had practically no other relations and that his own affairs took up all his time. He had put them in possession of Bly, which was healthy and secure, and had placed at the head of their little establishment — but below stairs only — an excellent woman, Mrs. Grosse, whom he was sure his visitor would like and who had formerly been maid to his mother. She was now housekeeper and was also acting for the time as superintendent to the little girl, of whom, without children of her own, she was, by good luck, extremely fond. There were plenty of people to help, but of course the young lady who should go down as governess would be in supreme authority. She would also have, in holidays, to look after the small boy, who had been for a term at school — young as he was to be sent, but what else could be done? — and who, as the holidays were about to begin, would be back from one day to the other. There had been for the two children at first a young lady whom they had had the misfortune to lose. She had done for them quite beautifully — she was a most respectable person — till her death, the great awkwardness of which had, precisely, left no alternative but the school for little Miles. Mrs. Grosse, since then, in the way of manners and things, had done as she could for Flora; and there were, further, a cook, a housemaid, a dairywoman, an old pony, an old groom, and an old gardener, all likewise thoroughly respectable.

So far had Douglas presented his picture when someone put a question, "And what did the former governess die of? — of so much respectability?"

Our friend's answer was prompt. "That will come out. I don't anticipate."

"Excuse me — I thought that was just what you ARE doing."

"In her successor's place," I suggested, "I should have wished to learn if the office brought with it —"

"Necessary danger to life?" Douglas completed my thought. "She did wish to learn, and she did learn. You shall hear tomorrow what she learned. Meanwhile, of course, the prospect struck her as slightly grim. She was young, untried, and nervous: it was a vision of serious duties and little company, of really great loneliness. She hesitated — took a couple of days to consult and consider. But the salary offered much exceeded her modest measure, and on a second interview she faced the music, she engaged." And Douglas, with this, made a pause that, for the benefit of the company, moved me to throw in —

"The moral of which was of course the seduction exercised by the splendid young man. She succumbed to it."

He got up and, as he had done the night before, went to the fire, gave a stir to a log with his foot, and then stood a moment with his back to us. "She saw him only twice."

"Yes, but that's just the beauty of her passion."

A little to my surprise, on this, Douglas turned round to me. "It WAS the beauty of it. There were others," he went on, "who hadn't succumbed. He told her frankly all his difficulty — that for several applicants the conditions had been prohibitive. They were, somehow, simply afraid. It sounded dull — it sounded strange; and all the more so because of his main condition."

"Which was —?"

"That she should never trouble him — but never, never: neither appeal nor complain nor write about anything; only meet all questions herself, receive all moneys from his solicitor, take the whole thing over and let him alone. She promised to do this, and she mentioned to me that when, for a moment, disburdened, delighted, he held her hand, thanking her for the sacrifice, she already felt rewarded."

"But was that all her reward?" one of the ladies asked.

"She never saw him again."

"Oh!" said the lady; which, as our friend immediately left us again, was the only other word of importance contributed to the subject till, the next night, by the corner of the hearth, in the best chair, he opened the faded red cover of a thin old-fashioned gilt-edged album. The whole thing took indeed more nights than one, but on the first occasion the same lady put another question.

"What is your title?"

"I haven't one."

"Oh, I have!" I said. But Douglas, without heeding me, had begun to read with a fine clearness that was like a rendering to the ear of the beauty of his author's hand.

I

I remember the whole beginning as a succession of flights and drops, a little seesaw of the right throbs and the wrong. After rising, in town to meet his appeal, I had at all events a couple of very bad days — found myself doubtful again, felt indeed sure I had made a mistake. In this state of mind I spent the long hours of bumping, swinging coach that carried me to the stopping place at which I was to be met by a vehicle from the house. This convenience, I was told, had been ordered, and I found, toward the close of the June afternoon, a commodious fly in waiting for me. Driving at that hour, on a lovely day, through a country to which the summer sweetness seemed to offer me a friendly welcome, my fortitude mounted afresh and, as we turned into the avenue, encountered a reprieve that was probably but a proof of the point to which it had sunk. I suppose I had expected, or had dreaded, something so melancholy that what greeted me was a good surprise. I remember as a most pleasant impression the broad, clear front, its open windows and fresh curtains and the pair of maids looking out; I remember the lawn and the bright flowers and the crunch of my wheels on the gravel and the clustered treetops over which the rooks circled and cawed in the golden sky. The scene had a greatness that made it a different affair from my own scant home, and there immediately appeared at the door, with a little girl in her hand, a civil person who dropped me as decent a curtsy as if I had been the mistress or a distinguished visitor. I had received in Harley Street a narrower notion of the place, and that, as I recalled it, made me think the proprietor still more of a gentleman, suggested that what I was to enjoy might be something beyond his promise.

I had no drop again till the next day, for I was carried triumphantly through the following hours by my introduction to the younger of my pupils. The little girl who accompanied Mrs. Grosse appeared to me on the spot a creature so charming as to make it a great fortune to have to do with her. She was the most beautiful child I had ever seen, and I afterward wondered that my employer had not told me more of her. I slept little that night — I was too much excited; and this astonished me, too, I recollect, remained with me, adding to my sense of the liberality with which I was treated. The large, impressive room, one of the best in the house, the great state bed, as I almost felt it, the full, figured draperies, the long glasses in which, for the first time, I could see myself from head to foot, all struck me — like the extraordinary charm of my small charge — as so many things thrown in. It was thrown in as well, from the first moment, that I should get on with Mrs. Grosse in a relation over which, on my way, in the coach, I fear I had rather brooded. The only thing indeed that in this early outlook might have made me shrink again was the clear circumstance of her being so glad to see me. I perceived within half an hour that she was so glad — stout, simple, plain, clean, wholesome woman — as to be positively on her guard against showing it too much. I wondered even then a little why she should wish not to show it, and that, with reflection, with suspicion, might of course have made me uneasy.

But it was a comfort that there could be no uneasiness in a connection with anything so beatific as the radiant image of my little girl, the vision of whose angelic beauty had probably more than anything else to do with the restlessness that, before morning, made me several times rise and wander about my room to take in the whole picture and prospect; to watch, from my open window, the faint summer dawn, to look at such portions of the rest of the house as I could catch, and to listen, while, in the fading dusk, the first birds began to twitter, for the possible recurrence of a sound or two, less natural and not without, but within, that I had fancied I heard. There had been a moment when I believed I recognized, faint and far, the cry of a child; there had been another when I found myself just consciously starting as at the passage, before my door, of a light footstep. But these fancies were not marked enough not to be thrown off, and it is only in the light, or the gloom, I should rather say, of other and subsequent matters that they now come back to me. To watch, teach, "form" little Flora would too evidently be the making of a happy and useful life. It had been agreed between us downstairs that after this first occasion I should have her as a matter of course at night, her small white bed being already arranged, to that end, in my room. What I had undertaken was the whole care of her, and she had remained, just this last time, with Mrs. Grosse only as an effect of our consideration for my inevitable strangeness and her natural timidity. In spite of this timidity — which the child herself, in the oddest way in the world, had been perfectly frank and brave about, allowing it, without a sign of uncomfortable consciousness, with the deep, sweet serenity indeed of one of Raphael's holy infants, to be discussed, to be imputed to her, and to determine us — I feel quite sure she would presently like me. It was part of what I already liked Mrs. Grosse herself for, the pleasure I could see her feel in my admiration and wonder as I sat at supper with four tall candles and with my pupil, in a high chair and a bib, brightly facing me, between them, over bread and milk. There were naturally things that in Flora's presence could pass between us only as prodigious and gratified looks, obscure and roundabout allusions.

"And the little boy — does he look like her? Is he too so very remarkable?"

One wouldn't flatter a child. "Oh, miss, MOST remarkable. If you think well of this one!"— and she stood there with a plate in her hand, beaming at our companion, who looked from one of us to the other with placid heavenly eyes that contained nothing to check us.

"Yes; if I do —?"

"You WILL be carried away by the little gentleman!"

"Well, that, I think, is what I came for — to be carried away. I'm afraid, however," I remember feeling the impulse to add, "I'm rather easily carried away. I was carried away in London!"

I can still see Mrs. Grosse's broad face as she took this in. "In Harley Street?"

"In Harley Street."

"Well, miss, you're not the first — and you won't be the last."

"Oh, I've no pretension," I could laugh, "to being the only one. My other pupil, at any rate, as I understand, comes back tomorrow?"

"Not tomorrow — Friday, miss. He arrives, as you did, by the coach, under care of the guard, and is to be met by the same carriage."

I forthwith expressed that the proper as well as the pleasant and friendly thing would be therefore that on the arrival of the public conveyance I should be in waiting for him with his little sister; an idea in which Mrs. Grosse concurred so heartily that I somehow took her manner as a kind of comforting pledge — never falsified, thank heaven! — that we should on every question be quite at one. Oh, she was glad I was there!

What I felt the next day was, I suppose, nothing that could be fairly called a reaction from the cheer of my arrival; it was probably at the most only a slight oppression produced by a fuller measure of the scale, as I walked round them, gazed up at them, took them in, of my new circumstances. They had, as it were, an extent and mass for which I had not been prepared and in the presence of which I found myself, freshly, a little scared as well as a little proud. Lessons, in this agitation, certainly suffered some delay; I reflected that my first duty was, by the gentlest arts I could contrive, to win the child into the sense of knowing me. I spent the day with her out-of-doors; I arranged with her, to her great satisfaction, that it should be she, she only, who might show me the place. She showed it step by step and room by room and secret by secret, with droll, delightful, childish talk about it and with the result, in half an hour, of our becoming immense friends. Young as she was, I was struck, throughout our little tour, with her confidence and courage with the way, in empty chambers and dull corridors, on crooked staircases that made me pause and even on the summit of an old machicolated square tower that made me dizzy, her morning music, her disposition to tell me so many more things than she asked, rang out and led me on. I have not seen Bly since the day I left it, and I daresay that to my older and more informed eyes it would now appear sufficiently contracted. But as my little conductress, with her hair of gold and her frock of blue, danced before me round corners and pattered down passages, I had the view of a castle of romance inhabited by a rosy sprite, such a place as would somehow, for diversion of the young idea, take all color out of storybooks and fairytales. Wasn't it just a storybook over which I had fallen a doze and a dream? No; it was a big, ugly, antique, but convenient house, embodying a few features of a building still older, half-replaced and half-utilized, in which I had the fancy of our being almost as lost as a handful of passengers in a great drifting ship. Well, I was, strangely, at the helm!

II

This came home to me when, two days later, I drove over with Flora to meet, as Mrs. Grosse said, the little gentleman; and all the more for an incident that, presenting itself the second evening, had deeply disconcerted me. The first day had been, on the whole, as I have expressed, reassuring; but I was to see it wind up in keen apprehension. The postbag, that evening, it came late contained a letter for me, which, however, in the hand of my employer, I found to be composed but of a few words enclosing another, addressed to himself, with a seal still unbroken. "This, I recognize, is from the headmaster, and the headmaster's an awful bore. Read him, please; deal with him; but mind you don't report. Not a word. I'm off!" I broke the seal with a great effort — so great a one that I was a long time coming to it; took the unopened missive at last up to my room and only attacked it just before going to bed. I had better have let it wait till morning, for it gave me a second sleepless night. With no counsel to take, the next day, I was full of distress; and it finally got so the better of me that I determined to open myself at least to Mrs. Grosse.

"What does it mean? The child's dismissed his school."

She gave me a look that I remarked at the moment; then, visibly, with a quick blankness, seemed to try to take it back. "But aren't they all —?"

"Sent home — yes. But only for the holidays. Miles may never go back at all."

Consciously, under my attention, she reddened. "They won't take him?"

"They absolutely decline."

At this she raised her eyes, which she had turned from me; I saw them fill with good tears. "What has he done?"

I hesitated; then I judged best simply to hand her my letter — which, however, had the effect of making her, without taking it, simply put her hands behind her. She shook her head sadly. "Such things are not for me, Miss."

My counselor couldn't read! I winced at my mistake, which I attenuated as I could, and opened my letter again to repeat it to her; then, faltering in the act and folding it up once more, I put it back in my pocket. "Is he really BAD?"

The tears were still in her eyes. "Do the gentlemen say so?"

"They go into no particulars. They simply express their regret that it should be impossible to keep him. That can have only one meaning." Mrs. Grosse listened with dumb emotion; she forbore to ask me what this meaning might be; so that, presently, to put the thing with some coherence and with the mere aid of her presence to my own mind, I went on: "That he's an injury to the others."

At this, with one of the quick turns of simple folk, she suddenly flamed up. "Master Miles! HIM an injury?"

There was such a flood of good faith in it that, though I had not yet seen the child, my very fears made me jump to the absurdity of the idea. I found myself, to meet my friend the better, offering it, on the spot, sarcastically. "To his poor little innocent mates!"

"It's too dreadful," cried Mrs. Grosse, "to say such cruel things! Why, he's scarce ten years old."

"Yes, yes; it would be incredible."

She was evidently grateful for such a profession. "See him, miss, first. THEN believe it!" I felt forthwith a new impatience to see him; it was the beginning of a curiosity that, for all the next hours, was to deepen almost to pain. Mrs. Grosse was aware, I could judge, of what she had produced in me, and she followed it up with assurance. "You might as well believe it of the little lady. Bless her," she added the next moment —"LOOK at her!"

I turned and saw that Flora, whom, ten minutes before, I had established in the schoolroom with a sheet of white paper, a pencil, and a copy of nice "round or's," now presented herself to view at the open door. She expressed in her little way an extraordinary detachment from disagreeable duties, looking to me, however, with a great childish light that seemed to offer it as a mere result of the affection she had conceived for my person, which had rendered necessary that she should follow me. I needed nothing more than this to feel the full force of Mrs. Grosse's comparison, and, catching my pupil in my arms, covered her with kisses in which there was a sob of atonement.

Nonetheless, the rest of the day I watched for further occasion to approach my colleague, especially as, toward evening, I began to fancy she rather sought to avoid me. I overtook her, I remember, on the staircase; we went down together, and at the bottom I detained her, holding her there with a hand on her arm. "I take what you said to me at noon as a declaration that YOU'VE never known him to be bad."

She threw back her head; she had clearly, by this time, and very honestly, adopted an attitude. "Oh, never known him — I don't pretend THAT!"

I was upset again. "Then you HAVE known him —?"

"Yes indeed, miss, thank God!"

On reflection I accepted this. "You mean that a boy who never is —?"

"Is no boy for ME!"

I held her tighter. "You like them with the spirit to be naughty?" Then, keep pace with her answer. "So do I!" I eagerly brought out. "But not to the degree to contaminate —"

"To contaminate?"— my big word left her at a loss. I explained it. "To corrupt."

She stared, taking my meaning in; but it produced in her an odd laugh. "Are you afraid he'll corrupt YOU?" She put the question with such a fine bold humor that, with a laugh, a little silly doubtless, to match her own, I gave way for the time to the apprehension of ridicule. But the next day, as the hour for my drive approached, I cropped up in another place. "What was the lady who was here before?"

"The last governess? She was also young and pretty — almost as young and almost as pretty, Miss, even as you."

"Ah, then, I hope her youth and her beauty helped her!" I recollect throwing off. "He seems to like us young and pretty!"

"Oh, he DID," Mrs. Grosse assented: "it was the way he liked everyone!" She had no sooner spoken indeed than she caught herself up. "I mean that's HIS way — the master's."

I was struck. "But of whom did you speak first?"

She looked blank, but she colored. "Why, of HIM."

"Of the master?"

"Of who else?"

There was so obviously no one else that the next moment I had lost my impression of her having accidentally said more than she meant; and I merely asked what I wanted to know. "Did SHE see anything in the boy —?"

"That wasn't right? She never told me."

I had a scruple, but I overcame it. "Was she careful — particular?"

Mrs. Grosse appeared to try to be conscientious. "About some things — yes."

"But not about all?"

Again she considered. "Well, miss — she's gone. I won't tell tales."

"I quite understand your feeling," I hastened to reply; but I thought it, after an instant, not opposed to this concession to pursue: "Did she die here?"

"No — she went off."

I don't know what there was in this brevity of Mrs. Grosse's that struck me as ambiguous. "Went off to die?" Mrs. Grosse looked straight out of the window, but I felt that, hypothetically, I had a right to know what young persons engaged for Bly were expected to do. "She was taken ill, you mean, and went home?"

"She was not taken ill, so far as appeared, in this house. She left it, at the end of the year, to go home, as she said, for a short holiday, to which the time she had put in had certainly given her a right. We had then a young woman — a nursemaid who had stayed on and who was a good girl and clever; and SHE took the children altogether for the interval. But our young lady never came back, and at the very moment I was expecting her I heard from the master that she was dead."

I turned this over. "But of what?"

"He never told me! But please, miss," said Mrs. Grouse, "I must get to my work."

Chapter 6 Sherwood Anderson

作者简介

Sherwood Anderson was born on September 13, 1876, in Camden, Ohio, and grew up in nearby Clyde. In 1898 he joined the U. S. Army and served in the Spanish-American War. In 1900 he enrolled in the Wittenberg Academy. The following year he moved to Chicago where he began a successful business career in advertising. Despite his business success, in 1912 Anderson walked away to pursue writing full time. His first novel was *Windy McPherson's Son*, published in 1916, and his second was *Marching Men*, published in 1917. The phenomenally successful *Winesburg, Ohio*, a collection of short stories about fictionalized characters in a small midwestern town, followed in 1919. Anderson wrote many novels including *The Triumph of the Egg*, *Poor White*, *Many Marriages*, and *Dark Laughter*, but it was his short stories that made him famous. Through his short stories he revolutionized short fiction and altered the direction of the modern short story. He is credited with influencing such writers as William Faulkner, Ernest Hemingway and F. Scott Fitzgerald. Anderson died in March 1941, of peritonitis suffered during a trip to South America. The epitaph he wrote for himself proclaims, "Life, not death, is the great adventure."

1876年9月13日,舍伍德·安德森出生于俄亥俄州的卡姆登,并在附近的克莱德长大。1898年,他加入了美国军队,曾参与了美国与西班牙的作战。1900年进入维滕贝格科学院。第二年他搬到芝加哥,在那里他开始了一个成功的商业广告事业。尽管他在商业上取得成功,但在1912年安德森开始追求全职写作。他的第一部小说是《温迪麦克弗森的儿子》,在1916年出版。他的第二部小说《前进的人们》发表在1917并大获成功。1919年,《温斯堡,俄亥俄州》问世,并获得了极大的成功。《温斯堡,俄亥俄州》是一部短篇小说集,讲述了几个生活在中西部小镇的人物的故事。安德森的小说包括《鸡》、《穷》、《多》、《阴》等。但真正令他名声大噪的是他的短篇小说。他掀起了一股短篇小说的革命,扭转了现代短篇小说发展的方向。威廉·福克纳厄斯特·海明威和弗朗西斯·斯科特·菲茨杰拉德都受了他的影响。1941年,安德森在去南非的途中死于腹膜炎。他在自己的墓志铭中写道:"生而不是死,才是伟大的冒险。"

作品及导读

作品 1

The Triumph of the Egg

导 读

The Triumph of the Egg is the work by Sherwood Anderson who was an American realistic writer of short stories and novels. He was a fighter against industrialization and mechanization and found modern industrial life degrading, humiliating and discouraging. In his work, he wrote about lonely, sad people, and he also showed his sympathy for emotionally stunted people, who were the victims of modern existence.

The story is about "my" father's failure in his so-called rising in the world and is told in the point of "the son" as a witness or an observer. As the key character of this story, father is dynamic with changes. At the very beginning, father is carefree, seemed to be cheerful and contended about his life. But after his marriage, changes took place. Father was bald-headed and no longer happy but insane, frustrated and desperate instead. Sherwood Anderson was so good at using symbolism as a key to extend meaning of something that stands for something else by reason of relationship, association, convention, or accidental resemblance. In *The Story of the Egg*, the egg is a visible sign of things invisible.

The egg symbolizes father's American Dream. In the forth paragraph egg is first mentioned "They rented ten acres of poor stony land on Griggs's Road… and launched into chicken rising." Father dreamed that the hen-and-chicken cycle would lead them to a wealthy future because it was a time that American passion took possession of everyone tightly included my father.

But then "one unversed in such matters can have no notion of the many and tragic things can happen to a chicken." Chicken on the farm could not run away form the fate of getting diseases or dying. As indicated, father's hope was dreadfully disillusioned even though he was so hard working.

The writer described poultry monstrosities at length and it was what represents father's twisty dreams. "All during our ten years on the chicken farm… most of the money he had earned had been spent for remedies to cure chicken diseases." "My" father was so tortured by his failure that he even tried to make those grotesques alive at any rate.

After ten-year's struggle "my" parents finally gave up that farm and began anther — a restaurant. But father still took his greatest treasure with him — bottles of body of those little monstrous things. "I" see these bottles as symbolism of father's spiritual world — that unsound. Maybe the action stands for father's freemasonry between his unsuccessful life and terribly deformed chicken.

At the end of this story, father tried his best to entertain his customers by tricks but failed. He wailed with great grief. Father eventually defeated by fate and gave up "American Dream". "He laid the egg gently on the table and … went to sleep." If we step back to the American society, we could tell that it is industrialization that ruins this man when values are set that fortune is the only standard for success.

Sherwood Anderson used chicken and eggs to demonstrate people can't escape from the fate. The eggs actually symbolize the fate and life. The father tried to conquer the eggs and changed his fate, but in the end failed, sneered by others and fate. The American dream of freedom, equality, fairness of competition is wispy to people at the bottom of society.

《鸡蛋的胜利》是美国现实主义作家舍伍德·安德森的作品,他主要写过短篇小说和长篇小说。他反对现代工业化社会中的工业化和机械化,他发现了现代工业生活中令人觉得可耻的不好的一面。他的作品中经常包含孤独,悲苦的人们,表现了他对情感受挫的人们的同情,这些人都是现代生活的受害者。

这个故事是关于"我"父亲在他所谓的世界崛起时遭遇的失败的故事,并且作者是从儿子的角度去观察。作为这个故事的关键角色,父亲是动态的,变化的。在开始的时候,父亲是无忧无虑,是欢快的,很热爱他的生活。但结婚后,他发生了变化。父亲成了秃头,不再快乐,这些快乐由疯狂、沮丧和绝望代替。舍伍德·安德森用了很多象征性的东西作为作品重点的延伸,在《鸡蛋的胜利》的故事中,鸡蛋是一种标志和象征:

鸡蛋象征着父亲的美国梦。在第四段第一次提到"他们租了十亩不怎么肥沃的土地作为养鸡场,并把精力投入在养鸡的事情上。"父亲梦见母鸡带领他们到达一个富有的未来。在这时候,美国梦的激情紧紧地包围着所有美国人,包括"我"的父亲。

但随后"这些我们想象中的事情没有一件实现。"鸡不能逃脱得病或死亡的命运,而这些暗示着,父亲的希望破灭,尽管他是如此努力工作。

作者描述了这些鸡在不同时间的大小以及在此时它代表了父亲什么样的梦想。"在养鸡场十年来他所赚来的大部分钱已经都花在补救措施上,以治愈鸡的疾病。""我"的父亲深受自己的失败所带来的折磨,他甚至试图让那些畸形的鸡无论如何必须活着来减轻那种折磨。

经过10年的奋斗,"我"的父母终于放弃了那个农场,并开始努力经营一家餐厅。但父亲还是随身带着他最珍贵的财宝,也就是那些死去的鸡的尸体,"我"认为这些瓶子其实具有作为父亲的精神世界的象征意义,他的精神世界已经开始变得畸形了。

在这个故事的结尾,父亲竭力通过技巧来招待他的客户,但失败了,他带着极大的悲痛哭着说自己的过往。父亲最终被命运打败,进而放弃了"美国梦"。"他把鸡蛋轻轻地放在桌子上,睡觉去了。"如果我们退一步到美国社会中,我们可以知道是这个工业化的社会把这位父亲毁掉了,让他以为只有成功这一个标准才能体现生命的意义。

舍伍德·安德森用鸡、鸡蛋映射到人们无法逃脱的命运。鸡蛋其实象征着命运和生活。父亲试图用鸡蛋来改变他的命运，但最终失败了，因此被别人嘲笑。美国梦的自由、平等、竞争、公平在社会的最底层那些人中几乎是不存在的。

选　文

The Triumph of the Egg

MY FATHER was, I am sure, intended by nature to be a cheerful, kindly man. Until he was thirty-four years old he worked as a farmhand for a man named Thomas Butterworth whose place lay near the town of Bidwell, Ohio. He had then a horse of his own and on Saturday evenings drove into town to spend a few hours in social intercourse with other farmhands. In town he drank several glasses of beer and stood about in Ben Head's saloon — crowded on Saturday evenings with visiting farmhands. Songs were sung and glasses thumped on the bar. At ten o'clock father drove home along a lonely country road, made his horse comfortable for the night and himself went to bed, quite happy in his position in life. He had at that time no notion of trying to rise in the world.

It was in the spring of his thirty-fifth year that father married my mother, then a country schoolteacher, and in the following spring I came wriggling and crying into the world. Something happened to the two people. They became ambitious. The American passion for getting up in the world took possession of them.

It may have been that mother was responsible. Being a schoolteacher she had no doubt read books and magazines. She had, I presume, read of how Garfield, Lincoln, and other Americans rose from poverty to fame and greatness and as I lay beside her — in the days of her lying-in — she may have dreamed that I would someday rule men and cities. At any rate she induced father to give up his place as a farmhand, sell his horse and embark on an independent enterprise of his own. She was a tall silent woman with a long nose and troubled grey eyes. For herself she wanted nothing. For father and myself she was incurably ambitious.

The first venture into which the two people went turned out badly. They rented ten acres of poor stony land on Griggs's Road, eight miles from Bidwell, and launched into chicken rising. I grew into boyhood on the place and got my first impressions of life there. From the beginning they were impressions of disaster and if, in my turn, I am a gloomy man inclined to see the darker side of life, I attribute it to the fact that what should have been for me the happy joyous days of childhood were spent on a chicken farm.

One unversed in such matters can have no notion of the many and tragic things that can happen to a chicken. It is born out of an egg, lives for a few weeks as a tiny fluffy thing such as you will see pictured on Easter cards, then becomes hideously naked, eats quantities of corn and meal bought by the sweat of your father's brow, gets diseases called pip, cholera, and other names, stands looking with stupid eyes at the sun, becomes sick and dies. A few hens and now and then a rooster intended to serve God's mysterious ends, struggle through to maturity. The hens lay eggs out of which come other chickens and the dreadful cycle is thus made complete. It is all unbelievably complex. Most philosophers must have been raised on chicken farms. One hopes for so much from a chicken and is so dreadfully disillusioned. Small chickens, just setting out on the journey of life, look so bright and alert and they are in fact so dreadfully stupid. They are so much like people they mix one up in one's judgments of life. If disease does not kill them they wait until your expectations are thoroughly aroused and then walk under the wheels of a wagon — to go squashed and dead back to their maker. Vermin infest their youth, and fortunes must be spent for curative powders. In later life I have seen how a literature has been built up on the subject of fortunes to be made out of the raising of chickens. It is intended to be read by the gods who have just eaten of the tree of the knowledge of good and evil. It is a hopeful literature and declares that much may be done by simple ambitious people who own a few hens. Do not be led astray by it. It was not written for you. Go hunt for gold on the frozen hills of Alaska, put your faith in the honesty of a politician, believe if you will that the world is daily growing better and that good will triumph over evil, but do not read and believe the literature that is written concerning the hen. It was not written for you.

I, however, digress. My tale does not primarily concern itself with the hen. If correctly told it will center on the egg. For ten years my father and mother struggled to make our chicken farm pay and then they gave up that struggle and began another. They moved into the town of Bidwell, Ohio and embarked in the restaurant business. After ten years of worry with incubators that did not hatch, and with tiny — and in their own way lovely — balls of fluff that passed on into semi-naked puller hood and from that into dead hen hood, we threw all aside and packing our belongings on a wagon drove down Griggs's Road toward Bidwell, a tiny caravan of hope looking for a new place from which to start on our upward journey through life.

We must have been a sad looking lot, not, I fancy, unlike refugees fleeing from a battlefield. Mother and I walked in the road. The wagon that contained our goods had been borrowed for the day from Mr. Albert Griggs, a neighbor. Out of its sides stuck the legs of cheap chairs and at the back of the pile of beds, tables, and boxes filled with kitchen utensils was a crate of live chickens, and on top of that the baby carriage in which I had been wheeled about in my infancy. Why we stuck to the baby carriage I don't know. It was unlikely other children would be born and the wheels were broken. People who have few possessions cling tightly to those they have. That is one of the facts that make life so discouraging.

Father rode on top of the wagon. He was then a bald-headed man of forty-five, a little fat and from long association with mother and the chickens he had become habitually silent and discouraged. All during our ten years on the chicken farm he had worked as a laborer on neighboring farms and most of the money he had earned had been spent for remedies to cure chicken diseases, on Wilmer's White Wonder Cholera Cure or Professor Bidlow's Egg Producer or some other preparations that mother found advertised in the poultry papers.

◂ ◂ ◂ ◂ THE AMERICAN PART

There were two little patches of hair on father's head just above his ears. I remember that as a child I used to sit looking at him when he had gone to sleep in a chair before the stove on Sunday afternoons in the winter. I had at that rime already begun to read books and have notions of my own and the bald path that led over the top of his head was, I fancied, something like a broad road, such a road as Caesar might have made on which to lead his legions out of Rome and into the wonders of an unknown world. The tufts of hair that grew above father's ears were, I thought, like forests. I fell into a half-sleeping, half-waking state and dreamed I was a tiny thing going along the road into a far beautiful place where there were no chicken farms and where life was a happy egg less affair.

One might write a book concerning our flight from the chicken farm into town. Mother and I walked the entire eight miles — she to be sure that nothing fell from the wagon and I to see the wonders of the world. On the seat of the wagon beside father was his greatest treasure. I will tell you of that.

On a chicken farm where hundreds and even thousands of chickens come out of eggs, surprising things sometimes happen. Grotesques are born out of eggs as out of people. The accident does not often occur — perhaps once in a thousand births. A chicken is, you see, born that has four legs, two pairs of wings, two heads or what not. The things do not live. They go quickly back to the hand of their maker that has for a moment trembled. The fact that the poor little things could not live was one of the tragedies of life to father. He had some sort of notion that if he could but bring into hen hood or rooster hood a five-legged hen or a two-headed rooster his fortune would be made. He dreamed of taking the wonder about to county fairs and of growing rich by exhibiting it to other farmhands.

At any rate he saved all the little monstrous things that had been born on our chicken farm. They were preserved in alcohol and put each in its own glass bottle. These he had carefully put into a box and on our journey into town it was carried on the wagon seat beside him. He drove the horses with one hand and with the other clung to the box. When we got to our destination the box was taken down at once and the bottles removed. All during our days as keepers of a restaurant in the town of Bidwell, Ohio, the grotesques in their little glass bottles sat on a shelf back of the counter. Mother sometimes protested but father was a rock on the subject of his treasure. The grotesques were, he declared, valuable. People, he said, liked to look at strange and wonderful things.

Did I say that we embarked in the restaurant business in the town of Bidwell, Ohio? I exaggerated a little. The town itself lay at the foot of a low hill and on the shore of a small river. The railroad did not run through the town and the station was a mile away to the north at a place called Pickleville. There had been a cider mill and pickle factory at the station, but before the time of our coming they had both gone out of business. In the morning and in the evening busses came down to the station along a road called Turner's Pike from the hotel on the main street of Bidwell. Our going to the out-of-the-way place to embark in the restaurant business was mother's idea. She talked of it for a year and then one day went off and rented an empty store building opposite the railroad station. It was her idea that the restaurant would be profitable. Traveling men, she said, would be always waiting around to take trains out of town and town people would come to the station to await incoming trains. They would come to the restaurant to buy pieces of pie and drink coffee. Now that I am older I know that she had another motive in going. She was ambitious for me. She wanted me to rise in the world, to get into a town school and become a man of the towns.

At Pickleville father and mother worked hard as they always had done. At first there was the necessity of putting our place into shape to be a restaurant. That took a month. Father built a shelf on which he put tins of vegetables. He painted a sign on which he put his name in large red letters. Below his name was the sharp command —"EAT HERE"— that was so seldom obeyed. A showcase was bought and filled with cigars and tobacco. Mother scrubbed the floor and the walls of the room. I went to school in the town and was glad to be away from the farm and from the presence of the discouraged, sad-looking chickens. Still I was not very joyous. In the evening I walked home from school along Turner's Pike and remembered the children I had seen playing in the town school yard. A troop of little girls had gone hopping about and singing. I tried that. Down along the frozen road I went hopping solemnly on one leg. "Hippity hop to the barber shop," I sang shrilly. Then I stopped and looked doubtfully about. I was afraid of being seen in my gay mood. It must have seemed to me that I was doing a thing that should not be done by one who, like myself, had been raised on a chicken farm where death was a daily visitor.

Mother decided that our restaurant should remain open at night. At ten in the evening a passenger train went north past our door followed by a local freight. The freight crew had switching to do in Pickleville and when the work was done they came to our restaurant for hot coffee and food. Sometimes one of them ordered a fried egg. In the morning at four they returned northbound and again visited us. A little trade began to grow up. Mother slept at night and during the day tended the restaurant and fed our boarders while father slept. He slept in the same bed mother had occupied during the night and I went off to the town of Bidwell and to school. During the long nights, while mother and I slept, father cooked meats that were to go into sandwiches for the lunch baskets of our boarders. Then an idea in regard to getting up in the world came into his head. The American spirit took hold of him. He also became ambitious.

In the long nights when there was little to do father had time to think. That was his undoing. He decided that he had in the past been an unsuccessful man because he had not been cheerful enough and that in the future he would adopt a cheerful outlook on life. In the early morning he came upstairs and got into bed with mother. She woke and the two talked. From my bed in the corner I listened.

It was father's idea that both he and mother should try to entertain the people who came to eat at our restaurant. I cannot now remember his words, but he gave the impression of one about to become in some obscure way a kind of public entertainer. When people, particularly young people from the town of Bidwell, came into our place, as on very rare occasions they did, bright entertaining conversation was to be made. From father's words I gathered that something of the jolly innkeeper effect was to be sought. Mother must have been doubtful from the first, but she said nothing discouraging. It was father's notion that a passion for the company of himself and mother would spring up in the breasts of the younger people of the town of Bidwell. In the evening bright happy groups would come singing down Turner's Pike. They would troop shouting with joy and laughter into our place. There would be song and festivity. I do not mean to give the impression that father spoke so elaborately of the matter. He was as I have said an uncommunicative man. "They want some place to go. I tell you they want some place to go," he said over and over. That was as far as he got. My own imagination has filled in the blanks.

For two or three weeks this notion of father's invaded our house. We did not talk much but in our daily lives tried earnestly to make smiles take the place of glum looks. Mother smiled at the boarders and I, catching the infection, smiled at our cat. Father became a little feverish in his anxiety to please. There was no doubt lurking somewhere in him a touch of the spirit of the showman. He did not waste much of his ammunition on the railroad men he served at night but seemed to be waiting for a young man or woman from Bidwell to come in to show what he could do. On the counter in the restaurant there was a wire basket kept always filled with eggs, and it must have been before his eyes when the idea of being entertaining was born in his brain. There was something pre-natal about the way eggs kept themselves connected with the development of his idea. At any rate an egg ruined his new impulse in life. Late one night I was awakened by a roar of anger coming from father's throat. Both mother and I sat upright in our beds. With trembling hands she lighted a lamp that stood on a table by her head. Downstairs the front door of our restaurant went shut with a bang and in a few minutes father tramped up the stairs. He held an egg in his hand and his hand trembled as though he were having a chill. There was a half insane light in his eyes. As he stood glaring at us I was sure he intended throwing the egg at either mother or me. Then he laid it gently on the table beside the lamp and dropped on his knees beside mother's bed. He began to cry like a boy and I, carried away by his grief, cried with him. The two of us filled the little upstairs room with our wailing voices. It is ridiculous, but of the picture we made I can remember only the fact that mother's hand continually stroked the bald path that ran across the top of his head. I have forgotten what mother said to him and how she induced him to tell her of what had happened downstairs. His explanation also has gone out of my mind. I remember only my own grief and fright and the shiny path over father's head glowing in the lamplight as he knelt by the bed.

As to what happened downstairs for some unexplainable reason I know the story as well as though I had been a witness to my father's discomfiture. One in time gets to know many unexplainable things. On that evening young Joe Kane, son of a merchant of Bidwell, came to Pickleville to meet his father, who was expected on the ten o'clock evening train from the south. The train was three hours late and Joe came into our place to loaf about and to wait for its arrival. The local freight train came in and the freight crew was fed. Joe was left alone in the restaurant with father.

From the moment he came into our place the Bidwell young man must have been puzzled by my father's actions. It was his notion that father was angry at him for hanging around. He noticed that the restaurant keeper was apparently disturbed by his presence and he thought of going out. However, it began to rain and he did not fancy the long walk to town and back. He bought a five-cent cigar and ordered a cup of coffee. He had a newspaper in his pocket and took it out and began to read. "I'm waiting for the evening train. It's late," he said apologetically.

He was no doubt suffering from an attack of stage fright. As so often happens in life he had thought so much and so often of the situation that now confronted him that he was somewhat nervous in its presence.

For one thing, he did not know what to do with his hands. He thrust one of them nervously over the counter and shook hands with Joe Kane. "How-de-do," he said. Joe Kane put his newspaper down and stared at him. Father's eye lighted on the basket of eggs that sat on the counter and he began to talk. "Well," he began hesitatingly, "well, you have heard of Christopher Columbus, eh?" He seemed to be angry. "That Christopher Columbus was a cheat," he declared emphatically. "He talked of making an egg stand on its end. He talked, he did, and then he went and broke the end of the egg."

My father seemed to his visitor to be beside himself at the duplicity of Christopher Columbus. He muttered and swore. He declared it was wrong to teach children that Christopher Columbus was a great man when, after all, he cheated at the critical moment. He had declared he would make an egg stand on end and then when his bluff had been called he had done a trick. Still grumbling at Columbus, father took an egg from the basket on the counter and began to walk up and down. He rolled the egg between the palms of his hands. He smiled genially. He began to mumble words regarding the effect to be produced on an egg by the electricity that comes out of the human body. He declared that without breaking its shell and by virtue of rolling it back and forth in his hands he could stand the egg on its end. He explained that the warmth of his hands and the gentle rolling movement he gave the egg created a new center of gravity, and Joe Kane was mildly interested. "I have handled thousands of eggs," father said. "No one knows more about eggs than I do."

He stood the egg on the counter and it fell on its side. He tried the trick again and again, each time rolling the egg between the palms of his hands and saying the words regarding the wonders of electricity and the laws of gravity. When after a half hour's effort he did succeed in making the egg stand for a moment, he looked up to find that his visitor was no longer watching. By the time he had succeeded in calling Joe Kane's attention to the success of his effort, the egg had again rolled over and lay on its side.

Afire with the showman's passion and at the same time a good deal disconcerted by the failure of his first effort, father now took the bottles containing the poultry monstrosities down from their place on the shelf and began to show them to his visitor. "How would you like to have seven legs and two heads like this fellow?" he asked, exhibiting the most remarkable of his treasures. A cheerful smile played over his face. He reached over the counter and tried to slap Joe Kane on the shoulder as he had seen men do in Ben Head's saloon when he was a young farmhand and drove to town on Saturday evenings. His visitor was made a little ill by the sight of the body of the terribly deformed bird floating in the alcohol in the bottle and got up to go. Coming from behind the counter, father took hold of the young man's arm and led him back to his seat. He grew a little angry and for a moment had to turn his face away and force himself to smile. Then he put the bottles back on the shelf. In an outburst of generosity he fairly compelled Joe Kane to have a fresh cup of coffee and another cigar at his expense. Then he took a pan and filling it with vinegar, taken from a jug that sat beneath the counter, he declared himself about to do a new trick. "I will heat this egg in this pan of vinegar," he said. "Then I will put it through the neck of a bottle without breaking the shell. When the egg is inside the bottle it will resume its normal shape and the shell will become hard again. Then I will give the bottle with the egg in it to you. You can take it about with you wherever you go. People will want to know how you got the egg in the bottle. Don't tell them. Keep them guessing. That is the way to have fun with this trick."

Father grinned and winked at his visitor. Joe Kane decided that the man who confronted him was mildly insane but harmless. He drank the cup of coffee that had been given him and began to read his paper again. When the egg had been heated in vinegar, father carried it on a spoon to the counter and going into a back room got an empty bottle. He was angry because his visitor did not watch him as he began to do his trick, but nevertheless went cheerfully to work. For a long time he struggled, trying to get the egg to go through the neck of the bottle. He put the pan of vinegar back on the stove, intending to reheat the egg, then picked it up and burned his fingers. After a second bath in the hot vinegar, the shell of the egg had been softened a little but not enough for his purpose. He worked and worked and a spirit of desperate determination took possession of him. When he thought that at last the trick was about to be consummated, the delayed train came in at the station and Joe Kane started to go nonchalantly out at the door. Father made a last desperate effort to conquer the egg and make it do the thing that would establish his reputation as one who knew how to entertain guests who came into his restaurant. He worried the egg. He attempted to be somewhat rough with it. He swore and the sweat stood out on his forehead. The egg broke under his hand. When the contents spurted over his clothes, Joe Kane, who had stopped at the door, turned and laughed.

A roar of anger rose from my father's throat. He danced and shouted a string of inarticulate words. Grabbing another egg from the basket on the counter, he threw it, just missing the head of the young man as he dodged through the door and escaped.

    Father came upstairs to mother and me with an egg in his hand. I do not know what he intended to do. I imagine he had some idea of destroying it, of destroying all eggs, and that he intended to let mother and me see him begin. When, however, he got into the presence of mother something happened to him. He laid the egg gently on the table and dropped on his knees by the bed as I have already explained. He later decided to close the restaurant for the night and to come upstairs and get into bed. When he did so he blew out the light and after much muttered conversation both he and mother went to sleep. I suppose I went to sleep also, but my sleep was troubled. I awoke at dawn and for a long time looked at the egg that lay on the table. I wondered why eggs had to be and why from the egg came the hen who again laid the egg. The question got into my blood. It has stayed there, I imagine, because I am the son of my father. At any rate, the problem remains unsolved in my mind. And that, I conclude, is but another evidence of the complete and final triumph of the egg — at least as far as my family is concerned.

7 F. Scott Fitzgerald

作者简介

F. Scott Fitzgerald was born on September 24, 1896, in St. Paul, Minnesota. His first novel's success made him famous and let him marry the woman he loved, but he later descended into drinking and his wife had a mental breakdown. Following the unsuccessful *Tender is the Night*, Fitzgerald moved to Hollywood and became a scriptwriter. He died of a heart attack in 1940, at age 44, his final novel only half completed. With its beautiful lyricism, pitch-perfect portrayal of the Jazz Age, and searching critiques of materialism, love and the American Dream, *The Great Gatsby* is considered Fitzgerald's finest work.

弗·斯科特·菲茨杰拉德于1896年9月24日出生在美国中部的明尼苏达州。他的第一部小说使他成名,从而娶了他最爱的女人,但是后来他沉迷于酒吧,他的妻子也变得精神崩溃。随后,由于《温柔之夜》的发行不是很成功,菲茨杰拉德进军好莱坞,成为一名编剧。他于1940年死于心脏病,卒年44岁,而他的最后一部小说仅完成了一半。由于其美妙的讽刺艺术,对爵士时代精推到位的描述,及对物质主义,爱和美国梦的追寻,《了不起的盖茨比》成为菲茨杰拉德最出色的作品。

作品及导读

作品 1

The Great Gatsby

导读

As *The Great Gatsby* opens, Nick Carraway, the story's narrator, remembers his upbringing and the lessons his family taught him. Readers learn of his past, his education, and his sense of moral justice, as he begins to unfold the story of Jay Gatsby. The narration takes place more than a year after the incidents described, so Nick is working through the filter of memory in relaying the story's events. The story proper begins when Nick moves from the Midwest to West Egg, Long Island, seeking to become a "well-rounded man" and to recapture some of the excitement and adventure he experienced as a soldier in WWI. As he tries to make his way as a bond salesman, he rents a small house next door to a mansion which, it turns out, belongs to Gatsby.

Daisy Buchanan, Nick's cousin, and her husband, Tom, live across the bay in the fashionable community of East Egg. Nick goes to visit Daisy, an ephemeral woman with a socialite's luminescence, and Tom, a brutish, hulking, powerful man made arrogant through generations of privilege, and there he meets Jordan Baker, the professional golfer and a girlhood friend of Daisy's. As the foursome lounge around the Buchanans' estate, they discuss the day's most pressing matters: the merits of living in the East, what to do on the longest day of the year, reactionary politics, and other such shallow topics. When Tom takes a phone call, Jordan informs Nick that Tom's mistress is on the phone. Tom, known for his infidelities, makes no pretense to cover up his affairs. As Tom and Daisy work to set up Nick and Jordan, they seize the opportunity to question him about his supposed engagement to a girl back home. Nick reassures them there is no impending marriage, merely a series of rumors that cannot substitute for truth.

Upon returning home that evening, as he is sitting outside, Nick notices a figure emerging from Gatsby's mansion. Nick's initial impulse is to call out to Gatsby, but he resists because Gatsby "gave a sudden intimation that he was content to be alone." It was while watching Gatsby that Nick witnesses a curious event. Gatsby, standing by the waterside, stretches his arms toward the darkness, trembling. This gesture seems odd to Nick, because all he can make out is a green light, such as one finds at the end of a dock, across the Sound. Looking back at the mysterious figure Nick realizes that Gatsby has vanished.

随着《了不起的盖茨比》故事的展开,故事的叙述者尼克·卡拉维追忆他的成长经历还有家族的教诲。随着他讲述杰·盖茨比的故事,读者们逐渐知道关于他的过往、教育背景,还有他的道德正义观。故事的回顾在事件发生一年多以后,尼克抽丝剥茧地追忆了整个事件的经过。故事恰好就开始于尼克从美国中西部搬到长岛的西卵村,他一直想要成为一个"成熟"的男人,也盼望能重获在第一次世界大战中当士兵的那种酣畅和冒险的快感。他试图去当一名债券销售员,他租借在盖茨比府邸所属的一间小公寓里。

黛西·布坎南,尼克的表妹,和她的丈夫汤姆,住在海湾边上西卵村的时髦社区里。尼克去看望黛西,她是一个热衷于社交活动的、朝生暮死又魅力十足的名媛;而汤姆则是一个冷酷、魁梧笨重、盛气凌人、傲慢地坚信特权的人。在那儿他还碰到了黛西少女时代的朋友,同时也是一味职业高尔夫球员,约旦·贝克。这四个人在布坎南宅邸里闲逛,回忆最有趣的事情:住在东部的好处、在一年中最漫长的日子里干些什么、保守的政治言论等等诸如此类浅薄的话题。汤姆接了一个电话,约旦告诉尼克这是汤姆的情妇的来电。汤姆一直都对婚姻不忠,也没有为婚外情找借口。当汤姆和黛西准备送别尼克和乔丹时,他们逮着机会问尼克要娶回家的女孩儿。尼克说根本没有近斯结婚的打算,仅仅只是一派谣言。

在当天晚上回到家时,当尼克坐在屋子外面,他留意到盖茨比的家里出现了一个人影。尼克的第一反应就是喊盖茨比,但他没有这样做,因为盖茨比的家里出现了一个人影。尼克的第一反应就是喊盖茨比,但他没有这样做,因为盖茨比"好像表示他满足于独自待着",正当在观察盖茨比时,尼克发现了奇怪的事情。盖茨比他朝着幽暗的海水把两只胳膊伸了出去,颤抖着。尼克觉得这个姿势非常诡异,因为他说见的除了一束绿光外,什么也没有,那光也许是一座码头的尽头。等尼克再回头看神秘的影子,发现盖茨比已经不见踪影了。

选 文

The Great Gatsby
Chapter 1

In my younger and more vulnerable years my father gave me some advice that I've been turning over in my mind ever since.

"Whenever you feel like criticizing any one," he told me, "just remember that all the people in this world haven't had the advantages that you've had."

He didn't say any more, but we've always been unusually communicative in a reserved way, and I understood that he meant a great deal more than that. In consequence, I'm inclined to reserve all judgments, a habit that has opened up many curious natures to me and also made me the victim of not a few veteran bores. The abnormal mind is quick to detect and attach itself to this quality when it appears in a normal person, and so it came about that in college I was unjustly accused of being a politician, because I was privy to the secret grieves of wild, unknown men. Most of the confidences were unsought-frequently I have feigned sleep, preoccupation, or a hostile levity when I realized by some unmistakable sign that an intimate revelation was quivering on the horizon; for the intimate revelations of young men, or at least the terms in which they express them, are usually plagiaristic and marred by obvious suppressions. Reserving judgments is a matter of infinite hope. I am still a little afraid of missing something if I forget that, as my father snobbishly suggested, and I snobbishly repeat, a sense of the fundamental decencies is parceled out unequally at birth.

And, after boasting this way of my tolerance, I come to the admission that it has a limit. Conduct may be founded on the hard rock or the wet marshes, but after a certain point I don't care what it's founded on. When I came back from the East last autumn I felt that I wanted the world to be in uniform and at a sort of moral attention forever; I wanted no more riotous excursions with privileged glimpses into the human heart. Only Gatsby, the man who gives his name to this book, was exempt from my reaction-Gatsby, who represented everything for which I have an unaffected scorn. If personality is an unbroken series of successful gestures, then there was something gorgeous about him, some heightened sensitivity to the promises of life, as if he were related to one of those intricate machines that register earthquakes ten thousand miles away. This responsiveness had nothing to do with that flabby impressionability which is dignified under the name of the "creative temperament"— it was an extraordinary gift for hope, a romantic readiness such as I have never found in any other person and which it is not likely I shall ever find again. No-Gatsby turned out all right at the end; it is what preyed on Gatsby, what foul dust floated in the wake of his dreams that temporarily closed out my interest in the abortive sorrows and short-winded elations of men.

My family has been prominent, well-to-do people in this Middle Western city for three generations. The Carraways are something of a clan, and we have a tradition that we're descended from the Dukes of Buccleuch, but the actual founder of my line was my grandfather's brother, who came here in fifty-one, sent a substitute to the Civil War, and started the wholesale hardware business that my father carries on to-day.

I never saw this great-uncle, but I'm supposed to look like him-with special reference to the rather hard-boiled painting that hangs in father's office I graduated from New Haven in 1915, just a quarter of a century after my father, and a little later I participated in that delayed Teutonic migration known as the Great War. I enjoyed the counter-raid so thoroughly that I came back restless. Instead of being the warm centre of the world, the Middle West now seemed like the ragged edge of the universe — so I decided to go east and learn the bond business. Everybody I knew was in the bond business, so I supposed it could support one more single man. All my aunts and uncles talked it over as if they were choosing a prep school for me, and finally said, "Why — ye — es," with very grave, hesitant faces. Father agreed to finance me for a year, and after various delays I came east, permanently, I thought, in the spring of twenty-two.

The practical thing was to find rooms in the city, but it was a warm season, and I had just left a country of wide lawns and friendly trees, so when a young man at the office suggested that we take a house together in a commuting town, it sounded like a great idea. He found the house, a weather-beaten cardboard bungalow at eighty a month, but at the last minute the firm ordered him to Washington, and I went out to the country alone. I had a dog — at least I had him for a few days until he ran away-and an old Dodge and a Finnish woman, who made my bed and cooked breakfast and muttered Finnish wisdom to herself over the electric stove.

It was lonely for a day or so until one morning some man, more recently arrived than I, stopped me on the road.

"How do you get to West Egg village?" he asked helplessly.

I told him. And as I walked on I was lonely no longer. I was a guide, a pathfinder, an original settler. He had casually conferred on me the freedom of the neighborhood.

And so with the sunshine and the great bursts of leaves growing on the trees, just as things grow in fast movies, I had that familiar conviction that life was beginning over again with the summer.

◂ ◂ ◂ ◂ THE AMERICAN PART

There was so much to read, for one thing, and so much fine health to be pulled down out of the young breath-giving air. I bought a dozen volumes on banking and credit and investment securities, and they stood on my shelf in red and gold like new money from the mint, promising to unfold the shining secrets that only Midas and Morgan and Maecenas knew. And I had the high intention of reading many other books besides. I was rather literary in college-one year I wrote a series of very solemn and obvious editorials for the "Yale News"— and now I was going to bring back all such things into my life and become again that most limited of all specialists, the "well-rounded man." This isn't just an epigram-life is much more successfully looked at from a single window, after all.

It was a matter of chance that I should have rented a house in one of the strangest communities in North America. It was on that slender riotous island which extends itself due east of New York-and where there are, among other natural curiosities, two unusual formations of land. Twenty miles from the city a pair of enormous eggs, identical in contour and separated only by a courtesy bay, jut out into the most domesticated body of salt water in the Western hemisphere, the great wet barnyard of Long Island Sound. they are not perfect ovals — like the egg in the Columbus story, they are both crushed flat at the contact end — but their physical resemblance must be a source of perpetual confusion to the gulls that fly overhead to the wingless a more arresting phenomenon is their dissimilarity in every particular except shape and size.

I lived at West Egg, the — well, the less fashionable of the two, though this is a most superficial tag to express the bizarre and not a little sinister contrast between them. My house was at the very tip of the egg, only fifty yards from the Sound, and squeezed between two huge places that rented for twelve or fifteen thousand a season. the one on my right was a colossal affair by any standard — it was a factual imitation of some Hotel de Ville in Normandy, with a tower on one side, spanking new under a thin beard of raw ivy, and a marble swimming pool, and more than forty acres of lawn and garden. It was Gatsby's mansion. Or, rather, as I didn't know Mr. Gatsby, it was a mansion inhabited by a gentleman of that name. My own house was an eyesore, but it was a small eyesore, and it had been overlooked, so I had a view of the water, a partial view of my neighbor's lawn, and the consoling proximity of millionaires — all for eighty dollars a month.

Across the courtesy bay the white palaces of fashionable East Egg glittered along the water, and the history of the summer really begins on the evening I drove over there to have dinner with the Tom Buchanans. Daisy was my second cousin once removed, and I'd known Tom in college. And just after the war I spent two days with them in Chicago.

Her husband, among various physical accomplishments, had been one of the most powerful ends that ever played football at New Haven — a national figure in a way, one of those men who reach such an acute limited excellence at twenty-one that everything afterward savors of anti-climax. His family were enormously wealthy — even in college his freedom with money was a matter for reproach — but now he'd left Chicago and come East in a fashion that rather took your breath away: for instance, he'd brought down a string of polo ponies from Lake Forest. It was hard to realize that a man in my own generation was wealthy enough to do that.

Why they came east I don't know. They had spent a year in France for no particular reason, and then drifted here and there unrestfully wherever people played polo and were rich together. This was a permanent move, said Daisy over the telephone, but I didn't believe it — I had no sight into Daisy's heart, but I felt that Tom would drift on forever seeking, a little wistfully, for the dramatic turbulence of some irrecoverable football game.

And so it happened that on a warm windy evening I drove over to East Egg to see two old friends whom I scarcely knew at all. Their house was even more elaborate than I expected, a cheerful red-and-white Georgian Colonial mansion, overlooking the bay. The lawn started at the beach and ran toward the front door for a quarter of a mile, jumping over sun — dials and brick walks and burning gardens — finally when it reached the house drifting up the side in bright vines as though from the momentum of its run. The front was broken by a line of French windows, glowing now with reflected gold and wide open to the warm windy afternoon, and Tom Buchanan in riding clothes was standing with his legs apart on the front porch.

He had changed since his New Haven years. Now he was a sturdy straw-haired man of thirty with a rather hard mouth and a supercilious manner. Two shining arrogant eyes had established dominance over his face and gave him the appearance of always leaning aggressively forward. Not even the effeminate swank of his riding clothes could hide the enormous power of that body-he seemed to fill those glistening boots until he strained the top lacing, and you could see a great pack of muscle shifting when his shoulder moved under his thin coat. It was a body capable of enormous leverage — a cruel body.

His speaking voice, a gruff husky tenor, added to the impression of fractiousness he conveyed. There was a touch of paternal contempt in it, even toward people he liked — and there were men at New Haven who had hated his guts

"Now, don't think my opinion on these matters is final," he seemed to say, "just because I'm stronger and more of a man than you are." We were in the same senior society, and while we were never intimate I always had the impression that he approved of me and wanted me to like him with some harsh, defiant wistfulness of his own.

We talked for a few minutes on the sunny porch.

"I've got a nice place here," he said, his eyes flashing about restlessly.

Turning me around by one arm, he moved a broad flat hand along the front vista, including in its sweep a sunken Italian garden, a half acre of deep, pungent roses, and a snub-nosed motor-boat that bumped the tide offshore.

"It belonged to Demaine, the oil man." He turned me around again, politely and abruptly. "We'll go inside."

We walked through a high hallway into a bright rosy-colored space, fragilely bound into the house by French windows at either end. The windows were ajar and gleaming white against the fresh grass outside that seemed to grow a little way into the house. A breeze blew through the room, blew curtains in at one end and out the other like pale flags, twisting them up toward the frosted wedding-cake of the ceiling, and then rippled over the wine-colored rug, making a shadow on it as wind does on the sea.

The only completely stationary object in the room was an enormous couch on which two young women were buoyed up as though upon an anchored balloon. They were both in white, and their dresses were rippling and fluttering as if they had just been blown back in after a short flight around the house. I must have stood for a few moments listening to the whip and snap of the curtains and the groan of a picture on the wall. Then there was a boom as Tom Buchanan shut the rear windows and the caught wind died out about the room, and the curtains and the rugs and the two young women ballooned slowly to the floor.

The younger of the two was a stranger to me. She was extended full length at her end of the divan, completely motionless, and with her chin raised a little, as if she were balancing something on it which was quite likely to fall. If she saw me out of the corner of her eyes she gave no hint of it — indeed, I was almost surprised into murmuring an apology for having disturbed her by coming in.

The other girl, Daisy, made an attempt to rise-she leaned slightly forward with a conscientious expression — then she laughed, an absurd, charming little laugh, and I laughed too and came forward into the room.

"I'm p-paralyzed with happiness."

She laughed again, as if she said something very witty, and held my hand for a moment, looking up into my face, promising that there was no one in the world she so much wanted to see. That was a way she had. She hinted in a murmur that the surname of the balancing girl was Baker. (I've heard it said that Daisy's murmur was only to make people lean toward her; an irrelevant criticism that made it no less charming.) At any rate, Miss Baker's lips fluttered, she nodded at me almost imperceptibly, and then quickly tipped her head back again — the object she was balancing had obviously tottered a little and given her something of a fright. Again a sort of apology arose to my lips. Almost any exhibition of complete self-sufficiency draws a stunned tribute from me.

I looked back at my cousin, who began to ask me questions in her low, thrilling voice. It was the kind of voice that the ear follows up and down, as if each speech is an arrangement of notes that will never be played again. Her face was sad and lovely with bright things in it, bright eyes and a bright passionate mouth, but there was an excitement in her voice that men who had cared for her found difficult to forget: a singing compulsion, a whispered "Listen," a promise that she had done gay, exciting things just a while since and that there were gay, exciting things hovering in the next hour.

I told her how I had stopped off in Chicago for a day on my way East, and how a dozen people had sent their love through me.

"Do they miss me?" she cried ecstatically.

"The whole town is desolate. All the cars have the left rear wheel painted black as a mourning wreath, and there's a persistent wail all night along the north shore."

"How gorgeous! Let's go back, Tom. To-morrow!" Then she added irrelevantly: "You ought to see the baby."

"I'd like to."

"She's asleep. She's three years old. Haven't you ever seen her?"

"Never."

"Well, you ought to see her. She's —"

Tom Buchanan, who had been hovering restlessly about the room, stopped and rested his hand on my shoulder.

"What you doing, Nick?"

"I'm a bond man."

"Who with?" I told him.

"Never heard of them," he remarked decisively.

This annoyed me.

"You will," I answered shortly. "You will if you stay in the East. quot;

"Oh, I'll stay in the East, don't you worry," he said, glancing at Daisy and then back at me, as if he were alert for something more. "I'd be a God damned fool to live anywhere else."

At this point Miss Baker said: "Absolutely!" with such suddenness that I started-it was the first word she uttered since I came into the room. Evidently it surprised her as much as it did me, for she yawned and with a series of rapid, deft movements stood up into the room.

"I'm stiff," she complained, "I've been lying on that sofa for as long as I can remember."

"Don't look at me," Daisy retorted. "I've been trying to get you to New York all afternoon."

"No, thanks," said Miss Baker to the four cocktails just in from the pantry, "I'm absolutely in training."

Her host looked at her incredulously.

"You are!" He took down his drink as if it were a drop in the bottom of a glass. "How you ever get anything done is beyond me."

I looked at Miss Baker, wondering what it was she "got done." I enjoyed looking at her. She was a slender, small-breasted girl, with an erect carriage, which she accentuated by throwing her body backward at the shoulders like a young cadet. Her gray sun-strained eyes looked back at me with polite reciprocal curiosity out of a wan, charming, discontented face. It occurred to me now that I had seen her, or a picture of her, somewhere before.

"You live in West Egg," she remarked contemptuously. "I know somebody there."

"I don't know a single —"

"You must know Gatsby."

"Gatsby?" demanded Daisy. "What Gatsby?"

Before I could reply that he was my neighbor dinner was announced; wedging his tense arm imperatively under mine, Tom Buchanan compelled me from the room as though he were moving a checker to another square.

Splendidly, languidly, their hands set lightly on their hips, the two young women preceded us out onto a rosy-colored porch, open toward the sunset, where four candles flickered on the table in the diminished wind.

"Why candles?" objected Daisy, frowning. She snapped them out with her fingers. "In two weeks it'll be the longest day in the year." She looked at us all radiantly. "Do you always watch for the longest day of the year and then miss it? I always watch for the longest day in the year and then miss it."

"We ought to plan something," yawned Miss Baker, sitting down at the table as if she were getting into bed.

"All right," said Daisy. "What'll we plan?" She turned to me helplessly: "What do people plan?"

Before I could answer her eyes fast ended with an awed expression on her little finger.

"Look!" she complained. "I hurt it." We all looked — the knuckle was black and blue.

"You did it, Tom," she said accusingly. "I know you didn't mean to, but you did do it. That's what I get for marrying a brute of a man, a great, big, hulking physical specimen of a —"

"I hate that word hulking," objected Tom crossly, "even in kidding."

"Hulking," insisted Daisy.

Sometimes she and Miss Baker talked at once, unobtrusively and with a bantering inconsequence that was never quite chatter, which was as cool as their white dresses and their impersonal eyes in the absence of all desire. They were here, and they accepted Tom and me, making only a polite pleasant effort to entertain or to be entertained. They knew that presently dinner would be over and a little later the evening too would be over and casually put away. It was sharply different from the West, where an evening was hurried from phase to phase toward its close, in a continually disappointed anticipation or else in sheer nervous dread of the moment itself.

"You make me feel uncivilized, Daisy," I confessed on my second glass of corky but rather impressive claret. "Can't you talk about crops or something?"

I meant nothing in particular by this remark, but it was taken up in an unexpected way.

"Civilization's going to pieces," broke out Tom violently. "I've gotten to be a terrible pessimist about things. Have you read 'The Rise of the Colored Empires' by this man Goddard?"

"Why, no," I answered, rather surprised by his tone.

"Well, it's a fine book, and everybody ought to read it. The idea is if we don't look out the white race will be — will be utterly submerged. It's all scientific stuff; it's been proved."

"Tom's getting very profound," said Daisy, with an expression of unthoughtful sadness. "He reads deep books with long words in them. What was that word we —"

"Well, these books are all scientific," insisted Tom, glancing at her impatiently. "This fellow has worked out the whole thing. It's up to us, who are the dominant race, to watch out or these other races will have control of things."

"We've got to beat them down," whispered Daisy, winking ferociously toward the fervent sun.

"You ought to live in California —" began Miss Baker, but Tom interrupted her by shifting heavily in his chair.

"This idea is that we're Nordics. I am, and you are, and you are, and —" After an infinitesimal hesitation he included Daisy with a slight nod, and she winked at me again. "— And we've produced all the things that go to make civilization — oh, science and art, and all that. Do you see?"

There was something pathetic in his concentration, as if his complacency, more acute than of old, was not enough to him any more. When, almost immediately, the telephone rang inside and the butler left the porch Daisy seized upon the momentary interruption and leaned toward me.

"I'll tell you a family secret," she whispered enthusiastically. "It's about the butler's nose. Do you want to hear about the butler's nose?"

"That's why I came over tonight."

"Well, he wasn't always a butler; he used to be the silver polisher for some people in New York that had a silver service for two hundred people. He had to polish it from morning till night, until finally it began to affect his nose —"

"Things went from bad to worse," suggested Miss Baker.

"Yes. Things went from bad to worse, until finally he had to give up his position."

For a moment the last sunshine fell with romantic affection upon her glowing face; her voice compelled me forward breathlessly as I listened — then the glow faded, each light deserting her with lingering regret, like children leaving a pleasant street at dusk.

The butler came back and murmured something close to Tom's ear, whereupon Tom frowned, pushed back his chair, and without a word went inside. As if his absence quickened something within her, Daisy leaned forward again, her voice glowing and singing.

"I love to see you at my table, Nick. You remind me of a — of a rose, an absolute rose. Doesn't he?" She turned to Miss Baker for confirmation. "An absolute rose?"

This was untrue. I am not even faintly like a rose. She was only extemporizing, but stirring warmth flowed from her, as if her heart was trying to come out to you concealed in one of those breathless, thrilling words. Then suddenly she threw her napkin on the table and excused herself and went into the house.

Miss Baker and I exchanged a short glance consciously devoid of meaning. I was about to speak when she sat up alertly and said "Sh!" in a warning voice. A subdued impassioned murmur was audible in the room beyond, and Miss Baker leaned forward unashamed, trying to hear. The murmur trembled on the verge of coherence, sank down, mounted excitedly, and then ceased altogether.

"This Mr. Gatsby you spoke of is my neighbor —" I said.

"Don't talk. I want to hear what happens."

"Is something happening?" I inquired innocently.

"You mean to say you don't know?" said Miss Baker, honestly surprised. "I thought everybody knew."

"I don't."

"Why —" she said hesitantly, "Tom's got some woman in New York."

"Got some woman?" I repeated blankly.

Miss Baker nodded.

"She might have the decency not to telephone him at dinner time. Don't you think?";

Almost before I had grasped her meaning there was the flutter of a dress and the crunch of leather boots, and Tom and Daisy were back at the table.

"It couldn't be helped!" cried Daisy with tense gayety.

She sat down, glanced searchingly at Miss Baker and then at me, and continued, "I looked outdoors for a minute, and it's very romantic outdoors. There's a bird on the lawn that I think must be a nightingale come over on the Cunard or White Star Line. He's singing away —" Her voice sang: "It's romantic, isn't it, Tom?"

"Very romantic," he said, and then miserably to me: "If it's light enough after dinner, I want to take you down to the stables."

The telephone rang inside, startlingly, and as Daisy shook her head decisively at Tom the subject of the stables, in fact all subjects, vanished into air. Among the broken fragments of the last five minutes at table I remember the candles being lit again, pointlessly, and I was conscious of wanting to look squarely at every one, and yet to avoid all eyes. I couldn't guess what Daisy and Tom were thinking, but I doubt if even Miss Baker, who seemed to have mastered a certain hardy skepticism, was able utterly to put this fifth guest's shrill metallic urgency out of mind. To a certain temperament the situation might have seemed intriguing — my own instinct was to telephone immediately for the police.

The horses, needless to say, were not mentioned again. Tom and Miss Baker, with several feet of twilight between them, strolled back into the library, as if to a vigil beside a perfectly tangible body, while, trying to look pleasantly interested and a little deaf, I followed Daisy around a chain of connecting verandas to the porch in front. In its deep gloom we sat down side by side on a wicker settee.

Daisy took her face in her hands as if feeling its lovely shape, and her eyes moved gradually out into the velvet dusk. I saw that turbulent emotions possessed her, so I asked what I thought would be some sedative questions about her little girl.

"We don't know each other very well, Nick," she said suddenly. "You didn't come to my wedding."

"I wasn't back from the war."

"That's true." She hesitated. "Well, I've had a very bad time, Nick, and I'm pretty cynical about everything."

Evidently she had reason to be. I waited but she didn't say any more, and after a moment I returned rather feebly to the subject of her daughter.

"I suppose she talks, and-eats, and everything."

"Oh, yes." She looked at me absently. "Listen, Nick; let me tell you what I said when she was born. Would you like to hear?"

"Very much."

"It'll show you how I've gotten to feel about — things. Well, she was less than an hour old and Tom was God knows where. I woke up out of the ether with an utterly abandoned feeling, and asked the nurse right away if it was a boy or a girl. She told me it was a girl, and so I turned my head away and wept. 'All right,' I said, 'I'm glad it's a girl. And I hope she'll be a fool — that's the best thing a girl can be in this world, a beautiful little fool."

"You see I think everything's terrible anyhow," she went on in a convinced way. "Everybody thinks so — the most advanced people. And I know. I've been everywhere and seen everything and done everything." Her eyes flashed around her in a defiant way, rather like Tom's, and she laughed with thrilling scorn. "Sophisticated — God, I'm sophisticated!"

The instant her voice broke off, ceasing to compel my attention, my belief, I felt the basic insincerity of what she had said. It made me uneasy, as though the whole evening had been a trick of some sort to exact a contributory emotion from me. I waited, and sure enough, in a moment she looked at me with an absolute smirk on her lovely face, as if she had asserted her membership in a rather distinguished secret society to which she and Tom belonged."

Inside, the crimson room bloomed with light. Tom and Miss Baker sat at either end of the long couch and she read aloud to him from the "Saturday Evening Post"— the words, murmurus and uninflected, running together in a soothing tune. The lamp-light, bright on his boots and dull on the autumn-leaf yellow of her hair, glinted along the paper as she turned a page with a flutter of slender muscles in her arms.

When we came in she held us silent for a moment with a lifted hand.

"To be continued," she said, tossing the magazine on the table, "in our very next issue."

Her body asserted itself with a restless movement of her knee, and she stood up.

"Ten o'clock," she remarked, apparently finding the time on the ceiling.

THE AMERICAN PART

"Jordan's going to play in the tournament to-morrow," explained Daisy, "over at Westchester."

"Oh — you're Jordan Baker."

I knew now why her face was familiar — its pleasing contemptuous expression had looked out at me from many rotogravure pictures of the sporting life at Asheville and Hot Springs and Palm Beach. I had heard some story of her too, a critical, unpleasant story, but what it was I had forgotten long ago.

"Good night," she said softly. "Wake me at eight, won't you."

"If you'll get up."

"I will. Good night, Mr. Carraway. See you at noon."

"Of course you will," confirmed Daisy. "In fact I think I'll arrange a marriage. Come over often, Nick, and I'll sort of-oh-fling you together. You know — lock you up accidentally in linen closets and push you out to sea in a boat, and all that sort of thing —"

"Good night," called Miss Baker from the stairs. "I haven't heard a word."

"She's a nice girl," said Tom after a moment. "They oughtn't to let her run around the country this way."

"Who oughtn't to?" inquired Daisy coldly.

"Her family."

"Her family is one aunt about a thousand years old. Besides, Nick's going to look after her, aren't you, Nick? She's going to spend lots of week-ends out here this summer. I think the home influence will be very good for her."

Daisy and Tom looked at each other for a moment in silence.

"Is she from New York?" I asked quickly.

"From Louisville. Our white girlhood was passed together there. Our beautiful white —"

"Did you give Nick a little heart to heart talk on the veranda?" demanded Tom suddenly.

"Did I?" She looked at me. "I can't seem to remember, but I think we talked about the Nordic race. Yes, I'm sure we did. It sort of crept up on us and first thing you know —"

"Don't believe everything you hear, Nick," he advised me.

I said lightly that I had heard nothing at all, and a few minutes later I got up to go home. They came to the door with me and stood side by side in a cheerful square of light. As I started my motor Daisy peremptorily called: "Wait!" "I forgot to ask you something, and it's important. We heard you were engaged to a girl out West."

"That's right," corroborated Tom kindly. "We heard that you were engaged."

"It's libel. I'm too poor."

"But we heard it," insisted Daisy, surprising me by opening up again in a flower-like way. "We heard it from three people, so it must be true."

Of course I knew what they were referring to, but I wasn't even vaguely engaged. The fact that gossip had published the banns was one of the reasons I had come east. You can't stop going with an old friend on account of rumors, and on the other hand I had no intention of being rumored into marriage.

Their interest rather touched me and made them less remotely rich — nevertheless, I was confused and a little disgusted as I drove away. It seemed to me that the thing for Daisy to do was to rush out of the house, child in arms — but apparently there were no such intentions in her head. As for Tom, the fact that he "had some woman in New York" was really less surprising than that he had been depressed by a book. Something was making him nibble at the edge of stale ideas as if his sturdy physical egotism no longer nourished his peremptory heart.

Already it was deep summer on roadhouse roofs and in front of wayside garages, where new red gas-pumps sat out in pools of light, and when I reached my estate at West Egg I ran the car under its shed and sat for a while on an abandoned grass roller in the yard. The wind had blown off, leaving a loud, bright night, with wings beating in the trees and a persistent organ sound as the full bellows of the earth blew the frogs full of life. The silhouette of a moving cat wavered across the moonlight, and turning my head to watch it, I saw that I was not alone — fifty feet away a figure had emerged from the shadow of my neighbor's mansion and was standing with his hands in his pockets regarding the silver pepper of the stars. Something in his leisurely movements and the secure position of his feet upon the lawn suggested that it was Mr. Gatsby himself, come out to determine what share was his of our local heavens.

I decided to call to him. Miss Baker had mentioned him at dinner, and that would do for an introduction. But I didn't call to him, for he gave a sudden intimation that he was content to be alone — he stretched out his arms toward the dark water in a curious way, and, far as I was from him, I could have sworn he was trembling. Involuntarily I glanced seaward — and distinguished nothing except a single green light, minute and far away, that might have been the end of a dock. When I looked once more for Gatsby he had vanished, and I was alone again in the unquiet darkness.

相关链接

The American Dream: is a national ethos of the United States, a set of ideals in which freedom includes the opportunity for prosperity and success, and an upward social mobility achieved through hard work.

The idea of the American Dream is rooted in *the United States Declaration of Independence* which proclaims that "all men are created equal" and that they are "endowed by their Creator with certain inalienable Rights" including "Life, Liberty and the pursuit of Happiness." The meaning of the "American Dream" has changed over the course of history, and includes both personal components (such as home ownership and upward mobility) and a global vision. The ethos today implies an opportunity for Americans to achieve prosperity through hard work. According to The Dream, this includes the opportunity for one's children to grow up and receive a good education and career without artificial barriers. It is the opportunity to make individual choices without the prior restrictions that limited people according to their class, caste, religion, race, or ethnicity. Immigrants to the United States sponsored ethnic newspapers in their own language; the editors typically promoted the American Dream.

The American Dream, which has lured tens of millions of all nations to American shores in the past century, has not been a dream of merely material plenty, though that has doubtlessly counted heavily. It has been much more than that. It has been a dream of being able to grow to fullest development as man and woman, unhampered by the barriers which had slowly been erected in the older civilizations, unrepressed by social orders which had developed for the benefit of classes rather than for the simple human being of any and every class.

Martin Luther King, Jr., in his *Letter from a Birmingham Jail* (1963) rooted the civil rights movement in the black quest for the American Dream: "We will win our freedom because the sacred heritage of our nation and the eternal will of God are embodied in our echoing demands ... when these disinherited children of God sat down at lunch counters they were in reality standing up for what is best in the American dream and for the most sacred values in our Judeo-Christian heritage, thereby bringing our nation back to those great wells of democracy which were dug deep by the founding fathers in their formulation of the Constitution and the *Declaration of Independence*."

The Lost Generation was the generation that came during World War I. The term was popularized by Ernest Hemingway, who used it as one of two contrasting epigraphs for his novel, *The Sun Also Rises*. This generation included distinguished artists such as F. Scott Fitzgerald, T·S·Eliot, John Dos Passos, Waldo Peirce, Isadora Duncan, Abraham Walkowitz, Alan Seeger, and Erich Maria Remarque.

In literature, this term originated with Gertrude Stein who, after being unimpressed by the skills of a young car mechanic, asked the garage owner where the young man had been trained. The garage owner told her that while young men were easy to train, it was those in their mid-twenties to thirties, the men who had been through WWI, whom he considered a "lost generation."

8 William Faulkner

作者简介

William Faulkner was born in New Albany, Mississippi. While he was still a child, the family moved to Oxford, Mississippi. Faulkner's education was irregular after the fifth grade. Although he attended high school for a period and later took courses at the University of Mississippi, he never earned a degree. In 1918, he was refused admission into the armed force because of his size. Determined to fight in World War I, he enlisted in the Royal Canadian Air Force and had basic training in Toronto. But the war was over before he could make his first solo flight.

After the war he studied literature at the University Mississippi for a short time. He published his first collection of poems entitled *The Marble Faun* in 1924. Despite his desire to be a poet, he had come to realize that his talent was for prose. In 1926 he published his first novel, *Soldier's Pay*. Then he traveled to Europe, where he learned the experimental writing of James Joyce and the psychoanalysis of Sigmund Freud, thus widening his vision further. In 1929 Faulkner published his ambitious work, *The Sound and the Fury*, in which he portayed the decline of aristocratic family, by the technique of allowing the main characters to tell the story in internal monologues. His other four works, *As I Lay Dying* (1930), *Light in August* (1932), *Absalom, Absalom*! (1936), and *Go Down, the Moses* (1942), are all considered, masterpiece of modernist fiction.

In 1929, Faulkner married Estelle Oldham, his childhood sweetheart, who had recently divorced her husband. The Next year he published the traditional southern pillared house in Oxford, which he named Roman Oak. To earn money to support his wife and children, Faulkner worked over the next 20 years in Hollywood on several screenplays. Faulkner received the 1949 Nobel Prize for literature and the 1954 Pulitzer Prize for his novel *The Fable*. During the last years of his life, besides his problems with alcohol, his wife's drug addiction and declining health shadowed his life.

Faulkner was particularly noted for the eloquent richness of his prose style and for the unique blend of tragedy and humor in his works. He was also a brilliant literary technician, making frequent use of convoluted time sequences and of the stream-of-consciousness technique. He borrowed cinematic devices experimented with rambling interior monologues. The language of his characters is based on popular Southern speech, and can be foul, funny, brilliantly metaphorical, savage, and exciting. Thus, Faulkner has been considered America's greatest novelist in the modern period. The best of his fictions rank among the most enduring of world literature. In writing about his land and about man in the ageless, eternal struggles, Faulkner speaks for both his people and humanity.

福克纳出生在密西西比州新阿尔巴尼镇,当他还很小的时候,他的家就搬到了密西西比州牛津镇。福克纳的教育经历在他五年级之后就变得非同寻常。尽管他上了一段时间的中学,而且后来还在密西西比大学学了些课程,但是他却从未取得过学位。在1918年,他参军却因为身体矮小而遭到拒绝。但是他已下定决心参加一战,后来他编入了加拿大皇家空军而且在多伦多接受了些基础的训练。但是一直到一战结束前他都没有机会进行独自飞行。

战后,他在密西西比大学学习了一段时间文学,然后在1924年发表了他的第一部诗集《玉石雕像卷》。尽管他渴望成为一名诗人,但是他却慢慢意识到了他在散文创作方面的才能。1926年,出版了他的第一部小说《士兵的报酬》,然后他游历欧洲,在那里学习到了詹姆斯·乔伊斯写作技巧和西格蒙德·弗洛伊德的心理分析,自此,他的眼界变得更加开阔,在1929年,福克纳发表了他的一篇充满雄心壮志的作品——《喧哗与躁动》,在这首诗中,他允许主要角色以内心独白的方式来讲述故事,以此描述了贵族阶层的衰落,他其他的四部作品——《我弥留之际》(1930)、《八月之光》(1932)、《押沙龙,押沙龙》(1936)、《去吧,莫西》(1936)都被认为是现代小说的杰出作品。

1929年,福克纳娶了与他青梅竹马的,刚刚与她丈夫离婚的奥尔丹。第二年,他公开了位于牛津镇的南方的一个传统柱状房子,他把这座房子命名为罗马橡树。为了挣钱养活他的妻子和孩子,在接下来的20多年,福克纳一直在好莱坞为几部荧幕电影工作。1949年,福克纳获得了诺贝尔文学奖,1954又因他的小说《寓言》斩获普利策奖。在他生命的最后几年,他酗酒成瘾,他的妻子沉溺于毒品,健康状况每况愈同步,给他的生活蒙上了阴影。

福克纳极其显著的特点是,他的诗歌风格隽永而又意涵丰富,将悲剧的氛围与幽默的氛围,以一种独特的方式结合起来。他也是一位富有智慧的文学巨匠,能熟练地使用复杂的时间序列和一系列的意识。他借助了电影的策略,并与多位小说家一起研讨,在简单的故事情节中植入了松散的内心独白。他小说中的人物语言基于南部流行的演讲,语言滑稽、有趣,富有深刻的比喻义,粗野,同时又激动人心。因此,福克纳也被看做美国现代最伟大的小说家。福克纳最好的文学作品对世界文学有持久的影响力。在作品中,他写了自己祖国及人民永恒的,持久地挣扎,福克纳既是为本国人民在呐喊,也是为世界人民在呐喊。

作品及导读

作 品 1

Absalom, Absalom!

导 读

Absalom, Absalom! tells that in September 1909, in Yoknapatawpha County, near Jefferson, Mississippi, Quentin Compson is sent a handwritten note from an old woman named Miss Rosa Coldfield, summoning him to meet her that afternoon, so that he can hear the story of her youth and of the destruction of her family. Quentin, a young man from a prominent Jefferson family — his grandfather was a general in the Civil War — is perplexed as to why she would want to talk to him, and asks his father about it. Mr. Compson explains that Quentin's grandfather had been involved in the story, because he was a friend of a man named Thomas Sutpen, whom Rosa Coldfield considers the demon responsible both for her family's ruination and her own.

Quentin goes to see Rosa Coldfield; they sit in the musty room she calls the "office," with the shutters shut so tightly that only thin slits of light shine into the room, and he listens to her story. She explains to him that she has heard he is preparing to attend Harvard — perhaps he would have literary ambitions, and perhaps he would like to write down the story one day. Quentin realizes that she wants the story to be told, so that its hearers will understand how God could have let the South lose the war — because the South was in the hands of men like Thomas Sutpen, who had valor and strength but neither pity nor compassion.

Miss Rosa's narrative is told with an intense, smoldering bitterness: she has spent the last four decades burning up in her obsession with the events she now recounts. In 1833, she says, Thomas Sutpen descended upon Jefferson with nothing more than a horse and two pistols and unknown past (with a group of savage slaves and a French architect in tow, Sutpen at their forefront like a demon — this is how Quentin pictures the event). Sutpen was little better than a savage himself, holding fights between his slaves — fights in which he often participated — and horse races, luring men to his plantation for events indescribable to young girls. Thirsting for respectability, Sutpen married Ellen Coldfield, the older sister of Miss Rosa, who was yet to be born), and the daughter of a local Methodist merchant. Sutpen had two children by Ellen, Henry in 1839 and Judith a year later, but being a father did not temper his wild, violent behavior. One night Ellen discovered her husband participating in a fight with a negro before a bloodthirsty crowd, with the children watching — Henry crying and upset, Judith (who had snuck there to watch with a little negro girl) in rapt attention. Judith seemed to possess her father's temperament: when his reckless carriage races before the church were stopped by the minister's complaints, the six-year-old girl began to cry insensibly.

Later details in the story become somewhat vague in Miss Rosa's narration: Thomas Sutpen and his son Henry both fought in the war, she says, and she describes Ellen on her deathbed. Just before she died, Ellen asked Rosa, then a young girl, to look out for Judith — even though Judith was older than Rosa. Rosa replied that the only thing the children needed protection from was themselves. But other than these glimpses, details are scarce — except for one central event which Rosa refers to several times: on Judith's wedding day, just before the wedding was to take place, her brother Henry killed her fiancé in front of the gates of Sutpen's Hundred.

文章讲述1909年的9月,在约克纳帕塔法郡,靠近密苏里州的杰弗逊,昆丁·康普生收到了一个名叫罗沙·科德菲尔德小姐的老妇人手写的一个便条,便条上写到让他那天下午去见她,这样他可以听到她年轻时和她家庭衰落的故事。昆丁是著名的杰弗生家族的一个年轻人,他的祖父在南北战争中是一位将军,他很困惑为什么这位老妇人会想跟他说话,而且还提到了他的父亲。其父康普生先生解释说,昆丁祖父在这个故事中有涉及,因为他是一个名叫托马斯·萨德本的人的朋友,罗沙·科德菲尔德认为萨德本便是毁掉她的家庭和她自己的一个恶魔。

昆丁去见了罗沙·科德菲尔德,他们坐在发霉的房间,她称之为"办公室",百叶窗关得紧紧的,只有一点点光可以照进房间,他听着她讲故事。她提到她听说了他正要准备上哈佛大学,也许他有文学方面的抱负,也许有一天会把这个故事写下来。昆丁意识到她想要把这个故事讲出来,这样听者会明白上帝如何能让南方输掉这场战争,因为南方人掌控在像萨德本这样的人手中,他只有蛮力而没有一点点怜悯和同情心。

罗沙小姐的叙述带着强烈的痛苦:她在过去的40多年中都痴迷于讲述这个故事,在1833年,她说,托马斯·萨德本来到杰弗逊时,什么都没有,只有一匹马和两支手枪,没有人知道他的过去(和一群野蛮的奴隶和一个法国建筑师在一起,萨德本站在他们的前面就像是一个恶魔一样——这是昆丁脑海中浮现的画面)。萨德本作为奴隶比其他的奴隶稍好一些,经常在奴隶中挑起战争,而且也经常参加。举行赛马,引诱男人来到他的农场,有时只是为了一些年轻女孩们无法理解的事情。渴望被尊重,他和艾伦·科德菲尔德(那正是罗沙小姐的姐姐,那时罗沙即将出世)结婚了,她是一个当地卫理公会的商人的女儿。萨德本和艾伦有两个孩子,亨利生于1839年,朱迪思生于一年后。作为一个父亲,他不曾对他的孩子发脾气,也不曾施暴。一天晚上,艾伦发现她丈夫在一个嗜血的人群与一个黑人在打斗,他的孩子也看到了,亨利哭了而且变得心烦意乱,朱迪思(她已经和一个黑人小女孩偷偷地溜到那里)全神贯注地观看着。朱迪思似乎拥有了她父亲的气质:当他鲁莽地在教堂前方举行马车比赛时因牧师的投诉而停止,这个6岁的小女孩不知不觉地哭了。

故事中后来的细节在罗沙小姐的叙述中逐渐变得模糊:托马斯·萨德本和他的儿子亨利都参加了战争,她说,她描述了艾伦临死的时候的情景。艾伦让罗沙来照料朱迪思,尽管朱迪思比罗沙要年长。罗沙回答道,孩子所需的唯一想要得到保护的就是他们自己。但除了这些一知半解,具体细节却很少——除了一件罗沙多次提及的中心事件:在朱迪思的婚礼上,婚礼即将举行,她的哥哥亨利却在"萨德本百里地"的门前杀害了她的未婚夫。

选 文

Absalom, Absalom!
(Chapter 1)

From a little after two o'clock until almost sundown of the long still hot weary dead September afternoon they sat in what Miss Coldfield still called the office because her father had called it that — a dim hot airless room with the blinds all closed and fastened for forty-three summers because when she was a girl someone had believed that light and moving air carried heat and that dark was always cooler, and which (as the sun shone fuller and fuller on that side of the house) became latticed with yellow slashes full of dust motes which Quentin thought of as being flecks of the dead old dried paint itself blown inward from the scaling blinds as wind might have blown them.

There was a wisteria vine blooming for the second time that summer on a wooden trellis before one window, into which sparrows came now and then in random gusts, making a dry vivid dusty sound before going away: and opposite Quentin, Miss Coldfield in the eternal black which she had worn for forty-three years now, whether for sister, father, or not husband none knew, sitting so bolt upright in the straight hard chair that was so tall for her that her legs hung straight and rigid as if she had iron shinbones' and ankles, clear of the floor with that air of impotent and static rage like children's feet, and talking in that grim haggard amazed Voice until at last listening would renege and hearing-sense self-confound and the long-dead object of her impotent yet indomitable frustration would appear, as though by outraged recapitulation evoked, quiet inattentive and harmless, out of the biding and dreamy and victorious dust.

Her voice would not cease, it would just vanish. There would be the dim coffin-smelling gloom sweet and oversweet with the twice-bloomed wisteria against the outer wall by the savage quiet September sun impacted distilled and hyper distilled, into which came now and then the loud cloudy flutter of the sparrows like a flat limber stick whipped by an idle boy, and the rank smell of female old flesh long embattled in virginity while the wan haggard face watched him above the faint triangle of lace at wrists and throat from the too tall chair in which she resembled a crucified child; and the voice not ceasing but vanishing into and then out of the long intervals like a stream, a trickle running from patch to patch of dried sand, and the ghost mused with shadowy docility as if it were the voice which he haunted where a more fortunate one would have had a house. Out of quiet thunderclap he would abrupt (man-horse-demon) upon a scene peaceful and decorous as a school prize water color, faint sculpture-reek still in hair clothes and beard, with grouped behind him his band of wild niggers like beasts half tamed to walk upright like men, in attitudes wild and reposed, and manacled among them the French architect with his air grim, haggard, and taller-ran. Immobile, bearded, and hand palm lifted the horseman sat; behind him the wild blacks and the captive architect huddled quietly, carrying in bloodless paradox the shovels and picks and axes of peaceful conquest. Then in the long unamaze Quentin seemed to watch them overrun suddenly the hundred square miles of tranquil and astonished earth and drag house and formal gardens violently out of the soundless Nothing and clap them down like cards upon a table beneath the up-palm immobile and pontific, creating the Sutpen's Hundred, the Be Sutpen's Hundred like the olden time Be Light. Then hearing would reconcile and he would seem to listen to two separate Quentins now the Quentin Compson preparing for Harvard in the South, the deep South dead since 1865 and people with garrulous outraged baffled ghosts, listening, having to listen, to one of the ghosts which had refused to lie still even longer than most had, telling him about old ghost-times; and the Quentin Compson who was still too young to deserve yet to be a ghost, but nevertheless having to be one for all that, since he was born and bred in the deep South the same as she was the two separate Quentins now talking to one another in the long silence of not people, in not language, like this: It seems that this demon — his name was Sutpen (Colonel Sutpen) — Colonel Sutpen. Who came out of nowhere and without warning upon the land with a band of strange niggers and built a plantation —(Tore violently a plantation, Miss Rosa Coldfield says)— tore violently. and married her sister Ellen and begot a son and a daughter which —(without gentleness begot, Miss Rosa Coldfield says)— without gentleness.

Which should have been the jewels of his pride and the shield and comfort of his old age, only —(Only they destroyed him or something or he destroyed them or something and died) — and died. Without regret, Miss Rosa Coldfield says —(Save by her) Yes, save by her. (And by Quentin Compson) Yes. And by Quentin Compson.

"Because you are going away to attend the college at Harvard they tell me," Miss Coldfield said. "So I don't imagine you will ever come back here and settle down as a country lawyer in a little town like Jefferson, since Northern people have already seen to it that there is little left in the South for a young man. So maybe you will enter the literary profession as so many Southern gentlemen and gentlewomen too are doing now and maybe some day you will remember this and write about it. You will be married then I expect and perhaps your wife will want a new gown or a new chair for the house and you can write this and submit it to the magazines. Perhaps you will even remember kindly then the old woman who made you spend a whole afternoon sitting indoors and listening while she talked about people and events you were fortunate enough to escape yourself when you wanted to be out among young friends of your own age." "Yessum," Quentin said. Only she doesn't mean that, he thought. It's because she wants it told. It was still early then. He had yet in his pocket the note which he had received by the hand of a small Negro boy just before noon, asking him to call and see her — the quaint, stiffly formal request which was actually a summons, out of another world almost — the queer archaic sheet of ancient good notepaper written over with the neat faded cramped script which, due to his astonishment at the request from a woman three times his age and whom he had known all his life without having exchanged a hundred words with her or perhaps to the fact that he was only twenty years old, he did not recognize as revealing a character cold, implacable, and even ruthless. He obeyed it immediately after the noon meal, walking the half mile between his home and hers through the dry dusty heat of early September and so into the house. It too was somehow smaller than its actual size — it was of two stories — unpainted and a little shabby, yet with an air, a quality of grim endurance as though like her it had been created to fit into and complement a world in all ways a little smaller than the one in which it found itself. There in the gloom of the shuttered hallway whose air was even hotter than outside, as if there were poisoned in it like in a tomb all the suspiration of slow heat laden time which had recurred during the forty-five years, the small figure in black which did not even rustle, the wan triangle of lace at wrists and throat, the dim face looking at him with an expression speculative, urgent, and intent, waited to invite him in.

It's because she wants it told, he thought, so that people whom she will never see and whose names she will never hear and who have never heard her name nor seen her face will read it and know at last why God let us lose the war: that only through the blood of our men and the tears of our women could He slay this demon and efface his name and lineage from the earth. Then almost immediately he decided that neither was this the reason why she had sent the note, and sending it, why to him, since if she had merely wanted it told, written, and even printed, she would not have needed to call in anybody — a woman who even in his (Quentin's) father's youth had already established herself as the town's and the county's poetess laureate by issuing to the stern and meager subscription list of the county newspaper poems, ode, eulogy, and epitaph, out of some bitter and implacable reserve of undefeated.

It would be three hours yet before he would learn why she had sent for him because part of it, the first part of it, Quentin already knew.

It was a part of his twenty years' heritage of breathing the same air and hearing his father talk about the man Sutpen; a part of the town's — Jefferson's — eighty years' heritage of the same air which the man himself had breathed between this September afternoon in 1909 and that Sunday morning in June in 1833 when he first rode into town out of no discernible past and acquired his land no one knew how and built his house, his mansion, apparently out of nothing and married Ellen Coldfield and begot his two children — the son who widowed the daughter who had not yet been a bride — and so accomplished his allotted course to its violent (Miss Coldfield at least would have said, just) end.

Quentin had grown up with that; the mere names were interchangeable and almost myriad. His childhood was full of them; his very body was an empty hall echoing with sonorous defeated names; he was not a being, an entity, he was a commonwealth.

He was a barracks filled with stubborn back looking ghosts still recovering, even forty-three years afterward, from the fever which had cured the disease, waking from the fever without even knowing that it had been the fever itself which they had fought against and not the sickness, looking with stubborn recalcitrance backward beyond the fever and into the disease with actual regret, weak from the fever yet free of the disease and not even aware that the freedom was that of impotence. ("But why tell me about it?" he said to his father that evening, when he returned home, after she had dismissed him at last with his promise to return for her in the buggy; "why tell me about it? What is it to me that the land of the earth or whatever it was got tired of him at last and turned and destroyed him? What if it did destroy her family too? It's going to turn and destroy us all some day, whether our name happens to be Sutpen or Coldfield or not."

"Ah," Mr. Compson said. "Years ago we in the South made our women into ladies. Then the War came and made the ladies into ghosts. So what else can we do, being gentlemen, but listen to them being ghosts?" Then he said, "Do you want to know the real reason why she chose you?" They were sitting on the gallery after supper, waiting for the time Miss Coldfield had set for Quentin to call for her. "It's because she will need someone to go with her — a man, a gentleman, yet one still young enough to do what she wants, do it the way she wants it done. And she chose you because your grandfather was the nearest thing to a friend Sutpen ever had in this county, and she probably believes that Sutpen may have told your grandfather something about himself and her, about that engagement which did not engage, that troth which failed to plight. Might even have told your grandfather the reason why at the last she refused to marry him. — And that your grandfather might have told me and I might have told you. And so, in a sense, the affair, no matter what happens out there tonight, will still be in the family; the skeleton (if it be a skeleton) still in the closet. She may believe that if it hadn't been for your grandfather's friendship, Sutpen could never have got a foothold here, and that if he had not got that foothold, he could not have married Ellen. So maybe she considers you partly responsible through heredity for what happened to her and her family through him."

"Whatever her reason for choosing him, whether it was that or not, the getting to it, Quentin thought, was taking a long time. Meanwhile, as though in inverse ratio to the vanishing voice, the invoked ghost of the neither man whom she could neither forgive nor revenge herself upon began to assume a quality almost of solidity, permanence. Itself circumambient and enclosed by its effluvium of hell, its aura of unregeneration, it mused (mused, thought, seemed to possess sentience, as if, though dispossessed of the peace — who was impervious anyhow to fatigue — which she declined to give it, it was still irrevocably outside the scope of her hurt or harm) with that quality peaceful and now harmless and not even very attentive — the ogre-shape which, as Miss Coldfield's voice went on, resolved out of itself before Quentin's eyes the two half-ogre children, the three of them forming a shadowy background for the fourth one. This was the mother, the dead sister Ellen: this Niobe without tears who had conceived to the demon in a kind of nightmare, who even while alive had moved but without life and grieved but without weeping, who — now had an air of tranquil and unwitting desolation, not is if she had either outlived the others or had died first, but as if she had never lived at all. Quentin seemed to see them, the four of them arranged into-the conventional family group of the period, with formal and lifeless decorum, and seen now as the fading and ancient photograph itself would have been seen enlarged and hung on the wall behind and above the voice and of whose presence there the voice's owner was not even aware, as if she (Miss Coldfield) had never seen this room before — a picture, a group which even to Quentin had a quality strange, contradictory, and bizarre; not quite comprehensible, not (even to twenty) quite right — a group the last member of which had been dead twenty-five years and the first, fifty, evoked now out of the airless gloom of a dead house between an old woman's grim and implacable unforgiving and the passive chafing of a youth of twenty telling himself even amid the voice maybe you have to know anybody awful well to love them but when you have hated somebody for forty-three years you will know them awful well so maybe it's better then, maybe it's fine then because after forty-three years they cant any longer surprise you or make you either very contented or very mad. And maybe it (the voice, the talking, the incredulous and unbearable amazement) had even been a cry aloud once, Quentin thought, long ago when she was a girl of young and indomitable unregretful of indictment of blind circumstance and savage event; but not now: now only the lonely thwarted old female flesh embattled for forty-three years in the old insult, the old unforgiving outraged and betrayed by the final and complete affront which was Sutpen's death:

"He wasn't a gentleman. He wasn't even a gentleman. He came here with a horse and two pistols and a name which nobody ever heard before, knew for certain was his own any more than the horse was his own or even the pistols, seeking some place to hide himself, and Yoknapatawpha County supplied him with it. He sought the guarantee of reputable men to barricade him from the other and later strangers who might come seeking him in turn, and Jefferson gave him that. Then he needed respectability, the shield of a virtuous woman, to make his position impregnable even against the men who had given him protection on that inevitable day and hour when even they must rise against him in scorn and horror and outrage; and it was mine and Ellen's father who gave him that. Oh, I hold no brief for Ellen: blind romantic fool who had only youth and inexperience to excuse her even if that; blind romantic fool, then later blind woman mother fool when she no longer had either youth or inexperience to excuse her, when she lay dying in that house for which she had exchanged pride and peace both and nobody there but the daughter who was already the same as a widow without ever having been a bride and was, three years later, to be a widow sure enough without having been anything at all, and the son who had repudiated the very roof under which he had been born and to which he would return but once more before disappearing for good, and that as a murderer and almost a fratricide; and he, fiend blackguard and devil, in Virginia fighting, where the chances of the earth's being rid of him were the best anywhere under the sun, yet Ellen and I both knowing that he would return, that every man in our armies would have to fall before bullet or ball found him; and only I, a child, a child, mind you, four years younger than the very niece I was asked to save, for Ellen to turn to and say, "Protect her. Protect Judith at least."

Yes, blind romantic fool, who did not even have that hundred miles of plantation which apparently moved our father nor that big house and the notion of slaves underfoot day and night which reconciled, I wont say moved, her aunt. No: just the face of a man who contrived somehow to swagger even on a horse — a man who so far as anyone (including the father who was to give him a daughter in marriage) knew either had no past at all or did not dare reveal it — a man who rode into town out of nowhere with a horse and two pistols and a herd of wild beasts that he had hunted down single-handed because he was stronger in fear than even they were in whatever heathen place he had fled from, and that French architect who looked like he had been hunted down and caught in turn by the Negroes — a man who fled here and hid, concealed himself behind respectability, behind that hundred miles of land which he took from a tribe of ignorant Indians, nobody knows how, and a house the size of a courthouse where he lived for three years without a window or door or bedstead in it and still called it Sutpen's Hundred as if it had been a king's grant in unbroken perpetuity from his great grandfather — a home, position: a wife and family which, being necessary: to concealment, he accepted along with the rest of respectability as he would have accepted the necessary discomfort and even pain of the briers and thorns in a thicket if the thicket could have given him the protection he sought. Marrying Ellen or marrying ten thousand Ellens could not have made him one. Not that he wanted to be one, or even be taken for one. No. That was not necessary, since all he would need would be Ellen's and our father's names on a wedding license (or on any other patent of respectability) that people could look at and read just as he would have wanted our father's (or any other reputable man's) signature on a note of hand because our father knew who his father was in Tennessee and who his grandfather had been in Virginia and our neighbors and the people we lived among knew that we knew and we knew they knew we knew and we knew that they would have believed us about whom and where he came from even if we had lied, just as anyone could have looked at him once and known that he would be lying about who and where and why he came from by the very fact that apparently he had to refuse to say at all. — And the very fact that he had had to choose respectability to hide behind was proof enough (if anyone needed further proof) that what he fled from must have been some opposite of respectability too dark to talk about.

He was too young that he was just twenty-five and a man of twenty-five does not voluntarily undertake the hardship and privation of clearing virgin land and establishing a plantation in a new country just for money; not a young man without any past that he apparently cared to discuss, in Mississippi in 1833 with a river full of steamboats loaded with drunken fools covered with diamonds and bent on throwing away their cotton and slaves before the boat reached New Orleans — not with all this just one night's hard ride away and the only handicap or obstacle being the other blackguards or the risk of being put ashore on a sandbar, and at the remotest, a hemp rope. And he was no younger son sent out from some old quiet country like Virginia or Carolina with the surplus Negroes to take up new land, because anyone could look at those Negroes of his and tells that they may have come (and probably did) from a much older country than Virginia or Carolina but it wasn't a quiet one. And anyone could have looked once at his face and known that he would have chosen the river and even the certainty of the hemp rope, to undertaking what he undertook even if he had known that he would find gold buried and waiting for him in the very land which he had bought.

No. I hold no more brief for Ellen than I do for myself. I hold even less for myself, because I had had twenty years in which to watch him, where Ellen had had but five. And not even those five to see him but only to hear at second hand what he was doing, and not even to hear more than half of that, since apparently half of what he actually did during those five years nobody at all knew about, and half of the remainder no man would have repeated to a wife, let alone a young girl; he came here and set up a raree show which lasted five years and Jefferson paid him for the entertainment by at least shielding him to the extent of not telling their women folks what he was doing.

But I had had all my life to watch him in, since apparently and for what reason Heaven has not seen fit to divulge, my life was destined to end on an afternoon in April forty-three years ago, since anyone who even had as little to call living as I had had up to that time would not call what I have had since living. I saw what had happened to Ellen, my sister. I saw her almost a recluse, watching those two doomed children growing up whom she was helpless to save. I saw the price which she had paid' for that house and that pride; I saw the notes of hand on pride and contentment and peace and all to which she had put her signature when she walked into the church that night, begin to fall due in succession. I saw Judith's marriage forbidden without rhyme or reason or shadow of excuse; I saw Ellen die with only me, a child, to turn to and ask to protect her remaining child; I saw Henry repudiate his home and birthright and then return and practically fling the bloody corpse of his sister's sweetheart at the hem of her wedding gown; I saw that man return the evil's source and head which had outlasted all its victims — who had created two children not only to destroy one another and his own line, but my line as well, yet I agreed to marry him.

No. I hold no brief for myself. I don't plead youth, since what creature in the South since 1861, man woman nigger or mule, had had time or opportunity not only to have been young, but to have heard what being young was like from those who had. I don't plead propinquity: the fact that I, a woman young and at the age for marrying and in a time when most of the young men whom I would have known ordinarily were dead on lost battlefields, that I lived for two years under the same roof with him. I don't plead material necessity: the fact that, an orphan a woman and a pauper, I turned naturally not for protection but for actual food to my only kin: my dead sister's family: though I defy anyone to blame me, an orphan of twenty, a young woman without resources, who should desire not only to justify her situation but to vindicate the honor of a family the good name of whose women has never been impugned, by accepting the honorable proffer of marriage from the man whose food she was forced to subsist on. And most of all, I do not plead myself: a young woman emerging from a holocaust which had taken parents security and all from her, who had seen all that living meant to her fall into ruins about the feet of a few figures with the shapes of men but with the names and statures of heroes — a young woman, I say, thrown into daily and hourly contact with one of these men who, despite what he might have been at one time and despite what she might have believed or even known about him, had fought for four honorable years for the soil and traditions of the land where she had been born.

And the man who had done that, villain dyed though he be, would have possessed in her eyes, even if only from association with them, the stature and shape of a hero too, and now he also emerging from the same holocaust in which she had suffered, with nothing to face what the future held for the South but his bare hands and the sword which he at least had never surrendered and the citation for valor from his defeated Commander-in-Chief. Oh, he was brave. I have never gainsaid that. But that our cause, our very life and future hopes and past pride, should have been thrown into the balance with men like that to buttress it — men with valor and strength but without pity or honor.

9 Ernest Miller Hemingway

作者简介

Ernest Miller Hemingway (July 21, 1899 – July 2, 1961) was an American author and journalist. His economical and understated style had a strong influence on 20th-century fiction, while his life of adventure and his public image influenced later generations. Hemingway produced most of his work between the mid-1920s and the mid-1950s, and won the Nobel Prize in Literature in 1954. He published seven novels, six short story collections, and two non-fiction works. Three novels, four collections of short stories, and three non-fiction works were published posthumously. Many of his works are considered classics of American literature.

Hemingway was raised in Oak Park, Illinois. After high school he reported for a few months for *The Kansas City Star*, before leaving for the Italian front to enlist with the World War I ambulance drivers. In 1918, he was seriously wounded and returned home. His wartime experiences formed the basis for his novel *A Farewell to Arms*. In 1921, he married Hadley Richardson, the first of his four wives. The couple moved to Paris, where he worked as a foreign correspondent and fell under the influence of the modernist writers and artists of the 1920s "Lost Generation" expatriate community. *The Sun Also Rises*, Hemingway's first novel, was published in 1926.

After his 1927 divorce with Hadley Richardson, Hemingway married Pauline Pfeiffer; they divorced after he returned from the Spanish Civil War where he had been a journalist, and after which he wrote *For Whom the Bell Tolls*. Martha Gellhorn became his third wife in 1940; they separated when he met Mary Welsh in London during World War II. He was present at the Normandy Landings and the liberation of Paris.

Shortly after the publication of *The Old Man and the Sea* in 1952, Hemingway went on safari to Africa, where he was almost killed in two successive plane crashes that left him in pain or ill health for much of the rest of his life. Hemingway had permanent residences in Key West, Florida

(1930s) and Cuba (1940s and 1950s), and in 1959, he bought a house in Ketchum, Idaho, where he committed suicide in the summer of 1961.

厄内斯特·海明威(1899年7月21日—1961年7月2日)美国作家兼记者。他的简朴和低调风格对20世纪的小说产生了巨大的影响,同时他的冒险的生活和他的公众形象也影响了后人。海明威的大部分作品产生于20世纪20年代中期和20世纪50年代中期,他在1954年获得诺贝尔文学奖。他出版了七部小说、六部短篇小说集和两部纪实小说。其中有三部小说,四部短篇故事合集和三部纪实小说类作品是在他去世后出版的。他的许多作品被认为是美国文学的经典之作。

海明威在伊利诺伊州的橡树公园区长大。高中毕业后,他在《堪萨斯城星报》做了几个月的记者,之后才前往意大利,应征入伍成为一战时的救护车司机。1918年,他受了重伤,回到了家里。他战时的经历奠定了小说《永别了,武器》的基础。1921年,他和哈德利·理查森结婚,是他4个妻子中的第一任。这对夫妇搬到巴黎,在那里他担任外国记者,受到现代主义作家和20年代"迷茫的一代"艺术家的影响。《太阳依旧升起》是海明威的第一部小说,于1926年出版。

海明威1927年离婚后,他又娶了波琳·菲佛。在西班牙内战时,他是一名记者。当他从西班牙内战回来后,他们就离婚了,之后,他便写了《丧钟为谁而鸣》。玛莎·葛尔宏在1940年成为他的第三任妻子。他们分开时,他于二战期间在伦敦邂逅了玛丽·威尔士,就和玛莎·葛尔宏分开了。他还参加了诺曼底登陆和巴黎解放战争。

1952年,《老人与海》出版后不久,海明威去非洲狩猎,在连续两次飞机事故中几乎丧生,这让他在痛苦和疾病中度过余生。海明威在佛罗里达州的基弗斯特(20世纪30年代),和古巴(20世纪40和50年代)都有固定住所。1959年,他在爱达荷州的凯彻么买了一所房子,并于1961年夏天,在那里自杀。

作品及导读

作 品 1

The killer

导 读

The story is set in a cafe late in the evening. Two waiters are waiting for their last customers to leave so they can close the cafe. The younger of the two is impatient, because he wants to get home to his wife and warm bed. The older one has more patience for he has nothing to do in the evening and he understands the old customer and feels pity for him. The old man is deaf. He is desperate in life and once attempts suicide. Finally the younger waiter refuses to sell brandy to the old man and closes the cafe. The older waiter goes to a bar unconsciously while thinking about the nihility of life. And that is all about this story. Although the plot of the story is brief and simple, the theme is deep and profound.

故事以深夜的一个咖啡厅为背景。两名服务员在等待他们最后一位顾客离开,这样他们就可以打烊了。两个中年轻的侍者很不耐烦,因为他想回他妻子身边和温暖的被窝。中年侍者很有耐心,因为他在夜里也无事可做,此外他也很同情年老的顾客。这个老年顾客对生活无望,自杀未遂。最终年轻待者拒绝给老年顾客提供白兰地并关了咖啡馆。老年侍者便去酒吧没有意识地思考人生的虚无。这就是这个故事,尽管故事情节简短,但主题意义深远。

选 文

The Killer

It was very late and everyone had left the cafe except an old man who sat in the shadow the leaves of the tree made against the electric light. In the day time the street was dusty, but at night the dew settled the dust and the old man liked to sit late because he was deaf and now at night it was quiet and he felt the difference. The two waiters inside the cafe knew that the old man was a little drunk, and while he was a good client they knew that if he became too drunk he would leave without paying, so they kept watch on him.

"Last week he tried to commit suicide," one waiter said.

"Why?"

"He was in despair."

"What about?"

"Nothing."

"How do you know it was nothing?"

"He has plenty of money."

They sat together at a table that was close against the wall near the door of the cafe and looked at the terrace where the tables were all empty except where the old man sat in the shadow of the leaves of the tree that moved slightly in the wind. A girl and a soldier went by in the street. The street light shone on the brass number on his collar. The girl wore no head covering and hurried beside him.

"The guard will pick him up," one waiter said.

"What does it matter if he gets what he's after?"

"He had better get off the street now. The guard will get him. They went by five minutes ago."

The old man sitting in the shadow rapped on his saucer with his glass. The younger waiter went over to him.

"What do you want?"

The old man looked at him. "Another brandy," he said.

"You'll be drunk," the waiter said. The old man looked at him. The waiter went away.

"He'll stay all night," he said to his colleague. "I'm sleepy now. I never get into bed before three o'clock. He should have killed himself last week."

The waiter took the brandy bottle and another saucer from the counter inside the cafe and marched out to the old man's table. He put down the saucer and poured the glass full of brandy.

"You should have killed yourself last week," he said to the deaf man. The old man motioned with his finger. "A little more," he said. The waiter poured on into the glass so that the brandy slopped over and ran down the stem into the top saucer of the pile. "Thank you," the old man said. The waiter took the bottle back inside the cafe. He sat down at the table with his colleague again.

"He's drunk now," he said.

"He's drunk every night."

"What did he want to kill himself for?"

"How should I know?"

"How did he do it?"

"He hung himself with a rope."

"Who cut him down?"

"His niece."

"Why did they do it?"

"Fear for his soul."

"How much money has he got?" "He's got plenty."

"He must be eighty years old."

"Anyway I should say he was eighty."

"I wish he would go home. I never get to bed before three o'clock. What kind of hour is that to go to bed?"

"He stays up because he likes it."

"He's lonely. I'm not lonely. I have a wife waiting in bed for me."

"He had a wife once too."

"A wife would be no good to him now."

"You can't tell. He might be better with a wife."

"His niece looks after him. You said she cut him down."

"I know." "I wouldn't want to be that old. An old man is a nasty thing."

"Not always. This old man is clean. He drinks without spilling. Even now, drunk. Look at him."

"I don't want to look at him. I wish he would go home. He has no regard for those who must work."

The old man looked from his glass across the square, then over at the waiters.

"Another brandy," he said, pointing to his glass. The waiter who was in a hurry came over.

"Finished," he said, speaking with that omission of syntax stupid people employ when talking to drunken people or foreigners. "No more tonight. Close now."

"Another," said the old man.

"No. Finished." The waiter wiped the edge of the table with a towel and shook his head.

The old man stood up, slowly counted the saucers, took a leather coin purse from his pocket and paid for the drinks, leaving half a peseta tip. The waiter watched him go down the street, a very old man walking unsteadily but with dignity.

"Why didn't you let him stay and drink?" the unhurried waiter asked. They were putting up the shutters. "It is not half-past two."

"I want to go home to bed."

"What is an hour?"

"More to me than to him."

"An hour is the same."

"You talk like an old man yourself. He can buy a bottle and drink at home."

"It's not the same."

"No, it is not," agreed the waiter with a wife. He did not wish to be unjust. He was only in a hurry.

"And you? You have no fear of going home before your usual hour?"

"Are you trying to insult me?"

"No, humble, only to make a joke."

"No", the waiter who was in a hurry said, rising from pulling down the metal shutters. "I have confidence. I am all confidence."

"You have youth, confidence, and a job," the older waiter said. "You have everything."

"And what do you lack?"

"Everything but work."

"You have everything I have."

"No. I have never had confidence and I am not young."

"Come on. Stop talking nonsense and lock up."

"I am of those who like to stay late at the cafe," the older waiter said.

"With all those who do not want to go to bed. With all those who need a light for the night."

"I want to go home and into bed."

"We are of two different kinds," the older waiter said. He was now dressed to go home. "It is not only a question of youth and confidence although those things are very beautiful. Each night I am reluctant to close up because there may be some one who needs the cafe."

"Hombre, there are bodegas open all night long."

"You do not understand. This is a clean and pleasant cafe. It is well lighted. The light is very good and also, now, there are shadows of the leaves."

"Good night," said the younger waiter.

"Good night," the other said. Turning off the electric light he continued the conversation with himself, It was the light of course but it is necessary that the place be clean and pleasant. You do not want music. Certainly you do not want music. Nor can you stand before a bar with dignity although that is all that is provided for these hours. What did he fear? It was not a fear or dread, it was a nothing that he knew too well. It was all a nothing and a man was a nothing too. It was only that and light was all it needed and a certain cleanness and order.

"What's yours?" asked the barman.

"Nada."

"Otro loco mas," said the barman and turned away.

"A little cup," said the waiter.

The barman poured it for him.

"The light is very bright and pleasant but the bar is unpolished," the waiter said.

The barman looked at him but did not answer. It was too late at night for conversation.

"You want another copita?" the barman asked.

"No, thank you," said the waiter and went out. He disliked bars and bodegas. A clean, well-lighted cafe was a very different thing. Now, without thinking further, he would go home to his room. He would lie in the bed and finally, with daylight, he would go to sleep. After all, he said to himself, it's probably only insomnia. Many must have it.

Chapter 10 Ezra Pound

作者简介

Ezra Pound (1885 – 1972), American poet and critic, was born in Idoho, America. In 1980, he came to London and intiated a imagism movement cohich amied to change the poetry style of that time, and thus started the modernism period of American.. After the world war I, he move to Paris, the center of the world's culture. In 1924, he went to Italy and drew closer to the national socialism of Mussolini and Hitler. He supported fascism and made some speeches about fighting against the jews and supporting fascists through the radio in Rome. After the War, he was caught by the American army and sent to America waiting for the trial. He was then imprisoned into a mental hospital because of his mental problems and the help of celebrities like Hemingway and frost. In 1958, Pound went back to Italy after 12 years of imprisonment in the hospital, and live there until death.

Pound was a prolific writer. His works includ "Personae"(1909). "The cartos"(1917 – 59) and so on. Besides, he also wrote man literary reviews. His early poems followed theories of imagism by using accurate, bright and implicit imapes to make poetic statement. His verses were simple and full of musical beauty. Some of his works criticized capitalism. Commer cialization and bourgeois in the western society. However, his poems also had such defects as vagueness, formalism and self-centeredness.

Pound is undoubtedly one of the most influential figures in the field of American modernist poetry and review. He has exerted great influence on the youth in the modernism movements after the world war I. He was almost a legend to them.

In a Station of the Metro is a master work of his imagism poetry. The poet combines the visual image with the intonation with just two lines. Different faces in the metro station imply the humane aspect of city life, while the rusing implyer some wonderful moments of people's lives.

Hugh Selwyn Mauberly is a long poem consisting of 18 short poems, which are a defence of Pound's poetry belief, and an attack against serious artists. Like Pound, Mouberly appreciates ancient classics. He lives in a simple society, which force him to sacrifice for a symbol.

埃兹拉·庞德(1885—1972)美国诗人、评论家。1885年生于美国的爱达荷州。1908年,他来到伦敦,发起了一场旨在改变当时文坛诗风的意象派运动,开创了美国现代派文学的先声。第一次世界大战后,庞德迁居到当时的世界文化中心巴黎。1924年庞德去往意大利,并在政治上开始向墨索里尼和希特勒的国家社会主义靠拢。第二次世界大战期间,他公开支持法西斯主义,并在罗马电台的对美国广播中发表数百次亲法西斯、反犹太人的演说。战争结束后,他被美军逮捕,押回本土等候受审。后因医生证明他精神失常,再加上海明威和弗罗斯特等名人的奔走说情,他只被关入一家精神病院。1958年,庞德结束了12年的精神病院监禁,重返意大利居住,直至去世。

庞德一生的著述颇多,主要作品有《面具》(1909)、《反击》(1912)、《献祭》(1916)、《休·西尔文·毛伯莱》(1920)和《诗章》(1917—1959)等。此外,他还写了不少文学评论文章。他的早期诗歌遵循意象派的理论,用准确、鲜明、含蓄的意象来表达事物,文字简洁,通俗上口,并富有流畅的音乐美。他的某些诗在一定程度上抨击了资本主义制度,讽刺了西方社会中商品化倾向和市侩气息对文艺的侵蚀,反映了当时知识分子的险恶境遇。不过,他的诗也有内容空泛、一味追求形式和个人色彩太浓的缺点。

埃兹拉·庞德在美国现代诗坛和评坛上无可非议是最有影响的人物,他对第一次世界大战后兴起的现代文学运动的一代青年有着巨大的影响,几乎是一位传奇式的人物。

《地铁站上》是其意象诗歌的代表作。诗人仅用两行诗句便将鲜明的视觉意象与引申含义有机地融为一体。地铁站在张张面孔暗示城市生活中的人格化,而匆忙紊乱暗示出人类生活本身的绝妙片刻。

《休·赛尔温·莫伯利》是由18节短诗构成的长诗,这些诗的含意是对庞德自己诗歌信仰的贬义性的自卫,是对拒绝严肃艺术家的社会嘲讽的攻击。同庞德一样,莫伯利赞赏古代,中古代的古典文学,如弗洛伯特,他身居在一个轻松、实利的社会,迫使他为一种象征而献身。

作品及导读

作品 1

The Cantos

导 读

The Cantos by Ezra Pound is a difficult and ambiguous modern poem, which has aroused many studies in different perspectives. It has been a controversial issue for a long time on whether there is a unified structure in *The Cantos* or not. This article, based on many studies about the issue, presents an analysis of The Cantos' structure. It traces back the forming process of *The Cantos*, and explores Pound's ways of constructing *The Cantos*. Meanwhile it presents a review of different ideas on the structure in *The Cantos*. It concludes that *The Cantos* is a very important modern poem, no matter whether there is a unified structure in it or not.

庞德的《诗章》是一部晦涩难懂的现代诗,学界已有许多著作从不同的方面研究。关于《诗章》是否有统一的结构,学界中一直存在争议。但无论如何,《诗章》都不失为一部重要的现代诗。

选 文

The Cantos 49

Dedicated to the seven lakes, do not know who made the poem,
The rain, the vast river, far away
Frozen in the fire, in the twilight of rain,
The house under the eaves of a lamp.
Reed was heavy, bow,
Bamboos whisper, like cry.
The autumn moon, mountains rise from the waters,
Against the sunset
The night like a cloud scene,
Wipe the Shiba, but laurel
Branches slender pierce the darkness,
The reeds in a sad melody plexus
The wind from the mountain side
A bell
In April October sailing past, maybe come back.
The ship is not found in silver, slowly,
Only the sun glowing in the river
In the autumn the direction flag capture,
Only a few wire smoke and sun cross.
Subsequently, snow fell in the river,
The whole world covered with snow,
The boat is like a lamp in the river,
The water is frozen, while in Shanyin
Others kef
Geese on the bar,
Cloud on the window

Expanse of water, the wild goose character and fall and the

Crow in the noisy fish lantern,

Moving to the north sky light

The children in the lift the stone shrimp.

One thousand seven hundred years Qing comes to these mountains

Light moves towards the southern sky.

The production of wealth in the country because of this and the debt

This is the scandal, as Gailiweng.

The river calm flow of Ten Shi

Although the old king built the canal is happy:

"Of the rotten Xi

Holiday season slowly come

The sun and the moon in Xi

Dan Fudan,

Chaoyang, labor

The setting sun, home

Wells for drinking water

Farming for food"

The imperial power? To us it is what meaning?

Fourth degrees, static

The power to defeat the beast.

作品 2

A girl

导 读

The poem describes the story of Daphne, the daughter of a river god. She was beautiful but shunned all suitors. One day Apollo, the sun god, saw her when she was hunting in the woods. He followed her but she was a fast runner, and fled. He called and called but she wouldn't stop, and for a long time he couldn't catch her; nymphs like Daphne knew it was too risky to have a god for a lover. As she approached the river she felt his breath on her neck, called out to her father for help, and immediately she began changing into a laurel tree. Apollo watched the change with dismay and grief.

这首诗歌讲述了河神女儿达芙妮,她是如此美丽却避开所有的追求者。有一天,太阳神阿波罗看见她在森林里狩猎。他跟着她,不过她跑得很快,逃开了。他叫唤,不过她怎么也不停。他追不上她。居于山林水泽的少女,比如达芙妮,知道要一个神来做爱人是件风险太大的事。当她接近河流的时候,她感觉到他的呼吸就在颈侧,大声地向父亲求救。立刻,她开始变成一棵月桂树。阿波罗看着这变化又是沮丧又是伤心。

选 文

A girl

The tree has entered my hands,
The sap has ascended my arms,
The tree has grown in my breast —
Downward,
The branches grow out of me, like arms.

Tree you are,
Moss you are,
You are violets with wind above them.
A child — so high — you are,
And all this is folly to the world.

Chapter 11 Wallace Stevens

作者简介

Wallace Stevens (October 2, 1879 - August 2, 1955) was an American Modernist poet. He was born in Reading, Pennsylvania, educated at Harvard and then New York Law School and he spent most of his life working as an executive for an insurance company in Hartford, Connecticut. His wife is Elsie Viola Kachel (1909 - 1955), and they have only one child, their daughter Holly Stevens (born 1924)

He received the National Book Award in 1951 and 1955, and he won the Pulitzer Prize for Poetry for his *Collected Poems* in 1955.

Some of his best-known poems include *Anecdote of the Jar*, *The Emperor of Ice-Cream*, *Sunday Morning*, *The Snow Man*, and *The Idea of Order at Key West*.

He believes that the poet should find beautifulness, joy, fun, stimulation and meanings in the dirty reality of the society. So he committed to study the inherent relationship between reality and art. The characters of his language in poetry are meticulous, full of wit, puns, and irony; meanwhile, it is difficult to understand.

Wallace Stevens' poetry has great influence on the western modernism and post modernism culture of the whole 20 century. In Stevens' poetry, imagination and reality seems to be the sole thesis. Every image in Stevens' poetry may not always have absolutely independent symbolic significance; it is up to the specific conception. When creating poetry, he didn't use the traditional meanings of the images but tried to create a new meaning which is ready to be explained. And his attitude towards those images is sometimes positive and sometimes negative, sometimes pessimistic and sometimes optimistic. All in all, the using of images is outstanding in Stevens' poetry.

Wallace Stevens regards writing poetry as a personal hobby, so he never communicates or gets in touch with anybody from the literature. But he may never thought of his name in the history of American liberation.

华莱士·史蒂文斯(Wallace Stevens,1879 年 10 月 2 日—1955 年 8 月 2

日)是美国现代主义诗人。他出生在宾夕法尼亚州里汀,一开始就读于哈佛大学,后进入纽约大学法学院,大部分生涯在康涅狄格州哈特福德保险公司作执行工作。他的妻子是艾乐思·维奥拉·卡希尔,他们只有一个女儿霍利。1951和1955年他获得美国国家图书奖,在1955年,他赢得了普利策诗歌奖。

史蒂文斯的代表作有《坛子轶事》、《冰激凌皇帝》、《星期天早晨》、《雪人》、《基维斯特的秩序观念》等等。

他认为诗歌应该发现社会中黑暗现实的美好、欢乐、喜悦、鼓舞和意义。所以他致力于研究现实和艺术的内在联系。他诗歌语言很细致、充满智慧。他还多用双关语、讽刺,所以他的诗歌是较难理解的。

史蒂文斯对整个20世纪西方现代主义和后现代主义文化产生了重要影响。在史蒂文斯的诗歌中,想象和现实几乎是唯一的主题。这个主题是通过反复出现的意象得以重申和强调的。史蒂芬斯诗歌中的每一种意象都不是绝对地有独立的象征意义,而是取决于具体的意境。在诗歌创造中,他并不沿用意象的传统含义,而是试图创造一种有待于阐释的新的意义。他本人对待这些意象的态度也是时而肯定,时而否定,时而悲观,时而乐观的。总之,意象的使用在史蒂文斯的诗歌中表现得极为突出。

史蒂文斯视写作为纯然私人的兴趣,因此终生不与文学界人士来往。但他可能都想不到,自己的名字会出现在美国的文学史里。

作品及导读

作品 1

Anecdote of the Jar

导 读

On the stage of 20th century American literature, Wallace Stevens, T. S. Eliot, Ezra Pound, Robert Frost and William Carlos Williams are called the "five poetic giants." Stevens is also known as the "poet of poets." He is one of the most influential American poets in the 20th century. The critic Geoffrey Moore once likened Stevens as the "hero of our time," who only has the qualification to compare with T. S. Eliot. *Anecdote of the Jar* is an exquisite poem in Stevens' first collection of poems *Harmonium*. Stevens is a great man who becomes famous late in life, and this poem is one of the most famous poems when the poet published when he was 44 years old. It shows us a strange but eloquent picture, and initiates interests and thinking of the scholars. This poem also gives inspiration, courage and strength to the people in the modern society.

在20世纪的美国文坛上,华莱士·史蒂文斯与特·斯·艾略特、埃兹拉·庞德、罗伯特·弗罗斯特和威廉姆·卡洛斯·威廉姆斯并称为诗坛的"五巨擎"。史蒂文斯又被称为"诗人中的诗人",他是20世纪最具有影响力的美国诗人之一,评论家摩尔曾把他比作唯一能同艾略特相比的"我们这个时代的英雄"。《坛子轶事》是史蒂文斯第一部诗集《管风琴》中的一首精致小诗。坛子轶事是大器晚成的美国诗人华莱士·史蒂文斯在44岁发表的名诗,这首诗向我们展示了一副奇特而又意味深长的画面,引发众多学者的浓厚兴趣和深思。《坛子轶事》给现代人以启迪、勇气和力量的真实写照。

选 文

Anecdote of the Jar

I placed a jar in Tennessee,
And round it was, upon a hill,
It made the slovenly wilderness
Surround that hill.
The wilderness rose up to it,
And sprawled around, no longer wild,
The jar was round upon the ground
And tall and of a port in air.
It took dominion everywhere.
The jar was gray and bare.
It did not give of bird or bush,
Like nothing else in Tennessee.

作 品 2

The Snow Man

导 读

As a poet with strong theory-practice consciousness, Wallace Stevens probes the essential way nature works upon observer's imagination in his masterpiece short poem *The Snow Man* while stressing the constructive role played by the poet's observation and imagination in the construction of the artistic world. Stevens illuminates the strong color of American Romanticism — Transcendentalism and notion of phenomenology, emphasizes the integration and unification of Man and Nature, demonstrates the state of "transparent self" proposed by Emerson and displays the return of Romanticism in the modernism dominant poetry in the 20th century of the United States.

作为一位诗歌理论和实践一致的诗人,史蒂文斯在其短篇诗歌杰作《雪人》中探讨了自认在人类精神生活中的重要作用,同时强调诗人的观察力和想象力对于艺术世界构建的重要作用。史蒂文斯在这首短诗中流露出强烈的美国浪漫主义——超验主义色彩和现象学的理念,强调人与自然的融合和统一,实现爱默生所谓的"透明的我"的状态,展现出20世纪美国现代诗风主导的诗坛中浪漫主义风格的回归。

The Snow Man

One must have a mind of winter
To regard the frost and the boughs
Of the pine-trees crusted with snow;

And have been cold a long time
To behold the junipers shagged with ice,
The spruces rough in the distant glitter

Of the January sun; and not to think
Of any misery in the sound of the wind,
In the sound of a few leaves,

Which is the sound of the land
Full of the same wind
That is blowing in the same bare place

For the listener, who listens in the snow
And, nothing himself, beholds
Nothing that is not there and the nothing that is

作 品 3

The Emperor of Ice-Cream

导 读

Wallace Stevens is one of the most important American Modernist poets. One outstanding feature of his poems is the using of images. Some of main images appear again and again, so it make up with a pretty stable system. "*The Emperor of Ice-Cream*" studies the meaning of the image ice-cream. Not only did this image make up the main part of this poem, but also strengthen the sole thesis: the relationship between life and death. The Emperor of Ice-Cream is a celebrated poem from Wallace Stevens' first collection of poetry, *Harmonium*, which was first published in 1922.

华莱士·史蒂文斯是美国最重要的现代派诗人之一。意象的运用,是他诗歌的一个突出特点。一些主要意象的反复出现,构成了一个相对稳定的象征体系。《冰激凌皇帝》探讨了诗中冰激凌的意象意义。这个意象不仅构成了诗歌的主体,并不断地强化了史蒂文斯这首诗中近乎唯一的主题:生存和死亡之间的对立关系。《冰激凌皇帝》选自史蒂文斯在1922年第一次出版第一部诗集《管风琴》。

选 文

The Emperor of Ice-Cream

Call the roller of big cigars,
The muscular one, and bid him whip
In kitchen cups concupiscent curds
Let the wenches dawdle in such dress
As they are used to wear, and let the boys
Bring flowers in last month's newspapers.
Let be finale of seem.
The only emperor is the emperor of ice-cream.

Take from the dresser of deal.
Lacking the three glass knobs, that sheet
On which she embroidered fantails once
And spread it so as to cover her face.
If her horny feet protrude, they come
To show how cold she is, and dumb.
Let the lamp affix its beam.
The only emperor is the emperor of ice-cream.

Chapter 12 Robert Frost

作者简介

Robert Frost was born in San Francisco on March 26, 1874. He moved to New England at the age of eleven and became interested in reading and writing poetry during his high school years in Lawrence, Massachusetts. He was enrolled at Dartmouth College in 1892, and later at Harvard, though he never earned a formal degree.

Frost drifted through a string of occupations after leaving school, working as a teacher, cobbler, and editor of the Lawrence Sentinel. His first professional poem, "My Butterfly," was published on November 8, 1894, in the New York newspaper *The Independent*.

In 1895, Frost married Elinor Miriam White, who became a major inspiration in his poetry until her death in 1938. The couple moved to England in 1912, after their New Hampshire farm failed, and it was abroad that Frost met and was influenced by such contemporary British poets as Edward Thomas, Rupert Brooke, and Robert Graves. While in England, Frost also established a friendship with the poet Ezra Pound, who helped to promote and publish his work.

By the time Frost returned to the United States in 1915, he had published two full-length collections, *A Boy's Will* and *North of Boston*, and his reputation was established. By the nineteen-twenties, he was the most celebrated poet in America, and with each new book — including *New Hampshire* (1923), *A Further Range* (1936), *Steeple Bush* (1947), and *In the Clearing* (1962) — his fame and honors (including four Pulitzer Prizes) increased.

Though his work is principally associated with the life and landscape of New England, and though he was a poet of traditional verse forms and metrics who remained steadfastly aloof from the poetic movements and fashions of his time, Frost is anything but a merely regional or minor poet. The author of searching and often dark meditations on universal themes, he is a quintessentially modern poet in his adherence to language as it is actually spoken, in the psychological complexity of his portraits, and in the degree to which his work is infused with layers of ambiguity and irony.

In a 1970 review of *The Poetry of Robert Frost*, the poet Daniel Hoffman describes Frost's early work as "the Puritan ethic turned astonishingly lyrical and enabled to say out loud the sources of its own delight in the world," and comments on Frost's career as The American Bard: "He became a national celebrity, our nearly official Poet Laureate, and a great performer in the tradition of that earlier master of the literary vernacular, Mark Twain."

About Frost, President John F. Kennedy said, "He has bequeathed his nation a body of imperishable verse from which Americans will forever gain joy and understanding."

Robert Frost lived and taught for many years in Massachusetts and Vermont, and died in Boston on January 29, 1963.

1874年3月26日,罗伯特·弗罗斯特出生于美国旧金山。在他11岁时他搬到了新英格兰。在马萨诸塞州的劳伦斯曼彻斯特学校上高中时就对阅读和写诗特别感兴趣。1982年他在达特茅斯上了大学,后来上了哈佛,但他从未获得过正式的学位。

弗罗斯特在离开学校后写了许多作品,如《一位老师》、《修鞋匠》和《有知觉的劳伦斯编辑》。他的第一部个人诗集《我的蝴蝶》出版于1894年11月8日。在纽约的《独立报》上发表。

1895年弗罗斯特和妻子结婚,直到她去世以前,妻子一直是弗罗斯特创作的灵感来源。1912年他们夫妇搬到了英格兰,也就是在他们在新罕布什尔的农场经营失败后。在那里,他结识了很多英国诗人,比如,托马斯布鲁克和格雷夫斯。在英国,弗罗斯特也与诗人庞德建立了友谊,庞德曾帮助他改进和出版作品。

到1915年返回美国之时,弗罗斯特已经发表了两部未删减版的诗集《少年心愿》和《波士顿以北》,此时,他已名声大噪。到了20世纪20年代,他已成为美国诗坛最著名的诗人,随着《新罕布什尔》(1923)、《以一片牧场》(1936)、《尖塔丛林》(1947)以及《林空间地》1962的发表,名声和荣誉(包括四次普利策奖)不断向他涌来。

弗罗斯特的作品大都与新英格兰的生活与风景有关,讲究形式与押韵,与同时代的诗歌运动与新诗风尚格格不入,但他决不仅仅是一个乡土诗人或次要诗人。他是一位不断探寻,摸索宇宙奥秘的伟大诗人。弗罗斯特崇尚不加雕琢的天然文字,其内心世界复杂而丰富,作品充满隐晦与讽刺,从这一方面来讲,他完全是一个典型的现代诗人。

1970年,诗人丹尼尔·郝福曼在评价《罗伯特·弗曼斯特诗集》时说到,弗罗斯特早期的诗歌是"诗意化的清教思想,能够大声表达对世界的无限热爱",同时郝福曼还称弗罗斯特是美国的吟游诗人:"他是全国人民心中的大亨,是大家公认的桂冠诗人,是一个马克·吐温式的文学巨匠。"

肯尼迪总统评价弗罗斯特时说:"他的诗歌是他对美国人民永不泯灭的馈赠,永远传播着喜悦和理解。"

罗伯特·弗罗斯特在马萨诸塞州和维蒙特州生活和从教多年,于1963年1月29日在波士顿逝世。

作品及导读

作品 1

The Road Not Taken

导 读

Robert Frost is the most distinguished modern poet in the 20th century of America. His lyric poetry has a unique artistic charm, and describes the natural pastoral scenery with the background of countryside in New England, and his poetry was still created with the background of rural scenery, with the subject matters of his own life experience, and with traditional writing form, which contributed to his great success. We can analyze his poems of autobiography theme with case study of *Home Burial* and *The Road Not Taken*, so as to explore the life prototype of his poems.

罗伯特·弗罗斯特是20世纪美国最杰出的现代诗人,他的诗具有独特的艺术魅力,大多数是以新英格兰的乡村为背景,描写田园自然景色,具有浓郁的乡土气息的抒情诗,罗伯特·弗罗斯特以自己的生活经历作为诗歌创作的主题,保持传统的诗歌创作形式,并获得了巨大的成功。从弗罗斯特的这首名诗《没有选择的路》可探索其自传主题诗,发掘其诗歌创作的生活原型。

选 文

The Road Not Taken

Two roads diverged in a yellow wood,
And sorry I could not travel both
And be one traveler, long I stood
And looked down one as far as I could
To where it bent in the undergrowth;

Then took the other, as just as fair,
And having perhaps the better claim,

Because it was grassy and wanted wear;
Though as for that the passing there
Had worn them really about the same,

And both that morning equally lay
In leaves no step had trodden black.
Oh, I kept the first for another day!
Yet knowing how way leads on to way,
I doubted if I should ever come back.

I shall be telling this with a sigh
Somewhere ages and ages hence:
Two roads diverged in a wood, and I —
I took the one less traveled by,
And that has made all the difference.

作 品 2

Mending Wall

导 读

Robert Frost, an American poet, was considered the pastoral poet of the industrial age. His poetry, with simple and new language, free and rhythmic style, developed a school of his own in American circle of poets. His poem *Mending Wall* seems very simple but very profound. Readers need to read through it with close attention, so as to explore its rich connotation and deep meanings.

美国著名诗人罗伯特·弗罗斯特被称为工业时代的田园诗人。他的诗歌以质朴、清新的语言,自由而又富有韵律的诗风在20世纪美国诗坛上独树一帜。他的《修墙》一诗看似简单,实则蕴意深邃,需要仔细研读,认真品味,才能挖掘其丰富内涵和深刻含义。

选 文

Mending Wall

Something there is that doesn't love a wall,
That sends the frozen-ground-swell under it,
And spills the upper boulders in the sun;
And makes gaps even two can pass abreast.
The work of hunters is another thing:
I have come after them and made repair
Where they have left not one stone on a stone,

But they would have the rabbit out of hiding,
To please the yelping dogs. The gaps I mean,
No one has seen them made or heard them made,
But at spring mending-time we find them there.
I let my neighbor know beyond the hill;
And on a day we meet to walk the line
And set the wall between us once again.
We keep the wall between us as we go.
To each the boulders that have fallen to each
And some are loaves and some so nearly balls
We have to use a spell to make them balance:
— Stay where you are until our backs are turned!
We wear our fingers rough with handling them.
Oh, just another kind of outdoor game,
One on a side. It comes to little more:
There where it is we do not need the wall:
He is all pine and I am apple orchard.
My apple trees will never get across
And eat the cones under his pines, I tell him.
He only says,— Good fences make good neighbors.
Spring is the mischief in me, and I wonder
If I could put a notion in his head:
— Why do they make good neighbors? Isn't it
Where there are cows? But here there are no cows.
Before I built a wall I'd ask to know
What I was walling in or walling out,
And to whom I was like to give offense.
Something there is that doesn't love a wall,
That wants it down. I could say 'Elves' to him,
But it's not elves exactly, and I'd rather
He said it for himself. I see him there
Bringing a stone grasped firmly by the top
In each hand, like an old-stone savage armed.
He moves in darkness as it seems to me,
Not of woods only and the shade of trees.
He will not go behind his father's saying,
And he likes having thought of it so well
He says again, "Good fences make good neighbors".

Chapter 13 William Carlos Williams

作者简介

"Something Urgent I Have to Say to You": *The Life and Works of William Carlos Williams*. Herbert Leibowitz.

To his patients in Rutherford, New Jersey, **William Carlos Williams** was just the local boy who had become their local doctor. And yet, as he made house calls, administered vaccinations or listened to their complaints, he heard not just what they said, but how they said it. A doctor but also a poet, Williams spent his life trying to capture the "infinite variety" of American speech, and to use it to create a uniquely American form of poetic verse.

It was not an easy task. As Herbert Leibowitz's new biography shows, Williams remained on the periphery of 20th-century literature as he spent a lifetime in the "grey-brown landscapes" of suburbia. He was disgruntled, with a severe dislike of many of his fellow poets, especially T. S. Eliot (Williams was both admiring and disdainful of "The Waste Land"), but his poems are now held up as some of the most daring examples of modern American poetry, and he was posthumously awarded the Pulitzer Prize in 1963.

During his lifetime, however, Williams was "Ill Bill" to his bigger, more successful friend Ezra Pound, who laughed at his insistence on staying in Rutherford. The son of immigrants who never naturalized, William's dedication to America did not flag, though it was a country that often disappointed him. Peopling his poems with "nurses and prostitutes, policemen and religious fanatics, farmers and fish peddlers, drunkards … blues singers and barbers," Williams wanted to pin down the whole messy country with his short, punchy lines of poetry. Sometimes he succeeded, as when he described the euphoric crowds at a baseball game, or when he catches a glimpse of "A big young bareheaded woman in an apron" on the pavement, bending down to remove a nail from her shoe. With the eyes of a doctor, he recorded the quotidian and the overlooked. He coined the maxim "*no ideas but in things.*" To his critics, the saying exposed him as an anti-intellectual, or as a poet who could only create "American speech barking at song."

赫伯特·雷伯茨曾写过**威廉·卡洛斯·威廉姆斯**的生活与作品:《有些事我必须要告诉你》。

对于他在新泽西拉瑟福德的病人来说,威廉·卡洛斯·威廉姆斯只是一个成为当地医生的男孩。但当他上门问诊,接种疫苗或是倾听抱怨时,他不仅仅是去听他们说了什么,而且还留意他们说话的方式。作为一名医生兼诗人,威廉姆斯毕生都致力于研究美国语音的"多样性"。

这不是个简单的任务。在郝伯特·雷伯茨的新传记里,威廉姆斯因为致力于研究郊区语音混杂的现象而被纳入了20世纪文学家之列。之后的许多诗人都不太喜欢威廉姆斯,这让他很郁闷,特别是T·S·艾略特(威廉姆斯对他的《荒原》有赞美,也有鄙视),但是现在威廉姆斯的诗被认为是美国现代诗歌的杰出代表,并于1963年,在他逝世后,被授予普利策奖。

在威廉姆斯生前,他的朋友埃兹拉·庞德曾笑他坚持待在拉瑟福德。他随父母移民到美国,但未加入美国国籍,尽管这个国家一直让他失望,但他造福国家的热情一直未减。在威廉的诗中有各种各样的人"护士、妓女、警察、宗教狂热者、农民和卖鱼的小贩、醉汉、布鲁斯歌手和理发师",威廉姆斯想在他简短有力的诗歌中改变整个国家的混乱。当他描述棒球比赛中激动的人群时,当他写到"一个身材高大的光头女青年穿着围裙在街头徘徊,弯腰将鞋上的钉子拿开"的情形时,他成功了。站在一个医生的角度,他记录着每天都会发生却被人们忽略的事情。他创造了那句格言"只有想不到,没有做不到"。在他的批评者看来,这句话暴露了他是一个反知识分子者,或一个只会以五十步笑百步的诗人。

作品及导读

作 品 1

Silence

导 读

"Silence" was selected from *Prologue* published during the Second World War. The artistic work is not so much what poet said, but what he created. "Silence" is a poem composed of colors and images to present a picture of a silent morning. The sky falls, with red leaves in yellow woods while the silence is suddenly broken by a bird perching on a peach tree branch with green buds. Image with warm colors in the background is contrasted with red and yellow in the foreground. The peach tree branch is shaking with the little bird, which gives some rues of life to the silent woods and in turn, strengthens the silence. Thus, a poem is intertwined with a picture and silence with motion. Readers are placed as if right present in the scene, to feel the silence presented by the picture.

《寂静》选自发表于第二次世界大战期间的诗集《楔子》。作品的艺术性并不在于诗人说了些什么,而在于他创造出什么。《寂静》呈现的是诗人用色彩和意象创造出的凌晨万籁俱寂的画面。天空低垂,满目红叶黄林。静悄悄中一只小鸟摇动了长着绿叶的桃树枝。寥寥数笔,画意入诗。画面以暖色为背景,红黄相间,然而着意涂抹的则是冷色调的绿色,对比强烈。小树枝被小鸟抖动了,小鸟则若隐若现,不仅使寂静中有了生机,也更显出树林的静谧。诗中有画,静中有动,有虚有实。使人如临其境,如睹其景,留下了悠悠不尽之意。

选 文

Silence

Under a low sky —
This quiet morning
Of red and
Yellow leaves —
A bird disturbs
No more than one twig
Of the green leaved
Peach

作品 2

Spring and All

导 读

This poem depicts an early spring scene, which is quite different from the gentle and bright spring that we learn from traditional poems. The spring in this poem is dirty, messy, "lifeless", "eye dizzy" and cannot bring sensual pleasure to the readers. In fact, the "cold wind" from the northeast already indicates the coming of the spring. Although the messenger of the spring —"the grass"— appears in the middle, the focus of the poet's attention is still the wild carrots. Seemingly, the wild carrots do not have any change. But the spring is working a major change inside them. And the same thing goes with the trees and wild plants in the woods. The poet is not writing about a full-blown spring, but a spring with endless vitality and possibility. It is not that sweet and lovely as many expect, but it is the real early spring in the countryside.

这首诗描写早春景象,和我们熟悉的传统诗文里柔美、明媚的春天形象不同。诗人笔下的春天,肮脏、杂乱、"没有生气"、"目光昏眩",并不能给读者带来感官的愉悦。如果没有题目的提示,粗心的读者几乎会以为这是在写冬天。其实,诗歌开头写的从东北吹来的冷风就透露了春天已然来到的信息,诗的中间点出报春使者——小草已经出现,不过诗人关注的重点还是野胡萝卜。从外表上看野胡萝卜没有什么变化,但春天已经对它们产生作用,它们的内部正酝酿着"重大的变化"。再回过头看,那些野地里的树木和野生植物不也同野胡萝卜一样吗?可以说,诗人写的不是已经大肆铺展开的春天,而是包含着无限生机、无限可能的春天,它不那么甜美、可爱,还残留着冬天的痕迹,而这不正是乡野早春的本来面目吗!

选 文

Spring and All

By the road to the contagious hospital
Under the surge of the blue
Mottled clouds driven from the
Northeast comes a cold wind. Beyond, the
Waste of broad, muddy fields
Brown with dried weeds, standing and fallen

Patches of standing water
The scattering of tall trees

All along the road the reddish
Purplish, forked, understanding, twiggy
Stuff of bushes and small trees

with dead, brown leaves under them
Leafless vines —
Lifeless in appearance, sluggish
Dazed spring approaches —
They enter the new world naked,
cold, uncertain of all
Save that they enter. All about them
the cold, familiar wind —
Now the grass, tomorrow
The stiff curl of wild carrot leaf
One by one object are defined —
It quickens: Clarity, outline of leaf
But now the stark dignity of
Entrance — still, the profound change
has come upon them; rooted, they
Grip down and begin to awaken

14 Eugene Gladstone O'Neill

作者简介

Eugene Gladstone O'Neill is unquestionably America's greatest playwright. He won the Pulitzer Prize four times and was the only dramatist ever to win a Nobel Prize (1936). He is widely acclaimed "founder of the American drama" and "the American Shakespeare" in the history of American drama.

O'Neill was born in New York on October 16, 1888 into a theatrical family. His father is an actor, and he grew up in New London, Connecticut, and spent his early years with his parents on theatrical road tours. He received university education for one year and later traveled all over the world. He avidly read up on dramatic literature, and cultivated an interest in play writing. In 1914, he attended Professor George Pierce Baker's drama workshop at Harvard, where his career as a dramatist began. Since then, O'Neill had been wholly dedicated to the mission as a dramatist. Although he was a great playwright, he had a tragic life. He experienced an unhappy marriage, his oldest son committed suicide, the younger son had drug addiction and mental illness. When he got old, he had the Parkinson's disease.

His career as a playwright can be divided into three periods. Early realist plays: He wrote about his own experiences, especially as a seaman. He was influenced by philosopher Frederic Nietzsche, psychologists Sigmund Freud and Carl Jung, and Swedish playwright August Strindberg. (He rejected realism in this period). Later period: He returned to idealism. (His life experience was used as the clues and themes of this works). Altogether O'Neill wrote and published about forty-nine plays of various lengths. He wrote some one-act melodramatic plays at first, including *Bound East for Cardiff* (1916), which described the dying sailor Yank and his dream about the security and peace which could never exist. It marked the beginning of O's long and successful dramatic career and ushered in the modern era of the American theatre. O'Neill's first full-length play,

Beyond the Horizon, made a great hit and won him the first Pulitzer Prize. Its theme is the choice between life and death, the interaction of subjective and objective factors, and this theme is dramatized more explicitly in *The Straw* (1921) and *Anna Christie* (1921). *Anna Christie* is more of a success because it deploys the developing complexity of O'Neill's personal vision, showing us that life is a closed circle of possibilities from which it is impossible to escape.

O'Neill was the first playwright to explore serious themes in the theater and to carry out his continual, vigorous, courageous experiments about theatrical conventions. His plays had been translated and staged all over the world. Four Pulitzer Prizes (1920, 1922, 1928, 1957) and the Noble Prize in 1936 showed his achievement and influence at home and abroad.

尤金·奥尼尔(1888—1952),无疑是美国最伟大的剧作家。他4次获得普利策奖并且是获得诺贝尔奖的唯一一位剧作家。他被誉为美国戏剧历史上的"美国戏剧之父"和"美国的莎士比亚"。

奥尼尔1888年10月16日出生于纽约一个演员家庭,父亲是一名演员,他在新伦敦长大,早年随父母四处流浪表演戏剧,他接受过一年的大学教育后来又周游世界。他积极地阅读戏剧文学,并且在1914年萌生了写作的兴趣,不久进入著名的哈佛大学"第47号戏剧研习班",在乔治贝克教授指导下,他的戏剧创作生涯开始了。从此之后,他完全投入到了戏剧创作之中。尽管他是一个伟大的剧作家,但他的生活却充满了悲剧性,他有一段不幸的婚姻,他的大儿子自杀了,小儿子沉迷于毒品并且有精神病。晚年,奥尼尔患上帕金森氏症,并与妻子卡罗塔爆发矛盾。

在他作为一个剧作家的生涯中,包括3个阶段。早期的现实主义创作,叙述了他的个人经历,特别是作为一个海员的个人经历,并且受到了心理学家卡尔·荣格的影响,一位瑞典的作家也对他产生了影响(这一时期他反对理想主义)。后期创作:又回到了理想主义(以他的生活经历作为线索和故事主题)。奥尼尔创作并出版了大约59部不同长度的戏剧。起初,他创作了几部独幕剧,其中一部《东航加迪夫》描绘了一位快死的船员杨克和他那对和平与安全的不切实际的幻想,促进了当代美国戏剧的发展。1920年,奥尼尔的《天边外》在百老汇上演,取得了巨大的轰动并获普利策奖,由此奠定了他在美国戏剧界的地位。它的主题是生与死的抉择,主客观因素的相互影响,剧作《草》和《安娜·克里斯蒂》更具戏剧化,但《安娜·克里斯蒂》更为成功。因为它展示了奥尼尔个人观点的复杂性,向我们展示出生活就是一个封闭的难以逃脱的圈。

奥尼尔是20世纪中叶美国最伟大的剧作家,他是首位在戏剧中探索严肃主题的作家,并且对传统戏剧进行了持续的,有勇气的探索实验。他的戏剧被翻译到各国并且被搬上舞台,他的4次普利策奖和一次诺贝尔奖显示了他的成就对国内外的影响,以及对美国戏剧的发展有划时代的影响。

作品及导读

作品 1

Desire Under the Elms

导 读

Desire Under the Elms is O'Neill's first effort at writing in the style of Greek tragedy. It is concerned with the tragedy of a New England family. In this family, there is no love between the father and the sons. Cabot, the father, is indifferent, obstinate and isolated. He trades his sons as working tools. His sons hate him and hope that Cabot would die early so that they could inherit his farm. In order to hold the farm, Cabot shows little love to his wife and sons. He just compels them to work like animals. Under his cruel oppression, his former two wives die consecutively. As to his wife, Abbie, he not only forces her to work diligently, but also hopes that she could give birth to a child to inherit the farm. Abbie, who has suffered a vagrant life and is young enough to be Cabot's daughter, just intends to get the farm. Eben, Cabot's third son, thinks that the farm is his mother's property and casts his covetous eyes on it. In order to realize their ulterior motives, Abbie and Eben make use of each other. At first, they hate each other, but with time going on, they fall in love with each other, which leads to a sad ending.

《榆树下的欲望》是尤金·奥尼尔第一次尝试写希腊式的悲剧。故事发生在新英格兰的一个农场家庭。在家庭里,父子之间毫无感情可言。卡伯特冷漠、顽固、孤僻,他将他的儿子们视为工作工具。他的儿子们憎恨他,并希望卡伯特早日死去,好让他们继承农场。为了农场不被抢去,卡伯特吝于向妻儿表达爱意,反而像对待动物般驱使他们干活。在他残酷的压迫下,他的前两任妻子相继死去。对于他的现任妻子,艾比,他不仅强迫她辛勤劳动,更希望她以为他生个孩子,继承家业。艾比过惯了流浪的生活。她年轻得足以当卡伯特的女儿,只想获得农场。埃本·卡伯特的第三个儿子,认为农场是他母亲的财产,并觊觎它。为了达到最终目的,艾比和埃本相互利用。一开始两个相互憎恨,但随着时间流逝,他们附入爱河,并酿成悲剧。

选 文

Desire Under the Elms

(*Scene* 4)

It is after dawn. The sky is brilliant with the sunrise. In the kitchen, Abbie sits at the table, her body limps and exhausted, her head bowed down over her arms, her face hidden. Upstairs, Cabot is still asleep but awakens with a start. He looks toward the window and gives a snort of surprise and irritation — throws back the covers and begins hurriedly pulling on his clothes. Without looking behind him, he begins talking to Abbie, whom he supposes beside him.

CABOT — Thunder 'n' lightnin', Abbie! I hain't slept this late in fifty year! Looks's if the sun was full riz a'most. Must've been the dancin 'an' likker. Must be gittin' old. I hope Eben's t' wuk. Ye might've tuk the trouble t' rouse me, Abbie. (*He turns — sees no one there — surprised*) Waal — whar air she? Gittin' vittles, I calc'late. (*He tiptoes to the cradle and peers down — proudly*) Mornin', sonny. Putty's a picter! Sleepin' sound. He don't beller all night like most o' 'em. (*He goes quietly out the door in rear — a few moments later enters kitchen — sees Abbie — with satisfaction*) So thar ye be. Ye got any vittles cooked?

ABBIE —(*without moving*) No.

CABOT —(*coming to her, almost sympathetically*) Ye feelin' sick?

ABBIE — No.

CABOT —(*pats her on shoulder. She shudders.*) Ye'd best lie down a spell. (*half jocularly*) Yer son'll be needin' ye soon. He'd ought t' wake up with a gnashin' appetite, the sound way he's sleepin'.

ABBIE —(*shudders — then in a dead voice*) He hain't never goin' t' wake up.

CABOT —(*jokingly*) Takes after me this mornin'. I hain't slept so late in . . . .

ABBIE — He's dead.

CABOT —(*stares at her —bewilderedly*) What . . . .

ABBIE — I killed him.

CABOT —(*stepping back from her — aghast*) Air ye drunk —'r crazy —'r . . . !

ABBIE —(*suddenly lifts her head and turns on him — wildly*) I killed him, I tell ye! I smothered him. Go up an' see if ye don't b'lieve me! (*Cabot stares at her a second, then bolts out the rear door, can be heard bounding up the stairs, and rushes into the bedroom and over to the cradle. Abbie has sunk back lifelessly into her former position. Cabot puts his hand down on the body in the crib. An expression of fear and horror comes over his face.*)

CABOT —(*shrinking away — tremblingly*) God A'mighty! God A'mighty. (*He stumbles out the door — in a short while returns to the kitchen — comes to Abbie, the stunned expression still on his face — hoarsely*) Why did ye do it? Why? (*As she doesn't answer, he grabs her violently by the shoulder and shakes her.*) I ax ye why ye done it! Ye'd better tell me 'r . . . !

ABBIE —(*gives him a furious push which sends him staggering back and springs to her feet — with wild rage and hatred*) Don't ye dare tech me! What right hev ye t' question me 'bout him? He wan't yewr son! Think I'd have a son by yew? I'd die fust! I hate the sight o' ye an' allus did! It's yew I should've murdered, if I'd had good sense! I hate ye! I love Eben. I did from the fust. An' he was Eben's son — mine an' Eben's — not your'n!

CABOT —(*stands looking at her dazedly — a pause — finding his words with an effort — dully*) That was it — what I felt — pokin' 'round the corners — while ye lied — holdin' yerself from me — sayin' ye'd a'ready conceived —(*He lapses into crushed silence — then with a strange emotion*) He's dead, sart'n. I felt his heart. Pore little critter! (*He blinks back one tear, wiping his sleeve across his nose.*)

ABBIE —(hysterically) Don't ye! Don't ye! (She sobs unrestrainedly.)

CABOT —(*with a concentrated effort that stiffens his body into a rigid line and hardens his face into a stony mask — through his teeth to himself*) I got t' be — like a stone — a rock o' jedgment! (*A pause. He gets complete control over himself — harshly*) If he was Eben's, I be glad he air gone! An' mebbe I suspicioned it all along. I felt they was somethin' onnateral — somewhars — the house got so lonesome — an' cold — drivin' me down t' the barn — t' the beasts o' the field .... Ay-eh. I must've suspicioned — somethin'. Ye didn't fool me — not altogether, leastways — I'm too old a bird — growin' ripe on the bough .... (*He becomes aware he is wandering, straightens again, looks at Abbie with a cruel grin.*) So ye'd liked t' hev murdered me 'stead o' him, would ye? Waal, I'll live to a hundred! I'll live t' see ye hung! I'll deliver ye up t' the jedgment o' God an' the law! I'll git the Sheriff now. (*starts for the door*)

ABBIE —(*dully*) Ye needn't. Eben's gone fur him.

CABOT —(*amazed*) Eben — gone fur the Sheriff?

ABBIE — Ay-eh.

CABOT — T' inform agen ye?

ABBIE — Ay-eh.

CABOT —(*considers this — a pause — then in a hard voice*) Waal, I'm thankful fur him savin' me the trouble. I'll git t' wuk. (*He goes to the door — then turns — in a voice full of strange emotion*) He'd ought t' been my son, Abbie. Ye'd ought t' loved me. I'm a man. If ye'd loved me, I'd never told no Sheriff on ye no matter what ye did, if they was t' brile me alive!

ABBIE —(*defensively*) They's more to it nor yew know, makes him tell.

CABOT —(*dryly*) Fur yewr sake, I hope they be. (*He goes out — comes around to the gate — stares up at the sky. His control relaxes. For a moment he is old and weary. He murmurs despairingly*) God A'mighty, I be lonesomer'n ever! (*He hears running footsteps from the left, immediately is himself again. Eben runs in, panting exhaustedly, wild-eyed and mad looking. He lurches through the gate. Cabot grabs him by the shoulder. Eben stares at him dumbly.*) Did ye tell the Sheriff?

EBEN —(*nodding stupidly*) Ay-eh.

CABOT —(*gives him a push away that sends him sprawling — laughing with withering contempt*) Good fur ye! A prime chip o' yer Maw ye be! (*He goes toward the barn, laughing harshly. Eben scrambles to his feet. Suddenly Cabot turns — grimly threatening)* Git off this farm when the Sheriff takes her — or, by God, he'll have t' come back an' git me fur murder, too! (*He stalks off. Eben does not appear to have heard him. He runs to the door and comes into the kitchen. Abbie looks up with a cry of anguished joy. Eben stumbles over and throws himself on his knees beside her — sobbing brokenly)*

EBEN — Fergive me!

ABBIE — (*happily*) Eben! (*She kisses him and pulls his head over against her breast.*)

EBEN — I love ye! Fergive me!

ABBIE —(*ecstatically*) I'd fergive ye all the sins in hell fur sayin' that! (*She kisses his head, pressing it to her with a fierce passion of possession.*)

EBEN —(*brokenly*) But I told the Sheriff. He's comin' fur ye!

ABBIE — I kin b'ar what happens t' me — now!

EBEN — I woke him up. I told him. He says, wait till I git dressed. I was waiting. I got to thinkin' o' yew. I got to thinkin' how I'd loved ye. It hurt like somethin' was bustin' in my chest an' head. I got t' cryin'. I knowed sudden I loved ye yet, an' allus would love ye!

ABBIE —(*caressing his hair —tenderly*) My boy, hain't ye?

EBEN — I begun t' run back. I cut across the fields an' through the woods. I thought ye might have time t' run away — with me — an' ....

ABBIE —(*shaking her head*) I got t' take my punishment — t' pay fur my sin.

EBEN — Then I want t' share it with ye.

ABBIE — Ye didn't do nothin'.

EBEN — I put it in yer head. I wisht he was dead! I as much as urged ye t' do it!

ABBIE — No. It was me alone!

EBEN — I'm as guilty as yew be! He was the child o' our sin.

ABBIE —(*lifting her head as if defying God*) I don't repent that sin! I hain't askin' God t' fergive that!

EBEN — Nor me — but it led up t' the other — an' the murder ye did, ye did 'count o' me — an' it's my murder, too, I'll tell the Sheriff — an' if ye deny it, I'll say we planned it t'gether — an' they'll all b'lieve me, fur they suspicion everythin' we've done, an' it'll seem likely an' true to 'em. An' it is true — way down. I did help ye — somehow.

ABBIE —(*laying her head on his — sobbing*) No! I don't want yew t' suffer!

EBEN — I got 't' pay fur my part 'o' the sin! An 'I'd suffer wuss leavin 'ye, goin' West, thinkin 'o' ye day an' night, bein' out when yew was in —(*lowering his voice*) 'R bein' alive when yew was dead. (*a pause*) I want t' share with ye, Abbie — prison 'r death 'r hell 'r anythin'! (*He looks into her eyes and forces a trembling smile.*) If I'm sharin' with ye, I won't feel lonesome, leastways.

ABBIE —(*weakly*) Eben! I won't let ye! I can't let ye!

EBEN —(*kissing her — tenderly*) Ye can't he'p yerself. I got ye beat fur once!

ABBIE —(*forcing a smile — adoringly*) I hain't beat — s'long's I got ye!

EBEN —(*hears the sound of feet outside*) Ssshh! Listen! They've come t' take us!

ABBIE — No, it's him. Don't give him no chance to fight ye, Eben. Don't say nothin'— no matter what he says. An' I won't, neither. (*It is Cabot. He comes up from the barn in a great state of excitement and strides into the house and then into the kitchen. Eben is kneeling beside Abbie, his arm around her, hers around him. They stare straight ahead.*)

CABOT —(*stares at them, his face hard. A long pause — vindictively*) Ye make a slick pair o' murderin' turtle doves! Ye'd ought t' be both hung on the same limb an' left thar t' swing in the breeze an' rot — a warnin' t' old fools like me t' b'ar their lonesomeness alone — an' fur young fools like ye t' hobble their lust. (*A pause. The excitement returns to his face, his eyes snap, he looks a bit crazy.*) I couldn't work today. I couldn't take no interest. T' hell with the farm. I'm leavin' it! I've turned the cows an' other stock loose. I've druv 'em into the woods whar they kin be free! By freein' 'em, I'm freein' myself! I'm quittin' here today! I'll set fire t' house an' barn an' watch 'em burn, an' I'll leave yer Maw t' haunt the ashes, an' I'll will the fields back t' God, so that nothin' human kin never touch 'em! I'll be a-goin' to Californi-a — t' jine Simeon an' Peter — true sons o' mine if they be dumb fools — an' the Cabots'll find Solomon's Mines t'gether! (*He suddenly cuts a mad caper.*) Whoop! What was the song they sung? "Oh, Californi-a! That's the land fur me." (*He sings this — then gets on his knees by the floorboard under which the money was hid.*) An' I'll sail thar on one o' the finest clippers I kin find! I've got the money! Pity ye didn't know whar this was hidden so's ye could steal .... (*He has pulled up the board. He stares — feels — stares again. A pause of dead silence. He slowly turns, slumping into a sitting position on the floor, his eyes like those of a dead fish, his face the sickly green of an attack of nausea. He swallows painfully several times — forces a weak smile at last.*) So — ye did steal it!

EBEN —(*emotionlessly*) I swapped it t' Sim an' Peter fur their share o' the farm — t' pay their passage t' Californi-a.

CABOT —(*with one sardonic*) Ha! (*He begins to recover. Gets slowly to his feet — strangely*) I calc'late God give it to 'em — not yew! God's hard, not easy! Mebbe they's easy gold in the West, but it hain't God's gold. It hain't fur me. I kin hear His voice warnin' me agen t' be hard an' stay on my farm. I kin see his hand usin' Eben t' steal t' keep me from weakness. I kin feel I be in the palm o' His hand, His fingers guidin' me. (*A pause — then he mutters sadly*) It's a-goin' t' be lonesomer now than ever it war afore — an' I'm gittin' old, Lord — ripe on the bough .... (*then stiffening*) Waal — what d'ye want? God's lonesome, hain't He? God's hard an' lonesome! (*A pause. The sheriff with two men comes up the road from the left. They move cautiously to the door. The sheriff knocks on it with the butt of his pistol.*)

SHERIFF — Open in the name o' the law! (*They start.*)

CABOT — They've come fur ye. (*He goes to the rear door.*) Come in, Jim! (*The three men enter. Cabot meets them in doorway.*) Jest a minit, Jim. I got 'em safe here. (*The sheriff nods. He and his companions remain in the doorway.*)

EBEN —(*suddenly calls*) I lied this mornin', Jim. I helped her do it. Ye kin take me, too.

ABBIE —(*brokenly*) No!

CABOT — Take 'em both. (*He comes forward — stares at Eben with a trace of grudging admiration.*) Putty good — fur yew! Waal, I got t' round up the stock. Good-by.

EBEN — Good-by.

ABBIE — Good-by. (*Cabot turns and strides past the men — comes out and around the corner of the house, his shoulders squared, his face stony, and stalks grimly toward the barn. In the meantime the sheriff and men have come into the room.*)

SHERIFF —(*embarrassedly*) Waal — we'd best start.

ABBIE — Wait, (*turns to Eben*) I love ye, Eben.

EBEN — I love ye, Abbie. (*They kiss. The three men grin and shuffle embarrassedly. Eben takes Abbie's hand. They go out the door in rear, the men following, and come from the house, walking hand in hand to the gate. Eben stops there and points to the sunrise sky.*) Sun's a-rizin'. Purty, hain't it?

ABBIE — Ay-eh. (*They both stand for a moment looking up raptly in attitudes strangely aloof and devout.*)

SHERIFF —(*looking around at the farm enviously — to his companion*) It's a jim-dandy farm, no denyin'. Wished I owned it!

15 Tennessee Williams

作者简介

Tennessee Williams(1911 – 1983), one of the most important American playwrights, left a great impact on American play, even the whole culture of American at that time. His works include *A Streetcar Named Desire*, *Cat on a Hot Tin Roof*, *Summer and Smoke*, *The Rose Tattoo*, *Orpheus Descending*, *Suddenly Last Summer*, and *The Sweet Bird of Youth*.

田纳西·威廉斯(1911—1983)是美国最重要的剧作家之一,他对20世纪的美国戏剧乃至文化产生了极大的影响。他的主要作品包括:《欲望号街车》《热铁皮屋顶上的猫》《夏日烟云》《玫瑰纹身》《俄耳甫斯下地狱》《夏日惊魂》和《可爱的青春小鸟》。

作品及导读

作 品

A Streetcar Named Desire

导 读

Tennessee Williams is one of the most famous writers in America, and *A Streetcar Named Desire* is one of his most well-known masterpieces and attractive plays. The reason why it is so attractive and pretty is that the leading character who named Blanche owes the unique characteristics. Different commentators with various opinions about Blanche had studied her image from a lot of stands. Some people appreciate her tenderness, pursuit and idealism; some people hold the opinion that she is a licentious woman who is full of vanity; and some people consider her as a lonely and mentally ill woman from a psychological perspective: on the one hand, she has the consciousness to control as most people do; on the other, she has unconscious desires. While the people for women's rights believe that she is a rebel and victim of the present society. All of her tenderness, sensitiveness, gracefulness are replaced by brutality. What she implies is the breaking up of people's mental thoughts in that period. The incompatible and complex characteristics of Blanche attracted the attention of the whole literary circle at that time. Standing in the opposing positions with the society not only troubled her existence but also her inner heart. She could dress gracefully but can't hide her obscene. In short, the strong desire is also a reflection of her despair moods to some degree.

《欲望号街车》是美国作家田纳西·威廉斯(Tennessee Williams)的主要成名作之一,也是美国最杰出的戏剧作品之一。这部作品之所以保持其独特的艺术魅力和吸引力主要归功于其有深度而形象的对女主人公布兰奇(Blanche)的独特人格魅力和吸引力的彰显。自古以来,各个评论家对布兰奇有着不同的理解和看法,促使他们从各个角度对她进行探索、分析和解释。有的人赞扬她具有女性温柔、追求理想;有的人则认为她是一个爱慕虚荣、道德败坏的淫荡之人;有的人从精神方面分析出布兰奇内心深处的孤独和精神上的分裂:一方面她具有人类普遍的有意识的控制,另一方面,她有无意识的欲望冲动;有的女性主义者则认为布兰奇是男权社会秩序的叛逆者和牺牲品,她的温柔、敏感和优雅被现代社会的野蛮慌乱所取代。女主人公反映了威廉斯对"人类精神世界的悲剧性分裂"的深刻探讨,布兰奇的性格中所呈现出的矛盾性、复杂性以及由此引发的她的悲剧的命运和遭遇,引起了文学界的极度关注。而她的悲剧命运不仅表现在她因为与社会对立所陷入的生存困境,更使她陷入内心上,及精神上的窘境。因此使得布兰奇的性格也陷于分裂对立的状态:她虽然外表纯洁,姿态优雅,但是精神淫荡,内心虚无,欲望越是无止境,越反映她的绝望。

选 文

A Streetcar Named Desire
(*Scene* 2)

It is six o'clock the following evening. Blanche is bathing. Stella is completing her toilette. Blanche's dress, a flowered print, is laid out on Stella's bed.

Stanley enters the kitchen from outside, leaving the door open on the perpetual 'blue piano' around the corner.

Stanley: What's this entire monkey doings?

Stella: Oh, Stan! [She jumps up and kisses him, which he accepts with lordly composure.] I'm taking Blanche to Galatoires' for supper and then to a show, because it's your poker night.

Stanley: How about my supper, huh? I'm not going to any Galatoires' for supper!

Stella: I put you a cold plate on ice.

Stanley: Well, isn't that just dandy!

Stella: I'm going to try to keep Blanche out till the party breaks up because I don't know how she would take it. So we'll go to one of the little places in the Quarter afterwards and you'd better give me some money.

Stanley: Where is she?

Stella: She's soaking in a hot tub to quiet her nerves. She's terribly upset.

Stanley: Over what?

Stella: She's been through such an ordeal.

Stanley: Yeah?

Stella: Stan, we've — lost Belle Reve.

Stanley: The place in the country?

Stella: Yes.

Stanley: how? Stella [vaguely]: Oh, it had to be — sacrificed or something. [There is a pause while Stanley considers. Stella is changing into her dress.] When she comes in be sure to say something nice about her appearance. And, oh! Don't mention the baby. I haven't said anything yet, I'm waiting until she gets in a quieter condition.

Stanley [ominously]: So?

Stella: And try to understand her and be nice to her, Stan.

Blanche [singing in the bathroom]:

'From the land of the sky blue water,

They brought a captive maid!'

Stella: She wasn't expecting to find us in such a small place. You see I'd tried to gloss things over a little in my letters.

Stanley: So?

Stella: And admire her dress and tell her she's looking wonderful. That's important with Blanche. Her little weakness!

Stanley: Yeah. I get the idea. Now let's skip back a little to where you said the country place was disposed of.

Stella: Oh. — yes...

Stanley: How about that? Let's have a few more details on that subject.

Stella: It's best not to talk much about it until she's calmed down.

Stanley: So that's the deal, huh? Sister Blanche cannot be annoyed with business details right now.

Stella: You saw how she was last night.

Stanley: Uh-hum, I saw how she was. Now let's have a gander at the bill of sale.

Stella: I haven't seen any.

Stanley: She didn't show you no papers, no deed of sale or nothing like that, huh?

Stella: It seems like it wasn't sold.

Stanley: Well, what in hell was it then, give away? To charity?

Stella: Shhh. She'll hear you.

Stanley: I don't care if she hears me. Let's see the papers.

Stella: There weren't any papers, she didn't show any papers, I don't care about papers.

Stanley: Have you ever heard of the Napoleonic code?

Stella: No, Stanley, I haven't heard of the Napoleonic code and if I have, I don't see what it —

Stanley: Let me enlighten you on a point or two, baby.

Stella: Yes?

Stanley: In the state of Louisiana we have the Napoleonic code according to which what belongs to the wife belongs to the husband and vice versa. For instance, if I had a piece of property, or you had a piece of property —

Stella: My head is swimming!

Stanley: All right. I'll wait till she gets through soaking in a hot tub and then I'll inquire if she is acquainted with the Napoleonic code. It looks to me like you have been swindled, baby, and when you're swindled under the Napoleonic code I'm swindled too. And I don't like to be swindled.

Stella: There's plenty of time to ask her questions later but if you do now she'll go to pieces again. I don't understand what happened to Belle Reve but you don't know how ridiculous you are being when you suggest that my sister or I or anyone of our family could have perpetrated a swindle on anyone else.

Stanley: Then where's the money if the place was sold?

Stella: Not Sold — lost, lost! [He stalks into bedroom, and she follows him.] Stanley! [He pulls open the wardrobe trunk standing in the middle of room and jerks out an armful of dresses.]

Stanley: Open your eyes to this stuff! You think she got them out of a teacher's pay.

Stella: Hush!

Stanley: Look at these feathers and furs that she come here to preen herself in What is this here? A solid-gold dress, I believe! And this one. What is these here? Fox-pieces! [He blows on them.] Genuine fox fur-pieces, a half a mile long! Where are your fox-pieces, Stella? Bushy snow-white ones, no less! Where are your white fox-pieces?

Stella: Those are inexpensive summer furs that Blanche has had a long time.

Stanley: I got an acquaintance who deals in this sort of merchandise. I'll have him in here to appraise it. I'm willing to bet you there's thousands of dollars invested in this stuff here!

Stella: Don't be such an idiot, Stanley!

[He hurls the furs to the daybed. Then he jerks open a small drawer in the trunk and pulls up a fistful of costume jewellery.]

Stanley: And what have we here? The treasure chest of a pirate

Stella: Oh, Stanley!

Stanley: Pearls! Ropes of them! What is this sister of yours, a deep-sea diver who brings up sunken treasures? Or is she the champion safe-cracker of all time! Where are your pearls and gold bracelets?

Stella: Shhh! Be still, Stanley!

Stanley: And diamonds. A crown for an empress!

Stella: A rhincstone tiara she wore to a costume ball.

Stanley: What's rhinestone?

Stella: Next door to glass.

Stanley: Are you kidding? I have an acquaintance that works in a jewellery store. I'll have him in here to make an appraisal of this. Here's your plantation, or what was left of it, here!

Stella: You have no idea how stupid and horrid you're being! Now close that trunk before she comes out of the bathroom! [He kicks the trunk partly closed and sits on the kitchen table.]

Stanley: The Kowalskia and the DuBois have different notions.

Stella [angrily]: Indeed, they have, thanks heavens! — I'm going outside. [She snatches up her white hat and gloves and crosses to the outside door.] You come out with me while Blanche is getting dressed.

Stanley: Since when do you give me orders?

Stella: Are you going to stay here and insult her?

Stanley: you're damn tootin' I'm going to stay here. [Stella goes out on the porch. Blanche comes out of the bathroom in a red satin robe.]

Blanche [airily]: Hello, Stanley! Here I am, all freshly bathed and scented, and feeling like a brand-new human being!

[He lights a cigarette.]

Stanley: That's good.

Blanche [drawing the curtains at the windows]: Excuse me while I slip on my pretty new dress!

Stanley: go right ahead, Blanche. [She closes the drapes between the rooms.]

Blanche: I understand there's to be a little card party to which we ladies are cordially not invited.

Stanley [ominously]: Yeah? [Blanche throws off her robe and slips into a flowered print dress.]

Blanche: Where's Stella?

Stanley: Out on the porch.

Blanche: I'm going to ask a favor of you in a moment.

Stanley: What could that be, I wonder?

Blanche: Some buttons in back! You may enter! [He crosses through drapes with a smoldering look.] How do I look?

Stanley: You look all right.

Blanche: Many thanks! Now the buttons!

Stanley: I can't do anything with them.

Blanche: You men with your big clumsy fingers. May I have a drag on your Cig?

Stanley: Have one for yourself.

Blanche: Why, thanks.... It looks like my trunk has exploded.

Stanley: I an' Stella were helping you unpack.

Blanche: Well, you certainly did a fast and thorough job of it!

Stanley: It looks like you raided some stylish shops in Paris.

Blanche: Ha-ha! Yes — clothes are my passion.

Stanley: What does it cost for a string of fur-pieces like that?

Blanche: Why, those were a tribute from an admirer of mine.

Stanley: He must have had a lot of — admiration.

Blanche: Oh, in my youth I excited some admiration. But look at me now! [She smiles at him radiantly] Would you think it possible that I was once considered to be — attractive?

Stanley: Your looks are okay.

Blanche: I was fishing for a compliment, Stanley.

Stanley: I don't go in for that stuff.

Blanche: What — Stuff?

Stanley: Compliments to women about their looks. I never met a woman that didn't know if she was good-looking or not without being told, and some of them give themselves credit for more than they've got I once went out with a doll who said to me, 'I am the glamorous type, I am the glamorous type!' I said, 'So what?'

Blanche: And what did she say then?

Stanley: she didn't say anything. That shut her up like clam.

Blanche: Did it end the romance?

Stanley: It ended the conversation — that was all. Some men are took in by this Hollywood glamour stuff and some men are not.

Blanche: I'm sure you belong to the second category.

Stanley: That's right.

Blanche: I cannot imagine any witch of a woman casting a spell over you.

Stanley: That's — right.

Blanche: You're simple, straightforward and honest, a little bit on the primitive side I should think. To interest you a woman would have to —[She pauses with an indefinite gesture]

Stanley [slowly]: Lay ... her cards on the table.

Blanche [smiling]: Yes — yes — cards on the table.... Well, life is too full of evasions and ambiguities, I think. I like an artist who paints in strong, bold colors, primary colors. I don't like pinks and creams and I never cared for wish-washy people. That was why, when you walked in here last night, I said to myself —'My sister has married a man.'— Of course that was all that I could tell about you.

Stanley [booming]: Now let's cut the re-bop!

Blanche [pressing hands to her ears]: Ouuuuu!

Stella [calling from the steps]: Stanley! You come out here and let Blanche finish dressing!

Blanche: I'm through dressing, honey.

Stella: Well, you come out, then.

Stanley: Your sister and I are having a little talk.

Blanche [lightly]: Honey, do me a favor. Run to the drug-store and get me a lemon-coke with plenty of chipped ice in it. Will you do that for me, Sweetie?

Stella [uncertainly]: Yes. [She goes round the comer of the building.]

Blanche: The poor thing was out there listening to us, and I have an idea she doesn't understand you as well as I do.... All right; now, Mr Kowalski, let us proceed without any more double-talk. I'm ready to answer all questions. I've nothing to hide. What is it?

Stanley: There is such a thing in this State of Louisiana as the Napoleonic code, according to which whatever belongs to my wife is also mine — and vice versa.

Blanche: My, but you have an impressive judicial air. [She sprays herself with her atomizer; then playfully sprays him with it. He seizes the atomizer and slams it down on the dresser. She throws back her head and laughs.]

Stanley: If I didn't know that you was my wife's sister I'd get ideas about you.

Blanche: Such as what?

Stanley: Don't play so dumb. You know what. — Where's the paper?

Blanche: Papers?

Stanley: Papers. That stuff people write on!

Blanche: Oh, papers, papers. Ha-ha! The first anniversary gift, all kinds of papers.

Stanley: I'm talking of legal papers. Connected with the plantation.

Blanche: There were some papers.

Stanley: You mean they're no longer existing?

Blanche: They probably are, somewhere.

Stanley: But not in the trunk.

Blanche: Everything that I own is in that trunk.

Stanley: Then why don't we have a look for them?

Blanche: These are love-letters, yellowing with antiquity, all from one boy. [He snatches them up. She speaks fiercely.] Give those back to me!

Stanley: I'll have a look at them first!

Blanche: The touch of your hands insults them!

Stanley: Don't pull that stuff!

[He rips off the ribbon and starts to examine them. Blanche snatches them from him,

THE AMERICAN PART

and they cascade to the floor.]

Blanche: Now that you've touched them I'll burn them!

Stanley [staring, baffled]: What in hell are they?

Blanche [on the floor gathering them up]: Poems a dead boy wrote. I hurt him the way that you would like to hurt me, but you can't! I'm not young and vulnerable any more. But my young husband was and I — never mind about that! Just give them back to me!

Stanley: What do you mean by saying you'll have to burn them?

Blanche: I'm sorry; I must have lost my head for a moment. Everyone has something he won't let others touch because of their — intimate nature.... [She now seems faint with exhaustion and she sits down with the strong box and puts on a pair of glasses and goes methodically through a large stack of papers.]

Stanley: What is Ambler & Ambler?

Blanche: A firm that made loans on the place.

Stanley: Then it was lost on a mortgage?

Blanche [touching her forehead]: That must've been what happened.

Stanley: I don't want any ifs, ands, or buts! What's all the rest of them papers? [She hands him the entire box. He carries it to the table and starts to examine the papers.]

Blanche [picking up a large envelope containing more papers]: There are thousands of papers, stretching back over hundreds of years, affecting Belle Reve as, piece by piece, our improvident grandfathers and father and uncles and brothers exchanged the land for their epic fornications to put it plainly! [She removes her glasses with an exhausted laugh.] Till finally all that was left — and Stella can verify that! — was the house itself and about twenty acres of ground, including a graveyard, to which now all but Stella and I have retreated. [She pours the contents of the envelope on the table.] Here all of them are all papers! I hereby endow you with them. Take them, peruse them — commit them to memory, even. I think it's wonderfully fitting that Belle Reve should finally be this bunch of old papers in your big, capable hands! ... I wonder if Stella's come back with my lemon-coke.

[She leans back and closes her eyes]

Stanley: I have a lawyer acquaintance who will study these out.

Blanche: Present them to him with a box of aspirin tablets.

Stanley [becoming somewhat sheepish]: You see, under the Napoleonic code — a man has to take an interest in his wife's affairs — especially now that she's going to have a baby.

[Blanche opens her eyes. The 'blue piano' sounds louder.]

Blanche: Stella? [Dreamily] I didn't know she was going to have a baby.

[She gets up and crosses to the outside door. Stella appears around the corner with a carton from the drug-store. Stanley goes into the bedroom with the envelope and the box. The inner rooms fade to darkness and the outside wall of the house is visible. Blanche meets Stella at the foot of the steps to the sidewalk.]

Blanche: Stella, Stella for Star! How lovely to have a baby! [She embraces her sister. Stella returns the embrace with a convulsive sob. Blanche speaks softly.] Everything is all right; we thrashed it out. I feel a bit shaky, but I think I handled it nicely. I laughed and treated it all as a joke, called him a little boy and laughed — and flirted Yes — I was flirting with your husband, Stella.

[Steve and Pablo appear carrying a case of beer.] The guests are gathering for the poker party. [The two men pass between them, and with a short, curious stare at Blanche, they enter the house.]

Stella: I'm sorry he did that to you.

Blanche: He's just not the sort that goes for jasmine perfume! But maybe he's what we need to mix with our blood now that we've lost Belle Reve and have to go on without Belle Reve to protect us.... How pretty the sky is! I ought to go there on a rocket that never comes down.

[A tamale vendor calls out as he rounds the corner.]

Vendor: Red hots! Red hots!

[Blanche utters a sharp, frightened cry and shrinks away; then she laughs breathlessly again.]

Blanche : Which way do we — go now — Stella?

Vendor: Re-e-d ho-o-ot!

Blanche: The blind are — leading the blind.

16 John Lawrence Ashbery

作者简介

John Lawrence Ashbery (born July 28, 1927) is an American poet. He has published more than twenty volumes of poetry and won nearly every major American award for poetry, including a Pulitzer Prize in 1976 for his collection *Self-Portrait in a Convex Mirror*. Renowned for its postmodern complexity and opacity, Ashbery's work still proves controversial. Ashbery stated that he wished his work to be accessible to as many people as possible, and not to be a private dialogue with himself. At the same time, he once joked that some critics still view him as "a harebrained, homegrown surrealist whose poetry defies even the rules and logic of Surrealism."

Ashbery was born in Rochester, New York, the son of Helen (née Lawrence), a biology teacher, and Chester Frederick Ashbery, a farmer. He was raised on a farm near Lake Ontario; his brother died when they were children. Ashbery was educated at Deerfield Academy. At Deerfield, an all-boys school, Ashbery read such poets as *W. H. Auden* and *Dylan Thomas*, and began writing poetry. Two of his poems were published in *Poetry* magazine, although under the name of a classmate who had submitted them without Ashbery's knowledge or permission. He also published a handful of poems, including a sonnet about his frustrated love for a fellow student, and a piece of short fiction in the school newspaper, the *Deerfield Scroll*. His first ambition was to be a painter. From the age of 11 until he was 15 Ashbery took weekly classes at the art museum in Rochester.

Ashbery graduated in 1949 with an A. B., *cum laude*, from Harvard College, where he was a member of the Harvard Advocate, the university's literary magazine, and the *Signet Society*. He wrote his senior thesis on the poetry of *W. H. Auden*. At Harvard he befriended fellow writers Kenneth Koch, Barbara Epstein, V. R. Lang, Frank O'Hara and Edward Gorey, and was a classmate of Robert Creeley, Robert Bly and Peter Davison. Ashbery went on to study briefly at New York University, and received an M. A. from Columbia in 1951.

约翰·劳伦斯·阿什贝利(生于1927年7月28日),美国诗人。他出版过超过20卷诗集,赢得了美国几乎所有的主要诗歌奖项,包括以诗集《凸面镜中的自画像》获得的1976年普利策奖。但阿什贝利的作品仍有很大争议。他的《文选》中收录了一篇评论伊丽莎白·毕晓普的文章,他将自己描述为"一个愚蠢、自产自销的超现实主义者,甚至无视超现实主义诗歌的规则和逻辑"。虽然阿什贝利以其作品的后现代复杂性与不透明性知名,他声称他希望自己的作品能为尽可能多的读者阅读,而不是自说自话。

阿什贝利生于纽约州罗切斯特,在安大略湖附近的一所农庄长大,童年时曾失去了一个哥哥。阿什贝利在迪尔菲尔德学院接受了教育。迪尔菲尔德是一所全男性的学院,阿什贝利在那儿读了威斯坦·休·奥登和狄兰·托马斯的诗歌,并开始写诗。其中一首诗登上了《诗歌》杂志,但是是以一位同学的名义发表的,他在没有阿什贝利允许的情况下发表了该诗歌。他还在校报《迪尔菲尔德纸卷》上发表了一打其他诗歌,其中一首是关于他和一位同性学生的失意恋爱,以及一篇短篇小说。他最初想当画家,11岁到15岁阿什贝利每周到罗切斯特的艺术博物馆上课。

阿什贝利1949年从哈佛学院毕业,获得A.B.荣誉,在那儿他是校园文学杂志《哈佛支持者》和图章社的成员,他的毕业论文是关于W.H.奥登的诗歌的。在哈佛他与肯尼斯·科克、芭芭拉·爱泼斯坦、V·R朗、弗兰克·奥哈拉和爱德华·戈里成了朋友,且是罗伯特·克里利、罗伯特·布莱和彼得·戴维森的同班同学。阿什贝利曾在纽约大学短暂学习,1951年在哥伦比亚大学拿到硕士学位。

作品及导读

作品 1

Syringa

导 读

Syringa sends Orpheus into "the nature of things to seen only once, as they happen along, bumping into other things." Orpheus proves most adaptable, shifting and changing his songs to extol and then to exhaust many measures of art, nature, love, and time. And in the end, he is not torn apart; rather, he is simply used up, burned out like a star, and the poem continues to its finish without Orpheus and yet with something of the beauty of his example, his fatal trajectory. The reckless economy of poetry teaches that "stellification is for the few," that out of many figures, only a handful resonate with enough life in enough time to set us the kind of example, that is, an exemplary self, in search of which we originally resort to the writing and reading of poems. In order to find these, the imagination tries and squanders a great deal, living carelessly off its only capital: the real and real time. The compact measures of bad poetry are niggardly; they refuse to waste words and try to pass off such parsimony as a virtue. Ashbery has taught me that I *must* waste words, lots of them, trying them against and upon one another, allowing them and their syntaxes to fall apart sometimes in order to find, not the true ones, but the ones that seem true at the time, the ones whose example I am willing to follow to their ultimately silent ends. The wasting and the falling apart are the circumstances, the medium of poetry.

《紫丁香》把俄耳甫斯带入了一个完全只有他自己的世界。"闪耀的紫色小花"是紫丁香，它在采石场的边缘生长。而俄耳甫斯的挽歌能使石头裂开，这种关联丰富了挽歌的意义。花用它的美劈裂岩石，肯定了荒凉之地的生命，这是传统挽歌的意义。当挽歌与花相匹敌，它把采石场的"裂缝"转变成一个生成的源头，"暗淡中午的井"。此诗另以对"紫丁香"的玩味加深了其含义，它起源于希腊语，意为潘神之笛。至此，紫丁香作为劈裂岩石的花与丧失的感知重合起来，挽歌的沉思力量虽然"不足够"但仍要继续。此诗明确激活了俄耳甫斯的神话，尤其是强调其复活和肢解后的重组方面。紫丁香也是山林女神西琳克斯的名字，她为保护贞操免受潘神玷污而变成芦苇，于是潘神就用它做成了潘神之笛。于是，诗的题目指向另一个象征——芦苇，而西琳克斯的故事就被俄耳甫斯的故事所取代，只是在诗的末尾暗示了一下。用这种置换，阿什贝利表明，存在两种诗歌模式。一方面是俄耳甫斯式的，另一方面，仅留下了一个名字的西琳克斯则代表了艺术超越自身技巧的需要，从所爱的事物向生活本身移动，调用那绝对的变形，正如被潘神抓住前所做的。而在最后，他并没有分裂，相反，他只是像一颗星星那样把自己燃烧殆尽。而这首诗还有待去完成，即使，没有他的唯美的轨迹。说出来的很多数字，只有少数具有足够的生活中有足够的时间来产生共鸣，我们设置的类的实例，也就是一个示范性的自我，寻找我们最初求助于写作和阅读诗歌。为了找到这些，他尝试和挥霍了很多，不惜关注唯一的品质：真正的和实时性。阿什贝利告诉我，我必须浪费的话，很多人，他们试图反对彼此，让他们和他们的语法土崩瓦解有时为了找到，而不是真正的人，而是那些看似真实的时候，在有些时候，语言的浪费是诗歌的一种媒介。

选 文

Syringa

Orpheus liked the glad personal quality
Of the things beneath the sky. Of course, Eurydice was a part
Of this. Then one day, everything changed. He rends
Rocks into fissures with lament. Gullies, hummocks
Can't withstand it. The sky shudders from one horizon
To the other, almost ready to give up wholeness.
Then Apollo quietly told him: "Leave it all on earth.
Your lute, what point? Why pick at a dull pavan few care to

Follow, except a few birds of dusty feather,
Not vivid performances of the past." But why not?
All other things must change too.
The seasons are no longer what they once were,
But it is the nature of things to be seen only once,
As they happen along, bumping into other things, getting along
Somehow. That's where Orpheus made his mistake.
Of course Eurydice vanished into the shade;
She would have even if he hadn't turned around.
No use standing there like a gray stone toga as the whole wheel
Of recorded history flashes past, struck dumb, unable to
utter an intelligent
Comment on the most thought-provoking element in its train.
Only love stays on the brain, and something these people,
These other ones, call life. Singing accurately
So that the notes mount straight up out of the well of
Dim noon and rival the tiny, sparkling yellow flowers
Growing around the brink of the quarry, encapsulizes
The different weights of the things.
But it isn't enough
To just go on singing. Orpheus realized this
And didn't mind so much about his reward being in heaven
After the Bacchantes had torn him apart, driven
Half out of their minds by his music, what it was doing to them.
Some say it was for his treatment of Eurydice.
But probably the music had more to do with it, and
The way music passes, emblematic
Of life and how you cannot isolate a note of it
And say it is good or bad. You must
Wait till it's over. "The end crowns all,"
Meaning also that the "tableau"
Is wrong. For although memories, of a season, for example,
Melt into a single snapshot, one cannot guard, treasure
That stalled moment. It too is flowing, fleeting;
It is a picture of flowing, scenery, though living, mortal,
Over which an abstract action is laid out in blunt,
Harsh strokes. And to ask more than this
Is to become the tossing reeds of that slow,
Powerful stream, the trailing grasses

Playfully tugged at, but to participate in the action
No more than this. Then in the lowering gentian sky
Electric twitches are faintly apparent first, then burst forth
Into a shower of fixed, cream-colored flares. The horses
Have each seen a share of the truth, though each thinks,
"I'm a maverick. Nothing of this is happening to me,
Though I can understand the language of birds, and
The itinerary of the lights caught in the storm is
fully apparent to me.
Their jousting ends in music much
As trees move more easily in the wind after a summer storm
And is happening in lacy shadows of shore-trees, now,
day after day."
But how late to be regretting all this, even
Bearing in mind that regrets are always late, too late!
To which Orpheus, a bluish cloud with white contours,
Replies that these are of course not regrets at all,
Merely a careful, scholarly setting down of
Unquestioned facts, a record of pebbles along the way.
And no matter how all this disappeared,
Or got where it was going, it is no longer
Material for a poem. Its subject
Matters too much, and not enough, standing there helplessly
While the poem streaked by, its tail afire, a bad
Comet screaming hate and disaster, but so turned inward
That the meaning, good or other, can never
Become known. The singer thinks
Constructively, builds up his chant in progressive stages
Like a skyscraper, but at the last minute turns away.
The song is engulfed in an instant in blackness
Which must in turn flood the whole continent
With blackness, for it cannot see. The singer
Must then pass out of sight, not even relieved
Of the evil burthen of the words. Stellification
Is for the few, and comes about much later
When all record of these people and their lives
Has disappeared into libraries, onto microfilm.
A few are still interested in them. "But what about
So-and-so?" is still asked on occasion. But they lie

Frozen and out of touch until an arbitrary chorus
Speaks of a totally different incident with a similar name
In whose tale are hidden syllables
Of what happened so long before that
In some small town, one different summer.

作品 2

Paradoxes and Oxymorons

导 读

Paradoxes and Oxymorons, while it doesn't express a Barthian or Pynchonian degree of interest in the construction of identity as a function of culture and history, is very much concerned with the post structural question of the relation between language and identity. The paradox at the heart of "Paradoxes and Oxymorons" is that what is revealed, in a text that represents a subject, is the very representational of that subject. Phrased as an oxymoron, the subject is true fiction.

This fiction of the subject, furthermore, is highly unstable. While the poem plays at being "plain"-spoken, it is too indeterminate for the speaker (objectified as "you") to comprehend. The speaker's response to his own question is evasive ("It is that") and vague ("other things"). And while he indirectly claims systematicity for poetic language in stanza two, that systematicity immediately turns out to involve "play." The transparency of the subject in language is "dreamed", a "role-pattern" which, like that of the Puritan saints, cannot be copied with assurance, since one's participation in "the division of grace" is "Without proof".

悖论与矛盾

悖论与矛盾,并没有巴特式神学和平钦式的功能结构、文化结构和历史结构,而是着重于语言与同一性的后结构主义。在悖论与矛盾中表现的悖论正是最具主题代表性的。而矛盾以矛盾来表现,主题就是真正虚构的。

这种主题的虚构,是极其不稳定的。诗歌是普通的,对说话者来说太不确定(主语"你")以致不能理解。说话者对自己问题的回应是逃辟的而又模糊的,("它是其他的事情")而且作者没有直接在第二诗节里表现诗歌语言的、与"游戏"相关联的系统性。主题语言的透明度是"被梦想的角色类型",就像清教徒圣人不能保证,因为一个人"优雅的分界线"是"没有证明的"。

选 文

Paradoxes and Oxymorons

This poem is concerned with language on a very plain level.
Look at it talking to you. You look out a window

THE AMERICAN PART

Or pretend to fidget. You have it but you don't have it.
You miss it, it misses you. You miss each other.

The poem is sad because it wants to be yours, and cannot.
What's a plain level? It is that and other things,
Bringing a system of them into play. Play?
Well, actually, yes, but I consider play to be

A deeper outside thing, a dreamed role-pattern,
As in the division of grace these long August days
Without proof. Open-ended. And before you knowknow
It gets lost in the steam and chatter of typewriters.

It has been played once more. I think you exist only
To tease me into doing it, on your level, and then you aren't there
Or have adopted a different attitude. And the poem
Has set me softly down beside you. The poem is you.

17 Arthur Miller

作者简介

Arthur Miller was born on October 17, 1915, in New York City. He was a famous American playwright and essayist. He was the second of three children of Isadora and Augusta Miller, Polish Jewish immigrants. His father manufactured women coats, but his business was devastated by the Depression. Due to his father's strained financial circumstances, Miller had to work for tuition money to attend the University of Michigan. It was at Michigan that he wrote his first plays. They were successes, earning him numerous student awards. In 1938, Miller received a BA in English. After graduation, he joined the Federal Theater Project, a New Deal agency established to provide jobs in the theater. He chose the theater project although he had an offer to work as a scriptwriter for 20th Century Fox. .

He was a prominent figure in American theatre, writing dramas that include plays such as *All My Sons* (1947), *Death of a Salesman* (1949), *The Crucible* (1953) and *A View from the Bridge* (one-act, 1955; revised two-act, 1956), as well as the film *The Misfits* (1961). His play *The Man Who Had All the Luck* (1944) and his novel *Focus* (1945) contained the basic themes of his work. In his play *All My Sons*, Miller portrayed the decline of the family of an industrialist who made a fortune during the war. The tragedy *Death of a Salesman*, which won the Pulitzer Prize, revealed the illusoriness of "success." Miller was died because of heart failure after a battle against cancer, pneumonia and congestive heart disease at his home in Roxbury, Connecticut. He died on the evening of February 10, 2005 (the 56th anniversary of the Broadway debut of Death of a Salesman), aged 89. Miller's career as a writer spanned over seven decades, and at the time of his death, Miller was considered to be one of the greatest dramatists of the twentieth century. After his death, many respected actors, directors, and producers paid tribute to Miller.

阿瑟·米勒于1915年12月17日出生于纽约,美国著名的剧作家和小说家。米勒生于波兰犹太裔移民家庭,是家里的第二个孩子。他的父亲伊萨德是成衣制造商,但是他的生意在美国大萧条中被击垮。由于家庭经济条件的拮据,米勒不得不自己挣钱交大学学费。在密歇根大学,米勒开始创作了他早期一些作品,而这些作品无疑都为米勒赢得了莫大的声誉,同时也获得了学校的很多奖励。1938年,米勒获得了密歇根大学的英语学位。毕业之后,他加入了联邦剧院工作。尽管当时他也收到了20世纪福克斯电影公司的邀请函,他还是选择了联邦剧院。

他是美国剧坛中有影响力的人物,创作了许多著名的作品。比如,《我所有的儿子们》、《推销员之死》、《炼狱》、《桥上一瞥》,以及电影巨作《花田错》。他的戏剧《天之骄子》和小说《焦点》蕴含了他的作品创作的基本主题。在他的作品《我所有的儿子们》中,米勒勾画了一个在战争中致富的一个家庭的没落。1949年创作的《推销员之死》获得了普利策奖,该剧揭示了对成功的一种错误认知与盲目追求。在2005年2月10日深夜,米勒因心脏衰竭在美国康涅狄格州的家中病逝,享年89岁。米勒的一生,写作时间长达70多年。米勒去世之后立即被誉为20世纪最伟大的剧作家。随后,许多著名的演员、导演、制片人等都对他做出了高度评价。

作品及导读

作品 1

Death of a Salesman

导 读

Death of a Salesman was the recipient of the 1949 Pulitzer Prize for Drama and Tony Award for Best Play. It brought Miller international fame, and become one of the major achievements of modern American theatre. This play rebates the tragic story of a salesman named Willy Loman, who chooses fame and wealth as the false goals for his life and is finally driven to suicide.

The first section in this theatre narrates that Willy Loman returns home exhausted after a lost business trip. Worried over Willy's state of mind and recent car "crashes", his wife Linda suggests that he ask his boss Howard Wagner to allow him to work in his home city so he will not have to travel. Willy complains to Linda that their son, Biff, has yet to make good on his life. Despite Biff's promise as an athlete in high school, he flunked senior year math and never went to college. Biff and his brother, Happy, who is also visiting, reminisce about their childhood together. They discuss their father's mental degeneration, which they have witnessed by his constant vacillations and talking to himself. When Willy walks in, angry that the two boys have never amounted to anything, Biff and Happy tell Willy that Biff plans to make a business proposition the next day in an effort to pacify their father.

Death of a Salesman traced the life of a common American and narrated a loser's poignant story. Willy's tragedy lies in his excessive fanatic in American Dream which eroded his soul and distorted his personality. The process of his failure was the period in which American Dream disillusioned. This work negates the success around American's Dream through two generation's failure, and gets high achievement in description of structure, space-time and figure.

　　1949年《推销员之死》这部作品获得了"普利策戏剧奖"和"托尼戏剧音乐奖"。这使得米勒成为国际知名作家。同时这部戏剧成为美国现代戏剧主要成就作品之一。它告诉我们一个关于名叫威利的推销员的悲剧故事。威利错误地用一生去追求名与利,最终死于自杀。

　　剧本的第一章讲述:取消了工作行程之后,威利精疲力竭地返回了家中。在家中威利讲了很多他回家途中的经历与感受,他的妻子琳达因为担心他,就建议威利去和自己的老板商量商量,让威利在纽约当差,省得途中劳顿。另外威利还向妻子抱怨他们的大儿子比夫,认为比夫无所事事,没有成就。即使比夫保证成为学校的一名运动员,但在数学考试中他没有及格,最终还是令人失望的。这时候比夫和他的弟弟哈皮在房间里追忆着他们儿时的童趣,他们还谈论了父亲身体恶化的情况,因为常常会看到和听到父亲自言自语。此时父亲气冲冲地走了进来,比夫和哈皮为了使父亲镇定些,准备告诉父亲比夫正在筹划一个商业计划。

　　《推销员之死》讲述了一个普通美国人经历的辛酸故事。威利的悲剧建立在大多数人的美国梦之上,这个梦摧毁了他的灵魂,更是腐蚀了他的人格。威利生活失败的时刻就是美国梦幻想破灭的时刻。作品通过两代人的失败,否定了人人都能成功的"美国梦",在结构上安排、时空上处理、人物形象刻画和内心复杂情感的描写上都取得了很高的成就。

选 文

Death of a Salesman
(ACT 1)

　　A melody is heard, played upon a flute. It is small and fine, telling of grass and trees and the horizon. The curtain rises. Before us is the Salesman's house. We are aware of towering, angular shapes behind it, surrounding it on all sides. Only the blue light of the sky falls upon the house and forestage; the surrounding area shows an angry glow of orange. As more light appears, we see a solid vault of apartment houses around the small, fragile-seeming home. An air of the dream dings to the place, a dream rising out of reality. The kitchen at center seems enough, for there is a kitchen table with three chairs, and a refrigerator. But no other fixtures are seen. At the back of the kitchen there is a draped entrance, which leads to the living room. To the right of the kitchen, on a level raised two feet, is a bedroom furnished only with a brass bedstead and a straight chair. On a shelf over the bed a silver athletic trophy stands. A window opens onto the apartment house at the side.

Behind the kitchen, on a level raised six and a half feet, is the boys' bedroom, at present barely visible. Two beds are dimly seen, and at the back of the room a dormer window. (This bedroom is above the unseen living room.) At the left a stairway curves up to it from the kitchen.

The entire setting is wholly or, in some places, partially trans-parent. The roof-line of the house is one-dimensional; under and over it we see the apartment buildings. Before the house lies an apron, curving beyond the forestage into the orchestra. This for-ward area serves as the back yard as well as the locale of all Willy's imaginings and of his city scenes. Whenever the action is in the present the actors observe the imaginary wall-lines, entering the house only through its door at the left. But in the scenes of the past these boundaries are broken, and characters enter or leave a room by stepping through a wall onto the forestage.

From the right, Willy Loman, the Salesman, enters, carrying two large sample cases. The flute plays on. He hears but is not aware of it. He is past sixty years of age, dressed quietly. Even a she crosses the stage to the doorway of the house, his exhaustion is apparent. He unlocks the door, comes into the kitchen, and thank-fully lets his burden down, feeling the soreness of his palms. A word-sigh escapes his lips — it might be "Oh, boy, oh, boy." He closes the door, then carries his cases out into the living room, through the draped kitchen doorway.

Linda, his wife, has stirred in her bed at the right. She gets out and puts on a robe, listening. Most often jovial, she has developed an iron repression of her exceptions to Willy's behavior — she more than loves him, she admires him, as though his mercurial nature, his temper, his massive dreams and little cruelties, served her only as sharp reminders of the turbulent longings within him, longings which she shares but lacks the temperament to utter and follow to their end.

LINDA (hearing Willy outside the bedroom, calls with some trepidation): Willy!

WILLY: It's all right. I came back.

LINDA: Why? What happened? (Slight pause.) Did something happen, Willy?

WILLY: No, nothing happened.

LINDA: You didn't smash the car, did you?

WILLY (with casual irritation): I said nothing happened. Didn't you hear me?

LINDA: Don't you feel well?

WILLY: I'm tired to the death. (The flute has faded away. He sit son the bed beside her, a little numb.) I couldn't make it. I just couldn't make it, Linda.

LINDA (very carefully, delicately): Where were you all day? You look terrible.

WILLY: I got as far as a little above Yonkers. I stopped for a cup of coffee. Maybe it was the coffee.

LINDA: What?

WILLY (after a pause): I suddenly couldn't drive any more. The car kept going off onto the shoulder, y'know?

LINDA (helpfully): Oh. Maybe it was the steering again. I don't think Angelo knows the Studebaker.

WILLY: No, it's me, it's me. Suddenly I realize I'm goin' sixty miles an hour and I don't remember the last five minutes. I'm — I can't seem to — keep my mind to it.

LINDA: Maybe it's your glasses. You never went for your new glasses.

WILLY: No, I see everything. I came back ten miles an hour. It took me nearly four hours from Yonkers.

LINDA (resigned): Well, you'll just have to take a rest, Willy, you can't continue this way.

WILLY: I just got back from Florida.

LINDA: But you didn't rest your mind. Your mind is over active, and the mind is what counts, dear.

WILLY: I'll start out in the morning. Maybe I'll feel better in the morning. (She is taking off his shoes.) These god dam arch sup-ports are killing me.

LINDA: Take an aspirin. Should I get you an aspirin? It'll soothe you.

WILLY (with wonder): I was driving along, you understand? And I was fine. I was even observing the scenery. You can imagine, me looking at scenery, on the road every week of my life. But it's so beautiful up there, Linda, the trees are so thick, and the sun is warm. I opened the windshield and just let the warm air bathe over me. And then all of a sudden I'm goin' off the road! I'm tellin' ya, I absolutely forgot I was driving. If I'd've gone the other way over the white line I might've killed somebody. So I went on again — and five minutes later I'm dreaming again, and I nearly ... (He presses two fingers against his eyes.) I have such thoughts, I have such strange thoughts.

LINDA: Willy, dear. Talk to them again. There's no reason why you can't work in New York.

WILLY: They don't need me in New York. I'm the New England man. I'm vital in New England.

LINDA: But you're sixty years old. They can't expect you to keep traveling every week.

WILLY: I'll have to send a wire to Portland. I'm supposed to see Brown and Morrison tomorrow morning at ten o'clock to show the line. Goddammit, I could sell them! (He starts putting on his jacket.

LINDA (taking the jacket from him): Why don't you go down to the place tomorrow and tell Howard you've simply got to workin New York? You're too accommodating, dear.

WILLY: If old man Wagner was alive I'd been in charge of New York now! That man was a prince, he was a masterful man. But that boy of his, that Howard, he doesn't appreciate. When I went north the first time, the Wagner Company didn't know where New England was!

LINDA: Why don't you tell those things to Howard, dear?

WILLY (encouraged): I will, I definitely will. Is there any cheese?

LINDA: I'll make you a sandwich.

WILLY: No, go to sleep. I'll take some milk. I'll be up right away. The boys in?

LINDA: They're sleeping. Happy took Biff on a date tonight.

WILLY (interested): That so?

LINDA: It was so nice to see them shaving together, one behind the other, in the bathroom. Are u going out together. You notice? The whole house smells of shaving lotion.

WILLY: Figure it out. Work a lifetime to pay off a house. You finally own it, and there's nobody to live in it.

LINDA: Well, dear, life is a casting off. It's always that way.

WILLY: No, no, some people — some people accomplish something. Did Biff say anything after I went this morning?

LINDA: You shouldn't have criticized him, Willy, especially after he just got off the train. You mustn't lose your temper with him.

WILLY: When the hell did I lose my temper? I simply asked him if he was making any money. Is that a criticism?

LINDA: But, dear, how could he make any money?

WILLY (worried and angered): There's such an undercurrent in him. He became a moody man. Did he apologize when I left this morning?

LINDA: He was crestfallen, Willy. You know how he admires you. I think if he finds himself, then you'll both be happier and not fight any more.

WILLY: How can he find himself on a farm? Is that a life? A farmhand? In the beginning, when he was young, I thought, well, a young man, it's good for him to tramp around, take a lot of different jobs. But it's more than ten years now and he has yet to make thirty-five dollars a week!

LINDA: He's finding himself, Willy.

WILLY: Not finding yourself at the age of thirty-four is a disgrace!

LINDA: Shh!

WILLY: The trouble is he's lazy, goddammit!

LINDA: Willy, please!

WILLY: Biff is a lazy bum!

LINDA: They're sleeping. Get something to eat. Go on down.

WILLY: Why did he come home? I would like to know what brought him home.

LINDA: I don't know. I think he's still lost, Willy. I think he's very lost.

WILLY: Biff Loman is lost. In the greatest country in the world a young man with such — personal attractiveness, gets lost. And such a hard worker. There's one thing about Biff — he's not lazy.

LINDA: Never.

WILLY (with pity and resolve): I'll see him in the morning; I'll have a nice talk with him. I'll get him a job selling. He could be big in no time. My God! Remember how they used to follow him around in high school? When he smiled at one of them their faces lit up. When he walked down the street... (He loses himself in reminiscences.)

LINDA (trying to bring him out of it): Willy, dear, I got a new kind of American-type cheese today. It's whipped.

WILLY: Why do you get American when I like Swiss?

LINDA: I just thought you'd like a change.

WILLY: I don't want a change! I want Swiss cheese. Why am I always being contradicted?

LINDA (with a covering laugh): I thought it would be a surprise.

WILLY: Why don't you open a window in here, for God's sake?

LINDA (with infinite patience): They're all open, dear.

WILLY: The way they boxed us in here.

LINDA: We should've bought the land next door.

WILLY: The street is lined with cars. There's not a breath of fresh air in the neighborhood. The grass don't grow any more, you can't raise a carrot in the back yard. They should've had a law against apartment houses. Remember those two beautiful elm trees out there? When I and Biff hung the swing between them?

LINDA: Yeah, like being a million miles from the city.

WILLY: They should've arrested the builder for cutting those down. They massacred the neighborhood. (Lost.) More and more I think of those days, Linda. This time of year it was lilac and wisteria. And then the peonies would come out, and the daffodils. What fragrance in this room!

LINDA: Well, after all, people had to move somewhere.

WILLY: No, there are more people now.

LINDA: I don't think there are more people. I think

WILLY: There are more people! That's what's ruining this country! Population is getting out of control. The competition is maddening! Smell the stink from that apartment house! And another one on the other side... How can they whip cheese? (On Willy's last line, Biff and Happy raise themselves up in their beds, listening.)

LINDA: Go down, try it. And be quiet.

WILLY (turning to Linda, guiltily): You're not worried about me, are you, sweetheart?

BIFF: What's the matter?

HAPPY: Listen!

LINDA: You've got too much on the ball to worry about.

WILLY: You're my foundation and my support, Linda.

LINDA: Just try to relax, dear. You make mountains out of mole-hills.

WILLY: I won't fight with him any more. If he wants to go back to Texas, let him go.

LINDA: He'll find his way.

WILLY: Sure. Certain men just don't get started till later in life. Like Thomas Edison, I think. Or B. F. Goodrich. One of them was deaf. (He starts for the bedroom doorway.) I'll put my money on Biff.

LINDA: And Willy — if it's warm Sunday we'll drive in the country. And we'll open the windshield, and take lunch.

WILLY: No, the windshields don't open on the new cars.

LINDA: But you opened it today.

WILLY: Me? I didn't. (He stops.) Now isn't that peculiar! Isn't that a remarkable ... (He breaks off in amazement and fright as the flute is heard distantly.)

LINDA: What, darling?

WILLY: That is the most remarkable thing.

LINDA: What, dear?

WILLY: I was thinking of the Chevvy. (Slight pause.)

HAPPY (to Biff): Jesus, maybe he smashed up the car again!

LINDA (calling after Willy): Be careful on the stairs, dear! The cheese is on the middle shelf. (She turns, goes over to the bed, takes his jacket, and goes out of the bedroom.)

(Light has risen on the boys' room. Unseen, Willy is heard talking to himself, "eighty thousand miles," and a little laugh. Biff gets out of bed, comes downstage a bit, and stands attentively. Biff is two years older than his brother Happy, well built, but in these days bears a worn air and seems less self-assured. He has succeeded less, and his dreams are stronger and less acceptable than Happy's. Happy is tall, powerfully made. Sexuality is like a visible color on him, or a scent that many women have discovered. He, like his brother, is lost, but in a different way, for he has never allowed himself to turn his face toward defeat and is thus more confused and hard-skinned, although seemingly more content.)

HAPPY (getting out of bed): He's going to get his license taken away if he keeps that up. I'm getting nervous about him, y'know, Biff?

BIFF: His eyes are going.

HAPPY: I've driven with him. He sees all right. He just doesn't keep his mind on it. I drove into the city with him last week. He stops at a green light and then it turns red and he goes. (He laughs.)

BIFF: Maybe he's color-blind.

HAPPY: Pop? Why he's got the finest eye for color in the business. You know that.

BIFF (sitting down on his bed): I'm going to sleep.

HAPPY: You're not still sour on Dad, are you, Biff?

BIFF: He's all right, I guess.

WILLY (underneath them, in the living room): Yes, sir, eighty thousand miles — eighty-two thousand!

BIFF: You smoking?

HAPPY (holding out a pack of cigarettes): Want one?

BIFF: (taking a cigarette): I can never sleep when I smell it.

WILLY: What a simonizing job, heh?

HAPPY (with deep sentiment): Funny, Biff, y'know? Us sleeping inhere again? The old beds. (He pats his bed affectionately.)

BIFF: Yeah. Lotta dreams and plans.

HAPPY (with a deep and masculine laugh): About five hundred women would like to know what was said in this room. (They share a soft laugh.)

BIFF: Remember that big Betsy something — what the hell washer name — over on Bushwick Avenue?

HAPPY (combing his hair): With the collie dog!

BIFF: That's the one. I got you in there, remember?

HAPPY: Yeah, that was my first time — I think. Boy, there was a pig. (They laugh, almost crudely.) You taught me everything I know about women. Don't forget that.

BIFF: I bet you forgot how bashful you used to be. Especially with girls.

HAPPY: Oh, I still am, Biff.

BIFF: Oh, go on.

HAPPY: I just control it, that's all. I think I got less bashful and you got more so. What happened, Biff? Where's the old humor, the old confidence? (He shakes Biffs knee. Biff gets up and moves restlessly about the room.) What's the matter?

BIFF: Why does Dad mock me all the time?

HAPPY: He's not mocking you, he...

BIFF: Everything I say there's a twist of mockery on his face. I can't get near him.

HAPPY: He just wants you to make good, that's all. I wanted to talk to you about Dad for a long time, Biff. Something's — happening to him. He — talks to himself.

BIFF: I noticed that this morning. But he always mumbled.

HAPPY: But not so noticeable. It got so embarrassing I sent him to Florida. And you know something? Most of the time he's talking to you.

BIFF: What's he say about me?

HAPPY: I can't make it out.

BIFF: What's he say about me?

HAPPY: I think the fact that you're not settled, that you're still kind of up in the air...

BIFF: There's one or two other things depressing him, Happy.

HAPPY: What do you mean?

BIFF: Never mind. Just don't lay it all to me.

HAPPY: But I think if you just got started — I mean — is there any future for you out there?

BIFF: I tell ya, Hap, I don't know what the future is. I don't know — what I'm supposed to want.

HAPPY: What do you mean?

BIFF: Well, I spent six or seven years after high school trying to work myself up. And it's a measly manner of existence. To suffer fifty weeks of the year for the sake of a two-week vacation, when all you really desire is to be out doors, with your shirt off. And still — that's how you build a future.

HAPPY: Well, you really enjoy it on a farm? Are you content out there?

BIFF (with rising agitation): Hap, I've had twenty or thirty different kinds of jobs since I left home before the war, and it always turns out the same. I just realized it lately. In Nebraska when I herded cattle, and the Dakotas, and Arizona, and now in Texas. It's why I came home now, I guess, because I realized it. This farm I work on, its spring there now, see? And they've got about fifteen new colts. There's nothing more inspiring or — beautiful than the sight of a mare and a new colt. And it's cool there now, see? Texas is cool now, and it's spring. And when-ever spring comes to where I am, I suddenly get the feeling, my God, I'm not gettin' anywhere! What the hell am I doing, playing around with horses, twenty-eight dollars a week! I'm thirty-four, and I ought to be makin' my future. That's when I come running home. And now, I get here, and I don't know what to do with myself. (After a pause.) I've always made a point of not wasting my life, and every time I come back here I know that all I've done is to waste my life.

HAPPY: You're a poet, you know that, Biff? You're a — you're an idealist!

BIFF: No, I'm mixed up very bad. Maybe I oughta get married. Maybe I oughta get stuck into something. Maybe that's my trouble. I'm like a boy. I'm not married, I'm not in business, I just — I'm like a boy. Are you content, Hap? You're a success, aren't you? Are you content?

HAPPY: Hell, no!

BIFF: Why? You're making money, aren't you?

HAPPY (moving about with energy, expressiveness): All I can do now is wait for the merchandise manager to die. And suppose I get to be merchandise manager? He's a good friend of mine, and he just built a terrific estate on Long Island. And he lived there about two months and sold it, and now he's building an-other one. He can't enjoy it once it's finished. And I know that's just what I would do. I don't know what the hell I'm workin' for. Sometimes I sit in my apartment — all alone. And I think of the rent I'm paying. And it's crazy. But then, it's what I always wanted. BIFF (with enthusiasm): Listen, why don't you come out West with me?

HAPPY: You and I, heh?

BIFF: Sure, maybe we could buy a ranch. Raise cattle, use our muscles. Men built like we are should be working out in the open.

HAPPY (avidly): The Loman Brothers, heh?

BIFF (with vast affection): Sure, we'd be known all over the counties!

HAPPY (enthralled): That's what I dream about, Biff. Sometimes I want to just rip my clothes off in the middle of the store and out box that goddam merchandise manager. I mean I can out-box, outrun, and out lift anybody in that store, and I have to take orders from those common, petty sons-of-bitches till I can't stand it any more.

BIFF: I'm tellin' you, kid, if you were with me I'd be happy out there.

HAPPY (enthused): See, Biff, everybody around me is so false that I'm constantly lowering my ideals ...

BIFF: Baby, together we'd stand up for one another, we'd have someone to trust.

HAPPY: If I were around you.

BIFF: Hap, the trouble is we weren't brought up to grub for money. I don't know how to do it.

HAPPY: Neither can I!

BIFF: Then let's go!

HAPPY: The only thing is — what can you make out there?

BIFF: But look at your friend. Builds an estate and then hasn't the peace of mind to live in it.

HAPPY: Yeah, but when he walks into the store the waves part in front of him. That's fifty-two thousand dollars a year coming through the revolving door, and I got more in my pinky finger than he's got in his head.

BIFF: Yeah, but you just said ...

HAPPY: I gotta show some of those pompous, self-important executives over there that Hap Loman can make the grade. I want to walk into the store the way he walks in. Then I'll go with you, Biff. We'll be together yet, I swear. But take those two we had tonight. Now weren't they gorgeous creatures?

BIFF: Yeah, yeah, most gorgeous I've had in years.

HAPPY: I get that any time I want, Biff. The only trouble is, it gets like bowling or something. I just keep knockin' them over and it doesn't mean anything. You still run around a lot?

BIFF: Naa. I'd like to find a girl — steady, somebody with sub-stance.

HAPPY: That's what I long for.

BIFF: Go on! You'd never come home.

HAPPY: I would! Somebody with character, with resistance! Like Mom, y'know? You're gonna call me a bastard when I tell you this. That girl Charlotte I was with tonight is engaged to be married in five weeks. (He tries on his new hat.)

BIFF: No kiddin'!

HAPPY: Sure, the guy's in line for the vice-presidency of the store. I don't know what gets into me, maybe I just have an overdeveloped sense of competition or something, but I went and ruined her, and furthermore I can't get rid of her. And he's the third executive I've done that to. Isn't that a crummy characteristic? And to top it all, I go to their weddings! Manufacturers offer me a hundred-dollar bill now and then to throw an order their way. You know how honest I am, but it's like this girl, see. I hate myself for it. Because I don't want the girl, and still, I take it and — I love it!

BIFF: Let's go to sleep.

HAPPY: I guess we didn't settle anything, heh?

BIFF: I just got one idea that I think I'm going to try.

HAPPY: What's that?

BIFF: Remember Bill Oliver?

HAPPY: Sure, Oliver is very big now. You want to work for him again?

BIFF: No, but when I quit he said something to me. He put his arm on my shoulder, and he said, "Biff, if you ever need any-thing, come to me."

HAPPY: I remember that. That sounds good.

BIFF: I think I'll go to see him. If I could get ten thousand or even seven or eight thousand dollars I could buy a beautiful ranch.

HAPPY: I bet he'd back you. That's why I say to come back here, and we both have the apartment. And I'm tel-lin' you, Biff, any babe you want...

BIFF: No, with a ranch I could do the work I like and still be something. I just wonder though. I wonder if Oliver still thinks I stole that carton of basketballs.

HAPPY: Oh, he probably forgot that long ago. It's almost ten years. You're too sensitive. Anyway, he didn't really fire you.

BIFF: Well, I think he was going to. I think that's why I quit. I was never sure whether he knew or not. I know he thought the world of me, though. I was the only one he'd let lock up the place.

WILLY (below): You gonna wash the engine, Biff?

HAPPY: Shh!

(Biff looks at Happy, who is gazing down, listening. Willy is mumbling in the parlor.)

HAPPY: You hear that? (They listen. Willy laughs warmly.)

BIFF (growing angry): Doesn't he know Mom can hear that?

WILLY: Don't get your sweater dirty, Biff! (A look of pain crosses Biff's face.)

HAPPY: Isn't that terrible? Don't leave again, will you? You'll find a job here. You gotta stick around. I don't know what to do about him, it's getting embarrassing.

WILLY: What a simonizing job!

BIFF: Mom's hearing that!

WILLY: No kiddin', Biff, you got a date? Wonderful!

HAPPY: Go on to sleep. But talk to him in the morning, will you?

BIFF (reluctantly getting into bed): With her in the house. Brother!

HAPPY (getting into bed): I wish you'd have a good talk with him. (The light of their room begins to fade.)

BIFF (to himself in bed): That selfish, stupid...

HAPPY: Sh... Sleep, Biff. (Their light is out. Well before they have finished speaking, Willy's form is dimly seen below in the darkened kitchen. He opens the refrigerator, searches in there, and takes out a bottle of milk. The apartment houses are fading out, and the entire house and surroundings become covered with leaves. Music insinuates itself as the leaves appear.)

WILLY: Just wanna be careful with those girls, Biff, that's all. Don't make any promises. No promises of any kind. Because a girl, y'know, they always believe what you tell 'em, and you're very young, Biff, you're too young to be talking seriously to girls.

Chapter 18 Joseph Heller

作者简介

  Joseph Heller, an American novelist, one of the representative writers of Black Humor. He was born on May 1, 1923, in Brooklyn, New York. His upbringing was mostly secular. Some critics have speculated that the environment in which he grew up is credited as a major source of the wry humor and irony that was his literary trademark. Heller graduated as an honored student from Abraham Lincoln High School in 1941, and then in 1942 enlisted in the Army Air Corps, which sent him to Corsica two years later. While in the Mediterranean theatre, he flew 60 combat missions and was awarded an Air Medal and a Presidential Unit Citation. After his discharge from the army in 1945, he married Shirley Held. Heller then went back to school under the G. I. Bill, earning a B. A. in English from New York University in 1948, an M. A. from Columbia in 1949, and then attending Oxford for a year on a Fulbright Scholarship. Heller was then employed as a lecturer in English at what were then Pennsylvania State College, Yale University and New York University. He was selected as one of the members of the American Academy of Arts and Letters.

  Catch-22 was published in 1961, and it immediately assured Heller a place in literary history. After the great success of his first novel, he published a series of novels, such as *Something Happened*, *Good as Gold*, *God Knows*, *Picture This*, *Closing Time*. Besides, Heller also wrote plays, such as *We Bombed in New Haven*, *Clevinger's Trial*. However, while Heller was achieving professional success, his marriage was failing, and in 1984 he and his wife divorced. In 1986, he became ill with Guillain-Barré syndrome, a nervous system disease that left him paralyzed for several months. In 1987, Heller remarried, wedding Valerie Humphries, a nurse who had tended him during his illness. Heller continued to write until his death in 1999 of a heart attack at home in East Hampton, New York. He was 76 years old at that year. His friend and fellow novelist Kurt Vonnegut described his death as a "calamity for American letters".

约瑟夫·海勒,美国小说家,《黑色幽默》代表作家之一。1923年5月1日出生于纽约布鲁克林的科尼岛区。他的教育大多是世俗的,批评家认为,海勒玩世不恭、街头式的机智幽默的独特特点就是童年在布鲁克林的科尼岛的火热生活中形成的。1941年海勒于亚伯拉罕·林肯高中毕业,1942年10月参加美国空军第12军团,两年后驻防科西嘉,并作为侧翼投弹手执行轰炸任务共60次。1945年海勒作为空军上尉退役,同年9月3日与雪莉·海尔德结婚,随即按美国兵役法就读于南卡罗莱纳大学,1948年获得伦敦大学英语学士学位、1949年又于哥伦比亚大学获硕士学位,并作为富布莱特学者赴牛津大学访学一年。此后,他曾先后在宾夕法尼亚州立大学、耶鲁大学和纽约大学任教,当选为美国艺术文学院成员。

1961年,约瑟夫·海勒发表了《第二十二条军规》,该作品一举成名,奠定了海勒在文学史上的地位。在他的第一部小说获得伟大成就后,他陆续发表了一系列小说,比如《出了毛病》、《像戈尔德一样好》、《上帝知道》、《设想一下》、《最后时光》。此外,他还创作和改编剧本《轰炸纽黑文》、《克莱文杰的审判》。然而,正当海勒事业蒸蒸日上的时候,他的婚姻却逐渐走向破灭。1984年,他和他的妻子离婚了。1987年,他患上了巴雷综合征,可怕的病痛折磨了他几个月。1987年,海勒和在他生病期间照顾他的一个护士再婚。海勒坚持创作,直到1999年他因心脏病发作在纽约东汉普顿的家中逝世,享年76岁。他的朋友和后来的小说家库特冯内古特认为他的逝世是"美国文学的损失"。

作品及导读

作 品 1

Catch-22

导 读

Catch-22 is a satirical novel by the American author Joseph Heller. He began writing it in 1953, and the novel was first published in 1961. It is set during World War II in 1943 and is frequently cited as one of the great literary works of the twentieth century. It uses a distinctive non-chronological third-person omniscient narration, describing events from different characters' points of view and out of sequence so that the time line develops along with the plot.

The novel follows Captain John Yossarian, a U. S. Army Air Forces B-25 bombardier. Most of the events in the book occur while the fictional 256th squadron is based on the island of Pianosa, in the Mediterranean Sea west of Italy. The novel looks into the experiences of Yossarian and the other airmen in the camp, and their attempts to keep their sanity in order to fulfill their service requirements, so that they can return home.

Among other things, *Catch*-22 is a general critique of bureaucratic operation and reasoning. Resulting from its specific use in the book, the phrase "Catch-22" became a commonly used idiom meaning "a no-win situation" or "a double bind" of any type. Within the book, "Catch-22" is a military rule, the self-contradictory circular logic that, for example, prevents anyone from avoiding combat missions. Other forms of "Catch-22" are invoked throughout the novel to justify various bureaucratic actions. At one point, victims of harassment by military police quote the MPs' explanation of one of Catch-22's provisions: "*Catch*-22 states that agents enforcing Catch-22 need not prove that Catch-22 actually contains whatever provision the accused violator is accused of violating." Another character explains: "Catch-22 says they have a right to do anything we can't stop them from doing." Yossarian comes to realize that Catch-22 does not actually exist, but because the powers that be claim it does, and the world believes it does, it nevertheless has potent effects. Indeed, because it does not exist, there is no way it can be repealed, undone, overthrown, or denounced. The combination of force with specious and spurious legalistic justification is one of the book's primary motifs.

Catch-22 is a microcosm of the twentieth-century world as it might look to someone dangerously sane. It is a novel that lives and moves and grows with astonishing power and vitality.

《第二十二条军规》是美国作家约瑟夫·海勒的一部讽刺小说。这部小说的创作始于1953年，并于1961年首次出版。它以二战为背景，一度被评为是20世纪最伟大的文学作品。它使用富有特色完全第三人称叙述方式，从不同人物角度描写事件，没有时间顺序，而是随着情节的展开铺展开来。

主人公约翰·约瑟连上尉（Captain John Yossarian）是美国陆军第27航空队B-25轰炸机上的一名领航员兼投弹手。本书主要情节发生于意大利西部地中海的一个美国空军基地——皮亚诺塞小岛上。小说深入描写了尤索林以及其他飞行员在营地的经历，也刻画了他们想要保持头脑清醒，以完成任务最终能够得以返回家园的努力。

一般说来，《第二十二条军规》是对官僚行径的一种批判。源于此书对这一名词的独特使用，它已成为象征"无获胜境地"和"双重束缚"这类情境的惯用语。在书中，"第二十二条军规"是一种自相矛盾的，具有环形式逻辑的军规，例如，它可以防止任何人违抗执行任务。第二十二条军规贯穿全篇，证明了各种官僚主义行为的存在。被军队警察骚扰的受害者引用了MP对其中一个条款的解释："第二十二条军规规定，执行者不需要证明其是否包涵了这些被控违规者所侵犯的条款。"另一个人物对它的解释是："第二十二条军规让他们有权做任何事，而且我们无法阻止。"约瑟连意识到其实第二十二条军规并不存在，但是由于人们赋予它的力量，以及世界对它的存在的认可，它有着不可小觑的影响。也正是因为它的不存在，别人反而奈何不了它。为假意尊重法律而找的华而无实的，虚伪的理由是本书的主旨之一。

这部小说是20世纪世界的一个缩影，它关注了那个时代极度疯狂的那些人，它是一部具有神奇力量和活力的小说。

选 文

Catch-22
(Excerpt)

There was, of course, a catch.

"Catch-22?" inquired Yossarian.

"Of course," Colonel Korn answered pleasantly, after he had chased the mighty guard of massive M. P. s out with an insouciant flick of his hand and a slightly contemptuous nod — most relaxed, as always, when he could be most cynical. His rimless square eyeglasses glinted with sly amusement as he gazed at Yossarian. "After all, we can't simply send you home for refusing to fly more missions and keep the rest of the men here, can we? That would hardly be fair to them."

"You're goddam right!" Colonel Cathcart blurted out, lumbering back and forth gracelessly like a winded bull, puffing and pouting angrily. 'I'd like to tie him up hand and foot and throw him aboard a plane on every mission. That's what I'd like to do."

Colonel Korn motioned Colonel Cathcart to be silent and smiled at Yossarian. "You know, you really have been making things terribly difficult for Colonel Cathcart," he observed with flip good humor, as though the fact did not displease him at all. "The men are unhappy and morale is beginning to deteriorate. And it's your entire fault."

"It's your fault," Yossarian argued, "for raising the number of missions."

"No, it's your fault for refusing to fly them," Colonel Korn retorted. "The men were perfectly content to fly as many missions as we asked as long as they thought they had no alternative. Now you've given them hope, and they're unhappy. So the blame is all yours."

"Doesn't he know there's a war going on?" Colonel Cathcart, still stamping back and forth, demanded morosely without looking at Yossarian.

"I'm quite sure he does," Colonel Korn answered. "That's probably why he refuses to fly them."

"Doesn't it make any difference to him?" "Will the knowledge that there's a war going on weaken your decision to refuse to participate in it?" Colonel Korn inquired with sarcastic seriousness, mocking Colonel Cathcart.

"No, sir," Yossarian replied. "I was afraid of that," Colonel Korn remarked with an elaborate sigh, locking his fingers together comfortably on top of his smooth, bald, broad, shiny brown head. "You know, in all fairness, we really haven't treated you too badly, have we? We've fed you and paid you on time. We gave you a medal and even made you a captain."

"I never should have made him a captain," Colonel Cathcart exclaimed bitterly. "I should have given him a court-martial after he loused up that Ferrara mission and went around twice."

THE AMERICAN PART

"I told you not to promote him," said Colonel Korn, "but you wouldn't listen to me."

"No you didn't. You told me to promote him, didn't you?"

"I told you not to promote him. But you just wouldn't listen."

"I should have listened."

"You never listen to me," Colonel Korn persisted with relish. "That's the reason we're in this spot."

"All right, gee whiz. Stop rubbing it in, will you?" Colonel Cathcart burrowed his fists down deep inside his pockets and turned away in a slouch. "Instead of picking on me, why don't you figure out what we're going to do about him?"

"We're going to send him home, I'm afraid." Colonel Korn was chuckling triumphantly when he turned away from Colonel Cathcart to face Yossarian. "Yossarian, the war is over for you. We're going to send you home. You really don't deserve it. Since there's nothing else we can risk doing to you at this time, we've decided to return you to the States. We've worked out this little deal to —"

"What kind of deal?" Yossarian demanded with defiant mistrust.

Colonel Korn tossed his head back and laughed. "Oh, a thoroughly despicable deal, make no mistake about that. It's absolutely revolting. But you'll accept it quickly enough."

"Don't be too sure."

"I haven't the slightest doubt you will, even though it stinks to high heaven. Oh, by the way. You haven't told any of the men you've refused to fly more missions, have you?"

"No, sir," Yossarian answered promptly.

Colonel Korn nodded approvingly. "That's good. I like the way you lie. You'll go far in this world if you ever acquire some decent ambition."

"Doesn't he know there's a war going on?" Colonel Cathcart yelled out suddenly, and blew with vigorous disbelief into the open end of his cigarette holder.

"I'm quite sure he does," Colonel Korn replied acidly, "since you brought that identical point to his attention just a moment ago." Colonel Korn frowned wearily for Yossarian's benefit, his eyes twinkling swarthily with sly and daring scorn. Gripping the edge of Colonel Cathcart's desk with both hands, he lifted his flaccid haunches far back on the corner to sit with both short legs dangling freely. His shoes kicked lightly against the yellow oak wood, his sludge-brown socks, garterless, collapsed in sagging circles below ankles that were surprisingly small and white. "You know, Yossarian," he mused affably in a manner of casual reflection that seemed both derisive and sincere, "I really do admire you a bit. You're an intelligent person of great moral character who has taken a very courageous stand. I'm an intelligent person with no moral character at all, so I'm in an ideal position to appreciate it."

"These are very critical times," Colonel Cathcart asserted petulantly from a far corner of the office, paying no attention to Colonel Korn.

"Very critical times indeed," Colonel Korn agreed with a placid nod. "We've just had a change of command above, and we can't afford a situation that might put us in a bad light with either General Scheisskopf or General Peckem. Isn't that what you mean, Colonel?"

"Hasn't he got any patriotism?"

"Won't you fight for your country?" Colonel Korn demanded, emulating Colonel Cathcart's harsh, self-righteous tone. "Won't you give up your life for Colonel Cathcart and me?"

Yossarian tensed with alert astonishment when he heard Colonel Korn's concluding words. "What's that?" he exclaimed. "What have you and Colonel Cathcart got to do with my country? You're not the same."

"How can you separate us?" Colonel Korn inquired with ironical tranquility.

"That's right," Colonel Cathcart cried emphatically. "You're either for us or against us. There's no two ways about it."

"I'm afraid he's got you," added Colonel Korn. "You're either for us or against your country. It's as simple as that."

"Oh, no, Colonel. I don't buy that."

Colonel Korn was unruffled. "Neither do I, frankly, but everyone else will. So there you are."

"You're a disgrace to your uniform!" Colonel Cathcart declared with blustering wrath, whirling to confront Yossarian for the first time. 'I'd like to know how you ever got to be a captain, anyway.'

"You promoted him," Colonel Korn reminded sweetly, stifling a snicker. "Don't you remember?"

"Well, I never should have done it."

"I told you not to do it," Colonel Korn said. "But you just wouldn't listen to me."

"Gee whiz, will you stop rubbing it in?" Colonel Cathcart cried. He furrowed his brow and glowered at Colonel Korn through eyes narrow with suspicion, his fists clenched on his hips. "Say, whose side are you on, anyway?"

"Your side, Colonel. What other side could I be on?"

"Then stop picking on me, will you? Get off my back, will you?"

"I'm on your side, Colonel. I'm just loaded with patriotism."

"Well, just make sure you don't forget that." Colonel Cathcart turned away grudgingly after another moment, incompletely reassured, and began striding the floor, his hands kneading his long cigarette holder. He jerked a thumb toward Yossarian. "Let's settle with him. I know what I'd like to do with him. I'd like to take him outside and shoot him. That's what I'd like to do with him. That's what General Dreedle would do with him."

"But General Dreedle isn't with us any more," said Colonel Korn, 'so we can't take him outside and shoot him. Now that his moment of tension with Colonel Cathcart had passed, Colonel Korn relaxed again and resumed kicking softly against Colonel Cathcart's desk. He returned to Yossarian. "So we're going to send you home instead. It took a bit of thinking, but we finally worked out this horrible little plan for sending you home without causing too much dissatisfaction among the friends you'll leave behind. Doesn't that make you happy?"

"What kind of plan? I'm not sure I'm going to like it."

"I know you're not going to like it." Colonel Korn laughed, locking his hands contentedly on top of his head again. "You're going to loathe it. It really is odious and certainly will offend your conscience. But you'll agree to it quickly enough. You'll agree to it because it will send you home safe and sound in two weeks, and because you have no choice. It's that or a court-martial. Take it or leave it."

Yossarian snorted. "Stop bluffing, Colonel. You can't court-martial me for desertion in the face of the enemy. It would make you look bad and you probably couldn't get a conviction."

"But we can court-martial you now for desertion from duty, since you went to Rome without a pass. And we could make it stick. If you think about it a minute, you'll see that you'd leave us no alternative. We can't simply let you keep walking around in open insubordination without punishing you. All the other men would stop flying missions, too. No, you have my word for it. We will court-martial you if you turn our deal down, even though it would raise a lot of questions and be a terrible black eye for Colonel Cathcart."

Colonel Cathcart winced at the words "black eye" and, without any apparent premeditation, hurled his slender onyx-and-ivory cigarette holder down viciously on the wooden surface on his desk. "Jesus Christ!" he shouted unexpectedly. "I hate this goddam cigarette holder!" The cigarette holder bounced off the desk to the wall, ricocheted across the window sill to the floor and came to a stop almost where he was standing. Colonel Cathcart stared down at it with an irascible scowl. "I wonder if it's really doing me any good."

"It's a feather in your cap with General Peckem, but a black eye for you with General Scheisskopf," Colonel Korn informed him with a mischievous look of innocence.

"Well, which one am I supposed to please?"

"Both."

"How can I please them both? They hate each other. How am I ever going to get a feather in my cap from General Scheisskopf without getting a black eye from General Peckem?"

"March."

"Yeah, march. That's the only way to please him. March. March." Colonel Cathcart grimaced sullenly. "Some generals! They're a disgrace to their uniforms. If people like those two can make general, I don't see how I can miss."

"You're going to go far." Colonel Korn assured him with a flat lack of conviction, and turned back chuckling to Yossarian, his disdainful merriment increasing at the sight of Yossarian's unyielding expression of antagonism and distrust. "And there you have the crux of the situation. Colonel Cathcart wants to be a general and I want to be a colonel, and that's why we have to send you home."

"Why does he want to be a general?"

"Why? For the same reason that I want to be a colonel. What else have we got to do? Everyone teaches us to aspire to higher things. A general is higher than a colonel, and a colonel is higher than a lieutenant colonel. So we're both aspiring. And you know, Yossarian, it's a lucky thing for you that we are. Your timing on this is absolutely perfect, but I suppose you took that factor into account in your calculations."

"I haven't been doing any calculating," Yossarian retorted.

"Yes, I really do enjoy the way you lie," Colonel Korn answered. "Won't it make you proud to have your commanding officer promoted to general — to know you served in an outfit that averaged more combat missions per person than any other? Don't you want to earn more unit citations and more oak leaf clusters for your Air Medal? Where's your 'sprit de corps? Don't you want to contribute further to this great record by flying more combat missions? It's your last chance to answer yes."

"No."

"In that case, you have us over a barrel —" said Colonel Korn without rancor.

"He ought to be ashamed of himself!"

"— and we have to send you home. Just do a few little things for us, and —"

"What sort of things?" Yossarian interrupted with belligerent misgiving.

"Oh, tiny, insignificant things. Really, this is a very generous deal we're making with you. We will issue orders returning you to the States — really, we will — and all you have to do in return is..."

"What? What must I do?"

Colonel Korn laughed curtly. "Like us."

Yossarian blinked. "Like you?"

"Like us."

"Like you?"

"That's right," said Colonel Korn, nodding, gratified immeasurably by Yossarian's guileless surprise and bewilderment. "Like us. Join us. Be our pal. Say nice things about us here and back in the States. Become one of the boys. Now, that isn't asking too much, is it?"

"You just want me to like you? Is that all?"

"That's all."

"That's all?"

"Just find it in your heart to like us."

Yossarian wanted to laugh confidently when he saw with amazement that Colonel Korn was telling the truth. "That isn't going to be too easy," he sneered.

"Oh, it will be a lot easier than you think," Colonel Korn taunted in return, undismayed by Yossarian's barb. "You'll be surprised at how easy you'll find it to like us once you begin." Colonel Korn hitched up the waist of his loose, voluminous trousers. The deep black grooves isolating his square chin from his jowls were bent again in a kind of jeering and reprehensible mirth. "You see, Yossarian, we're going to put you on easy street. We're going to promote you to major and even give you another medal. Captain Flume is already working on glowing press releases describing your valor over Ferrara, your deep and abiding loyalty to your outfit and your consummate dedication to duty. Those phrases are all actual quotations, by the way. We're going to glorify you and send you home a hero, recalled by the Pentagon for morale and public-relations purposes. You'll live like a millionaire. Everyone will lionize you. You'll have parades in your honor and make speeches to raise money for war bonds. A whole new world of luxury awaits you once you become our pal. Isn't it lovely?"

Yossarian found himself listening intently to the fascinating elucidation of details. "I'm not sure I want to make speeches."

"Then we'll forget the speeches. The important thing is what you say to people here." Colonel Korn leaned forward earnestly, no longer smiling. "We don't want any of the men in the group to know that we're sending you home as a result of your refusal to fly more missions. And we don't want General Peckem or General Scheisskopf to get wind of any friction between us, either. That's why we're going to become such good pals."

"What will I say to the men who asked me why I refused to fly more missions?"

"Tell them you had been informed in confidence that you were being returned to the States and that you were unwilling to risk your life for another mission or two. Just a minor disagreement between pals, that's all."

"Will they believe it?"

"Of course they'll believe it, once they see what great friends we've become and when they see the press releases and read the flattering things you have to say about me and Colonel Cathcart. Don't worry about the men. They'll be easy enough to discipline and control when you've gone. It's only while you're still here that they may prove troublesome. You know, one good apple can spoil the rest," Colonel Korn concluded with conscious irony. "You know — this would really be wonderful — you might even serve as an inspiration to them to fly more missions."

"Suppose I denounce you when I get back to the States?"

"No one would believe you, the Army wouldn't let you, and why in the world should you want to? You're going to be one of the boys, remember? You'll enjoy a rich, rewarding, luxurious, privileged existence. You'd have to be a fool to throw it all away just for a moral principle, and you're not a fool. Is it a deal?"

"I don't know."

"It's that or a court-martial."

"That's a pretty scummy trick I'd be playing on the men in the squadron, isn't it?"

"Odious," Colonel Korn agreed amiably, and waited, watching Yossarian patiently with a glimmer of private delight.

"But what the hell!" Yossarian exclaimed. "If they don't want to fly more missions, let them stand up and do something about it the way I did. Right?"

"Of course," said Colonel Korn.

"There's no reason I have to risk my life for them, is there?"

"Of course not."

Yossarian arrived at his decision with a swift grin. "It's a deal!" he announced jubilantly.

"Great," said Colonel Korn with somewhat less cordiality than Yossarian had expected, and he slid himself off Colonel Cathcart's desk to stand on the floor. He tugged the folds of cloth of his pants and undershorts free from his crotch and gave Yossarian a limp hand to shake. "Welcome aboard."

"Thanks, Colonel. I —"

"Call me Blackie, John. We're pals now."

"Sure, Blackie. My friends call me Yo-Yo. Blackie, I —"

"His friends call him Yo-Yo," Colonel Korn sang out to Colonel Cathcart. "Why don't you congratulate Yo-Yo on what a sensible move he's making?"

"That's a real sensible move you're making, Yo-Yo," Colonel Cathcart said, pumping Yossarian's hand with clumsy zeal.

"Thank you, Colonel, I —"

"Call him Chuck," said Colonel Korn.

"Sure, call me Chuck," said Colonel Cathcart with a laugh that was hearty and awkward. "We're all pals now."

"Sure, Chuck."

"Exit smiling," said Colonel Korn, his hands on both their shoulders as the three of them moved to the door.

"Come on over for dinner with us some night, Yo-Yo," Colonel Cathcart invited hospitably. "How about tonight? In the group dining room."

"I'd love to, sir."

"Chuck," Colonel Korn corrected reprovingly.

"I'm sorry, Blackie. Chuck. I can't get used to it."

"That's all right, pal."

"Sure, pal."

"Thanks, pal."

"Don't mention it, pal."

"So long, pal."

Yossarian waved goodbye fondly to his new pals and sauntered out onto the balcony corridor, almost bursting into song the instant he was alone. He was home free, he had pulled it off; his act of rebellion had succeeded; he was safe, and he had nothing to be ashamed of to anyone. He started toward the staircase with a jaunty and exhilarated air. A private in green fatigues saluted him. Yossarian returned the salute happily, staring at the private with curiosity. He looked strangely familiar. When Yossarian returned the salute, the private in green fatigues turned suddenly into Nately's whore and lunged at him murderously with a bone-handled kitchen knife that caught him in the side below his upraised arm. Yossarian sank to the floor with a shriek, shutting his eyes in overwhelming terror as he saw the girl lift the knife to strike at him again. He was already unconscious when Colonel Korn and Colonel Cathcart dashed out of the office and saved his life by frightening her away.

相关链接

Black Humor is an important term of America in 1960's. The phrase "black humor" comes from the name of a book, which is written by B. J. Friedman. Black humor refers primarily to a kind of bitter and often outrageous satire.

Mostly black humor is directed against greed, narrow-mindedness, complacency, and hypocrisy. Black humor frequently satirizes social institutions, including the government, the military, and large corporations, depicting them as dehumanizing organizations. Black humorists often attack the absurdity they see in life itself, as well as in the morbid society. People's moral consciousness is in line with the core of balck humor.

Black humor as a movement became prominent in the 1960's. But it also drew criticism from such writers as Jonathan Swift.

It is one of the most representative genres in the American literature in the 1960s. For instance, the works of such writers as Kurt Vonnegut, Thomas Pynchon, John Barth, Joseph Heller, and Philip Roth contain elements of black humor. It was usually used in literary dramas and films, where grotesque or morbid humor is used to express the absurdity, insensitivity, paradox, and cruelty of the modern world. Ordinary characters or situations are usually exaggerated far beyond the limits of normal satire or irony. Black humor uses devices associated with tragedy and is sometimes equated with tragic farce. On the whole, black humor is a comedy, but it is also a sick comedy with tragedy.

Black Humor is marked by the use of morbid, ironic, or grotesquely comic episodes that ridicule the stupidity of human begings. The term came into common use in the 1960s to describe the work of novelists such as Joseph Heller, whose *Catch-22* (1961) is an outstanding example.

黑色幽默是20世纪60年代一个很重要的术语。黑色幽默这个词来自于弗里德曼写的一本书。它的主要内容在于表现无可奈何的苦笑。

黑色幽默主要是和贪婪、狭隘、自满、虚伪相悖的,更多的是表现出对社会机构的挖苦,包括政府部门、军事部门、大型企业,把它们描述为丧失人性的组织。黑色幽默派的作家主要抨击他们在现实生活中看到的荒谬言行及病态的社会。人们的道德意识和黑色幽默的内涵是一致的。黑色幽默作为20世纪60年代主要的思潮,同时也引来的一些作家的批判,如乔纳森·斯威夫特等。

它是20世纪60年代最有代表性的一种体裁。库尔特·冯内古特,托马斯·皮休,约翰·巴斯,约瑟夫·海勒,菲利普·罗斯的作品中都渗透了黑色幽默的元素。黑色幽默作为一种体裁,也经常会被运用到文学戏剧,电影中。在这些领域的运用主要为了表达荒诞、相悖、冷漠以及现实世界的残酷。在作品中通常会采用夸张、悖论、反讽等表现手法。黑色幽默所用的表现手段一般都和悲剧有一定关系,有时就是一个悲剧性的闹剧。总之,黑色幽默就是一个喜剧,但它同时也是一个有着悲剧色彩的病态喜剧。

黑色幽默被标注上病态、讽刺、怪异、滑稽等特征,来折射出人类的愚昧。这个术语在约瑟夫·海勒的《第二十二条军规》中成功被运用。

19 Toni Morrison

作者简介

Toni Morrison, originally named Chloe Anthony Walford (born on February 18, 1931, Lorain, Ohio, U. S.), is perhaps the most celebrated contemporary American novelist. Awarded the Nobel Prize for literature in 1993, Morrison powerfully evokes in her fiction the legacies of displacement and slavery that have been bequeathed to the African-American community.

Morrison grew up in the American Midwest in a family that possessed an intense love of and appreciation for black culture. Storytelling, songs, and folktales were a deeply formative part of her childhood. She attended Howard University (B. A., 1953) and Cornell University (M. A., 1955). After teaching at Texas Southern University for two years, she taught at Howard from 1957 to 1964. In 1965 she became a fiction editor. From 1984 she taught writing at the State University of New York at Albany, leaving in 1989 to join the faculty of Princeton University.

Her eight major novels, *The Bluest Eye*, *Saul*, *Song of Solomon*, *Tar Baby*, *Beloved*, *Jazz*, *Paradise* and *Love* have received extensive critical acclaim. She received the National Book Critics Award in 1978 for *Song of Solomon* and the 1988 Pulitzer Prize for *Beloved*. Both novels were chosen as the main selections for *the Book of the Month Club* in 1977 and 1987 respectively. In 2006 *Beloved* was chosen by the *New York Times Book Review* as the best work of American fiction published in the last quarter-century. Ms. Morrison co-authored the Childers's books *Remember*, the *Who's Got Game?* series, *The Book of Mean People* and *The Big Box*. Her books of essays include *Playing in the Dark*, *Whiteness and Literary Imagination*.

Ms. Morrison's work deeply reflects the African-American's life, and all her works of racial dignity is based on the complete culture of the "colored". Her works have a close relationship with the America's history and culture. They are of great significance.

托尼·莫里森,原名克洛伊·安东尼·沃夫德(1931年2月18日生于美国俄亥俄州的洛雷恩),可以说是美国当代最著名的小说家,于1993年获得诺贝尔文学奖,在莫里森的小说中,她强烈呼吁遗产捐赠和取消非裔美国人的奴隶制度。

莫里森生长在美国中西部一个充满友爱和尊重黑人文化的家庭里。讲故事、唱歌和民间传说是她童年重要的组成部分。她进入耶鲁大学学习并在1953年获得学士学位,又在1955年获得了康奈尔大学的硕士学位;在南德克萨斯州立大学任教两年之后,于1957到1964年期间在哈佛大学任教;1965年,她成为一名小说编辑;从1989年开始她在美国奥尔巴尼州立大学教写作,于1989年离职;随后又成为普林斯顿大学的全职教师。

她的8部主要的小说作品《最蓝的眼睛》、《苏拉》、《所罗门之歌》、《柏油孩子》、《宠儿》、《爵士乐》、《乐园》和《爱》都获得了广泛的赞誉。她作品《所罗门之歌》于1978年获得了《国家图书》的评论奖,《宠儿》于1988年获得普利策奖,同时这两部小说都分别被《月刊》选为最佳书籍。在2006年《宠儿》还被《纽约时报书评》选为过去25年出版过的最优秀的小说。莫里森小姐还共同撰写了儿童文学作品《记住》和《谁叫那个名字》,以及《卑劣人之书》、《大盒子》系列。她的随笔包括《在黑暗中玩耍》、《文学想象》等。

莫里森的作品深刻地反映了非裔美国人的生活,她所有作品的种族尊严和身份都建立在一个相对完整的文化之上,并且与美国人的历史及文化息息相关,具有十分重要的意义!

作品及导读

作 品 1

Beloved

导 读

Beloved (1987) is the most mature and shocking novel of Toni Morrison and has been a classic novel now and one of the most well-sold works in American literature history. It wined the Pulitzer Prize-winning novel just one year after it was written in 1987. A survey of writers and literary critics conducted by *The New York Times* found *Beloved* the best work of American fiction of the past 25 years.

The novel is loosely based on the life and legal case of the slave Margaret Garner, a woman brutally kills her infant daughter rather than allow her to be enslaved. The name of the protagonist is Seth, and the novel traces her journey from slavery to freedom during and immediately following the Civil War. It mesmerizingly nartates the horrible past of seth: the incredible cruelties she endured as a slave, and the hardships she suffered in her journey north to freedom. Just as Seth finds the past too painful to remember, and the future just "a matter of keeping the past at bay," her story is almost too painful to read. Yet Morrison manages to imbue the wreckage of her characters' lives with compassion, humanity, and humor. Part ghost story, part history lesson, part folk tale, *Beloved* finds beauty in the unbearable, and lets us all see the enduring promise of hope that lies in everyone's future.

《宠儿》是托妮·莫里森最震撼人心、最成熟的代表作,现已经成为当代文学史上不朽的经典,也是美国文学史上最畅销的作品之一。小说完成于1987年,1988年即获得美国普利策小说奖。2006年《纽约时报》召集125位知名作家、评论家、编辑及文坛泰斗等选出自己心目中"25年来最佳美国小说",《宠儿》得票最高,名列第一。

《宠儿》的故事梗概基于一个叫玛格丽特·加纳的黑奴的一生及其所涉法律案件写成。小说的主人公是女性黑奴塞思,小说追述内战时期的塞思从奴隶身到自由身的逃难羁旅。迷离地叙述了塞思可怕的过去:做黑奴时忍受的无法想象的残酷对待,还有她往北方逃亡追寻自由路途上的艰辛。正如塞思后来所发现的,她的过去回忆起来太痛苦,而未来"只是关于抛下过去",她的故事读起来让人心痛。莫里森在小说人物的残破人生中渗透了同情、人性和幽默,时而是恐怖故事,时而给予历史教训,时而讲述民间故事。《宠儿》在不能承受的苦难中发现美,让我们看到藏在我们任何一个人的未来中的永不泯灭的希望。

选 文

Beloved

The grandmother, Baby Sughs, was dead, and the sons, Howard and Burglar, had run away by the time they were thirteen years old — as soon as merely looking in a mirror shattered it (that was the signal for Burglar); as soon as two tiny hand prints appeared in the cake (that was it for Howard). Neither boy waited to see more; another kettleful of chickpeas smoking in a heap on the floor; soda crackers crumbled and strewn in a line next to the door sill.

Nor did they wait for one of the relief periods: the weeks, months even, when nothing was disturbed. No. Each one fled at once — the moment the house committed what was for him the one insult not to be borne or witnessed a second time. Within two months, in the dead of winter, leaving their grandmother, Baby Sughs; Seth, their mother; and their little sister, Denver, all by themselves in the gray and white house on Bluestone Road. It didn't have a number then, because Cincinnati didn't stretch that far. In fact, Ohio had been calling itself a state only seventy years when first one brother and then the next stuffed quilt packing into his hat, snatched up his shoes, and crept away from the lively spite the house felt for them.

Baby Sughs didn't even raise her head. From her sickbed she heard them go but that wasn't the reason she lay still. It was a wonder to her that her grandsons had taken so long to realize that every house wasn't like the one on Bluestone Road. Suspended between the nastiness of life and the meanness of the dead, she couldn't get interested in leaving life or living it, let alone the fright of two creeping-off boys. Her past had been like her present — intolerable — and since she knew death was anything but forgetfulness, she used the little energy left her for pondering color.

"Bring a little lavender in, if you got any. Pink, if you don't." And Seth would oblige her with anything from fabric to her own tongue. Winter in Ohio was especially rough if you had an appetite for color. Sky provided the only drama, and counting on a Cincinnati horizon for life's principal joy was reckless indeed. So Seth and the girl Denver did what they could, and what the house permitted, for her. Together they waged a perfunctory there against the outrageous behavior of that place; against turned-over slop jars, smacks on the behind, and gusts of sour air. For they understood the source of the outrage as well as they knew the source of light.

Baby Sughs died shortly after the brothers left, with no interest whatsoever in their leave-taking orders, and right afterward Seth and Denver decided to end the persecution by calling forth the ghost that tried them so. Perhaps a conversation, they thought, an exchange of views or something would help. So they held hands and said, "Come on. Come on. You may as well just come on." The sideboard took a step forward but nothing else did.

"Grandma, Baby must be stopping it," said Denver.

Seth opened her eyes. "I doubt that," she said.

"Then why doest't it come?" "You forgetting how little it is," said her mother. "She wasn't even two years old when she died. Too little to understand. Too little to talk much even." "Maybe she don't want to understand," said Denver.

"Maybe. But if she'd only come, I could make it clear to her." Seth released her daughter's hand and together they pushed the sideboard back against the wall.

Outside a driver whipped his horse into the gallop local people felt necessary when they passed124.

"For a baby she throws a powerful spell," said Denver.

"No more powerful than the way I loved her," Seth answered and there it was again. The-welcoming cool of chiseler headstones; the one she selected to lean against on tiptoe, her knees wide open as any grave. Pink as a fingernail it was, and sprinkled with glittering chips. Ten minutes, he said. You got ten minutes I'll do it for free.

Ten minutes for seven letters. With another ten could she have gotten "Dearly" too? She had not thought to ask him and it bothered her still that it might have been possible — that for twenty minutes, a half hour, say, she could have had the whole thing, every word she heard the preacher say at the funeral (and all there was to say, surely) engraved on her baby's headstone: Dearly Beloved. But what she got, settled for, and was the one word that mattered. She thought it would be enough, rutting among the headstones with the engraver, his young son looking on, the anger in his face so old; the appetite in it quite new. That should certainly be enough. Enough to answer one more preacher, one more abolitionist and a town full of disgust.

Counting on the stillness of her own soul, she had forgotten the other one: the soul of her baby girl.

Who would have thought that a little old baby could harbor so much rage? Rutting among hearthstones under the eyes of the engraver's son was not enough. Not only did she have to live out her years in a house palsied by the baby's fury at having its throat cut, but those ten minutes she presidents up against dawn-colored stone studded with star chips, her knees wide open as the grave, were longer than life, more alive, more pulsating than the baby blood that soaked her fingers like oil. "We could move," she suggested once to her mother-in-law.

"What's being the point?" asked Baby Sughs. "Not a house in the country ins't packed to its rafter with some dead Negro's grief. We lucky this ghost is a baby. My husband's spirit was to come backing here? or yours? Don't talk to me. You lucky. You got three left.

"My first-born. All I can remember of her is how she loved the burned bottom of bread. Can you beat that? Eight children and that's all I remember." "That's all you let yourself remember," Seth had told her, but she was down to one herself — non lives, that is — the boys chased off by the dead one, and her memory of Bulbar was fading fast.

Howard at least had a head shape nobody could forget. As for the rest, she worked hard to remember as close to nothing as was safe. Unfortunately her brain was devious. She might be hurrying across a field, running practically, to get to the pump quickly and rinse the chamomile sap from her legs. Nothing else would be in her mind. The picture of the men coming to nurse her wises lifeless as the nerves in her back where the skin buckled like a washboard. Nor was there the faintest scent of ink or the cherry gum and oak bark from which it was made. And then sopping the chamomile away with pump water and rags, her mind fixed on getting every last bit of sap off — on her carelessness in taking a shortcut across the field just to save a half mile, and not noticing how high the weeds had grown until the itching was all the way to her knees. Then something. The plash of water, the sight of her shoes and stockings awry on the path where she had flung them; or Here Boy lapping in the puddle near her feet, and suddenly there was Sweet Home rolling, rolling, rolling out before her eyes, and although there was not a leaf on that farm that did not make her want to scream, it rolled itself out before her in shameless beauty. It never looked as terrible as it was and it made her wonder if hell was a pretty place too. Fire and brimstone all right, but hidden in lacy groves. Boys hang from the most beautiful sycamores in the world. It shamed her — remembering the wonderful soughing trees rather than the boys. Try as she might to make it otherwise, the sycamores beat out the children every time and she could not forgive her memory for that.

When the last of the chamomile was gone, she went around to the front of the house, collecting her shoes and stockings on the way.

As if to punish her further for her terrible memory, sitting on the porch not forty feet away was Paul D, the last of the Sweet Home men. And although she said, "Is that you?" "What's left." He stood up and smiled. "How you been, girl, besides barefoot?" When she laughed it came out loose and young. He made a face as though tasting a teaspoon of something bitter." I don't want to even hear about it.

"Always did hate that stuff." Seth balled up her stockings and jammed them into her pocket. "Come on in." "Porch is fine, Seth. Cool out here." He sat back down and looked at the meadow on the other side of the road, knowing the eagerness he felt would be in his eyes.

"Eighteen years," she said softly.

"Eighteen," he repeated. "And I swear I been walking every one of me. Mind if I join you?" Handed toward her feet and began unlacing his shoes.

"You want to soak them? Let me get you a basin of water." She moved closer to him to enter the house.

Is that what you came by for?" That's some of what I came for. The rest is you. But if all the truth be known, I go anywhere these days. Anywhere they let me sit down." You are looking good." Devil's confusion. He lets me look good long as I feel bad. "He looked at her and the word"bad "took on another meaning.

Seth smiled. This is the way they were — had been. All of the Sweet Home men, before and after Halle, treated her to a mild brotherly flirtation, so subtle you had to scratch for it.

Except for a heap more hair and some waiting in his eyes, he looked the way he had in Kentucky.

Peach stone skin; straight-backed.

For a man with an immobile face it was amazing how ready it was to smile or blaze or be sorry with you. As though all you had to do was get his attention and right away he produced the feeling you were feeling. With less than a blink, his face seemed to change — underneath it lay the activity.

"I wouldn't have to ask about him, would I You'd tell me if there was anything to tell, wouldn't you?" Seth looked down at her feet and saw again the sycamores.

"I'd tell you. Sure I'd tell you. I don't know any more now than I did then." Except for the churn, he thought, and you don't need to know that. "You must think he's still alive." No. I think he's dead. It's not being sure that keeps him alive. "What did Baby Sughs think?" Same, but to listen to her, all her children is dead. Claimed she felt each one go the very day and hour. "Eighteen fifty-five. The day my baby was born." You had that baby, did you? Never thought you'd make it. "He chuckled." Couldn't be no waiting. "She lowered her head and thought, as he did, how unlikely it was that she had made it. And if it hadn't been for that girl looking for velvet, she never would have. He was proud of her and annoyed by her."

Proud she had done it; annoyed that she had not needed Halle or him in the doing.

"Almost by myself. Not all by myself. A white girl helped me." Then she helped herself too, God bless her. "You could stay the night, Paul D." "You don't sound too steady in the offer." Seth glanced beyond his shoulder toward the closed door. "Oh it's truly meant. I just hope you'll pardon my house. Come on in. Talk to Denver while I cook you something." Paul D tied his shoes together, hung them over his shoulder and followed her through the door straight into a pool of red and undulating light that locked him where he stood.

"You got company?" he whispered, frowning.

"Off and on," said Seth.

"Good God." He backed out the door onto the porch. "What kind of evil you got in here?" "It's not evil, just sad. Come on. Just step through." He looked at her then, closely. Closer than he had when she first rounded the house on wet and shining legs, holding her shoes and stockings up in one hand, her skirts in the other. He had never seen her hair in Kentucky. And though her face was eighteen years older than when last he saw her, it was softer now. A face too still for comfort; irises the same color as her skin, which, in that still face, used to make him think of a mask with mercifully punched out eyes. Pregnant every year including the year she sat by the fire telling him she was going to run. Her three children she had already packed into a wagonload of others in a caravan of Negroes crossing the river. They were to be left with Hallie's mother near Cincinnati. Even in that tiny shack, leaning so close to the fire you could smell the heat in her dress, her eyes did not pick up a flicker of light. They were like two wells into which he had trouble gazing. Even punched out they needed to be covered, lidded, with some sign to warn folks of what that emptiness held. So he looked instead at the fire while she told him, because her husband was not there for the telling. Mr. Garner was dead and his wife had a lump in her neck the size of a sweet potato and unable to speak to anyone. She leaned as close to the fire as her pregnant belly allowed and told him, Paul D, the last of the Sweet Home men. There had been six of them who belonged to the farm, Seth the only female. Mrs. Garner, crying like a baby, had sold his brother to pay off the debts that surfaced the minute she was widowed. Then schoolteacher arrived to put things in order. But what he did broke three more Sweet Home men and punched the glittering iron out of Seethe's eyes, leaving two open wells that did not reflect firelight.

Now the iron was back but the face, softened by hair, made him trust her enough to step inside her door smack into a pool of pulsing red light.

She was right. It was sad. Walking through it, a wave of grief soaked him so thoroughly he wanted to cry. It seemed a long way to the normal light surrounding the table, but he made it — dry-eyed and lucky.

"You said she died soft. Soft as cream," he reminded her.

"That's not Baby Sughs," she said.

"My daughter. The one I sent ahead with the boys." "She didn't live?" "No. The one I was carrying when I run away is all I got left."

Boys went too. Both of me walked off just before Baby Sughs died. "Paul D looked at the spot where the grief had soaked him. The red was gone but a kind of weeping clung to the air where it had been."

Probably best, he thought. If a Negro got legs he ought to use them. Sit down too long, somebody will figure out a way to tie them up. Still ... if her boys were gone ...

"No man? You here by yourself?" "Me and Denver," she said.

"That all right by you?" "That's all right by me." She saw his skepticism and went on. "I cook at a restaurant in town. And I sew a little on the sly." Paul D smiled then, remembering the bedding dress. Seth was thirteen when she came to Sweet Home and already iron-eyed. She was a timely present for Mrs. Garner who had lost Baby Sughs to her husband's high principles. The five Sweet Home men looked at the new girl and decided to let her be. They were young and so sick with the absence of women they had taken to calves. Yet they let the iron-eyed girl be, so she could choose in spite of the fact that each one would have beaten the others to mush to have her. It took her a year to choose — a long, tough year of thrashing on pallets eaten up with dreams of her. A year of yearning, when rape seemed the solitary gift of life. The restraint they had exercised possible only because they were Sweet Home men — the ones Mr. Garner bragged about while other farmers shook their heads in warning at the phrase.

It was the reaction Garner loved and waited for. "Neither would I," he said. "Neither would I," and there was always a pause before the neighbor, or stranger, or peddler, or brother-in-law or whoever it was got the meaning. Then a fierce argument, sometimes a fight, and Garner came home bruised and pleased, having demonstrated one more time what a real Kentuckian was: one tough enough and smart enough to make and call his own niggers men.

And so they were: Paul D Garner, Paul F Garner, Paul A Garner, Halle Sughs and Silo, the wild man. All in their twenties, minus women, fucking cows, dreaming of rape, thrashing on pallets, rubbing their thighs and waiting for the new girl — the one who took Baby Sughs' place after Halle bought her with five years of Sundays.

Maybe that was why she chose him. A twenty-year-old man so in love with his mother he gave up five years of Sabbaths just to see her sit down for a change was a serious recommendation.

She waited a year. And the Sweet Home men abused cows while they waited with her. She chose Halle and for their first bedding she sewed herself a dress on the sly.

"Won't you stay on awhile? Can't nobody catch up on eighteen years in a day?" Out of the dimness of the room in which they sat, a white staircase climbed toward the blue-and white wall paper of the second floor.

Paul D could see just the beginning of the paper; discreet flecks of yellow sprinkled among blizzard of snowdrops all backed by blue.

The luminous white of the railing and steps kept him glancing toward it. Every sense he had told him the air above the stairwell was charmed and very thin. But the girl who walked down out of that air was round and brown with the face of an alert doll.

Paul D looked at the girl and then at Seth who smiled saying, "Here she is my Denver. This is Paul D, honey, from Sweet Home Good morning, Mr. D." "Garner, baby. Paul D Garner." "Yes sir." "Glad to get a look at you. Last time I saw your mama, you were pushing out the front of her dress." "Still is," Seethe smiled, "provided she can get in it?" Denver stood on the bottom step and was suddenly hot and shy. It had been a long time since anybody (good-willed white woman, preacher, speaker or newspaperman) sat at their table, their sympathetic voices called liar by the revulsion in their eyes. For twelve years, long before Grandma Baby died, there had been visitors of any sort and certainly no friends. No colored people. Certainly no hazel nut man (no) with too long hair and no notebook, no charcoal, no oranges, no questions. Someone her mother wanted to talk to and would even consider talking to while barefoot. Looking, in fact acting, like a girl instead of the quiet, queenly woman Denver had known all her life. The one who never looked away, who when a man got stomped to death by aware right in front of Sawyer's restaurant did not look away; and when a sow began eating her own litter did not look away then either. And when the baby's spirit picked up Here Boy and slammed him into the wall hard enough to break two of his legs and dislocate his eye, so hard he went into convulsions and chewed up his tongue, still her mother had not looked away. She had taken a hammer, knocked the dog unconscious, wiped away the blood and saliva, pushed his eye back in his head and set his leg bones. He recovered, mute and off-balance, more because of his untrustworthy eye than his bent legs, and winter, summer, drizzle or dry, nothing could persuade him to enter the house again.

Chapter 20 Maxine Hong Kingston

作者简介

Maxine Hong Kingston is an internationally-recognized contemporary Chinese-American writer, her ancestral home is Xinhui, Gouangdong, and she was born on October 27, 1940 in California, America. Her white, long hair is real impressive. She is the first of six children born. Her two older siblings had died early in China. Her father, Tom Hong, was a Cantonese poet and calligrapher who immigrated to China alone in 1924, working for 15 years as manager of a gambling business in order to put her mother, YingLan, through midwifery school. She eventually left her family's village in China to join him at his New York City laundry (they later opened another business in California). They worked long and hard, and Kingston's mother often had to pick up a second job as an agricultural worker in order to put her children through school. Raised on her mother's "talk-stories" of Chinese ancestors and ancient heroes, Kingston, a bright but shy child who suffered from her parents' expectations, developed a rich imagination hidden behind her silence at school and at home. She is currently a Professor Emeritus at the University of California, Berkeley where she graduated with a B.A. in English in 1962. Her works often reflect on her cultural heritage and blend fiction with non-fiction. Among her works are *The Woman Warrior: Memoirs of a Girlhood Among Ghosts* (1976), awarded the National Book Critics Award for Nonfiction, and *China Men* (1980), given the same award. She has written one novel, *Tripmaster Monkey: His Fake Book*, a story depicting a character based on the mythical Chinese character Sun Wu Kong. She likes the literature, the prose and the poetry since childhood, uses the spare time to be engaged in the creation frequently, and her poetry was selected into "the American Garland." In 1958s she obtained the scholarship to enter UC Berkeley to major first in Engineering then in British Literature. In 1962, She obtained the Bachelor of Arts degree. At the end of 1962, she married her classmate, Earl Kingston. After marriage, she served as an English teacher for many years in California Middle School and

Hawaiian Middle School. From 1970 – 1977, she worked as a British Literature professor in University of Hawaii, and then in University of Michigan. From 1990, She taught in University of California Berkeley. From 2001, she also served as a chief editor for *Califonia Literature*.

汤婷婷，国际上公认的一名现代华裔作家。她于 1940 年 10 月 27 日出生于美国加利福尼亚州蒙士得顿市，她白色的头发令人印象深刻。汤婷婷是家中六个孩子中的长女，她的两个姐姐很早就在中国去世了，父亲于 1924 年独身移民到中国，是一名广东诗人和书法家。她的父亲在广东从事赌博生意 15 年，主要是陪伴她母亲进入助产学校。他们家在加利福尼亚斯托克顿市开了一家洗衣店，工作很辛苦，为了供养孩子们完成学业，母亲找了两份兼职工作。她 1962 年毕业于加利福尼亚伯克利分校，现为其荣誉教授。她的作品通常反映了中国文化的影响，并且在小说中融合了非小说元素。她于 1976 年发表的《女勇士》，获国家图书评论奖，1980 年的《中国佬》也获得此殊荣。她的另一部小说《孙行者》以中国神话人物孙悟空为原型。自幼爱好文学、散文和诗歌，经常利用业余时间从事创作，她所创作的诗歌被选入《美国诗歌选》。1958 年获得奖学金进入加州大学伯克利分校就读，先念工程学系，后转念英国文学。1962 年取得文学士学位。1962 年底与同班同学 Earl Kingston 结婚。婚后曾在加州中学和夏威夷中学担任英文教师多年。1970 年至 1977 年曾任夏威夷大学英国文学系教授，后又担任东部密歇根大学英国文学系教授。1990 年起担任加州大学伯克利分校英国文学系教授。从 2001 年起她也担任《加利福尼亚文学》主编。

作品及导读

作品 1

The Woman Warrior: *Memoirs of Girlhood among Ghost*

导 读

The Woman Warrior: *Memoirs of Girlhood among Ghost* was written by Maxine Hong Kingston in 1976 which is the first book of Maxine Hong Kingston as well as her master piece. It is semi-autobiography, incorporating many elements of fiction. In any case, her work stands as an example of postmodernism in American Literature.

It consists of five parts: *No Name Woman*, *White Tigers*, *Shaman*, *At the Western Palace* and *A Song for a Barbarian Reed Pipe*. The book is told in the first person and blends with Chinese folktales about historical figures and life in the Chinatown. As a Chinese-American living in the U.S., Maxine Hong Kingston has not only inherited Chinese traditional culture but learned to think in American way and accustomed to the life there. Due to the fact that she is between the two cultures, she has a feeling of confusion and contradiction — she belongs to neither of them. This contradiction is indicated by *The Woman Warrior*, at the last part, where Cai Wenji's story reveals her wishes of establishing the social status of Chinese-Americans in America.

What results is a complex portrayal of the 20th Century experiences of Chinese-Americans living in the U.S. in the shadow of the Chinese Revolution. *The Woman Warrior* has been reported by the Modern Language Association as the most commonly taught text in modern university education. It has been used in disciplines as far reaching as American Literature, Anthropology, Asian Studies, Composition, Education, Psychology, Sociology, and Women Studies. In addition, it has also won the National Book Critics Circle Award and has been named one of *Time Magazine*'s top nonfiction books of the 1970s.

《女勇士:生活在群鬼中的女孩的回忆录》是汤婷婷1976年发表的作品,是她的第一部作品,也是她的成名作。它是一部半自传,书中结合了小说的许多元素。这部小说成为美国文学后现代主义的典范。

《女勇士》共分为5个部分:"无名女子"、"白虎山学道"、"乡村医生"、"西宫门外"、"羌笛夜曲"。书中汤婷婷以第一人称"我"进行叙述,其中夹杂着中国的神鬼故事,历史人物故事和唐人街的生活片段。作为一个生活在美国的第二代华裔作家,汤婷婷不仅传承了一些中国传统文化,还学会了美国人的思维方式和风俗习惯。由于身处两种文化之中,汤婷婷感到矛盾和困惑——她既不属于中国社会,又不被美国社会认可。她通过《女勇士》表达出了这种矛盾心理,并在该书的最后一部分通过蔡文姬的故事揭示了融合两种文化,确立华裔在美国的社会地位的愿望。

本书描绘了20世纪深受中国解放战争影响的华裔美国人的经历。现代语言协会曾报道说《女勇士》是现代大学教育中最普遍的教学读物,已广泛应用于诸如美国文学、人类学、亚洲研究、艺术作品、教育学、心理学、社会学和妇女研究方面。而且本书还获得了国家图书批评家的殊荣,并入围1970年《时代》杂志最受欢迎的纪实作品提名。

选 文

The Woman Warrior: Memoirs of Girlhood among Ghost
(*Chapter 1*)

"You must not tell anyone," my mother said, "what I am about to tell you. In China your father had a sister who killed herself. She jumped into the family well. We say that your father has all brothers because it is as if she had never been born."

"In 1924 just a few days after our village celebrated seventeen hurry-up weddings — to make sure that every young man who went 'out on the road' would responsibly come home — your father and his brothers and your grandfather and his brothers and your aunt's new husband sailed for America, the Gold Mountain. It was your grandfather's last trip. Those lucky enough to get contracts waved goodbye from the decks. They fed and guarded the stowaways and helped them off in Cuba, New York, Bali, Hawaii. "We'll meet in California next year," they said. "All of them sent money home."

"I remember looking at your aunt one day when she and I were dressing; I had not noticed before that she had such a protruding melon of a stomach. But I did not think, 'She's pregnant,' until she began to look like other pregnant women, her shirt pulling and the white tops of her black pants showing. She could not have been pregnant, you see, because her husband had been gone for years. No one said anything. We did not discuss it. In early summer she was ready to have the child, long after the time when it could have been possible."

"The village had also been counting. On the night the baby was to be born the villagers raided our house. Some were crying. Like agreat saw, teeth strung with lights, files of people walked zigzag across our land, tearing the rice. Their lanterns doubled in the disturbed black water, which drained away through the broken bunds. As the villagers closed in, we could see that some of them, probably men and women we knew well, wore white masks. The people with long hair hung it over their faces. Women with short hair made it stand up on end. Some had tied white bands around their foreheads, arms, and legs."

"At first they threw mud and rocks at the house. Then they threw eggs and began slaughtering our stock. We could hear the animals scream their deaths — the roosters, the pigs, a last great roar from the ox. Familiar wild heads flared in our night windows; the villagers encircled us. Some of the faces stopped to peer at us, their eyes rushing like searchlights. The hands flattened against the panes, framed heads, and left red prints."

"The villagers broke in the front and the back doors at the same time, even though we had not locked the doors against them. Their knives dripped with the blood of our animals. They smeared blood on the doors and walls. One woman swung a chicken, whose throat she had slit, splattering blood in red arcs about her. We stood together in the middle of our house, in the family hall with the pictures and tables of the ancestors around us, and looked straight ahead."

"At that time the house had only two wings. When the men came back, we would build two more to enclose our courtyard and a third one to begin a second courtyard. The villagers pushed through both wings, even your grandparents' rooms, to find your aunt's, which was also mine until the men returned. From this room a new wing for one of the younger families would grow. They ripped up her clothes and shoes and broke her combs, grinding them underfoot. They tore her work from the loom. They scattered the cooking fire and rolled the new weaving in it. We could hear them in the kitchen breaking our bowls and banging the pots. They overturned the great waist-high earthenware jugs; duck eggs, pickled fruits, vegetables burst out and mixed in acrid torrents. The old woman from the next field swept a broom through the air and loosed the spirits-of-the-broom over our heads.

'Pig.' 'Ghost.' 'Pig,' they sobbed and scolded while they ruined our house."

"When they left, they took sugar and oranges to bless themselves. They cut pieces from the dead animals. Some of them took bowls that were not broken and clothes that were not torn. Afterward we swept up the rice and sewed it back up into sacks. But the smells from the spilled preserves lasted. Your aunt gave birth in the pigsty that night. The next morning when I went for the water, I found her and the baby plugging up the family well."

"Don't let your father know that I told you. He denies her. Now that you have started to menstruate, what happened to her could happen to you. Don't humiliate us. You wouldn't like to be forgotten as if you had never been born. The villagers are watchful."

Whenever she had to warn us about life, my mother told stories that ran like this one, a story to grow up on. She tested our strength to establish realities. Those in the emigrant generations who could not reassert brute survival died young and far from home. Those of us in the first American generations have had to figure out how the invisible world the emigrants built around our childhoods fits in solid America.

The emigrants confused the gods by diverting their curses, misleading them with crooked streets and false names. They must try to confuse their offspring as well, who, I suppose, threaten them in similar ways — always trying to get things straight, always trying to name the unspeakable. The Chinese I know hide their names; sojourners take new names when their lives change and guard their real names with silence.

Chinese-Americans, when you try to understand what things in you are Chinese, how do you separate what is peculiar to childhood, to poverty, insanities, one family, your mother who marked your growing with stories, from what is Chinese? What is Chinese tradition and what are the movies?

If I want to learn what clothes my aunt wore, whether flashy or ordinary, I would have to begin, "Remember Father's drowned-in-the-well sister?" I cannot ask that. My mother has told me once and for all the useful parts. She will add nothing unless powered by Necessity, a riverbank that guides her life. She plants vegetable gardens rather than lawns; she carries the odd-shaped tomatoes home from the fields and eats food left for the gods.

Whenever we did frivolous things, we used up energy; we flew high kites. We children came up off the ground over the melting cones our parents brought home from work and the American movie on New Year's Day — Oh, You Beautiful Doll with Betty Grable one year, and She Wore a Yellow Ribbon with John Wayne another year. After the one carnival ride each, we paid in guilt; our tired father counted his change on the dark walk home.

Perhaps she had encountered him in the fields or on the mountain where the daughters-in-law collected fuel. Or perhaps he first noticed her in the marketplace. He was not a stranger because the village housed no strangers. She had to have dealings with him other than sex. Perhaps he worked an adjoining field, or he sold her the cloth for the dress she sewed and wore. His demand must have surprised, then terrified her. She obeyed him; she always did as she was told.

THE AMERICAN PART

When the family found a young man in the next village to be her husband, she had stood tractably beside the best rooster, his proxy, and promised before they met that she would be his forever. She was lucky that he was her age and she would be the first wife, an advantage secure now. The night she first saw him, he had sex with her. Then he left for America. She had almost forgotten what he looked like. When she tried to envision him, she only saw the black and white face in the group photograph the men had had taken before leaving.

The other man was not, after all, much different from her husband. They both gave orders: she followed. "If you tell your family, I'll beat you. I'll kill you. Be here again next week." No one talked sex, ever. And she might have separated the rapes from the rest of living if only she did not have to buy her oil from him or gather wood in the same forest. I want her fear to have lasted just as long as rape lasted so that the fear could have been contained. No drawn-out fear. But women at sex hazarded birth and hence lifetimes. The fear did not stop but permeated everywhere. She told the man, "I think I'm pregnant." He organized the raid against her.

On nights when my mother and father talked about their life back home, sometimes they mentioned an "outcast table" whose business they still seemed to be settling, their voices tight. In a commensally tradition, where food is precious, the powerful older people made wrongdoers eat alone. Instead of letting them start separate new lives like the Japanese, who could become samurais and geishas, the Chinese family, faces averted but eyes glowering sideways, hung on to the offenders and fed them leftovers. My aunt must have lived in the same house as my parents and eaten at an outcast table. My mother spoke about the raid as if she had seen it, when she and my aunt, a daughter-in-law to a different household, should not have been living together at all. Daughters-in-law lived with their husbands' parents, not their own; a synonym for marriage in Chinese is "taking a daughter-in-law." Her husband's parents could have sold her, mortgaged her, stoned her. But they had sent her back to her own mother and father, a mysterious act hinting at disgraces not told me. Perhaps they had thrown her out to deflect the avengers.

She was the only daughter; her four brothers went with her father, husband, and uncles "out on the road" and for some years became western men. When the goods were divided among the family, three of the brothers took land, and the youngest, my father, chose an education. After my grandparents gave their daughter away to her husband's family, they had dispensed all the adventure and all the property. They expected her alone to keep the traditional ways, which her brothers, now among the barbarians, could fumble without detection. The heavy, deep-rooted women were to maintain the past against the flood, safe for returning. But the rare urge west had fixed upon our family, and so my aunt crossed boundaries not delineated in space.

The work of preservation demands that the feelings playing about in one's guts not be turned into action. Just watch their passing like cherry blossoms. But perhaps my aunt, my forerunner, caught in a slow life, let dreams grow and fade and after some months or years went toward what persisted. Fear at the enormities of the forbidden kept her desires delicate, wire and bone. She looked at a man because she liked the way the hair was tucked behind his ears, or she liked the question-mark line of a long torso curving at the shoulder and straight at the hip. For warm eyes or a soft voice or a slow walk — that's all — a few hairs, a line, a brightness, a sound, a pace, she gave up family. She offered us up for a charm that vanished with tiredness, a pigtail that didn't toss when the wind died. Why, the wrong lighting could erase the dearest thing about him.

It could very well have been, however, that my aunt did not take subtle enjoyment of her friend, but, a wild woman, kept rollicking company. Imagining her free with sex doesn't fit, though. I don't know any women like that, or men either. Unless I see her life branching into mine, she gives me no ancestral help.

To sustain her being in love, she often worked at herself in the mirror, guessing at the colors and shapes that would interest him, changing them frequently in order to hit on the right combination. She wanted him to look back.

On a farm near the sea, a woman who tended her appearance reaped a reputation for eccentricity. All the married women blunt-cut their hair in flaps about their ears or pulled it back in tight buns. No nonsense. Neither style blew easily into heart-catching tangles. And at their weddings they displayed themselves in their long hair for the last time. "It brushed the backs of my knees," my mother tells me. "It was braided, and even so, it brushed the backs of my knees."

At the mirror my aunt combed individuality into her bob. A bun could have been contrived to escape into black streamers blowing in the wind or in quiet wisps about her face, but only the older women in our picture album wear buns. She brushed her hair back from her forehead, tucking the flaps behind her ears. She looped a piece of thread, knotted into a circle between her index fingers and thumbs, and ran the double strand across her forehead. When she closed her fingers as if she were making a pair of shadow geese bite, the string twisted together catching the little hairs. Then she pulled the thread away from her skin, ripping the hairs out neatly, her eyes watering from the needles of pain. Opening her fingers, she cleaned the thread, then rolled it along her hairline and the tops of her eyebrows. My mother did the same to me and my sisters and herself. I used to believe that the expression "caught by the short hairs" meant a captive held with a depilatory string. It especially hurt at the temples, but my mother said we were lucky we didn't have to have our feet bound when we were seven. Sisters used to sit on their beds and cry together, she said, as their mothers or their slaves removed the bandages for a few minutes each night and let the blood gush back into their veins. I hope that the man my aunt loved appreciated a smooth brow, that he wasn't just a tits-and-ass man.

She dug it out with a hot needle and washed the wound with peroxide.

More attention to her looks than these pullings of hairs and pickings at spots would have caused gossip among the villagers. They owned work clothes and good clothes, and they wore good clothes for feasting the new seasons. But since a woman combing her hair hexes beginnings, my aunt rarely found an occasion to look her best. Women looked like great sea snails — the corded wood, babies, and laundry they carried were the whorls on their backs. The Chinese did not admire a bent back; goddesses and warriors stood straight. Still there must have been a marvelous freeing of beauty when a worker laid down her burden and stretched and arched.

Such commonplace loveliness, however, was not enough for my aunt. She dreamed of a lover for the fifteen days of New Year's, the time for families to exchange visits, money, and food. She plied her secret comb. And sure enough she cursed the year, the family, the village, and herself.

Even as her hair lured her imminent lover, many other men looked at her. Uncles, cousins, nephews, brothers would have looked, too, had they been home between journeys. Perhaps they had already been restraining their curiosity, and they left, fearful that their glances, like a field of nesting birds, might be startled and caught. Poverty hurt, and that was their first reason for leaving. But another, final reason for leaving the crowded house was the never-said.

She may have been unusually beloved, the precious only daughter, spoiled and mirror gazing because of the affection the family lavished on her. When her husband left, they welcomed the chance to take her back from the in-laws; she could live like the little daughter for just a while longer. There are stories that my grandfather was different from other people, "crazy ever since the little Jap bayoneted him in the head." He used to put his naked penis on the dinner table, laughing. And one day he brought home a baby girl, wrapped up inside his brown western-style greatcoat. He had traded one of his sons, probably my father, the youngest, for her. My grandmother made him trade back. When he finally got a daughter of his own, he doted on her. They must have all loved her, except perhaps my father, the only brother who never went back to China, having once been traded for a girl.

Brothers and sisters, newly men and women, had to efface their sexual color and present plain miens. Disturbing hair and eyes, a smile like no other, threatened the ideal of five generations living under one roof. To focus blurs, people shouted face to face and yelled from room to room. The immigrants I know have loud voices, unmodulated to American tones even after years away from the village where they called their friendships out across the fields. I have not been able to stop my mother's screams in public libraries or over telephones. Walking erect and speaking in an inaudible voice, I have tried to turn myself American-feminine. Chinese communication was loud, public. Only sick people had to whisper. But at the dinner table, where the family members came nearest one another, no one could talk, not the outcasts nor any eaters. Every word that falls from the mouth is a coin lost. Silently they gave and accepted food with both hands. A preoccupied child who took his bowl with one hand got a sideways glare. A complete moment of total attention is due everyone alike. Children and lovers have no singularity here, but my aunt used a secret voice, a separate attentiveness.

She kept the man's name to herself throughout her labor and dying; she did not accuse him that he be punished with her. To save her inseminator's name she gave silent birth.

He may have been somebody in her own household, but intercourse with a man outside the family would have been no less abhorrent. All the villages were kinsmen, and the titles shouted in loud country voices never let kinship be forgotten. Any man within visiting distance would have been neutralized as a lover — "brother", "younger brother", "older brother" — one hundred and fifteen relationship titles. Parents researched birth charts probably not so much to assure good fortune as to circumvent incest in a population that has but one hundred surnames. Everybody has eight million relatives. How useless then sexual mannerisms, how dangerous.

As if it came from an atavism deeper than fear, I used to add "brother" silently to boys' names. It hexed the boys, who would or would not ask me to dance, and made them less scary and as familiar and deserving of benevolence as girls.

But, of course, I hexed myself also — no dates. I had no idea, though, how to make attraction selective, how to control its direction and magnitude. If I made myself American-pretty so that the five or six Chinese boys in the class fell in love with me, everyone else — the Caucasian, Negro, and Japanese boys — would too. Sisterliness, dignified and honorable, made much more sense.

Attraction eludes control so stubbornly that whole societies designed to organize relationships among people cannot keep order, not even when they bind people to one another from childhood and raise them together. Among the very poor and the wealthy, brothers married their adopted sisters, like doves. Our family allowed some romance, paying adult brides' prices and providing dowries so that their sons and daughters could marry strangers. Marriage promises to turn strangers into friendly relatives — a nation of siblings.

In the village structure, spirits shimmered among the live creatures, balanced and held in equilibrium by time and land. But one human being flaring up into violence could open up a black hole, a maelstrom that pulled in the sky. The frightened villagers, who depended on one another to maintain the real, went to my aunt to show her a personal, physical representation of the break she had made in the "roundness." Misallying couples snapped off the future, which was to be embodied in true offspring. The villagers punished her for acting as if she could have a private life, secret and apart from them.

If my aunt had betrayed the family at a time of large grain yields and peace, when many boys were born, and wings were being built on many houses, perhaps she might have escaped such severe punishment. But the men — hungry, greedy, tired of planting in dry soil — had been forced to leave the village in order to send food-money home. There were ghost plagues, bandit plagues, wars with the Japanese, floods. My Chinese brother and sister had died of an unknown sickness. Adultery, perhaps only a mistake during good times, became a crime when the village needed food.

The round moon cakes and round doorways, the round tables of graduated sizes that fit one roundness inside another, round windows and rice bowls — these talismans had lost their power to warn this family of the law: a family must be whole, faithfully keeping the descent line by having sons to feed the old and the dead, who in turn look after the family. The villagers came to show my aunt and her lover-in-hiding a broken house. The villagers were speeding up the circling of events because she was too shortsighted to see that her infidelity had already harmed the village, that waves of consequences would return unpredictably, sometimes in disguise, as now, to hurt her. This roundness had to be made coin-sized so that she would see its circumference: punish her at the birth of her baby. Awaken her to the inexorable. People who refused fatalism because they could invent small resources insisted on culpability. Deny accidents and wrest fault from the stars.

After the villagers left, their lanterns now scattering in various directions toward home, the family broke their silence and cursed her. "Aiaa, we're going to die. Death is coming. Death is coming. Look what you've done. You've killed us. Ghost! Dead ghost! Ghost! You've never been born." She ran out into the fields, far enough from the house so that she could no longer hear their voices, and pressed herself against the earth, her own land no more. When she felt the birth coming, she thought that she had been hurt. Her body seized together. "They've hurt me too much," she thought. "This is gall, and it will kill me." With forehead and knees against the earth, her body convulsed and then relaxed. She turned on her back, lay on the ground. The black well of sky and stars went out and out and out forever; her body and her complexity seemed to disappear. She was one of the stars, a bright dot in blackness, without home, without a companion, in eternal cold and silence. An agoraphobia rose in her, speeding higher and higher, bigger and bigger; she would not be able to contain it; there would no end to fear.

Flayed, unprotected against space, she felt pain return, focusing her body. This pain chilled her — a cold, steady kind of surface pain. Inside, spasmodically, the other pain, the pain of the child, heated her. For hours she lay on the ground, alternately body and space. Sometimes a vision of normal comfort obliterated reality: she saw the family in the evening gambling at the dinner table, the young people massaging their elders' backs. She saw them congratulating one another, high joy on the mornings the rice shoots came up. When these pictures burst, the stars drew yet further apart. Black space opened.

She got to her feet to fight better and remembered that old-fashioned women gave birth in their pigsties to fool the jealous, pain-dealing gods, who do not snatch piglets. Before the next spasms could stop her, she ran to the pigsty, each step a rushing out into emptiness. She climbed over the fence and knelt in the dirt. It was good to have a fence enclosing her, a tribal person alone.

Laboring, this woman who had carried her child as a foreign growth that sickened her every day, expelled it at last. She reached down to touch the hot, wet, moving mass, surely smaller than anything human, and could feel that it was human after all — fingers, toes, nails, nose. She pulled it up on to her belly, and it lay curled there, butt in the air, feet precisely tucked one under the other. She opened her loose shirt and buttoned the child inside. After resting, it squirmed and thrashed and she pushed it up to her breast. It turned its head this way and that until it found her nipple. There, it made little snuffling noises. She clenched her teeth at its preciousness, lovely as a young calf, a piglet, a little dog.

She may have gone to the pigsty as a last act of responsibility, she would protect this child as she had protected its father. It would look after her soul, leaving supplies on her grave. But how would this tiny child without family find her grave when there would be no marker for her anywhere, neither in the earth nor the family hall? No one would give her a family hall name. She had taken the child with her into the wastes. At its birth the two of them had felt the same raw pain of separation, a wound that only the family pressing tight could close. A child with no descent line would not soften her life but only trail after her, ghostlike, begging her to give it purpose. At dawn the villagers on their way to the fields would stand around the fence and look.

Full of milk, the little ghost slept. When it awoke, she hardened her breasts against the milk that crying loosens. Toward morning she picked up the baby and walked to the well.

Otherwise abandon it. Turn its face into the mud. Mothers who love their children take them along. It was probably a girl; there is some hope of forgiveness for boys.

"Don't tell anyone you had an aunt. Your father does not want to hear her name. She has never been born." I have believed that sex was unspeakable and words so strong and fathers so frail that "aunt" would do my father mysterious harm. I have thought that my family, having settled among immigrants who had also been their neighbors in the ancestral land, needed to clean their name, and a wrong word would incite the kinspeople even here. But there is more to this silence: they want me to participate in her punishment. And I have.

In the twenty years since I heard this story I have not asked for details nor said my aunt's name; I do not know it. People who can comfort the dead can also chase after them to hurt them further — a reverse ancestor worship. The real punishment was not the raid swiftly inflicted by the villagers, but the family's deliberately forgetting her. Her betrayal so maddened them, they saw to it that she would suffer forever, even after death. Always hungry, always needing, she would have to beg food from other ghosts, snatch and steal it from those whose living descendants give them gifts. She would have to fight the ghosts massed at crossroads for the buns a few thoughtful citizens leave to decoy her away from village and home so that the ancestral spirits could feast unharassed. At peace, they could act like gods, not ghosts, their descent lines providing them with paper suits and dresses, spirit money, paper houses, paper automobiles, chicken, meat, and rice into eternity — essences delivered up in smoke and flames, steam and incense rising from each rice bowl. In an attempt to make the Chinese care for people outside the family, Chairman Mao encourages us now to give our paper replicas to the spirits of outstanding soldiers and workers, no matter whose ancestors they may be. My aunt remains forever hungry. Goods are not distributed evenly among the dead.

My aunt haunts me — her ghost drawn to me because now, after fifty years of neglect, I alone devote pages of paper to her, though not origamied into houses and clothes. I do not think she always means me well. I am telling on her, and she was a spite suicide, drowning herself in the drinking water. The Chinese are always very frightened of the drowned one, whose weeping ghost, wet hair hanging and skin bloated, waits silently by the water to pull down a substitute.

21 Amy Tan

作者简介

Amy Tan was born in Oakland, California. She is the second of three children born to Chinese immigrants Daisy (née Li), and John Tan, an electrical engineer and Baptist minister. When Tan was 15 years old, her older brother Peter and father both are died of brain tumors within that year. Daisy moved Amy and her younger brother John Jr. to Switzerland, where Amy finished high school. During this period in her life, Amy learned about her mother's former marriage to an abusive man in China, of their four children (a son who died as a toddler, and three daughters) and how her mother was forced to leave her children from a previous marriage behind in Shanghai. This incident provided the basis for Tan's first novel, 1989 *New York Times* bestseller *The Joy Luck Club*. In 1987 Amy traveled with Daisy to China. There, Amy met her three half-sisters. Tan received her bachelor's and master's degrees in English and linguistics from San José State University, and later did doctoral linguistics studies at UC Santa Cruz and UC Berkeley.

Tan has written several other bestselling novels, including *The Kitchen God's Wife*, *The Bonesetter's Daughter*. In addition to these, Tan has written two children's books: *The Moon Lady* (1992) *and Sagwa*, *the Chinese Siamese Cat* (1994). Tan is also in a band with several other well-known writers, the Rock Bottom Remainders.

谭恩美出生在加利福尼亚州的奥克兰,她是中国移民黛西•李和约翰•谭,一个电气工程师和浸信会牧师所生的第三个孩子。谭恩美 15 岁的时候,她的哥哥彼得和父亲都在一年之内死于脑瘤。黛西把小艾米和她的弟弟约翰送到了瑞士,艾米在那里完成高中学业。在此期间,艾米得知母亲在中国时候的上一段不幸婚姻。前夫经常对她施暴,他们有过 4 个孩子(一个夭折了的儿子和 3 个女儿)。后来在上海,母亲被迫离开了女儿们。这一事件为她的第一部小说,1989 年《纽约时报》畅销书《喜福会》提供了基础。1987 年恩美与黛西前往中国。在那里,艾米遇见她的 3 个同母异父的妹妹。谭从圣何塞州立大学获得学士和硕士学位英语和语言学,加州大学圣塔克鲁兹分校和加州大学伯克利分校从事语言学研究。

她著有长篇小说《灶神之妻》《灵感女孩》和为儿童创作的《月亮夫人》《中国暹罗猫》等。她是一个具有罕见才华的优秀作家,能触及人们的心灵。

作品及导读

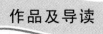

The Joy Luck Club

导 读

The Joy Luck Club (1989) is a best-selling novel written by Amy Tan. It focuses on four Chinese American immigrant families in San Francisco who start a club known as "the Joy Luck Club," playing the Chinese game of mahjong for money while feasting on a variety of foods. The book is structured somewhat like a mahjong game, with four parts divided into four sections to create sixteen chapters. The three mothers and four daughters (one mother, Suyuan Woo, dies before the novel opens) share stories about their lives in the form of vignettes. Each part is preceded by a parable relating to the game.

The Joy Luck Club consists of sixteen interlocking stories about the lives of four Chinese immigrant women and their four American-born daughters. In 1949, the four immigrants meet at the First Chinese Baptist Church in San Francisco and agree to continue to meet to play mahjong. They call their mahjong group the Joy Luck Club. The stories told in this novel revolve around the Joy Luck Club women and their daughters. Structurally, the novel is divided into four major sections, with two sections focusing on the stories of the mothers and two sections on the stories of the daughters.

《喜福会》(1989)是谭恩美所写的一部畅销小说,它关注四位华裔移民家庭在旧金山成立的名为"喜福会"的俱乐部,玩中国的麻将游戏,享用各种各样的食物。这本书的结构有点像麻将游戏,十六章节分为4个部分。3个母亲和4个女儿分享他们的生活小插曲。每个部分是之前是一个和游戏相关的比喻。

《喜福会》由16个连锁故事组成,主人公是4个中国移民妇女和她们的4个在美国出生的女儿。1949年,4个移民家庭在旧金山第一中国浸信会见面,同意约在一起打麻将。他们称之为麻将喜福会。这部小说的故事围绕着喜福会妇女和他们的女儿。从结构上看,这部小说分为4个主要部分,两个部分关注的母亲,另两个部分关注女儿。

选 文

The Joy Luck Club
(Excerpt)

Feathers From a Thousand Li Away

The old woman remembered a swan she had bought many years ago in Shanghai for a foolish sum. "This bird", boasted the market vendor, "was once a duck that stretched its neck in hopes of becoming a goose, and now look! — it is too beautiful to eat."

Then the woman and the swan sailed across an ocean many thousands of li wide, stretching their necks toward America. On her journey she cooed to the swan, "In America I will have a daughter just like me. But over there nobody will say her worth is measured by the loudness of her husband's belch. Over there nobody will look down on her, because I will make her speak only perfect American English. And over there she will always be too full to swallow any sorrow! She will know my meaning, because I will give her this swan — a creature that became more than what was hoped for."

But when she arrived in the new country, the immigration officials pulled her swan away from her, leaving the woman fluttering her arms and with only one swan feather for a memory. And then she had to fill out so many forms she forgot why she had come and what she had left behind.

Now the woman was old. And she had a daughter who grew up speaking only English and swallowing more Coca-Cola than sorrow. For a long time now the woman had wanted to give her daughter the single swan feather and tell her, "This feather may look worthless, but it comes from afar and carries with it all my good intentions." And she waited, year after year, for the day she could tell her daughter this in perfect American English.

Jing-Mei Woo

My father has asked me to be the fourth corner at the Joy Luck Club. I am to replace my mother, whose seat at the mah jong table has been empty since she died two months ago. My father thinks she was killed by her own thoughts.

"She had a new idea inside her head," said my father. "But before it could come out of her mouth, the thought grew too big and burst. It must have been a very bad idea."

The doctor said she died of a cerebral aneurysm. And her friends at the Joy Luck Club said she died just like a rabbit: quickly and with unfinished business left behind. My mother was supposed to host the next meeting of the Joy Luck Club.

The week before she died, she called me, full of pride, full of life: "Auntie Lin cooked red bean soup for Joy Luck. I'm going to cook black sesame-seed soup."

"Don't show off," I said.

"It's not show off." She said the two soups were almost the same, *chabudwo*. Or maybe she said *butong*, not the same thing at all. It was one of those Chinese expressions that means the better half of mixed intentions. I can never remember things I didn't understand in the first place.

My mother started the San Francisco version of the Joy Luck Club in 1949, two years before I was born. This was the year my mother and father left China with one stiff leather trunk filled only with fancy silk dresses. There was no time to pack anything else, my mother had explained to my father after they boarded the boat. Still his hands swam frantically between the slippery silks, looking for his cotton shirts and wool pants.

When they arrived in San Francisco, my father made her hide those shiny clothes. She wore the same brown-checked Chinese dress until the Refugee Welcome Society gave her two hand-me-down dresses, all too large in sizes for American women. The society was composed of a group of white-haired American missionary ladies from the First Chinese Baptist Church. And because of their gifts, my parents could not refuse their invitation to join the church. Nor could they ignore the old ladies' practical advice to improve their English through Bible study class on Wednesday nights and, later, through choir practice on Saturday mornings. This was how my parents met the Hsus, the Jongs, and the St. Clairs. My mother could sense that the women of these families also had unspeakable tragedies they had left behind in China and hopes they couldn't begin to express in their fragile English. Or at least, my mother recognized the numbness in these women's faces. And she saw how quickly their eyes moved when she told them her idea for the Joy Luck Club.

Joy Luck was an idea my mother remembered from the days of her first marriage in Kweilin, before the Japanese came. That's why I think of Joy Luck as her Kweilin story. It was the story she would always tell me when she was bored, when there was nothing to do, when every bowl had been washed and the Formica table had been wiped down twice, when my father sat reading the newspaper and smoking one Pall Mall cigarette after another, a warning not to disturb him. This is when my mother would take out a box of old ski sweaters sent to us by unseen relatives from Vancouver. She would snip the bottom of a sweater and pull out a kinky thread of yarn, anchoring it to a piece of cardboard. And as she began to roll with one sweeping rhythm, she would start her story. Over the years, she told me the same story, except for the ending, which grew darker, casting long shadows into her life, and eventually into mine.

"I dreamed about Kweilin before I ever saw it," my mother began, speaking Chinese. "I dreamed of jagged peaks lining a curving river, with magic moss greening the banks. At the tops of these peaks were white mists. And if you could float down this river and eat the moss for food, you would be strong enough to climb the peak. If you slipped, you would only fall into a bed of soft moss and laugh. And once you reached the top, you would be able to see everything and feel such happiness it would be enough to never have worries in your life ever again."

Bibliography

[1] HIGH P. B. An outline of American Literature[M]. London: Longman Group Ltd., 1986.
[2] KEARNS G. American Literature[M]. Macmillan Publishing Company, 1987.
[3] Liu Yan, ed. Guided Readings in American Poetry[M]. Beijing: Press of Beijing Languages and Cultures University, 2000.
[4] Luo, Lianggong. A Survey of English Poetry[M]. Wuhan: Wuhan University Press, 2002.
[5] THORNLEY G C, ROBERTS G. An outline of English Literature[M]. London: Longman Group Ltd., 1981.
[6] Rogers, Pat. An Outline of English Literature[M]. Oxford: Oxford University Press, 1998.
[7] Rubinstein, Annette T. The Great Tradition in English Literature from Shakespeare to Shaw[M]. Beijing: Foreign Language Teaching and Research Press, 1988.
[8] Toming, A. History of American Literature[M]. Nanjing: Yilin Press, 2002.
[9] VINON J. Great Writers of the English Language: Novelists and Prose Writers[M]. New York: St. Martin's Press, 1979.
[10] Williams, Tennessee. Cat on a Hot Tin Roof[M]. Penguin Books, 1987.
[11] 鲍秀文,王卫新. 美国文学名著故事梗概及作品导读[M]. 天津:天津人民出版社,2001.
[12] 常耀信. 美国文学简史[M]. 天津:南开大学出版社,1997.
[13] 常耀信. 美国文学选读[M]. 天津:南开大学出版社,1997.
[14] 陈嘉. 英国文学作品选读(第三册)[M]. 北京:商务印书馆,1984.
[15] 范凤祥,宫玉波. 英美文学[M]. 大连:大连海事大学出版社,1999.
[16] 桂扬清,吴翔林. 英美文学选读[M]. 北京:中国对外翻译出版公司,1995.
[17] 胡荫桐,美国文学新编[M]. 北京:外语教学与研究出版社,2001.
[18] 胡荫桐,刘树森. 美国文学教程[M]. 天津:南开大学出版社,1995.
[19] 李宜燮,常耀信. 美国文学选读[M]. 天津:南开大学出版社,1991.
[20] 刘炳善. 英国文学简史[M]. 上海:上海外语教育出版社,1985.
[21] 罗经国. 新编英国文学选读[M]. 北京:北京大学出版社,1996.
[22] 罗经国. 新编英国文学选读(上、下卷)[M]. 北京:北京大学出版社,2005.
[23] 钱青. 美国文学名著精选. 北京:商务印书馆,1994.
[24] 史志康. 美国文学背景概观[M]. 上海:上海外语教育出版社,1998.
[25] 汪玲. 美国文学作品选读[M]. 上海:上海交通大学出版社,2003.
[26] 王佐良,刘承沛. 英国文学名篇选注[M]. 北京:商务印书馆,1993.
[27] 吴伟仁. 英国文学史及选读[M]. 北京:外语教学与研究出版社,1990.
[28] 杨岂深,孙珠. 英国文学选读(三册)[M]. 上海:上海译文出版社,2003.
[29] 张伯香. 英国文学教程[M]. 武汉:武汉大学出版社,1997.
[30] 张伯香. 美国文学教程[M]. 北京:外语教学与研究出版社,2000.